SPECIAL

How God Found Me
Memoirs of an American Guru

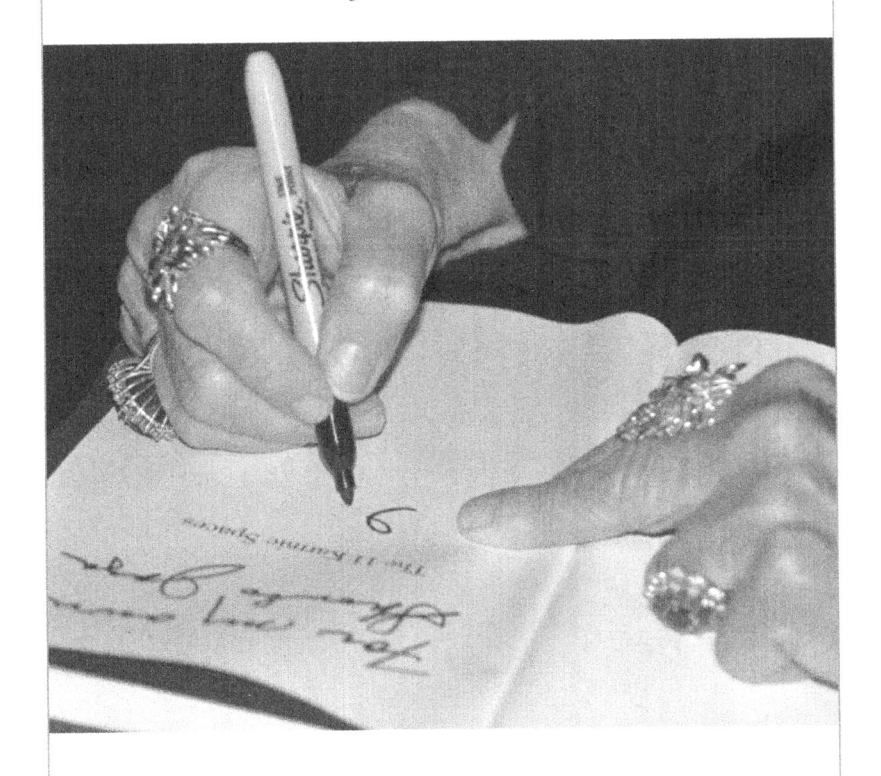

Praise for Ma Jaya and *How God Found Me*

While reading this book tears came, peace came, and inspiration flooded my heart as I learned the story of the one I called Ma. Simply said, it affirmed my belief that the Divine is real and can manifest on this planet.

—*Snatam Kaur*
Musician, Teacher of Kundalini Yoga and Sacred Sound

Forced to find her own path through life early on, Ma Jaya faced her challenges with panache, gusto, and love as she strove to align the world of spirit into which she was catapulted with the world of matter in which she was immured. Her life, an open book for those who had the eyes to read it, has now been distilled by her into a printed book, replete with teachings for those who can comprehend them. Kali Ma ki jai!

—*Dr. Robert Svoboda*
Teacher of Ayurveda, Tantra, and Jyotish astrology;
author of 12 books, including
Prakriti: Your Ayurvedic Constitution

This book is amazing! No one will believe it except those of us who were there. You cannot digest her words even with an open mind. She only will allow an open heart to absorb her. She is in death as she was in life, an enigma to the merely curious and bottomless well for the truly thirsty.

—*Arlo Guthrie*
American Folksinger

Ma Jaya Sati Bhagavati was the Guru we needed to emerge in this time and place to show us what it meant to live the love of the Divine out loud with no apologies or regret. She showed us what it meant to be free in this moment if we could only let go and let the Divine hold and heal us. She was loud, direct, opinionated, surprising, uncomfortable, as well as deeply loving, kind, patient, realized, devoted and honest.

I never had a chance to meet or study with Ma in this life. Yet, after having read about her life in her own words, I have felt as if she has become my teacher. She sits with me now teaching me to let go of being guarded and hurt and to open my heart to my own Beloved.

Her autobiography is desperately needed now as a pure light to illumine the darkness of our fear, hate, and loneliness that plagues our present and may overwhelm our future.

—Lama Rod Owens
Co-Author of Radical Dharma: Talking Love, Race, and Liberation

Ma had an extraordinary ability to cut through a wide variety of obscurations and shadows dimming the psyches of her students. This unique ability provided them an opportunity for true liberation from many forms of inner suffering.

She was also brilliant in revealing the shining essence that lies at the very heart of our Being. All this deep transformational support she provided from a space of great compassion.

During the times that I spent time with her and the Kashi family, I was deeply impressed by her loving commitment to the health and growth of both the Kashi spiritual community and in finding ways to reduce suffering in the outer world as well.

Ma was a very dear friend. I miss her.

—John P. Milton
Pioneering environmentalist; Meditation, Qigong and Tai Chi Master; author of Cultivating Natural Liberation

How God Found Me

Also by Ma Jaya Sati Bhagavati:

Deep and Simple Wisdom:
Spiritual Teachings of Ma Jaya Sati Bhagavati

First Breath, Last Breath:
Practices to Quiet the Mind and Open the Heart

The 11 Karmic Spaces:
Choosing Freedom from the Patterns That Bind You

How God Found Me
Memoirs of an American Guru

Ma Jaya Sati Bhagavati

KASHI

Kashi Publishing
Sebastian, Florida

Copyright © 2020
by The Ma Jaya Bhagavati Trust
All Rights Reserved.

No portion of this book, except for brief reviews, may be reproduced, stored in a retrieval system, or transmitted in any form or by any means—electronic, mechanical, photocopying, recording or otherwise—without written permission of the publisher. For information contact Kashi Publishing.

Published by Kashi Publishing
11155 Roseland Road
Sebastian, Florida 32958

Edited by Swami Matagiri Jaya
Cover and Book Design by Laurie Douglas
Front Cover Photograph by Durga
Back Cover Photograph by Kailash Shankara

Printed in the United States of America

ISBN: 978-0-9838228-7-5

For the book, Ma changed the names of some childhood friends, although the names of her family members remain unchanged. Privacy concerns led the editors to change the names of some people she worked with, including people with AIDS. Ma gave spiritual names to many of her students, and we have used these names. Public figures are named accurately.

Dedication

I dedicate this book to my beloved guru Neem Karoli Baba, who is the keeper of my heart and my soul, to my teacher Avadhut Swami Bhagawan Nityanada, and to my Mother Kali, the beautiful black goddess who is brilliant with her love.

I also dedicate this book to Swami Matagiri Jaya, who has been devoted to making this book a reality. I love you with all my heart and soul, and truly there would be no book without you. You are my love, my chela.

*I spent my youth in the fire
so I could spend my age in the ashes of truth.*

Contents

FOREWORD xiii

PREFACE xix

CHAPTERS

  1. Who Knew from Gurus in Brooklyn? 1
  2. Death, Here I Am 5
  3. Under the Boardwalk 12
  4. One Grain of Sand 17
  5. A Teacher's Heart 21
  6. The County Home 23
  7. The Furnace 27
  8. A Sadhu's Vision 31
  9. Spoonfed's Ashes 35
  10. A Star in the East 42
  11. A Walk with Harry 47
  12. Big Henry's Story 52
  13. My River 58
  14. Hot Corn 62
  15. Ping-Pong Champion 67
  16. Shabbos Queen 72
  17. Tirza the Wine Bath Girl 80
  18. ABC Beach Chairs 86
  19. I Sold My Heart to the Junk Man 92
  20. Pier Moon 100
  21. Illusion and Truth 110
  22. A Nickel for a Pickle 120
  23. Chews 129
  24. Haagen Das 134

25. Rescuing Grandma	137
26. Strange Fruit	149
27. The Soul's Color	154
28. Anna's Snowman	163
29. Make Them Laugh	166
30. Never Ask Why	169
31. Stop Praying for Me	178
Photos 1940–1970	187
32. Aunt Lily's Chicken Farm	199
33. Vinny's Lesson	203
34. Frankie Boy	211
35. Take Me to Kashi to Die	216
36. Sal	223
37. Jimmy Has Tits!	232
38. Cooking Italian	237
39. Professional Mourner	239
40. Hot Goods	245
41. The Cord Replica	249
42. Why Don't You Eat A Little?	256
43. Jack LaLanne's	261
44. I'm Jewish—You Got the Wrong House	266
45. Yearning and Terror	273
46. Teach All Ways	276
47. Mount Manresa	285
48. The Joy of God	289
49. Swami Bhagawan Nityananda	293
50. Nothing but Ash	298
51. Not a Kiddy Pool	302
52. Is Rudi Here?	307
53. Glimpses of Samadhi	312
54. Notes from My Blue Diary	316

55. The Third Eye	320
56. Faith	323
57. "Ram" on Every Page	326
Photos 1971–2000	332
58. Swami's Birthday	348
59. Hilda Charlton	353
60. God Intoxication	359
61. Billy	361
62. Let Them Touch Your Feet	367
63. The Stigmata	371
64. Kali	376
65. Cremation Grounds	381
66. Hanuman and Christ	385
67. Neem Karoli Baba	387
68. Save the Last Dance for Me	393
69. Baba's Blanket	398
70. Guru Is Everything	403
71. Ram Dass	410
72. Learning to Teach	415
73. Steam Rollin' Mama	420
74. Freedom	425
75. Montauk to Miami	428
76. Tell Them How I Died	433
77. The Parliament of the World's Religions	438
78. My Sacred Kashi	444
79. Home	452
AFTERWORD: AND THEN WHAT HAPPENED?	454
ACKNOWLEDGEMENTS	459
SUGGESTED READING	460
GLOSSARY	461
PHOTO CREDITS	469

Foreword

I first saw her in September of 1993. I was in a crowded foyer of the Palmer House in Chicago where much of the Parliament of the World's Religions was being held. Suddenly the milling crowd parted like the Red Sea, as a formidable force of nature and spirit moved through. It was Ma Jaya, and she was something else again. A street-smart lady of Jewish background and culture, she was living the life of a thirty-something Brooklyn matron, complete with three children and a Sicilian husband, when she had an enlightenment experience while doing yoga breathing exercises. This took her to India, a new life as an ecumenical Hindu adept, and becoming one of the most original spiritual teachers on the planet. Her heart is huge, and she has founded a center in Florida where she and her associates take care of babies as well as grown-ups infected with AIDS.

She came through the crowd, radiant with spirit, a vision in a billowing wine and gold sari, oriental jewelry, her vibrant face abrim with good humor, a *yenta* who is also a *yidam*.

Suddenly someone broke through her entourage, a pasty-faced man in a wrinkled seersucker suit. "Do you know Jesus?" he demanded accusingly.

Ma Jaya gave the man a ravishing smile. "Know him!" she exclaimed, and then added in her pungent Brooklyn accent, "Why, darling, I'm his Mother!"

I fell over myself laughing. And in reading this book, I continue to laugh, and cry, and experience a planet of emotions and feelings. For the life and times of Ma Jaya Sati Bhagavati alias Joya alias Joyce de Fiore alias Joyce Green is the stuff of legend. But it is also the heartbreaking, soul-charging tale of a woman who has seen everything, experienced just about everything, and there is little on this earth and time that she has not known or felt.

Her childhood alternates between the harrowing and the hilarious. In this she is in splendid company. One thinks of the great novels of childhood, almost always involving orphaned or disenfranchised children who fall into hard circumstances, but through their spirit and pluck change the world about them. In these stories the central characters' inner qualities give them the courage to act and be in remarkable ways. Thus each child takes on his or her own "Hero's Journey" and often becomes part of another kind of family or a different social class. Huckleberry Finn runs away from his brutish drunken father to launch himself down the deep river with Jim, a runaway slave. Dorothy is carried away on a tornado from dreary, bleak Kansas to the wonderful land of Oz where she acquires several extraordinary new friends. Joyce Green finds new family with homeless but richly wise black people under the Coney Island Boardwalk.

In their new home or reality, the children face serious or life-threatening antagonism: the Wicked Witch of the West is the daunting foe of Dorothy; Huck and Jim are taken advantage of by the fake nobility they meet on the river; Joyce confronts grinding poverty and prejudice. Still, through courage, cunning, and indomitable spirit and purity of heart, the child hero wins out over his or her antagonists, and a new order of reconciliation, or even redemption, prevails. Huck is eventually seen for the remarkable boy he is; Dorothy kills the Wicked Witch by throwing water on her and wins wonders for herself and her companions; and Joyce moves into ever-deepening compassion as well as discovers wildly original ways to best the world of its wrongs, preparing her for the tasks she later will assume. All are returned to their true state enhanced and exalted, and the world is the better for their journey.

One cannot help but wonder what happens to these child heroes when they grow up. We know nothing of forty-year-old Dorothy or fifty-year-old Huck Finn. But we do know quite a lot about sixty-year-old Ma Jaya, which may have been the path toward which both Dorothy and Huck were heading. This is the path of the World Server, the kind of person who, like Ma, knows perfectly well that the emperor has no clothes but then sets about making him some. This is the path of ones who recognize their spiritual genes and open up to the tasks that are theirs and ours in a spiritually conscious universe. This is the path that I believe was given to Ma Jaya in some time out of time, space out of space, but ended up in Brooklyn in the 1940s. This is the path of those who are being prepared to become a Bodhisattva.

The word "Bodhisattva" comes from the Sanskrit roots *bodhi*, meaning "awakening or enlightenment" and *sattva*, meaning "sentient being." *Sattva* has also been translated as "creative and resolute intention to wake up." In the traditional Eastern Buddhist belief, the Bodhisattva is one whose entire life and even lives are dedicated to helping all and everything to wake up to the glory of their beingness. Having known the sheer splendor of the Oneness of life and spirit, they feel the need to spread the word, offer help to those who are suffering, guide others onto a path of new possibilities, and be a companion and friend on the road of life.

One of the funniest accounts ever written of an awakening experience has got to be Ma's meeting with the Christ while doing her breathing exercises in an attempt to drop a hundred pounds or so. From this meeting came this yearning, and from this yearning, the passionate commitment to live the spiritual life in the world, and to do so in service to those from whom society turns its clucking face. Lest that seem like the tallest of all tall orders, we learn from Ma the ultimate Unity of all being and the fact that not one of us is really apart from the other.

Bodhisattvas have been described as "enlightening, radiant beings who exist in innumerable forms, valiantly functioning in helpful ways right in the midst of the busy-ness of the world." It is also recorded that Bodhisattvas can be awesome in their power, radiance, and wisdom. They also can be as ordinary and commonplace as your next-door neighbor. Well, that's Ma all right, radiant and neighborly, sacred and madly profane.

Many Bodhisattvas have had shadowed careers at one time or another; they have known the suffering and delusions of the world and fallen prey to them just as we all have. What is important, and what is different, I think, is that out of their experience has grown a deep concern and compassion for their fellow traveler on life's path. They do not hide out, roiling in regret and self-blame. Have you ever thought about it that way, that the wrong you have done to yourself and others can be harvested so as to bring forth a greater good? Think of it as the manure you put on the soil of your nature to grow a finer crop of goodness.

The fact is that Bodhisattvas enter into every kind of work to be of benefit in the world. *The Flower Ornament Sutra* offers a very interesting and comprehensive account of the different roles and ways of being a Bodhisattva: not only a spiritual teacher, but a priest, doctor, scientist, fortune-teller, king, beggar, engineer, bus driver, architect, construction contractor, laborer, songwriter, musician, householder, housewife, magician, teacher, writer, janitor, gardener, farmer, actor, soldier, storyteller, athlete, dancer, courtesan, child, politician, lawyer, and even, a tough little girl from Brooklyn.

So how does she do it, this Bodhisattva Ma, caring for so many, and doing so with unstinting compassion and practical know-how? The answer, I believe, is that the Bodhisattva life, the life of living from essence, has many more capacities than does the self that is conditioned and sustained by ordinary and unexamined living experience wherein one does not really ever get around to doing one's human homework. Or as Meister Eckhart said, "The outward work will never be puny if the inward work is great."

In the Bodhisattva life, the capacities are known as skillful means. These capacities are very subtle and can easily be overlooked, for although they participate in and gather information from the physical senses, they also have information and perceptions from "elsewhere." This information from elsewhere appears to transcend local time and space, belonging to space/time or hyperdimensional spaces and times.

The knowing that you have when in a state of essence is neither insight nor intuition, nor do you look at things randomly. It is direct and total knowing, involving you physically, mentally, emotionally, and spiritually. Observe Ma giving *darshan* or in some of her semi-private audiences. Her awareness seems to extend not just to the physical person before her, but also to their inner states and history, their promise as well as their pathos. Observe her further, and watch as she dives deep into the larger dynamic system of which our physical reality is a part.

Putting it in terms of quantum physics, it seems that Ma has a knowledge of not only the particle but also the wave. Thus the deepest values, purposes, and patterns for life, the richest potential coding for existence, the source level of creative patterns, innovative actions, and ideas are known to her in her Bodhisattva state. She knows them with a simultaneity of knowings that grasps the whole of anything or anybody. In her state of direct knowledge, there is a certainty, a clarity and precision, a rightness about it that you do not get from reasoning, intuition, or insight. From the perspective of essence, the power and action of a Ma Jaya is explicable; her sheer genius of perception and cutting through the nonsense make a marvelous sense; her goodness, perseverance, and social activism in spite of immense obstacles appear to be a natural calling and way of being.

As the remarkable story in these pages shows, this high-souled woman is living out of the mother matrix of reality, the moral flow of the universe, the very stuff of what is trying to emerge into space and time, the continuously creating universe. Thus she lives differently-dimensioned. She lives out of a fullness that empowers those who know her to become their finest selves, even at the moment of death. She lives out of dimensions that contain the coded energies of change and evolution. She lives out of the heart of never-failing love. And yet the world under the Boardwalk is never forgotten. Hudson and Big Henry and Joe Joe continue to live with her, as do the many men and women who have died in her arms.

She is Ma.

—*Dr. Jean Houston*

Preface

"I never teach from a piece of paper," Ma would say, and it was true. Hers was an oral teaching, and it was all in the moment.

Until recent times, the teachings of spiritual masters were passed down orally, and the transmission from master to student is always about much more than words. There is, in the presence of a great spiritual being, an essence that is absorbed not through the mind but through the heart and soul. In India, this is described by the word *darshan*, which means "being in the presence of" as well "seeing" or "glimpse." The real lesson is the presence, the Holy Spirit in its many manifestations. When you sat with Ma, the depth of her presence was such that you might listen intently to every word, feel profoundly moved, but later not be able to remember a single thing she said. And yet your life would be forever changed.

Ma might start an explanation of some esoteric topic, then something would trigger a story, and with the comic timing of a professional standup she would have us laughing and gasping for breath, and then just as suddenly she would remind us to sit up straight and hold the essence of God. The laughter, it turned out, often had a purpose. Ma would call it a "speed check," a distraction to keep us from noticing or getting scared as she led us to a deeper place, or a higher place, from which we might better absorb a teaching. Or it could be just laughter for the sake of laughter, or to shake us out of our self-importance.

Even though Ma was a master storyteller, she often told us that the words didn't really matter, that we should attend to the silence between the words. Even so, we scurried after her with notebooks, cameras, and tape recorders, but she could never be fully contained.

In 1991, our efforts took a different direction. Ma was profoundly saddened by the too-early death of her beloved student Billy Byrom. Billy had begged her to write, so she taught herself to type and started on her memoirs. She often wrote a chapter a day, which she would read to us each night—the only time she taught from the written word. The chapters were sometimes about her childhood and youth and sometimes about the people she had been working with that day. By then, Ma and her *ashrams* were deeply engaged in her work with the destitute and the dying, especially people with AIDS. She sat with many of them as they took their last breaths and went home to write about them. In this way, Ma became a writer, yet always keeping the beautiful texture of the spoken word, and always showing how service is essential on a spiritual path. These chapters form the foundation of this memoir. With Ma's permission, we added the transcripts of stories she had told us over the years, in which she recounted her agonizing yet ecstatic metamorphosis from housewife to guru.

As I and others helped Ma to edit her work, people would always tell us, "Just don't lose Ma's voice." Oh, but she had so *many* voices! Sometimes she spoke with the voice and weight of ancient scripture. There were other times when she would drift far away, communing with a presence that we could feel but not see. Meanwhile her native Brooklyn accent and pitchman patter would come and go depending on what she was saying and who she was talking to.

Or she would interrupt herself to speak directly to one person. If someone needed a personal teaching *right now*, nothing else mattered.

And so the style can change from chapter to chapter, or even within chapters, because change itself is Ma's truest voice. This verbal dance is one expression of the feminine face of divinity, the play of form manifesting itself against the backdrop of the unknowable formless.

This memoir was essentially ready to be published in the late 1990s, but Ma, always so generous, was also intensely private. She chose not to go forward with the publication. But before she passed in 2012, she gave us permission to publish this history of her extraordinary journey. It offers us yet another "glimpse," another darshan, because, after all, she is the Mother, forever giving to us of herself and her love.

—*Swami Matagiri Jaya*

CHAPTER ONE

Who Knew from Gurus in Brooklyn?

My very fancy copper refrigerator showed every fingerprint, a record of all the people who opened it every day.

I looked down at my hands as I was scrubbing my refrigerator, and there was blood. It was Good Friday, 1974, more than a year since the night the Christ had first appeared to me in my living room in Brooklyn. "I'm a Jew," I said, "you got the wrong house address."

Then he told me, "Teach all ways, for all ways are mine."

At first I didn't understand, but in the months that followed I had fallen passionately in love with God in any form. I was teaching about Buddha, Christ, Mary, the Hindu gods, and my own heritage of Judaism. So much had happened since then, but my love for Christ had only grown deeper. I didn't know the word *stigmata*, but somehow I knew this blood came from loving Christ so passionately, something I would never deny.

I was so very afraid, but I was also in ecstasy, both at the same time.

Later, after it was all over, my daughter asked me, "Are you still my mother? Or are you a saint?"

I said, "I ain't no damned saint. This is just a freak accident."

My daughter told the priest at school, and he sent her to a psychologist. I didn't tell too many people what had happened. I wasn't looking to be a saint, a teacher, a holy person, and least of all a freak.

It's only now, so many years later, that I tell my story.

People call me a *guru*, but who knew from gurus in Brooklyn? I only knew from God. He lived in the old synagogue with Rabbi Rubenstein, and he sat with the men on the right side of the temple, far away from the women. It bothered me that God should think those old men with the beards were better than my mama, but in spite of the rabbi, I loved God, and I was sure that God loved me.

How could God not love me when he gave me Coney Island? It was ecstasy, it was a fairyland, it was constant doing, constant moving. Coney Island was like one grand illusion that had to be lived, that had to be played out, yet it was all for nothing, all without meaning. Coney Island taught me that all of life is an illusion.

My family lived in Mr. Krumpenholtz's house on Brighton 8th Street, more exactly in his cellar in the Brighton Beach section of Coney Island. To see out the windows, we would look up to where people's feet were passing on the street. There were pipes running all over our ceiling, and my brothers and I would swing on them like monkeys. Mama was a secretary for the IRS, and Papa was a gambler who didn't believe in doing a nine-to-five job even though he had four kids. There were times when Papa gambled away the food money. Sometimes at night when I was about to fall asleep, I would hear the rats running around, and I would wonder, "Are you a boy rat or a girl rat?" You see, the landlord gave us the cheese and the traps, but me and my brother Harvey ate the cheese and saved the rats by our own hunger.

I was a child brought up in the streets, a child who was starving for part of every year. Then for three or four months in the summer, I had the continuous Ferris Wheel and the beach. I ran around in a bathing suit, and no one knew who was poor, no one knew who was rich, no one knew who was starving. It taught me to take the moment, grab it, live it, run with it, because it's all a game. We were all urchins, we all lived in the streets, we all ate from the garbage pails behind Nathan's. We had the beach, we had the boardwalk, we had fireworks on a Tuesday night, we had life. It was rich.

There was always somebody being murdered under the Boardwalk, there was always somebody being mugged, there was always somebody being robbed, there was always somebody being happy, there was always somebody crying, and there was always somebody laughing. Everything I know, I learned on those streets.

We were orthodox Jews, so my earliest memory of God should be of the synagogue and the *Torah*, but it isn't. In spite of what the rabbi said, I always thought I had a personal connection to God, so very real, except that I called him "Mac." I don't remember exactly how I named God "Mac." Perhaps in those days in Coney Island everybody was called "Hey, Mac."

As soon as I was consciously aware, I would hear the word "Ma," repeated over and over, coming from a place deep down in my chest and exploding at times in my head. Thinking everyone heard it, I ignored it when I could. I never really thought too much about it, except for the few solitary times by the ocean when the sound was louder than the waves, or even at times when the roar of thunder couldn't stop it.

मा

Although now I am known to many as a guru or spiritual teacher, I never wanted to teach. I only wanted to share my life with anyone who would listen. There is a sacred river in India called the Ganga. She's so brilliant in her love, this Mother Ganga, that she continuously flows toward every human being, and everyone that comes toward her is blessed and purified. All are greeted by an astonishing amount of beauty. Even those who are filled with corruption and hate are never judged.

My wish when I first got started in spirituality was that I could always be like that river. I wanted only to reach out arms to hold

Note: The symbol between paragraphs is the word "Ma" in Sanskrit, in Ma Jaya's handwriting.

and hands to touch. Now when there is so much pain in the world, the whole river is in my heart, and the river has overflowed its banks.

I acknowledge my river in my own way, sometimes with bells and incense and oils, other times with the fury of a woman who faces injustice every moment of her life. I acknowledge my river by meeting those injustices with an open heart and a quiet mind.

I don't tell my story to make idle conversation or to impress anyone. I tell it because I want to see you come into her waters; I want to see you feel her gentle flow, taste her richness, and create a moment in your life that is so full that it will go on and on, beyond life, beyond death, beyond fulfillment, even beyond emptiness.

With this book, I give you my history, primitive as it is, my history of learning how to live in a world that is filled with so much hate and at the same moment filled with so much beauty and love. To understand this Ma, you must understand Brooklyn, which I call the holy land, for it was there that divinity first visited me.

CHAPTER TWO

Death, Here I Am

The Palm Beach County Home was bustling. I had brought plenty of bananas and cookies to the AIDS ward. It was 1992, and AIDS was still a death sentence for most. The residents didn't get fresh fruit too often, so when my *chelas* and I appeared with a trolley of fruit and cookies, everybody kind of woke up. I was going from room to room as I always did—feeding, touching, kissing, laughing, crying. I looked up, and there was Bruce (I had named him Shiva Baba), the head of the People with AIDS Coalition of West Palm Beach, a man who gave his heart and soul to anyone with AIDS. Like me, he visited the AIDS ward regularly. As soon as I saw him, I knew something wasn't right.

"What did the doctor say this morning?" I asked him.

"I'm going into the hospital in about an hour. The doc wants to see why I'm coughing up blood, even though we both know why."

"How long did he say you have?" I had always been straight and honest with this man, whom I loved so much.

"About a week."

"Okay, son, we'll take the next week's journey together."

He insisted on going to the hospital alone to get settled in. "I'll see you later," he said, as he waved goodbye to the people in the Haney Wing, the AIDS ward. He walked out, his shoulders back and his head high. He was a slim man and proud of his build. I never loved him more than at that moment when he was walking away from life itself.

Later that day when we arrived at the hospital to see him, we found him lying in bed looking ever so slight. The Kaposi's sarcoma lesions on his face were already more raised and pronounced. Both lungs were full of lesions, and he was beginning to drown in his own blood. The sound of hissing oxygen filled the room. He laid his head back on the pillow. The pain that he had kept hidden earlier was making him weak.

I knew I soon would have to let him go—this man who had been around the block so many times he forgot to count; this man who had once been married and had the courage to come out of the closet, despite how painful it was; this man who now lived and breathed to help other people with AIDS—my gentleman, my scholar, my streetwise student, my bum, and, most of all, my beloved chela, or spiritual student.

Several of my chelas had come with me. He looked around the room and asked, with only a trace of sarcasm, "Can I be alone with the Holy One for a while?" I told him okay and asked everyone to leave except Yashoda, my assistant. He didn't mind since he was used to seeing her with me.

When everyone was gone, I sat close to him on the bed. "Well, Shiva Baba, I'm all yours and I hope this is not going to be true confessions because, if it is, you don't have enough time. One week won't do it."

He laughed, and began spitting up blood. I asked if I should call a nurse. "No," he said, "it will stop." Glancing at his nightstand, I noticed a pile of paperwork for the Coalition. To the end, he was taking care of his own.

When the coughing ceased, he said, "You know, Ma, there are two things I am going to ask of you, and I want you to promise to do both of them." He continued, "You are the greatest teacher in the world, yet the thing I love best is to watch you enjoy sweets."

"Oh, what are you talking about? I would never cheat on my diet!"

He pointed to one of the trays of cookies and cakes we had brought for the nurses. My chelas and I manage to visit a lot of hospital wards where we might not otherwise be welcomed; we have found that nothing opens the door like a huge tray of cookies for the staff. We always bring food—cookies for the nurses, fresh fruit for the patients. My guru always said, "Feed everyone," and so we do, whether with cookies or with food for the hungry heart. While I sat with Shiva Baba, the chelas I had brought with me were visiting other patients, so many of whom were forgotten and unwanted.

"Okay, I will have to let you have your death wish." He still had plenty of life in him, so this was not exactly a deathbed wish, but it was close enough to give me an excuse to get off my diet. He smiled at me, a smile that reached his eyes, and pointed to the night stand. When I opened the drawer, I saw a Diet Pepsi marked with magic marker: "For Ma." I placed the soda on his tray and brought over a plate of cookies. "One for me and one for me," I said as I sat on the bed with my cookies, my soda, and my Shiva Baba.

His breathing was quite labored, and he looked as though he was sleeping. As I started to turn off the light, his bony hand reached up as if returning from the grave and grabbed my hand. "Ma," he said, "two deathbed requests."

"Go ahead, son, what is it?" My mouth was already filled with chocolate cookies.

"Ma, I want you to tell me a story about your birth, and I want to know what you were like when you were a child."

I was so touched that I began to speak. Before I could get two words out, he said, "Promise to wake me if I doze off."

Between bites of cookie, I began to tell my story.

HOW GOD FOUND ME

मा

One day when Mama was pregnant, she had very bad pains that didn't feel like labor pains at all. She was rushed to the hospital, where her appendix burst. The hospital tracked my father down at a neighbor's house where he was playing cards. They told him that my mother didn't have long to live and to come right away. For fear of losing the baby, Mama was refusing to allow an operation to remove her appendix.

When Papa got there, he signed the papers, and she had the operation. She not only survived, but the next day delivered a baby who managed to live in spite of the odds. Mama had told them to put the name "Joy" on my birth certificate, but someone at the hospital made a mistake and wrote "Joyce" instead, and it remained that way.

Mama was written up in medical journals for a while after that. Some people said it was a miracle that we both lived. But that wasn't the greatest miracle. When Mama was a little girl in Brooklyn, just off the boat from Russia, everybody used to shoot off guns for the Fourth of July, and when she was five she was hit in the stomach. Her mother was told that the bullet had entered the child's womb and that she would never be able to have children. My mama, Anna, grew into a beautiful, intelligent young woman, yet she always felt sad at the thought of never being able to have a child.

When Harry Green started coming around, Mama fell head over heels in love. He was very dapper, very charming, a dancer on the vaudeville stage. When Mama told him she couldn't have children, Harry was thrilled. What would a man like him do with a bunch of kids? Not only was Anna gorgeous, but her family had a little gelt, as Papa used to say. He also used to say, "Never put your hand in your own pocket when it can fit in someone else's."

Grandma Rachel caught on fast, so Mama never got a penny while she was married to my papa, and that was for the rest of her life.

After a while, Mama defied all odds and began getting pregnant. She gave birth to my sister, Shirley, and my two brothers, Melvin and Harvey. I was the fourth child. There was no money for a crib, and so they brought me home and put me in a dresser drawer.

Once, when I was older, I asked, "Mama, was I an accident?" Why would anyone so poor want a fourth child? She answered, "I lived through the gunshot wound at the age of five, and I probably will die some day on the Fourth of July to complete the circle. Having you was a miracle I am proud of." She didn't talk nice like that to me too often, so those words had to last.

Shiva Baba whispered, "Ma, did she die on the Fourth of July?"

"Yes," I answered. "Mama was my spiritual teacher for the first thirteen years of my life. She used to say, 'Joyala, you were born into the house of the dead. Now make good use of your life'."

"How were you born into the house of the dead?" Shiva Baba asked. He looked really interested.

"That is another story."

"Bullshit," he said sweetly.

As I write all this down, I can't help but look at the urn that holds my Shiva Baba's ashes and think, "This turned out to be some long story."

Mama lay very still in the charity ward of Israel Zion Hospital. She had just been operated on for the burst appendix, and the nurses were watching her closely, thinking she wouldn't last through the night. As she lay there, a young woman in the next bed died after giving birth. A nurse covered Mama's face with the sheet, so as not to let her awaken to the sight of death. The attendant who came to collect the other woman's body took my mama instead. He was already inside the morgue when he saw something move beneath the sheet. It was the baby kicking as Mama began to go into labor. "So, yes," I said, "I was born in the house of death, or at least I started to be born there."

Shiva Baba began to spit up blood again. Between coughs, he said, "I am not going to die in a hospital. I'm coming home to Kashi to die in my own house of death, by your river and in your arms." Kashi is the name of my *ashram*, but it is also a place in India, the holy city on the banks of the sacred Ganges River. It is said that those who die in Kashi achieve liberation.

"Ma, what an ending for me, to hear your story and watch you eat your sweets, and to hear about the house of death bringing life to a baby named Joy. Don't worry about gaining weight. You look like a little girl sitting there with the tears running down your face and three cookies in your hand."

या

Shiva Baba did make it home to Kashi to die. For the last two weeks of his life, he would come with his oxygen tank to the Dattatreya Temple, the room where I teach almost every night. Every once in a while, he would turn to the window to look at our pond, our own sacred Ganga. He knew that this pond is a part of the sacred river and that this was where his ashes would be scattered. I had taught him a poem by Ramprasad. Sometimes, from my couch, I could see his lips moving, and I knew he was reciting his poem. Only two nights before his death, I stopped whatever I was teaching about and went over to the couch where he sat. Together we whispered the words:

> *All right, Death, here I am.*
> *I have drawn a circle around me with Kali's name.*
> *The great death, Shiva, with Kali on his chest,*
> *Has taken her feet to his heart.*
> *Remembering that her feet cancel all fear,*
> *Who needs to fear death?*

For a while all we could hear was the sound of the oxygen. He took my hand, and the river of life and death flowed through our hands as I taught my other chelas about death, which to me is just a short interruption in the flow of the sacred river of life. My Shiva Baba had no fear, and death took this gentle man two nights later. By allowing my chelas to witness his dying, he gave us all a gift.

CHAPTER THREE

Under the Boardwalk

I was alone in our cellar home, and I had fallen asleep on the floor. When I woke up, I felt I was the only little girl left in the world. I wanted my papa, and I knew he would be in the alley. It was still light outside, yet there was some coolness in the air. It was the time of the yard's shadows, and Mama should have been home from work by now, but she wasn't. My sister Shirley was working at night, and I had no idea where my brothers were.

The familiar stench of the garbage piled near the door made me feel better as I made my way out of the shadowy yard into the alleyway that ran between the houses. I saw my papa playing cards as usual, his face so still in the shadows of the dark alley. "Always let them think you're bluffing, Joyala," my papa said time and time again.

I walked quietly up to Papa, wanting him to see my tears and take me on his lap. I was only five years old, and my eyes were at the level of the table. I could see there was quite a pot in front of Papa and his friends. "Papa, I don't want to be alone anymore." It was as if I had just woken up from a dream in which I realized that I was, and always had been, alone.

"You're not alone. I'm here. I raise you a nickel," he said without skipping a beat. "Joyala," he said under his breath, "don't you have your friends to play with?"

My friends were Kathy, who lived on the next block, and Joe Joe, who lived in the cellar of the building right behind our cellar. But I didn't know where they were, and I said so.

"Go play with them and don't cross the street."

"They're not here," I said, looking around to see if they would appear.

"Then go find new ones."

I had never felt so alone in my life. Even my grandmother wasn't around, and even if she was, she always locked herself in the old mop room, the only room in our house that had a locked door. Sometimes she would tell me tales of Minsk and her life in Russia, but not very often. I was the one she loved the best, but she hated my papa. When I asked her why, she said in Yiddish that it was because of the way he made my mama live, whatever that meant.

"Goodbye, Papa," I said. "I am going to find new friends."

"Don't cross the street. Okay, Joyala?"

I ran and ran down Brighton 8th Street, stopping here and there to look in windows, wanting to be part of the families I could see inside. But it wasn't those people I wanted; I wanted my own family to sit down and have a meal together like these people were having.

When I got to the end of the block, I realized that I had never gone this far by myself before. But I knew, too, that if I went around the block, I would end up where I had begun—alone. Brighton 8th is a little hidden street that runs into Brighton 7th, which goes out to Brighton Beach Avenue. I turned down Brighton 7th.

When I stood alone on Brighton Beach Avenue, I was in awe. There were at least four lanes of traffic weaving in and out between the big black legs of the elevated train. I walked toward a long black staircase leading up to the El and decided to climb it. When I got to the top, I thought maybe I had reached heaven, so I began to talk to my friend, Mac, which was my name for God. "Well, now what, Mac?" I asked, noticing the man who made the change in the little cage staring at me. Mac must have been listening because an idea came to me. I screamed, "Mama, I'm coming!" and ran right past the ticket man to another staircase that went back down to the other side of the street.

I climbed down the stairs, holding tight to the railing, and got to the other side of the street right in front of the five-and-ten. Peeking in the windows, I saw electric fans and made a wish that one day we could have one for my mama for when she came home from work. I squashed my face on the glass. A little boy eating at the counter turned and saw me. He said something to his mama, and she looked where he pointed. I stuck out my tongue at the little boy, and the mama held her heart as if she thought I had stuck my tongue out at her. I started to run.

I ran to the corner of Coney Island Avenue and Brighton Beach Avenue, stopped there for a moment, then made a fast turn down toward the beach and the best years of my life.

There were plenty of shadows now because of the big apartment buildings. At the end of the street were some benches and then a concrete ramp. I didn't think. I just ran straight down the ramp and right under the Boardwalk.

In the cool dimness under the Boardwalk were a few large cardboard boxes covered in tar, and one of them had legs sticking out. I ran past them and straight into the largest man I had ever seen. He was standing with his back toward the beach. He took me by the shoulders and asked in a kind voice if I was okay. He kept looking behind me. "Where is your mama?"

I looked up at this black giant with a gray beard, and I told him the truth: I didn't know where my mama was.

"Where is your papa?"

"He's playing cards, and he wants me to find some new friends."

The man bent down. He had the scent of salt, old clothes, and the beach. "Don't tell me you're here all alone?"

"No," I said, "I'm with you." I wasn't trying to be funny. I really meant it.

"Are you jiving me, child?"

I started to cry even though my mama always said tears were a waste of time. He lifted me up and held me close.

"It's okay. You got a friend now."

"Hey Henry, whatcha doing with a white baby?" I turned around in the big man's arms and saw a frail man on wooden crutches.

"Hudson," said the big man, "shut your mouth and come here and meet this baby girl, our new friend."

I wasn't crying anymore. That was for babies. So I said, "I am not a baby, and you'd better believe it, you fuck." Both men looked shocked.

"Well, little girl, I have to put you down and get me some soap. Wash out that mouth."

I understood that my new friend didn't want me to say "fuck," so I told him I wouldn't, a promise I tried to keep in the years to come, but I didn't always manage it, growing up in the streets as I did.

People were starting to leave the beach. Young children were being carried by their papas, and babies were in their mothers' arms. I felt safe in the big man's arms. I almost wanted to stay there forever.

"Now, what is your name, little girl?" the big man asked, as he put me down.

"My name is Joyce or sometimes it's Joyala." The man on the crutches hobbled over, and he stooped down like the big one. It looked like we were going to play ring-around-the-rosy.

"I am Hudson," said the man on crutches, "and this large fellow is called Big Henry."

I wanted to give my friends a gift, so I told them God's name was Mac, and then Big Henry told me that Mac's other name was Jesus. That reminded me that Kathy's father had said that me and my brother Harvey killed Jesus. It seems that her father told her that whenever he had a drink.

"No," Big Henry said, quietly, "you and your brother didn't kill Lord Jesus. It was life that did it."

"Well," I said, "will you tell him that? I don't want him to be mad at us."

The older man said, with a little choking sound, "Why, ain't you a special one?"

म्रा

That was the beginning of me being with the under-the-Boardwalk people almost every day, or every night, or whenever I could sneak away.

Papa would always say to me, "Don't cross the street, Joyala," as if those were the magic words that made him a father. And I never did; I always crossed over the El.

CHAPTER FOUR

One Grain of Sand

"Ma, you're the Mother, always flowing."

Often I ask my guru, Neem Karoli Baba, "What is it that I am? What is it that I can tell people I am?"

"That may sound simple to you, Baba, but how am I going to explain it to normal people, like my guys with AIDS? Not everybody knows all this Indian stuff."

"Explain yourself to yourself first, and then, through writing, it will become easier to explain who you are."

मा

I begin with what I always knew, even before God found me. All my life I've desperately wanted to serve humanity. Wherever I was—Coney Island, Brighton Beach, Red Hook—and at whatever age, I always wanted the ability to give. One night I was sitting on the beach with Big Henry and Hudson. "Joyce, touch some sand," Big Henry suddenly said.

"We sitting on sand anyway," said Hudson. The two men were sharing red wine out of a bottle with no label.

Henry ignored him. "If you touch one little grain of sand, you change the shape of the whole beach." Hudson made a face. Henry kept talking. "If you touch one person, you can change the shape of their life."

Hudson interrupted. "Change your life good if a cop sees us sitting here gabbing with a white child."

"I tell you the way it is," Henry continued. "If no one touches anyone, nothing ever changes. Where could God put his beauty, if nothing grows?"

We were away from the Boardwalk, closer to the ocean, yet not quite where the sand begins to get damp. I picked up a little sand. "Look," I said, "I just changed something, so did I change everything?"

Henry lay down on his side on the sand, half of his face looking white in the moonlight. Both men were lying in front of the great big ocean, as comfortable as could be. I wondered if they could see the beauty of the sea if they were drunk. They were asleep now, so I'd have to ask my mother.

Once again, I ran home over the El. By now I had learned the ticket taker's name—Mr. McDonald. I was sneaking out the bathroom window and crossing over the El almost every night, and he never stopped me.

I went straight to Mama's bed. "Mama," I said, "do people see other stuff when they're drunk?" I sometimes saw things that nobody else seemed to see, and I wanted to understand. I'd tried a sip of Henry's bottle one time, but it just made me sick.

"Are you crazy? Go back to sleep. You'll wake up Papa."

"So what? He doesn't go to work. You do."

"Then why didn't you wake him up in the first place? And why aren't you in your underwear?"

"Oh, I just thought I would save time in the morning if I slept with my clothes on."

She looked more closely at me. "You have sand on your hands and sneakers. Where the hell have you been?"

"Out back," I said, quickly.

"Out back where?"

"Out back there." I pointed toward the alley.

Mama closed her eyes for a second. "Listen, I don't have the strength to question you hard, but if you're lying to me, I'm going to tan your hide."

"Mama, I would never lie."

She just laughed. "Go to bed."

"Does being drunk feel nice, Mama?"

"No, it hides the world from people's eyes. Why are you asking me this?"

"If I was drunk, does it mean I won't see the plaster falling from the ceiling?"

Papa was up now. "Listen, Joyala, some day the landlord will paint this dump. Meanwhile, you're making memories." He always said that, as if being poor was special.

"These memories she don't need. Get Krumpenholtz to paint."

Papa suddenly looked very white beneath the small light overhead. "Harry," Mama said, "did he give you the money for paint?"

"Oh, Anna, I had a good tip."

So much for the paint job. The fighting began. I got out of there fast, but I was thinking about what Henry said. I went back in the bedroom.

"Mama, let me touch you."

"What? Get out of here. I'm talking to your father."

"Let her touch you. It's not the kid's fault I gambled the paint money."

I touched her face ever so lightly. I loved my mama so much, and it hurt my heart to see her upset. Mama grabbed me and held me tight, a thing she rarely did.

"Mama, Papa, it works! Touching works!"

They went to sleep after that, and I swore to Mac, "I will go on touching people forever."

CHAPTER FIVE

A Teacher's Heart

If my sister Shirley wasn't home, nobody paid much attention to me. There wasn't a lot of food in the house, or really much of anything. One time, I must have been in first grade, I couldn't find any clothes to put on, so I put on an old red bathing suit that was a hand-me-down from my cousin. Papa didn't say anything about it when he left me in the schoolyard.

The kids started to giggle and point at me. That happened sometimes, because my clothes were often raggedy, so I ignored them, but this time it was more than usual.

When my teacher Mr. Lipshitz got there, he looked around and said, "Look at Joyce. Isn't that a great idea? She can go straight to the beach without having to change." The other kids looked shocked. He continued, "Why don't you children all wear bathing suits tomorrow and bring a change of clothes. We'll go out in the school yard and turn on the sprinklers."

I couldn't wait for the next day to wear my bathing suit to school again. When Mama came home that night, all tired and cranky from the heat and traveling, I told her all about it. She was furious—at me.

"But Mama, there was no clothes for me to wear."

She got off the old sofa and went into the cardboard box where the dirty clothes were sometimes kept. She found a cotton dress and began to wash it in the sink. When she was finished, she went into the furnace room that was part of the cellar and put the dress on the water heater. I didn't care. I was going to wear my bathing suit anyway. She then went into the dresser and took out the bathing suit. She knotted it up and threw it into the garbage. "Tell Papa you need a new one." I was going to argue, but I looked at her lying on the sofa again, and she just looked so tired.

I went to the alley. "Papa, I need a new bathing suit."

"Sure, just let me win this game."

Later that night while everyone else was asleep, I was playing jacks on the floor, waiting for my papa to come and give me money.

"I guess you'll have to wait a little bit more," he said, as he came in and took off his jacket. I knew that, but I always waited for him anyway.

The next day it rained and the bathing suit was forgotten.

A few years later, Mr. Lipschitz disappeared. But before that there were fliers around: "Lipschitz Commie." It was the beginning of the McCarthy era, and this was a man who used to talk all the time about equality between black and white. I heard later that he killed himself. Forty years later, when I had the first big gallery show of my paintings, I dedicated the catalogue to Joseph Lipschitz. Everybody was trying to figure out who he was. That's who he was: a teacher who had the heart of awareness to help a child and get her through a very hard time in her life, a time when she thought she was different from other people.

CHAPTER SIX

The County Home

In the 1980s and '90s, the AIDS epidemic kept growing, and I found myself working more and more with the brave people who lived and died of this plague. On my first visit to the AIDS wing at the Palm Beach County Home, the supervisor watched me like a hawk.

"I'm Lee, the head of Social Services," he said. "We don't preach anything here."

I said in my very heaviest Brooklyn accent, "I don't preach anything, Sir. I love everyone, and that is the extent of what I do. Anyway, you don't look filled up with volunteers."

Lee gave a look as if to say, "How long will this one last?" Then he took me over to a black man in his eighties. I knew right away that he was introducing me to a real hard case. "This is Ma, Mr. Tillman. She's brought you fruit and cookies."

"Why?" he asked in a menacing voice. "What do you bring me your white girl shit for?"

In front of the huge Lee, I answered very sweetly, "Well, Mr. Tillman, this shit was made by little children's hands just to make you happy."

"Why?" he asked again and added, without shame, "Bitch."

Once again answering like a lady, I said, "My name is Ma, not Bitch."

"That is a stupid name. Don't you know that?"

At this point, Lee left us. He must have figured he was leaving me in good hands and that I couldn't do too much damage.

"Listen, bitch," the old man said, "lower this chair down, if you can do something as easy as that."

Now, no one calls me "bitch" more than once, especially if I'm not being bitchy. "Mr. Tillman," I said softly, "you fuck with me and you fuck with the wrong one." Well, the silence was the loudest I've ever heard. Then, all of the sudden, a weird sound came from this old man. I thought maybe I had killed him and this was some kind of weird death rattle.

"Girl, girl."

"Yes, Sir," I answered. "Are you okay?"

"Where'd you learn to speak my language like that?"

He laughed so loud that the nurses came in. "Are you okay, Mr. T?"

"Fine," answered my newfound friend. "Now, get the hell out of here and leave me be with this good lady."

"Wow," I thought, "this one was hard." But I loved him right from the beginning, in the same way I loved my dad. Over the months that followed, Mr. Tillman and I talked often about Harry's life. He loved the idea that Harry, having never worked for more than a few days at a time, died at eighty-eight having been unemployed for his whole life.

"Now lay me down in this old chair," he said again. I had never seen a chair like Mr. Tillman's. It was heavy and long, with a lot of buttons. I pressed the one I was sure would lower his head. Whoosh went the chair, and Mr. T's head was by the floor, his legs straight up in the air. "Holy shit, girl, whatcha doing? Don't you knows I got AIDS? You want it to go to my head?"

I pushed another button, and the old man shot straight upright. It was a good thing he was strapped in so tight.

"What you tryin' to do, kill me?" At that moment two aides came in and got everything straightened out.

"Well, Mr. T," said the aide, "now you see how it feels when you sneak into people's rooms and press the controls while they're asleep." I guess he was strapped in for more than medical reasons.

I was almost out the door when Mr. T screamed, "Ma, girl, would you please feed me my watermelon?"

The aide said, "You can sure enough feed yourself."

With a voice that would melt butter, the old gentleman pointed to me and said, "That white girl got more guts in her little finger than all of Harlem."

That was the beginning of a friendship that lasted until his death, and it was the start of my regular weekly visits to the County Home.

A week before, one of my chelas had said she was sending me a book. She had met the author, Paul Monette, and the book was called *Borrowed Time*. The book had arrived that morning as we were loading the van, and it went into my bag. Now Mr. Tillman was going through my stuff while I was getting his watermelon.

"Get out of the damn bag, you old bandit," I said.

"Shut your mouth girl, and read this to me." He had seen the words "AIDS" on the cover.

"I'm not reading you any book about AIDS."

"I got AIDS, and you think I can't read something written about this thing I got?"

"It's not that, Mr. T, I think it's going to be boring."

"You let me be the judge."

"All right, close your eyes and let me read." He was looking pretty tired now, and I wanted him to shut up and rest. I began to read:

"I don't know if I will be alive to finish this book...." The beginning words caught my attention and I read on. I must have been reading a long time. Before I knew it, I was on page 116 and still reading. When I heard a cough behind me, I turned around to see a whole group of patients, some in wheelchairs, a new nurse, and a couple of aides, all listening.

Well, I thought, Mr. T must be in a real deep sleep to allow this. I was just about to shoo everyone out when the old man woke up.

"What you stopping for? Read on."

He kept his eyes closed so he wouldn't have to see the other people, and I kept reading on, choking down my own emotions. *"The most casual things took a twist, as if to remind you that nothing in the body was to be taken for granted anymore. That is what aging feels like, isn't it? It's common among gay men now to say we're all eighty years old, our friends dying off like Florida pensioners."*

Mr. T began to chuckle, yet there were tears in his eyes. "Now all you lazy people get out of my room. I got AIDS, and I need to rest."

I bent to kiss him goodbye, and he told me, "Meet this man that wrote the book and make him your friend." And I did. I met Paul on my next trip to Los Angeles, and he loved hearing how I read his book to the forgotten people in the County Home.

CHAPTER SEVEN

The Furnace

It was a hot sticky morning. By 7:30, the temperature had already reached eighty-two degrees. Mama had gone to work, and Papa was making a thermos of iced coffee to take into the alleyway with him.

"Are you planning to spend the day in the alleyway, Papa?"

"Where else should I be on such a nice morning?"

Soon I was with my friend Kathy in the basement of her big apartment building. I had gotten the idea that coal dust could make us rich, so we were down in the coal bin rubbing the chunks of coal against the metal edge to make dust. Even Kathy was having fun, and Kathy very rarely laughed. I could never figure it out. She at least had plenty of food and a real cot to sleep on. And she always had nice clothes to wear, even if I thought they were all sissy looking.

We heard a screech that would have woken the dead. It was Aunt Mary. "Kathy Magee, I had to work hard to get the money for that dress!"

"What is it, Aunt Mary?" I asked, innocently, while looking for a route out of there. I was inside the coal bin, and Kathy was standing just outside of it. She only had some coal dust on her face, dress, and hands. I was covered with it from head to toe. I could feel it in my nostrils, and it was burning my mouth. "Don't worry, Aunt Mary. We're all going to be rich."

"How, in the name of Christ, Joyce Green, are we going to become rich?" Aunt Mary screeched at me.

I felt like a cornered rat as I tried to explain about coal dust. Well, that was it. As Aunt Mary grabbed me by my long black hair, she screamed, "You fool! It's *gold* dust that would be making the likes of us rich. Now, you get out of here and stay away from Kathy."

The next day, I was alone in the alleyway behind Kathy's apartment. I kept throwing stones at her window until I saw her face appear.

"Why are you here? My mama said you shouldn't come around until the end of the summer." Aunt Mary said that a lot, and we both knew she'd forget. Now I heard her screeching, "Don't you dare do anything to get your clothes dirty!" Kathy had white slacks on, and a white blouse. I was in Harvey's old dungarees and polo shirt. My sneakers looked like they were three hundred years old, but I felt comfortable, and I felt sorry for Kathy having to wear white. This might be a problem, but I wanted to get another look at that furnace.

"Let's go down and see that furnace again. I want to see how it works."

"What if I get my pants dirty? I wish I could live like you."

"No, you don't. No one wants to live like me. I'm the only one in the world who would enjoy my own life." In later years I found myself saying that often: "I loved my life, but I would never want another kid to live it."

"We won't get dirty, I promise. We won't touch anything."

In the basement, Kathy suddenly said, "Do you know some people get burnt in furnaces when they're dead?"

"Oh, come on, who told you that?"

"I read it in school. In a place called India, they burn the dead bodies."

"No way," I said. Then something happened to me. A river flashed in front of my eyes, and the scent of burning flesh entered into my being. "Kathy, do you smell that?"

"Smell what? That's just the old furnace."

"For a second I wasn't here."

She looked confused. "I see you. You're right here."

"No, for real. Spit my blood and swear on my life. I wasn't here. I was someplace far away."

"How did you get there?" she asked.

"I don't know. It was like a beautiful river, and something as hot as that furnace was behind me. And it smelled. But I wasn't afraid." She looked scared. "Don't be afraid. We're too young to have anything bad happen to us."

"How could you say that? Everything bad happens to your family."

"Does not!"

"Does too!"

"What's bad that happens to my family?"

"My mama said that you're just a kid who needs a lot of love and attention."

"Well, Kathy Magee, I don't want to go around in white pants in the middle of the summer."

She was serious again. "What did you smell?"

"I don't know. It smelled like chopped meat burning."

"What did it feel like?"

"I think I felt death."

"Joyce, you're scaring me for real. Let's both go tell the priest. Or you can go tell your rabbi."

"I can't. The rabbi don't like me."

It was true; I had been thrown out of synagogue because I insisted on running up the aisle to kiss the Torah. "If she can't behave, better she doesn't come at all," said the rabbi. Most of the time now I went to Catholic church with Kathy. The nuns were kind to me and took me on field trips to the zoo and all over. I told them I was an orphan, and it didn't bother them that I was Jewish.

या

Every once in a while, even at seven, I would have flashbacks to another time. I never knew what they were, but I didn't worry about it. There was a longing growing in me, though, which would eventually succeed in making me who I am today. The furnace had brought me to a moment of yesterday and, perhaps, to one in the future.

I walk so close to death these days. The scent of death has continuously filled my nostrils as I've worked with so many people with AIDS. But there was always the ocean air to remind me of Brighton Beach and the days when I looked upon the sea and knew that God loved me.

CHAPTER EIGHT

A Sadhu's Vision

It was September 1977. For the first time this life, I was in Mother India. I walked through the streets of Kashi in a daze, catching hold of the different scents from the funeral pyres, the smell of burning flesh entering my nostrils. Cows strayed all around, in and out of holy places, as if they owned the world—in India they certainly do. You could hear the sound of their bells everywhere, even on the steps to the *ghats* leading to the sacred river, the Ganga. The scents, the sounds, all entered fully into my being, and I knew I was home. I had traveled throughout India, going to shrines and temples built in honor of my guru. I met many people and was honored as "The Mother," a title given to a holy woman.

One morning, on the steps to the raging Ganga in Haridwar, I was approached by an old lady dressed in the simple cloth of a renunciate. *"Mataji, Mataji,"* she said, then continued in English, "Many children wait for you to tell them about this river."

"How do you know that?" I asked. I'd been talking about the river for years. My guru had taught me a poem, part of an ancient song about his beloved Ganga, which I would often recite. Now this stranger was telling me that I must speak even more about the river. I was impressed that she spoke English.

At that moment, my chelas came by, and the old woman dashed off.

"Who was that?"

"Just a *sadhu* lady," I answered.

We sat there, looking at the river. I began to speak the words of the river song my guru had taught me:

> *Children play by my River*
> *Sadhus stay by my River*
> *Cities old by my River*
> *Temples made of gold by my River*
> *Cows stray by my River*
> *Ghats burn by my River,*
> *Old Man, why do you cry by my River?*
> *Did I not die by my River*
> *And live on by my River?*
> *Kashi, Kashi, by my River....*

We remained sitting there in silence, watching the river flow.

The following day, I put on my all-white sari, wrapping it around my body and tying it simply around my neck, as I'd seen the sadhu wear hers. I went outside, and there was the woman again, in her sadhu cloth. I bent and lightly touched her feet and asked her how she knew of my love for the Ganga and why she spoke English so well.

"One at a time, my daughter," she answered. "Number one, I know things that many people don't know, but I usually keep them to myself. As for speaking English, these clothes do not make one illiterate. I was a professor of literature in New Delhi for many years. Then the yearning to be by my Ganga every day of my life overtook all reason and sensibility. My children were grown, and my husband had been dead for many years. My yearning became more and more intense, so I decided to follow my heart. I never stay in one place more than one day."

"But, Mother," I said, "you are here again today."

"I was waiting for you."

"I am honored," I replied.

"You will have many come and want to die at your feet at the place where you dwell. You must not tell of this meeting before this occurs."

I became very frightened. "Mother, what are you saying? Are my children in danger?"

"All are your children. You must teach of the Ganga. Write, teach, and paint of the river of your heart."

"Paint?" I asked in shock. "I can't paint a stick figure!"

"You will paint the river from the memory of your past lives and from your trip to your motherland this life."

"I will try to do as you say, Mother. What is your name?"

She simply said, "Ma."

I once again touched her feet as she bade me farewell. She walked a few steps and turned back to me to *pranam*. I began to cry. I knew what she had told me would come true and that one day the dead and dying would come to me, either in the form of ash or flesh, to be near the River Ganga.

"I will make ready to receive them," I vowed to my river. "I will make ready."

The Ma had disappeared into the mist of the raging waters, as if she had never existed except in my mind and heart.

It was many, many years before I told anyone that story. Yet as I sit in my temple, facing the statue of the god Ganesh and thinking of all the memorial services we have conducted here by my pond, my own Ganga, I recall the story of the sadhu Ma who, in 1977, had me make ready to receive the dead and the dying—too many, too young, and too close to my heart.

या

Just a few days before, I had run toward the sacred river, hand in hand with my chela, Hanuman Giri. He joined me in her raging waters. A few years later as we walked together by the pond at Kashi Ashram, he asked me a very strange question: "Can I have my ashes in your Ganga?"

"What are you talking about? You're a young man, younger than me."

But he insisted until I made him that promise, to place his ashes in the pond, which had become our own sacred body of water, our Ganga. I didn't know it yet, but he had AIDS, and I would soon have to keep my promise. He would be one of the first of many whose ashes would grace our waters.

CHAPTER NINE

Spoonfed's Ashes

The full moon was directly overhead. My chelas, all in white, were singing the "Hanuman Chaleesa," forty verses of devotion to the god of service, Hanuman. The moon lit up their faces as the ancient melody went on, entering into my heart. The ashram's young adults and teenagers held urns and vases filled with the ashes of twenty-seven unknown souls who had died from AIDS. All these ashes had been left unclaimed.

There was one small bag of ashes, separate from the others, the ashes of a throwaway child. "Baby—Gender Unknown." Those words were typed on a label on the bottom of the plastic bag. I gently fingered the little femur bone that the crematorium hadn't consumed and began to talk of the loneliest of deaths. I moved to the edge of the dock overlooking my pond, my Ganga. Ashes were handed to me. We had a list of names, but we didn't know which names went with which ashes. The funeral parlor had carelessly mixed them all up, not caring. As the names were read aloud, I fed the ashes into the waiting water.

The moon allowed me to see my reflection staring back at me from the water's surface, my sari white and flowing, my hair blowing in the gentle wind. I remembered another dock and other ashes. The year was 1947.

या

"Juice, Juicey, what's you staring on that water so hard for, girl? You want to fall in?" Joe Joe's grandmother, Georgia, was trying to get my attention by using the name that seemed to be mine in Brighton Beach's black community. Joe Joe and his grandparents lived right behind us—the back of our cellar facing the back of his cellar.

I said, "I just like to see where the ashes went," but what I meant was, "Why did we put ashes in the ocean?"

As we were coming home from the schoolyard, Joe Joe had told me that his grandma and grandpa were going to put the ashes of Grandpa's brother, Spoonfed, in the ocean since Spoonfed always wanted to go out to sea. It was to happen late that night, "Cause," he said, "it ain't a legal thing to do."

"Why does old Spoonfed want his ashes to be in the ocean? Can I come and see?"

"No way, it's gonna be in the middle of the night."

In truth, I went out whenever I wanted to. Mama slept like the dead on vacation, and Shirley worked nights. "Is Spoonfed gonna be there?" I asked.

"Nah, I don't think so. Remember when Spoonfed's girlfriend was over the house? She said that Spoonfed got ten to twenty years on an island in California for armed burglary."

"Yeah, I remember. I'm going tonight. And that's that."

We held hands as we crossed Oceanview Avenue. We had finally figured that one out for ourselves. When Papa asked me if someone held my hand when I crossed the street, I could swear to God that someone did. Joe Joe said the same thing to his grandma when she came home from work. We just never told anyone that it was each other's hands we held.

We ran into the alleyway to see my papa. There he was in the middle of January, freezing cold and sitting on a folding chair, cards in hand. While there was no wind in the alley, the sun couldn't get in there between the houses either. Near the folding table and the four not-working men was a big garbage can with a great big fire in it, warming up the whole of the alley. I went over to the can and looked at the ashes that were flying all around. I saw nothing special, except for a funny thing in between my eyebrows that I had been seeing now and then all my life: a river flowing and free. I thought everyone could see what I saw.

"Papa, do you love your ashes?"

"Go have something to eat, and give Joe Joe something too," said my papa, looking at his cards as if he held a full house.

Joe Joe and I ran to the cellar and went right to the old icebox. There was nothing in it but one open Pepsi. We sat on the dirty wooden floor and took turns sipping the flat soda.

"I'm meeting you tonight. Where are you going to put your uncle's ashes in the ocean?"

"Grandma said that Spoonfed liked the pier off West 19th Street."

"Okay, what time?"

"Just watch my house, and stay behind us when you see us leave."

That night no one went to sleep at the right time. At 11 o'clock, Mama was still up and, for some reason unknown to us, was playing Mama. She wanted to make sure that I had a bath and had eaten my Rice Krispies. Finally, after playing the old turn-it-yourself Victrola and listening to Bessie Smith blast out the blues, she lay down on the dusty couch and fell asleep with her clothes still on. Papa was in the alleyway under a big spotlight that he and his gambler friends had hooked up so they could play late into the night. Shirley was working, Harvey was asleep, and Melvin was never home if he could help it.

I saw my chance. With my hair still wet from the forced bath, I climbed out the bathroom window just in time to see Joe Joe's family leave their basement and walk toward Brighton Beach Avenue. They walked the first long block, and I walked behind them, seemingly unseen.

When they reached the big street, Grandma Georgia called out into the still, cold night, "Juicey, you hold onto Grandpa's hand. You hear me, child?"

Joe Joe giggled, and so did I as I raced up to old Joe and took his rough hand. We crossed over and walked straight to the Boardwalk. In Grandpa's other hand was a cardboard box.

"What's in there, Grandpa?" I asked out of curiosity.

"That's Spoonfed's ashes, child."

"Oh," I said, still wondering why Spoonfed sent his ashes to Joe Joe's grandparents when we could have all the ashes we wanted from the under-the-Boardwalk crowd.

We got to the Boardwalk and watched the full moon reflecting on the great Atlantic. It was a clear, still, cold night. Looking as if we had on all the clothes that we owned, we walked the two or so miles to Coney Island's famous pier. When we finally got there, there were the fishermen who stay out all night. I had not come this far by myself, so I was on a new adventure. The pier looked like the finger of a giant wooden monster going out into the night. Behind us, walking slowly and singing was a procession of people I had at one time or another seen in Joe Joe's cellar or on the streets of Brighton Beach.

Joe Joe said, "What do you think is going on, Joycey?"

"I don't know, but it sure is weird."

When we got to the end, Grandma held the cardboard box containing the ashes and spilled some of them slowly into the waiting waters. Then we each took a turn. Behind us the soft voices of Joe Joe's kin swept into the night. The fishermen, strangers the moment before, joined in and sang with the others.

"Joe Joe, say something," said Grandma.

Joe Joe lowered his head, his dark curls falling on his face and said, "I love you, Uncle Spoonfed."

"Say something, Juicey, go on and speak," said Grandma.

"Spoonfed," I said, "when I see you I'm gonna ask you why you wanted to put your ashes in the water."

Everyone said something like, "Isn't she sweet?" or "How cute." I thought they were all nuts. We started for home. Me and Joe Joe walked in front with Grandma and Grandpa. Feeling like important big kids, we just pretended to understand everything. Everyone was silent as we made the long walk back to Brighton Beach in the cold night, hearing the sound of the waves hitting the shore.

"You know," I finally said, "this is the weirdest thing I ever saw done."

Grandma laughed into the night. "Don't you worry none, child, you did good, you honored old Spoonfed real nice."

We finally got to where we had to leave the Boardwalk. Joe Joe and I ran down the wooden ramp leading to the street, holding hands all the way. We stopped at the corner to wait for Grandma and Grandpa to catch up. In the light from the street lamp, I saw that Grandpa was crying. The tears were falling down his dark handsome face.

"I sure miss you, Spoonfed," he said, as he took my hand to cross the street.

"Well, why don't you go to that island in California and see him?" I asked, trying to stop the old man's tears.

"Can't see him no more, child."

All of a sudden Grandma Georgia came up and took my other hand. "Child, I am thinking that you and Joe Joe don't realize that what we put in the ocean was Spoonfed's ashes."

"I know that," said the indignant Joe Joe.

"So do I, Grandma."

"No," she said, as we reached the curb on the other side of the street. "No," she said again, as we turned the corner and began to walk down her street. "No, you don't know that Spoonfed was killed in Alcatraz Prison in a fight in the yard."

I stopped and stood still. Joe Joe had stopped too, and was standing still on the street corner. I can remember looking up at the street sign. "Brighton 7th Street," it read, and I could see the sign for Brighton 8th Street. That was my block. I wanted to run home in the darkness and pretend that I didn't understand. Instead I asked, "Spoonfed's dead?" He always had chicken corn candy and shared it with me and Joe Joe. I couldn't grasp the thought of never seeing him again—his toothless smile, handsome face, and wild and bushy gray hair.

"You mean to tell me," said Joe Joe, "that Uncle Spoonfed is dead?"

"Yes, son," she said, holding him close. "And that was his ashes, the ashes that was left after they burned his body in California."

"That was Uncle Spoonfed in the box?" shouted Joe Joe.

"How does a person become ash?" I asked.

We began to walk up the street. Georgia said, "We all gonna turn to ash when we die, honey child. Burning someone's body turns it to ash faster than burying it does. Now you go on through the back and get on home. Dream nice dreams of Spoonfed tossing you in the air and giving you lots of chicken candy."

"But, Grandma," I said, "he ain't gonna toss me or give me candy again."

"So sleep on the memories," she said, beginning to cry.

या

That night by my pond I remembered the moment when I put some of Spoonfed's ashes in the Atlantic, how the ash kept my fingers warm. I purposely didn't wash my hands as I got into the bed that I shared with Shirley in the front room. I usually was pretty good about washing up, yet that night I wanted to keep the ash on my fingers for as long as I could. At seven, that was the way I grieved for Spoonfed.

Many years later, the ashes of those unknown men, women, children, and babies coated my fingers, and the gentle breeze blew the ashes back at me as I scattered them into the Ganga. "I give them all to you, Mac, and I give them all to you, Christ. Take care of them." The big fountain in the middle of the pond rained down, and the ashes swirled together in the water beneath the full moon. They found a resting place where we will grieve for them and celebrate their lives. If we remember the dead, they live on.

CHAPTER TEN

A Star in the East

The steam was banging away on the pipes that ran along the ceiling of our cellar. I couldn't sleep, so I sang along with the pipes: "Boom, boom, pssssssssss, boom, boom, pssssssssss."

Shirley, who had been asleep, told me in no uncertain terms to shut up. I might as well get dressed and go to the beach. I ran to the bathroom. My brother Harvey was in there.

"Harvey, get the fuck out of there."

He opened the door. He was sitting on the closed toilet, studying the Bible.

"Harvey, that don't look like no Jewish Bible."

"It's not, stupid."

"What is it then?"

"It's the New Testament."

"Like the one Kathy has?"

"Yes, and where are you going with my jacket at 4:30 in the morning?"

"I am going out that window and then to the beach, and, if you open your mouth, I will tell Mama that you are reading some *goyisha* thing. You're supposed to be studying for your bar mitzvah."

"If you don't tell, then I won't tell how you sneak out."

"Deal," I said and spat three times in my hand, waiting for him to do the same.

He looked at me in absolute disgust. "Deal," he said, "but I'll be damned if I'm going to touch your spit to seal the deal."

"Harvey, you're such a sissy."

"Joyce," he said, serious now, without a drop of the sarcasm he usually had when he said my name, "where are you going?"

I looked at my brother sitting there on the closed toilet bowl in the filthy bathroom, his long *payot* curled on the sides of his face. He still wore his hair in the orthodox style even though he always used to get beat up on the streets. "Come with me," I said kindly.

He hesitated a moment. "Okay. Wait for me right here."

"Hurry up," I said, "I am sweating my balls off."

"You know, you have a mouth like a sewer."

"Hurry up or I'm going without you." He was back in two minutes with his Bible, and we were off.

The streets were quiet. When we got to Brighton Beach Avenue, Harvey took my hand. "Joyala, don't cross the street!" he said. Making fun of Papa was the main thing we had in common.

By the time we got to the beach, we were out of breath and cold. I didn't want to bring my brother to meet my friends for fear he would say something stupid, and anyway I wanted to be alone with him and hear about his new kind of Bible. He was still clutching it.

"Come on, I'll race you down to the water."

"I've never been on the beach in the middle of the night." He looked at me in the moonlight. "Aren't you afraid?"

"Shit yeah, I'm afraid of getting caught."

He smiled, and at that second I loved my brother more than ever before. We kept still. The night was the stillness. The moon was bright in the sky. The ocean was calm and singing her melody to the stars falling into her.

"Harvey," I whispered, "I wish we didn't have to go home." My brother took my hand. I asked him, "Why are you always so sad?"

"I'm lonely sometimes," said my twelve-year-old brother.

"So am I sometimes, but I have friends who live under the Boardwalk."

"Right."

"No, really."

Just then a huge star fell into the ocean. "Look, it's in the East," he said, like that mattered.

"Who cares where it is?" I didn't want a geography lesson. The wind began to blow and the sea got rougher. We cuddled up, my brother and I. It felt good, and warm.

"Joyce, do you know it's almost Christmas?"

"Yeah, and we'll get to go to Aunt Mary's and Uncle Fred's. And he will say me and you killed Christ, and then we'll get cookies."

"We didn't kill Christ. People who were afraid of his beauty killed him. They didn't understand him." I looked into his moonlit face. He was crying.

"Why are you crying, brother? Okay, shut up and tell me about Christ."

He began, like he was reading except that he wasn't. "Once, in the olden days, there was a virgin named Mary, who was to be married to a man named Joseph." It seemed to me as if the ocean and the stars were listening to him speak. "An angel came and visited Mary in the night and told her she was blessed among women."

His voice was a melody that was putting me to sleep. I laid my head in his lap. He just kept talking. "Funny," I thought, "I always thought I was smarter than Harvey. I bet he could teach me some things." The last words I remember hearing were "and the baby leaped in her womb."

When I woke up, it was almost light. Harvey was staring into the ocean.

"Shit, Harvey, we better get our asses out of here."

"Joyce, this night is our secret, okay?"

We brushed the sand off our bottoms and raced to the Boardwalk.

When we had climbed through the window, Harvey suddenly said, "I'm sorry for how you have to live."

In a moment of wisdom that hit me like a ton of bricks, I replied, "Don't be, I probably chose it. And thanks for the story. It was a good one."

"Shaindela," he said, using my Jewish name, "that was the story of Christmas."

"You didn't make it up?" We were in the filthy bathroom, yet the scent of the sea was still with me.

"No, but one day I hope to know the man that it was written about."

"Jesus?" I said.

"Yes, little sister," he said and walked out of the bathroom. I didn't know it then, but he was already thinking about becoming a Catholic. A few years later he did.

I looked back out the window after he was gone and said, "Hey, Mac, let my brother see you." As I looked up, a large star was falling. "Is that the East?" I asked the new morning. I bet that it was. "Let him see Christ. You still got *me*." I fell asleep, dreaming of the beach, the ocean, and the Eastern stars.

मा

Harvey continued to search, and finally his search took him far from his family. No one has seen or heard from him since the late sixties, although we hired detectives to find him. Every night, as I look at the stars over our sacred Kashi Ashram, I believe in my heart that my brother Harvey is also seeing the stars and thinking of his sister. Maybe one day my brother will hear these words and know that whatever got him lost in this big world is not as important as a sister's love and affection. I love you my brother. I always have and always will.

CHAPTER ELEVEN

A Walk with Harry

"Joyala! Joyala! Wake up!"

"Papa, I'm not sleeping. I'm wide awake."

In the cellar at 3014 Brighton 8th Street, the boys slept wherever they wanted. Shirley and I slept on an old couch that opened up. It was in the front room, which had windows that looked up at the street. All you could see through the windows was people's legs. Mama and Papa had a room in the back, and Grandma stayed in a little room that Mama called "the mop room."

"Do you want to come with me this morning?"

I jumped at the chance to miss school legitimately. "Where are we going?"

"We are gonna walk the Boardwalk. I need a break."

"A break from what?"

"Listen, playing cards isn't the easiest thing in the world."

"Papa," I said, "no one takes a break from no work. The opposite of no work is work."

He laughed as he pulled my braid. "Bite your tongue! Do you want to come with me, or not?"

"Sure, what time?"

"How about as soon as Mama goes to work?"

The morning brought a bright and cold day. After Mama left, Papa gave me Harvey's heavy pea coat, handed down from Melvin. It reached my ankles. I was wearing my knitted hat with the itchy straps wrapped around my neck and heavy woolly underwear from Aunt Lily under my dungarees. I looked like a little refugee child. Papa said if I was warm, what difference did it make?

"Can I wear Harvey's gloves?" My unsuspecting brother was taking a shower, and I knew he would be mad as hell when he saw the jacket missing. He would have to wear his old coat that was too small for him.

"No, just put your hands in your pockets."

I was yearning to have pretty little mittens pinned to my sleeves like the girls from Manhattan Beach. Papa somehow or other always had a warm coat and a nice hat; Mama made sure. When I asked for a new coat, the answer from my papa was usually something about how lucky I was to be making memories.

We were on our way.

"Why are we climbing the El? Are we going on a train?"

"Why did the chicken cross the street?"

I knew the ticket seller—the same man who had watched me cross over the tracks for so many nights—got off his shift mornings at eight. It was now five to eight. Papa went straight to the token booth. I thought about making a run for it.

"Give me Big Jock in the third, and if you're smart you'll put your own money down on him too." The man looked surprised that Papa would talk business in front of me. Yet he just gave me a wink and took Papa's money. I was dying to know where that money came from, but it was more important to me that he had kept my secret.

And Papa knew I wouldn't rat him out to Mama. Off we went, me and my papa sharing life's secrets.

The wind was blowing hard as we walked down the ramp on Coney Island Avenue to the beach. Under the Boardwalk, I could see a few folks still sleeping near garbage pails with fires going. I kept my face down toward the sand. I thought, "What if Hudson and Henry see me? They'll surely come over and want to meet my papa."

"Hey, Joyce!" Big Henry's voice called.

I didn't have the heart to ignore my friend, even if it got me in trouble. I turned. Papa looked curious. Henry came toward us. He looked cold. Please, God, don't let him be drunk. "Papa," I said real bold, "this is my friend, Big Henry."

"Hello Harry," said Henry to Papa, then turning to me, "I've known your father a long time."

Papa smiled. "Henry and I did soft-shoe way back when."

All of a sudden everything became a little clearer. Big Henry always seemed to know a little too much about my life.

"I've known Big Henry a long time too. We go way back since when I was five."

"Okay, let's walk."

After a little while, I asked him, "Why did Henry stop dancing?"

"The music stops sometimes, that's all. Now, we're going to get on the Boardwalk and keep going till we reach the end."

"That's Sea Gate," I said. Sea Gate was a place with a fence around it where wealthy people lived in big houses on the beach. Diamond Jim is said to have bought Mae West a house there. Yet if Papa said we were going to the end, then I knew we would somehow get in.

We walked fast till the cold wasn't cold anymore. Papa took my hand and we began skipping.

"Papa, working makes people old," I said, thinking of my mama.

He stopped short. "There are different things for different people. I chose freedom over work."

"Are you free?"

"No, but you are."

When we got to Sea Gate, Papa walked straight up to the guardhouse. The guard on duty looked bewildered. No one came to Sea Gate without a car. "Mr. Epstein is expecting us," said my father as if this was normal. The guard checked his clipboard and let us pass. I was shocked. Papa seemed excited and pulled me along. We came to a huge mansion on the beach. "Papa," I said, "this is the end, the end of the world."

Papa laughed and rang the doorbell. A lady answered and led us through a huge hallway and into a big room with lots of books where a frail old man was sitting in a wheelchair. Papa shook his hand. All the bones in the old man's hand showed; I was too afraid to touch it. I just said, "Hi."

"Do you know," the skeleton said, "that your papa was the best hoofer on my stage?"

"What's a hoofer?" I asked. I was eyeing the little sandwiches, baby knishes, and baby franks that the housekeeper was bringing on a tray.

"A dancer, child, a dancer of the soft-shoe."

"Oh, Seymour, I wasn't that good."

"Yes, you were. You and Henry both were the best. But for Henry that was only until his family was killed in that accident."

"My Henry?" I asked, wide-eyed.

Papa said, "Seymour, the kid is fond of Henry."

"Weren't we all?"

We stayed for a while, eating little baby sandwiches. When no one was looking, I filled my pockets to take to Henry. I never did take off that pea coat. When it was time to go, Mr. Epstein called the lady, and she gave me a bag full of the little delicious things. I wasn't a bit ashamed about having already stuffed my pockets.

We started to walk again, Papa holding my hand, yet not being there at all. By the time we got to the Boardwalk, Papa looked downhearted and his face was wet. "Sometimes," he said, "the music stops too soon. I could have been the best."

"You *are* the best."

It was 1949. Dinah Washington's big hit was "Laughing Boy." Mama always said Dinah sang it special for Papa. Now, seeing my always-cheerful father alone with his tears, I began to understand. All through the years, whenever I heard Dinah sing about the brokenhearted laughing boy, I would always remember that walk home from Sea Gate.

CHAPTER TWELVE

Big Henry's Story

"Henry," I said to the sleeping man under the Boardwalk who looked like a big bundle of rags. The fire in the garbage can was raging. It was about two in the morning and freezing cold. I was wrapped up in everything that I could find to put on, even Melvin's Cooper Union sweater. I knew he would have a fit if he found out. I didn't care as long as I was warm. There was no wind, which was surprising for the beach in January. I could hear the sound of the waves breaking. I felt good and at home on the beach. I could see the stars when I looked out and up.

"Henry, wake up. I need to talk to you."

From the other side of the can, a voice I recognized right away said, "Hey, girl, are you crazy bothering a man sleeping off a good drunk?"

It was Chicken Boy, the man with the scratchiest voice anyone ever heard. Chicken Boy was sometimes called Chicken Shit. Chicken usually stayed most of the cold months in Florida. I was surprised and happy to see him under the Boardwalk.

"Girl," he said, "you sure grew up pretty."

"Oh, Chicken, what are you doing home?"

"Florida got too hot, if you know what I mean."

I didn't know what he meant, but I would die before I admitted it. I knew that Chicken Boy loved the heat, so this confused me. He was shaking from the cold. I quickly took off Harvey's pea coat and then Melvin's favorite sweater.

"Here, wear this. It's okay, Melvin won't mind." I handed him the sweater and put the pea coat back on. I only intended to loan it to him, never thinking that I might have to face my big brother's wrath. He didn't hesitate. He pulled it over his head, ignoring the buttons like I did.

"What's all that racket?" It was Big Henry.

"It's Chicken Boy, Henry. Ain't you happy?"

I left Chicken and went over to my best friend. "I spent the day in Sea Gate!" I told him.

"Bullshit," said Chicken Boy, "the likes of you don't get into no Sea Gate."

But Henry was paying close attention now and sat up to look me square in the face.

"What's wrong?" I asked him.

"Nothing, just tell me what you were doing in Sea Gate." He looked strange.

"I was with Papa visiting his friend Mr. Seymour Epstein. He said you were the best soft-shoe dancer. And look, I brought us some food from his house."

Grabbing my shoulders, he shook me. "What did he tell you, child? Tell me now."

I was scared. Henry never treated me badly. I said, "He told me that you stopped dancing when you lost your family in an accident. Please, don't hurt me."

"I'm sorry, child, I didn't mean to scare you."

I started asking him questions about his family, hardly noticing that he didn't answer me. "Shush, and listen up," said Chicken Boy in his strange voice. "We let you be close to us drunks since you was little. Now you take us the way we are, or you don't take us at all. Ain't that right, Henry?"

Henry's eyes were looking up as if he was trying to see through the cracks in the Boardwalk. He started to get up. Boy, he sure did look tall under the Boardwalk that dark night. He had to stoop a little not to hit the boards. I just sat there with Chicken Boy, not saying a word, listening to the sound of the waves and feeling bad. I saw Henry walk out from under the Boardwalk onto the beach, and I watched until he disappeared into the moonless night. I wanted to go with him and apologize for talking so much.

I was about to get up when Chicken Boy said, "Wait." I waited. He continued, "Remember, we don't like to talk about what it is that makes us drink."

After a while I heard a whisper, "Joyce, girl, come here to me." Henry's voice was faint, yet clear on that still night.

"Go now," said Chicken Boy, "but you just listen, do you hear me?"

"Okay." I could hear someone digging, and I followed the soft sound. Big Henry was digging in the cold sand and looked to be making some sort of tunnel. I started digging too. I'd promised to keep quiet, so we just kept digging for a while until he began to speak.

"Many years ago, before you were born, my family would come to Coney Island to let the kids play in the sand." There was something in my friend's voice that broke my young heart. He continued, "My youngest child, Bo, loved to make tunnels in the sand so's our hands could meet in the middle."

The mound of sand was already getting pretty high. Now for the hard part, making a second hole without collapsing the whole thing.

"I had five kids, all boys," Henry continued. "I made my living like your papa, doing soft-shoe in the vaudeville theaters in New York. But I never gambled like your papa or drank."

I wasn't even mad at Henry for what he said about my papa. I guessed it was best at that moment to let him think that Papa was a real gambler. I would tell him later that it was all just a game to my papa.

"It was fifteen years ago a friend of mine loaned us an old Ford pickup. We packed the truck and took the highway down from Harlem and then the tunnel to Brooklyn."

Henry and I were both lying on our bellies on the beach with the pile of sand between us. He was talking and making the hole in the tunnel from his side. I was doing the same from my side. Then our hands touched. It felt good. His big, hard, callused hand holding mine made me feel safe and loved in a secret place in my heart.

He told me about a long day with his family at the beach. "At the end of the day," he said, "we all walked to where the truck was parked under the El. I remember little Bo was asleep in my arms. My oldest son, Little Henry, was saying how Bo was spoiled. I told all them boys to get into the back of the truck, and I took Bo and Pearl in the front with me."

Listening to Henry's story, I knew that I was hearing something he had never told anyone. I held tight to his hand in that damp tunnel, which was becoming warmed by our hands.

"We was about to make a turn when a big cement truck came at us from under the El. He was coming straight at us. I screamed out of the open window for the boys to jump out of the back of the truck. I couldn't see them at all. They had all fell asleep like little Bo. I threw myself over Pearl and the baby. The next thing I know is I woke up in Coney Island Hospital. All I had was broken bones, but my baby was dead. I suffocated him in his sleep with this big clumsy body. Pearl and my boys were crushed under the cement truck."

Henry was holding my hand too tightly in the tunnel. It began to hurt, but I didn't dare to move it. Henry was looking at me now as if he had just realized I was there. He loosened his hold on my hand. Both of us moving at the same time collapsed our tunnel.

"Is that why you drink so much, because you miss your family? You can't be drinking cause you killed your family...." I heard Henry gasp, but I kept going. "Because you didn't. I think it was better for Bo to be in your arms than to be crushed by a cement truck."

"Hush and come here. You said just enough, don't say no more." I got up and ran into my friend's arms. He was on his knees, and I fit right in his big arms. The scent of him was cheap sweet wine. "None of us, saints or sinners, have the answer to these things of life," he whispered into my hair. "Don't look for answers. Just give your love."

Then we walked hand-in-hand back to under the Boardwalk. Chicken Boy was sitting on Big Henry's cardboard, drinking, I assumed, from Big Henry's bottle. Seeing Big Henry and me, he dropped the bottle and ran away.

Henry picked up the bottle, but there was nothing left. Big tears began to run down his face. He told me, "Now go on home and be sure you stay out of your brother's way for a while."

"Why?"

He smiled in the firelight. "Cause Chicken Shit just ran off with your brother's school sweater."

"Shit!" I made to run after Chicken Boy.

"Don't even bother, girl. You can't catch that one. He'll bring it back when he realizes he has it. He has to sober up first, though."

"By then the sweater will be ruined."

"It's only a sweater," he said, "not a life."

CHAPTER THIRTEEN

My River

I began to take my chelas with me to the County Home, and then to other care facilities. First, we fed cookies and love to everyone in the lobby, and then we made our way with a trolley filled with food down the long hall to the AIDS wing.

"Got those smokes for me, Ma?" Mr. Daniels knew if I got caught giving him cigarettes I would be in big trouble, but for so many, a smoke was all they had left in the world to enjoy.

"Mr. Daniels, do you think I would dare not bring you your cigarettes?"

"You know I follow the rules. Now, you give me those cigarettes."

"You can have the cigarettes, but no matches. You're sitting right next to an oxygen tank."

"Well, that would be like giving me a woman. What would I do with her right now?"

"You just be careful." I knew he would go outside to the garden to sneak a smoke.

I walked into the other room where Charlie had his earphones on. The music he was listening to was turned up so loud that everyone could hear.

"Hey, Charlie, what's happening?"

"Hey, Ma, Mr. Daniels is buying it, ain't he?"

"He doesn't have enough money to buy it right now. What you listening to, Charlie?"

"I'm listening to the music that goes on in my head, and what's coming through these earphones is just background."

I handed Charlie his bananas and cookies, then walked down to see the next person, and the next.

Back in the hallway, I gave all the caregivers and nurses hugs and cookies, kisses, grapes, crackers, and lots of love.

One of my chelas came in. "Mr. Daniels is saying he wants to see you again, Ma."

When I got to back to his room, he screamed at me, "Ma, you didn't leave me no matches!" I sat down on his bed and handed him the matches. He looked at me seriously. "I'm so tired," he said after a moment. "Maybe you better start teaching me all about death." I was surprised by the question, although we both knew Mr. Daniels didn't have a lot of time left.

"What do you want to know?"

"Where is it I'm going?" he asked.

"You're going where there is no pain and suffering."

"Is it boring?" he asked, looking more like a child than a man in his fifties.

"No. How can it be boring when God is your companion? God's never boring."

"You know they operate on me next Thursday." His foot was being amputated, a result of the diabetes he had in addition to AIDS.

"I'll be there," I told him.

I gazed into his eyes and began to speak, letting the words take their own course: "All I know is about my river, a river that is so powerful and strong it cuts into death even while visiting life. It's not warm or cool as it rides its course through death. It just *is*. In life my River Ganga bathes her own people, she caresses her own people. Her people wash their clothes in the river, and the river waters her people's lands and soothes their souls. The children play upon her waters. The holy people come from all over to sit beside it. Sitting by the Ganga is like singing gospel by the river Jordan. The river is used, the river is wild, and the river is respected. Then there is a moment's interruption."

Mr. Daniels was listening intently.

"An interruption of breath, and when that breath ceases to be, the river keeps flowing right over the non-breath into eternity. There she continues to nourish the lands and allow the souls to swim in her waters of life and death. It does not matter to the river; it's just a second's interruption. Less than that."

I kissed him gently on his forehead. My eyes were misting; at that moment, I myself needed my river more than anything. Hearing my name being called, I got up and walked toward the next person who needed me. The need doesn't end, and sometimes all one can do is walk on to the next person, or the next bed. When you are dealing with so much suffering, when you are dealing with so much pain, emotionalism helps no one. The dying don't need your tears, they need your strength.

So I was taught by my beloved teacher Swami Nityananda. He showed me how to be in the presence of those in pain without bringing my own pain to them, by going into the *Chidakash*, or the Sky of Consciousness. I have taught this process to many caregivers to help them avoid burn out.

To reach the Chidakash, breathe deeply into your heart, let the breath out slowly, and focus your attention above your head. Do this three times, and your consciousness will be carried to the heart space over the head. There you are free of attachment, free of emotion, and yet still filled with love. When working with others, keep your awareness on this space above the head. It may feel cold at first, but it brings forth the clearest, truest love. It is a clear space of heart consciousness: love without attachment.

मा

The following Thursday dawned bright and sunny. We arrived at the hospital, and in my own subtle way I barged into the place with trays of cookies. When we reached Mr. Daniels' floor, we found that he had just come up from recovery. He was still very groggy. He opened his eyes and had the sweetest smile, a smile that has stayed in my heart to this day. He spoke in a long, soft drawl. "Ma, Ma," he said, "I'm still here, but I saw the other side of that river, and it's pretty nice."

मा

My river is filled with people I have loved and held. The river just continuously flows on and touches everyone without a thought of who it's touching. All are welcomed, including my people: the whores, the junkies, the dying, the people no one wants to touch—the river touches them all. If the world would take time to know them, they would see the beauty of God shining through their eyes. My people open their arms wide to anyone who can see through the veils of poverty. They are open to anyone who gives them a kind word. Their beauty is there for anyone to see, and it's the same beauty as my river, the Ganga.

CHAPTER FOURTEEN

Hot Corn

Brooklyn grew real cold in the winter. The winter I was eight, the togetherness of family meals was an illusory thing at 3014 Brighton 8th Street. Still, Mama called a powwow in the room that most resembled a kitchen, the one with a sink and an old wooden table in it.

In the sink, I was soaking the socks of all three men in soapy water. I loved to skip rinsing them, leaving the soap still in them. I'd dry them on the steam pipes overhead so they'd be stiff as sticks when my brothers tried to put them on. Boy, did they throw a fit! That was the only time I would pretend to be my age. Only Papa didn't seem to mind.

Mama had us all sitting down. "Now isn't this nice, us all together?"

"Mama," I said, wise-guy-like, "are you going to cook us a meal?" She looked at me as if I had asked her to go to Mars. As I remember it, it wasn't a look of guilt as much as genuine shock. "It's okay," I said, "I wouldn't know you if you cooked."

She breathed out a sigh of relief. "Joyala, make some peanut butter and jelly sandwiches."

My brother Mel announced, "I'm on a diet."

Papa said, "Good, son, you're living in the right place."

Shirley didn't think any of this was funny. The weight of us not being a real family seemed to fall on her, though she didn't know what to do about it. Even so, she seemed to think our parents could do no wrong.

"Papa's gonna work in Coney Island," Mama announced.

"A real job?" I asked.

"Of course," Mama replied, real dignified. "Papa is gonna run a hot corn stand."

"Yay, food!" I said. I was busy preparing the one meal that we might eat together, if my timing was good. Shirley and Melvin looked a little skeptical, like, "What is this adventure gonna cost us?" Harvey was in Never-Never land as usual, sitting there with a book in his hands.

"Now, that means you might have to be alone, days," said Papa.

"That's fine," I answered. I was usually alone anyway, which Papa didn't seem to notice.

"Come on, Joyala," he said, jumping up. "I'll teach you to dance to Sioux City Sue." He began to dance and sing, teaching me the soft-shoe. I was in my glory. If Mr. Krumpenholtz wasn't home, we didn't have heat, but now the pipes began banging as the heat was being sent up, which was a good beat to dance to. Soon the whole cellar would be like a sauna, and we would have to open the windows to the freezing cold.

We had all winter long to think of eating hot corn on hot summer nights. Little did we know that hot corn was all we were going to eat, except for the watermelon that Frank was selling. His stand was attached to Papa's hot corn stand, and he had eleven kids. Papa made more money than Frank, yet Papa got married to the rubber-ball poker machine where you won points in the form of coupons, which you traded in for things. That's how we got our first toaster, which cost about a thousand dollars worth of coupons.

The stand opened as soon as the weather warmed up, and by the time school was out, I was already a pro at boiling corn. Meanwhile Joe Joe's grandma Georgia was gonna teach me how to cook pickled pigs feet—but only after she sent me and Joe Joe all the way to the butcher in Coney Island. "If you come back here, Juicey, I'll let you watch me pickle the feet." She kept talking, telling me that Bubba the butcher would give us some pigskin so she could make the gravy for the black-eyed peas and potatoes. "You two be real nice, and Juicey can eat over tonight. Ain't nothing like my black-eyed peas floating in my pigskin gravy."

"What about the pigs' feet?"

"Well, child, that takes a little doing. You got to wait for that meal."

Big Joe was Joe Joe's grandfather. Joe Joe's dad, who was away in jail, was also Joe, but everyone called him Junior. No one ever talked about Joe Joe's mother.

"Is pigs' feet kosher?" I asked Georgia.

"Child, pigs' feet is everything."

Joe Joe and I were off. We climbed the fence from Joe Joe's backyard to mine so we wouldn't have to go around the block. Papa's friend Max was talking seriously about taking a boat to Israel now that the war was over. I just gave Papa a kiss and said goodbye. He didn't notice us, so I just whispered that we were going to get pigs' feet.

"There," I said to Joe Joe, "I told him."

"Where's Israel?" Joe Joe asked me.

"Near Williamsburg," I answered smoothly. I'd heard them say Israel was the Jewish homeland, and Papa had said a lot of Jews lived in Williamsburg.

It was summer now, and we could do what we wanted. After we picked up the pigs' feet, we were going to get us some hot corn at my papa's stand, at least if he would open on time.

We walked about a whole hour, maybe more. The store was way down in the black section of Coney Island.

"Aren't you Big Joe's grandson?" asked the butcher, a man so skinny you wouldn't have seen him if he was standing sideways.

"Yes, Sir," Joe Joe answered. "My grandpa got a job," he said, "and Grandma Georgia said you was supposed to help us celebrate."

"Here you go, son. Good fresh pigs' feet and lots of pork skin for your grandma."

On our way again, we went past the Steeplechase and ran into the Bowery, where we saw Papa at his hot corn stand.

"Joycey, girl, watch the pot for me. I got a real good feeling. This feels like my lucky day."

Joe Joe and I asked Frank, who was receiving an ice delivery, if we could have a piece of watermelon.

"Sure, kids, anything you want."

While we were eating our watermelon, I got a great idea: to boil some pork skin in the hot corn pot and make nice gravy for Papa's corn. Joe Joe couldn't decide whether to do it or not, so I just grabbed the package out of his hands and pushed a piece of the skin into the big pot.

"Put it all in," Joe Joe said, so I did.

Papa came back while we were confusing a lady with the wrong change for her corn. Frank was laughing too much to be any help.

After giving the lady her change, Papa whispered in my ear, "What is that smell?"

A thick fat-like substance formed a layer at the top of the pot. Papa pulled out a corn, took some bites and said it was the best corn he'd ever tasted. Then a look of understanding began to dawn on his face. Looking at us sharply, he said, "I don't care what's in this corn and neither do you two." The lady came back for another hot corn for her Hasidic husband. Papa almost choked as he gave it to her. We couldn't figure out what was going on with him, but who cared?

Papa gave us a whole lot of cooked corn to take to Joe Joe's family. Grandma Georgia was waiting for us. "What took you kids so long?"

"Papa gave me some corn cooked in your pork skin."

"What you say, child?" She sniffed the corn and began to laugh. "Well, at least you didn't cook the pigs' feet, did you now?"

"No, Grandma," we answered together.

That night she made a delicious corn pudding, and I'm sure everything was kosher, one way or another.

CHAPTER FIFTEEN

Ping-Pong Champion

You could smell summer, and its scent held a secret of its own.

All the kids in the neighborhood belonged to the Brighton Beach Baths, all except me, Kathy, and Joe Joe. It was situated right on the beach and had tennis courts and at least three pools. It was a huge complex, and it cost a fortune to get a season pass, never mind a one-day ticket. Located just down Coney Island Avenue from us, the Baths called to us just because we couldn't afford to go.

"Come on, Kathy, I'll show you something," I said one very hot day.

We walked under the Boardwalk until we got to where the Brighton Beach Baths crowd got their hands stamped to get back in after they went into the ocean.

"Mister, mister?" I asked an aging Jewish man wearing a great big *mezuzah* in the brightest gold I ever saw around his neck. He looked like a safe choice.

"Yes, little girl," he answered, not unkindly.

"Me and my sister lost our beach bag with our season passes in it. Our mama is going to kill us." I asked him to let me transfer the ink from his fresh stamp onto my hand.

"Well," he said, looking us over, "that will take care of your problem. What about your sister?" Kathy looked nothing like me. "My name is Mr. Cohen. Come with me," he said, so we followed him to another gate.

"Hello, Mary," he said, "will you let my grandchildren go in this way?"

With a wave of her arm, she let us pass. I turned and thanked the man. "Never lie," he said, "at least not if you can help it."

"Goodbye, Sir," I said, then whispered to Kathy, "and what did he just do?"

"Would you look at the size of the pool?" Kathy said.

Were we ever in awe! We were in shorts, not bathing suits, so I made believe I pushed Kathy in, and then she grabbed my foot and pulled me in. We thought we were two smart kids fooling the world. Little did we know that no one gave a damn about two little kids on the loose.

Then I spotted the ping-pong tables. I had learned how to play in the first grade at the after-school center of PS 253, whenever Papa forgot to pick me up, which was pretty often if he had a good hand. Here at the Baths two boys were beating the hell out of the paddles and table, and betting money. I knew I was better than both of them. "I'll take the winner," I said, in my drooping shorts and wet polo shirt that came down to my knees.

"Oh, my God, my hair," said Kathy, whose nice braids were dripping wet.

"Don't worry, I'll fix them as soon as I win these boys."

"Get lost, kid," they told me.

"What, are you chicken?" I asked. "I'll bet you a dime and I'll spot you five." I didn't have a dime, but I didn't plan to lose.

"You're on," said the cute blond one. "What's your name?"

Now, that scared me. I thought if the cops knew we had snuck in we would go to jail. "Shirley Green," I answered as smoothly as I could. I figured if I got caught my sister Shirley would take the rap and then get off simply because she was an adult. To my eyes, adults got away with everything. Look at Mr. Cohen.

We started playing. "Three and over," I said, real easy like. If I won fast, me and Kathy could have a nickel cherry coke apiece.

I began slamming every time I got the ball on my side, even the serves. I won him eleven to the five I spotted him.

"I was only warming up," Blondie said.

"Oh, shut your face," his friend told him, then said to me, "My name is Larry. Do you want to be my partner in the doubles match this afternoon?"

"What's the take?" I coolly asked.

"First prize is five dollars."

Kathy's eyes were bulging out of her head.

"Okay, I'll be there."

"Wait, Shirley, what's your cabana number?"

I replied, "My mama told me never to give out my address," and I walked away, dragging Kathy with me.

Kathy said, "Okay, smarty, now what?"

"First I got to fix your hair, so when the game is over, we're out of here."

We went into the open-air locker and cabana section and sat in a shady place. I did the best I could, but Kathy ended up looking like Joe Joe's little sister, with braids sticking up every which way.

"How does it look?"

"It looks a little different, but okay," I lied, because I had done the best I could. Her freckled face was already burned from the sun, and her hair looked like she'd put her finger in a socket.

All of a sudden I heard on the loudspeaker: "Shirley Green, Shirley Green, wanted at the ping-pong tables." We ran back toward the tables. There was a big crowd, mostly boys, with a few girls wearing little beach jackets that matched their bathing suits.

"Shirley, ready for the first set?" Larry was coming toward us with Blondie close on his heels.

Blondie spotted Kathy. "Oh, shit," he said, "what's that?"

"Say one more word, and I'll shove this paddle down your throat!"

"Children, children," a dressed-up lady was saying. She had a clipboard in her hands and was coming toward us. "What division are you in?" she asked me.

The only thing I knew about divisions was from my dad when he bet the fights. "Featherweight," I answered.

"Certainly, dear." She looked at her clipboard. "One minute, Shirley's name is nowhere on this list."

Larry gave me this look. Then I guess, between my drooping, wrinkled clothes and Kathy's hair, something clicked. "The slammer is my cousin from Queens."

"The Slammer," the lady wrote on her clipboard.

We were playing against two brothers. We got the serve. Larry offered me the ball, and I slam-served it five times straight. We won in a shutout, twenty-one to nothing.

"Wow," I said to my new cousin, "that was easy money."

"Shirley, we have to play two more games."

Kathy gulped. We were sure to get caught if we hung around any longer. I looked at the crowd, and there was Mr. Cohen. "Okay," I thought, "no one is gonna get me, not with Grandpa Cohen watching."

We quickly beat the other two teams. I was a hero. Larry asked if I would come and play the next day. "It's up to my grandfather," I sweetly said.

Mr. Cohen was beaming. "Clara," he called out to Mrs. Clipboard, "this little girl should get the prize money right now. I'll sign for it. No need to wait for her mother."

"That's fine, Uncle Aaron." Years later, when Mr. Cohen's obituary was in the *Daily News*, I found out that he was part owner of Brighton Beach Baths. No wonder he didn't need to stamp his hand.

Kathy and I now had five whole dollars. Larry had given me his half. He said he hardly hit the ball. That five dollars was our ruination for one whole year. We were afraid to break the biggest bill we ever saw for fear of someone thinking we stole it. I would keep it hidden in different places all over the cellar because no one ever cleaned our rooms, except me. At Kathy's, Aunt Mary would have found it for sure.

When Aunt Mary saw Kathy's hair, she went into some sort of shock. Kathy couldn't see me for a week, and some of her hair had to be cut off, but the worst thing of it all was that we never did get our cherry Cokes.

CHAPTER SIXTEEN

Shabbos Queen

"Ma, this night is for you, for you to remember, for you to become."

"Oh, right," I thought, "another teacher in my life."

I was with Rabbi Zalman Schachter-Shalomi and his beautiful wife, Eve, who I call Parvati Sati. I realized that the rabbi's schedule was as packed as mine, and that he was giving up his precious teaching and writing time to be with me.

"How I love this man," I thought, "but I hope he doesn't start with the heritage crap."

Everything that could represent a normal *Shabbos* night—in spite of us all being vegetarians—was ready to be served. The matzo ball and mock chicken soup looked delicious. The good rabbi was doing Shabbos in my home on my ashram in Florida, just for me. I had invited some of my Jewish chelas, but he had shooed them out. I really didn't care to do Shabbos—too much pain, too much sorrow, too many memories. "Rabbi," I said, as I stared into his beautiful deep brown eyes, "you know Yashoda has to stay." I was ready to stand my ground, and I was waiting for an argument.

"Of course," he said.

"Of course," I repeated, sounding like I was two years old. Go figure—the Jews had to leave, but the *shiksa* could stay.

मा

I thought for a moment of Rabbi Rubenstein's little synagogue in Brighton Beach. Although we were Orthodox Jews, I had never sat at a proper Shabbos table, I guess because my family was never together. I used to watch my grandmother light the candles in her private space in the cellar. Her space consisted of an orange crate, an old chair, and the two silver candelabras that belonged to only her and her memories of Minsk. Papa had his eyes on those candelabras for years—to sell. I was the only one in the family allowed to witness her rite. I yearned to touch the flame and feel my Jewishness, but I looked too much like my papa to have my grandma let me that close to her candles.

Suddenly I found myself flooded with memories I had put far behind me. I was high up in the rafters of the synagogue, over the right side. Below me were only boys and men, including Harvey. The rabbi was speaking to them about the name of God, or why one must never say out loud the name of God. I already knew God's name to be Mac, but still I listened, until I heard him say the word *"Adonai,"* which is used in addressing God in prayers. I thought, if this was God's secret name, all I had to do was say it and God would come to me. I tried it out, whispering at first, then a little louder, and then it seemed to take over and say itself, louder and louder, until I was shouting it. "Adonai! Adonai!"

Harvey knew right away it was me. "Get her!" he yelled.

I scurried across the dirty little space between the rafters, but something broke and I fell and landed in the middle of the congregation, luckily in some fat guy's lap. I was quick, and I made it out the door before they could grab me. I ran down the street with the rabbi and the cantor running after me. I tripped, and the cantor had me, grabbed me by my long braids and yanked them hard. I spun around and bit him. Oh, what a beating I got after that! He used his cane on me and beat me bloody right there in the street, beat me so badly I had to go to the hospital. I remember lying there on the sidewalk, looking up at the little stained-glass window with the Star of David. "That can't be God's sign," I thought, and then I passed out.

After that, I wasn't allowed back in the synagogue. I started going with Kathy to Our Lady of Solace, where I would tell my troubles to the statue of the lady outside the church, and I swear she listened to me.

या

Rabbi Zalman was staring into my eyes. I felt lost for a moment. "Hey," I thought, "I'm Ma. I touch; I'm not touched." But I kept still in the stillness.

"Ma, here is a present I had made for you in Israel," the rabbi said.

I thought, "I don't want anything that would commit me to this night. I'm only doing this for the rabbi"—as if the rabbi needed me to make Shabbos. He handed me a beautiful shawl made especially for me, with my own colors on the border.

"Don't cry," I said to myself. "This is just the Jewish drama that you expected." I touched the shawl, the gift from the rabbi's heart, and my tears began to flow.

The rabbi continued talking, ignoring my tears. He began to tell the story of the Shabbos Queen. He placed the shawl on my head and around my shoulders and showed me how to light the candles, a gift from him to me. He placed the prayer book in my hands and, in that moment, gave me everything that I was and will be. He gave me the moment, the moment of all Jewish women who light the candles all over the world.

I was, this night, the Shabbos Queen.

In that moment, I was lifted from the grief I'd unknowingly carried like a large bag of sand in my heart, and I was made whole. I felt my whole ashram stirring with emotion; the temple doors swung open wide with completion, and our Jewish shrine stirred with a newness. Something had been missing in my life, and that something was my heritage. I was a Jew, I am a Jew, and I will always be a Jew. But I am also a Jew who bows to the feet of my Christ; a Jew with a big red ribbon tattooed for life on my left hand, representing all the dead I have lost to AIDS; a Jew who is a Hindu and follows the monkey god of service, Hanuman; a Jew who loves the true Tantric merge of man into God; a Jew who is a devotee of India's black mother, Kali; a Jew who is the disciple of an Indian guru, Neem Karoli Baba; a Jew who worships the Buddha and tries to follow his life of compassion, love, and kindness; a Jew who listens to the ancient teachings of the Sikh gurus.

I heard Parvati Sati singing in her profoundly sweet voice, and my mind went spinning again, back in time and place.

मा

After climbing out the cellar window one night, I went looking for my friends, but they weren't there. The place we called home under the Boardwalk was empty. I walked the Boardwalk for a long time, until I was almost under the big Parachute ride. I went there often and felt quite safe in the crowd of mostly soldiers and sailors. Right in front of the Parachute was a bench where people sat and watched or waited to buy tickets. The line was always long. On the bench I spotted two candles in fancy glass holders.

"Hey, Joycey, whatcha doing out so late in the night?" asked Butchy, who had the night job of running the Parachute.

"I felt like walking," I said, eyeing the candles. "What are those candles?" I asked, knowing they were the candles that Jewish people lit for the dead. Grandma would light them every year for her husband and her parents, none of whom I'd met.

"They're some Jewish things," he said. "Don't touch them." Then it hit him that I was a Jewish kid. "Do you want them, Joyce?"

"Yeah," I answered, trying to seem indifferent.

"Well, go on, take them, and get out of here. You're too young to go on the Parachute unescorted." That was for show—we had both grown up begging rides on the big chute and getting them when it wasn't too crowded. I grabbed the glass candleholders with the Hebrew writing on them and felt sorry for the person who had forgotten them when he went on the Parachute.

I ran on the Boardwalk all the way to Brighton Beach, stopping for a moment to take a cool drink from the water fountain and to stare out at my ocean. The night was hot and sticky, and the sky was clear and filled with falling stars. I stared at the ocean and was glad to be alive. I walked over to a couple who were holding hands on a bench and, like me, gazing out toward the ocean.

"Is this still Thursday, or is it Friday yet?" I asked.

They looked startled. "Well," said the young man, "it's after twelve, so I guess it's Friday."

I began to run again, with the slightest hint of a breeze in my hair. When I reached our usual spot, I ran down the steps to the beach and started screaming for my friends. I could make out two figures in heavy overcoats down by the shore. The temperature must have been in the nineties, so I knew it could only be Big Henry and Old Hudson, wearing their entire wardrobes. They were sitting in the night, sharing a bottle of Homer's homemade booze. I ran to them.

"Please, Mac," I said, "please, don't let them be too drunk."

"Hey, Lady J," Big Henry called out, "whatcha screaming about?"

"Henry, Henry," I said throwing myself into his big arms, loving the scent of him and the scent of the beach, sea, and the night air. "Henry, we can *bentsch licht*."

"Whatcha talking about little girl? What kinda language is that?"

"It's English, Henry. My grandma bentsches licht every Friday, and the guy on the beach said that this is Friday, and I want to be the Shabbos Queen, okay?" I held the candles out for him to see. "Come on, let's go under the Boardwalk and light the candles."

"Well, they'd make good drinking glasses once they're burnt out," said Big Henry, slowly getting up.

We reached our home under the Boardwalk. Henry took off some layers of clothes and placed them in his house, a big fridge box. Hudson did the same. From his cardboard box, Hudson brought out a piece of wood about a foot and a half square. He placed it in front of us like a small table. I put my candles on the board and asked for a match.

Just then Chews came along. She lived in this section of under-the-Boardwalk too. She got her name because she had no teeth; every time she wanted to eat something, she put in some old dentures that didn't belong to her. They bobbed around because they didn't fit right. They'd been thrown out by mistake, and Chews had found them in a garbage can in front of an apartment building. She'd often tell the story of how she had watched the daughter of the teeth's owner looking through the garbage can.

I once asked her, "Chews, why didn't you give them back?"

"Cause I didn't want to." That seemed simple enough, so I never asked again.

"Whatcha doing?" she asked, as she stumbled over, carrying a greasy paper bag.

"Joycey is the Shabbos Queen," answered Hudson. "How's tricks?"

"Not too bad. I got some leftover pretzels from Hazel. What kinda queen, sweet thing?" she asked, as she handed me a pretzel.

"I'm going to bentsch licht."

"Okay, darling, whatever makes ya happy."

"Chews, do you have a match?"

She went into the little bag on a string around her neck and pulled out a butt and some matches. A small old cross fell from the bag and just lay there next to the candles for the dead. Chews went to pick it up, but stopped and left it.

"This was my baby boy's," she said.

We all looked at her in silence. None of us had ever heard Chews talk of family.

"Chews," I said, "where's your baby boy now?"

"Why, darling, he's with Lord Jesus. Now light this butt for me while I take off some of these smelly clothes. And don't you dare inhale. You're much too young."

I lit the Camel butt, inhaled deeply, and waited for Chews to come back. The men were getting sleepy now. Chews came to the little circle, her arms bare now and showing track marks in the moonlight. I kept quiet as I gave her the lit butt. Her face looked beautiful in the night. I lit the *Yahrzeit* candles, the candles for the dead, and thought of Chews' little boy. "What's his name?" I whispered into the night.

"Herbert," whispered Big Henry hoarsely.

I began the only prayer I could remember from Grandma. "*Baruch Atah Adonai, Eloheinu Melech Ha'olam.* And please, Mac, take care of little Herbert. And please, Mac, don't let me get caught being out. but if I do, let them care. Amen."

Everyone joined in and said, "Amen."

Sitting there under the Boardwalk, cuddled up to my friends, looking out and up at the full moon and the falling stars, I was the Shabbos Queen. It was my first real Friday Shabbos night.

या

Back in the present, I was swaying to the music around me, hearing Reb Zalman singing in his booming, compassionate voice. I opened my eyes; Parvati Sati was holding me. Me, Ma, who holds the dying, the babies, the young men and women whom very few visit. Me, whose people are the junkies, the prostitutes, the crack addicts. Me, who always holds—now I was being held. I felt like that little girl again, only safe and free now. I could see my ancestors from Russia before me, proud of the moment that marked the beginning of the renewal of my Judaism.

CHAPTER SEVENTEEN

Tirza the Wine Bath Girl

"Tirza, why do people pay you a dime to take a wine bath?"

"Listen, kid," she said, looking at me straight in my eye, Mae West style. "Everyone has to have a *shtick*. Life runs right over you if you don't start out with a shtick."

In the daylight hours, Tirza's dressing room in Coney Island looked kind of dingy, but I liked it. There were pictures of well-known strippers all over the walls and one big one of Dinah Washington.

"What's my shtick?"

"Kid, it will come. Here, get those Camels for me."

"Can I light it?"

"You're too young to light a match. Come here, I'll light it for you."

We lit up. Tirza, the Jewish stripper, already had a son older than me although the billboard said: "Tirza, The Seventeen Year Old Wine Bath Girl." I still believed everything, too young to know about the illusion of life's dramas, hiding one's truth behind well-concealed lies. Papa had made some kind of arrangement with Tirza to watch me while he worked the hot corn stand.

I inhaled deeply. Smoking for street kids was a very common thing to do. You just walked along and picked up people's butts. I always hated the ones with lipstick on them.

"Tirza, you know there is a real nice lady up near the church where Kathy goes to school."

"Don't you go around hanging with strangers."

"I told her all about you." That seemed to calm her down.

"Come here, kid. I'm gonna put Dinah Washington's latest record on—'Why Can't You Behave?'" The blues started floating around the dingy room, embracing us.

"Come with me one day to meet my lady friend," I pleaded.

"Shit, girl, I have to practice my dance, and I've got to try on this guy's new pasties."

"Let me try them on," I begged her.

"They're on the dresser. Be careful. They're supposed to stick on real well. Just wet them a little."

Tirza turned away from me, trying real hard not to laugh. "Anything growing there, Joycey Babe?"

With the utmost nervousness, I took off Harvey's undershirt and looked into the mirror. "Nothing yet. Anyway, I want to be a boy." It looked to me as if the boys had more fun.

"Put those frigging things on." She was laughing, and I was, too, by now. They stuck all right and took up my whole skinny chest. "Now, go like this," my mentor said. "Go with the music, nice and slow. Da Da *Boom*, Da Da *Boom*."

There was a loud knock on the door. "Tirza, Mr. Katz wants to see you."

"Ask him if he is still married, and if he isn't, send him in." She turned to me. "Come on, kid, let's get those pasties off of you. I wanna get out of here. Let's go see your lady friend."

"Hey, Tirza, this shit don't come off!"

"I guess they really work. Put on your shirt. We'll get them off later."

The sound of loud banging came from the door. "Tirza, let me in!"

She put a kimono over her huge breasts and tugged on a pair of skin-tight shorts. She quickly picked up the eyebrow pencil and placed a beauty mark on the left side of her chin. Then she carefully put clear nail polish over it to make it stay.

"Put one on me."

"Okay, okay, come here." She bent over and drew one on me. "Hold still while I put the nail polish on it." She smelled of her favorite perfume, Tabu. She grabbed the bottle and splashed it on her and me, and we were off and running.

Mr. Katz was waiting outside. "Excuse me," she said, "I got a kid to watch." He gave me this miserable dirty look. I immediately stuck out my tongue. "Look," said my protector, "here's how you give him the bird." She put up her middle finger. I would practice that move for days.

We were off for real by then. The pasties were itchy. I kept pulling on them, but they wouldn't budge. We crossed Surf Avenue and went on to Mermaid, where we made a left. We went quite a few blocks, and then I ran ahead of her to the church. Between Our Lady of Solace and the school was my lady. "Isn't she beautiful, Tirza?"

Tirza was looking real hard at my lady now. "Well, kid," she said softly, "if she makes you feel good, it's a good thing."

"Who is she?"

"I guess some people call her the Virgin. Her name is Mary."

Although I was getting real itchy now and the pasties were killing me, I kept still. Tirza was kneeling, like I saw all the Catholics do, and tears were rolling down her face. "One day, kid, when I'm not around, you go and tell this lady all about your troubles."

"Okay."

"Let's go now," she said. "I have a show to do."

"Goodbye, Virgin Lady. Please help get these pasties off, or else I'm in deep shit."

Tirza began to laugh. She wiped her eyes and we were off again.

After that, there were always three roses by my Lady. Now these many years later, I still like to think of Tirza running out before show time to place her roses before our friend, the Virgin.

मा

Tirza seemed to have a lot of boyfriends, and they would always be waiting outside her dressing room. One time I asked her, "Why do you always make your boyfriends wait so long for you?" I was putting powder all over my face while Tirza was putting on her famous beauty mark.

"Get us an ashtray, kid, and sit down." She thought I was too young for matches, but she lit up a Camel for herself, and one for me. I sat on her footstool, where I was the most comfortable, and took a long drag. Tirza used to play with my braids while she was talking, which made me feel good all over. "Now," she said, "tell me, if you were really hungry, how would a Nathan's hot dog taste to you?" She didn't give me a chance to answer before she answered herself: "It would taste much better than if you were full up."

I didn't tell her that a Nathan's hot dog bought fresh and warm from the counterman would taste good whether you were full or hungry, much better than the half-eaten ones we street kids got from the garbage cans.

"If Tony out there warms his buns for a while, he'll be more appreciative of my talents."

"What talents?" I asked. She almost knocked me off the stool.

"What the fuck did you do that for?" I protested.

"What the fuck do you mean 'what talents'? And don't curse. You're too young. Tell me what you meant."

I was trying not to cry. "I only wanted to know if you do the wine dance for Tony."

"Is that what you meant, kid?" Tirza asked, softening. "Here, have another cigarette, and you can light it yourself this time." My cigarette had gotten broken when she hit me. "Now, tell me why you said that."

I lit my cigarette and inhaled deeply. "The thing I want the most is to be like you or like my friend Chicky who lives under the Boardwalk. But if I become like Chicky then I wouldn't have any money to buy my mama pretty things. Not that Chicky couldn't take a wine bath if she wanted to, it's only that her closet is her back, at least that's what Big Henry says all the time."

"Well, you and Chicky are different," I continued. "She takes her men friends behind the bathrooms on the beach, and one time I heard her tell Big Henry, 'When they pay, you'd better be there on time.' So I figured I'd rather grow up like you, Tirza."

When I looked up, Tirza had tears in her eyes. I thought it was the smoke. "Kid, I gotta tell you something. Chicky and I are not much different, and you don't want to be either one of us. Now listen to me. When you're hungry, food tastes much better to you. So if I keep Tony waiting, he'll get hungrier and hungrier."

"I thought all he wants to do is show you his new car."

Tirza slipped on her bright red summer dress. She was popping out of the top of it. She grabbed a pair of red wedge sandals, put them on her feet, and took my hand. "Kid, now you're going to ride in your first foreign car. Act cool."

We walked out of the dressing room into the front room where the stage with its big empty tank was and where she did her famous wine dance. Tirza had just changed her hair color from dark black to flaming red. She looked like a beautiful house on fire. Tony whistled and hugged her tight. I liked this man a whole lot.

"Hey, kid, do you want to take a ride with us?"

"Aren't you hungry, Tony?" I asked. He looked confused. Tirza gave me a gentle kick with her left sandal.

"The kid is always hungry," said the beautiful Tirza.

"Well," said Tony, "let's jump into the Bentley and get the kid a frank at Nathan's."

I looked at Tony like he was crazy. "Nathan's is right across the street!"

Tirza said, "Tony wants to show off his new car and bust everyone's chops."

"Come on, you two," said the very handsome Tony. "It's not only the car I want to show off, it's my two beautiful ladies."

I was thrilled to my toes. I almost danced out the door into the hot afternoon air. There, in front of Tirza's place, was the biggest car I'd ever seen, a 1948 Bentley. Tony opened the door for Tirza and me. Tirza looked me in the eye. "See, Baby, keep them hungry."

CHAPTER EIGHTEEN

ABC Beach Chairs

I was dancing to Dinah Washington on the new linoleum floor, which was covered with faded boats. Mama had picked it up for nothing from the linoleum man on Brighton Beach Avenue. She said we were all getting splinters from the old wooden floor and told Papa she didn't care if the linoleum was meant for a little boy's room. It was our first luxury, and I loved it. Plus, ABC Beach Chairs had hired me to carry chairs and umbrellas for tips.

I was in bliss. I was a working girl now. I had a job. Earning money! All alone in the basement, I had no one to tell, so I just kept singing along with Dinah, "The Richest Man in the Graveyard," about how you can't take it with you.

I was making her a promise: I'm gonna spend it, Dinah! I'm gonna buy my mama a flower every day of her life, and I'm gonna take violin lessons from Mr. Rivelli on Coney Island Avenue for fifty cents a week, even though he touches everyone's titties. And I'll let Big Henry sleep on a chair under an umbrella all day.

I put on my only shorts with pockets and a fairly new polo shirt which Aunt Lily had sent. I turned off the music and ran to the alleyway.

"Papa," I yelled, "I'm gonna work for the beach chairs in Coney Island. The owner said to be there at nine. His place is on the same block as the Cyclone. Papa, Papa! Pay attention. I won't be home till later."

Boy, was I ever high. Joe Joe wasn't around. He had gotten a job with the junk man and thought of himself as quite the man about town. Now, at the ages of nine and ten, we both worked. Kathy had to practice her piano all the time now, so I didn't see her as much. Aunt Mary was giving her real piano lessons, which is how I knew he touched everybody's titties, even though we didn't yet have anything to touch. Kathy was afraid to tell her mama. I was hoping for violin lessons anyway.

"He'd better not touch mine," I told Kathy.

I had gotten over wanting to be a boy. Tirza had explained that boys can't take wine baths because no one would pay a dime to see them.

So here I was, still climbing over the El and waving to the new guy in the booth. I just smiled my biggest smile as I walked past him to the other side, and he didn't ask any questions. I ran all the way to the Boardwalk. It was the middle of July. The sun was already hot and red-looking. I thanked the sun for shining on my day and making it bright enough for people to want umbrellas. I would get off the Boardwalk where the men played handball and walk the rest of the way to the Cyclone.

At the Cyclone, there were a bunch of older kids hanging out. They had on black motorcycle jackets and great big garrison belts, which is why they called their gang the Garrisons. I walked over to a kid called Blackie. He was tough, but he always gave me his cigarettes before he put them out so they were almost new and not like the ones from the gutter.

"Where you going, Joycey Babe?"

"I got a job. I'm gonna save up and get me some violin lessons."

"Violin lessons?" he said, like I was talking about going to the moon.

"Yeah," I answered, real tough-like.

"You'd better get your Garrison jacket and belt first, so no one busts your chops about the violin."

"Now I really gotta work," I thought as I walked away. "I gotta save up for a garrison belt, a motorcycle jacket, flowers for Mama, violin lessons for me, and a chair and umbrella for Big Henry." I laughed as I went through the door of the dingy storefront under the sign "ABC Beach Chairs."

या

"Girlie, girlie," a big fat lady in the red and white polka dot bathing suit that could have fit a baby whale was saying to me, "can you put the umbrella over there, please?"

"Sure, ma'am," I answered, in my give-me-a-nice-tip voice. This was the third place this lady had made me stick the umbrella, and I still had to run back to the stand under the Boardwalk for her beach chair, which I was sure she wasn't gonna fit into anyway.

"Now, you run along and get me my chair. Hurry! Hurry! I can't stand here all day!"

I ran as quickly as I could. I was the only girl in a crew of six boys assigned to that bay. At only 9:30 in the morning the hot July sun was already beating on my back. When I got under the Boardwalk, the damp coolness greeted me like a cold shower. I was working the bay on West Tenth Street, just south of where the Cyclone had its home. On the Boardwalk, you could be fed, entertained, have your weight guessed, win a Kewpie doll—if you had the money. Under the Boardwalk, the stands sold everything from drugs to sodas to booze to counterfeit tickets for some of the rides.

I was racing back for the chair when I spotted Big Henry, Hudson, and Chicky. I ran to my friends, forgetting Mrs. Polka Dot for a minute. "Wait here," I said, when I got to them.

I said to Mitch, the kid who stamped the tickets that you got when you received the chairs and umbrellas, "Mitch," I said, "loosen up on the time of three chairs and umbrellas." Most people who rented chairs didn't pay attention to the time on their ticket; by the time they brought the stuff back, they were so tired from spending the day in the sun that they just paid their ten cents an hour and got the hell out of there. If you didn't time stamp it when they came in, you could resell the same umbrella later on that day and pocket the money. I knew Mitch stole what he could. He would even throw me a fifty-cent piece once in a while, which was more like insurance than a bribe. I didn't care. I already had the reputation of being closemouthed about the goings-on in the street. Mama always said, "Talk all day, Joyala, but say nothing."

I grabbed the chair and ran to the polka dot lady, who was consuming two knishes at a time, one in each hand. The knish lady was waiting to be paid. She was a good lady, very old. Her name was Rifka. She made the knishes in her basement on Mermaid Avenue and West 17th Street. She had a beautiful house, full of her children and grandchildren. She made all her money from selling knishes. No one knew where Rifka's husband was, and no one asked.

Polka Dot was eating her knishes before paying. Rifka looked like she was gonna hit her with the big mustard spoon. I said to Polka Dot, "You better pay up, lady. Rifka is off the wall."

"Where have you been?" she said, her giant mouth filled with chewed-up knish.

"Why, I've been here the whole time."

She looked skeptical but let it go and turned to Rifka. "Give me another knish."

"Give me my twenty cents," Rifka answered. The lady reluctantly handed her two dimes. "Give the kid a good tip. She's the daughter of a beat cop here, and he likes his kid to make what she's worth." Rifka smiled at me as she pushed her knish wagon away through the sand.

"What tip?" Polka Dot asked me. "I thought it was included in the price."

"Okay, lady," I answered, as I dropped the complicated wooden chair in the sand, "you put it together." I was about to uproot the umbrella, which I had so painstakingly dug into the sand.

"No, no!" she screamed and handed me a quarter.

A whole quarter! No one ever gave any of us carriers a whole quarter. I fixed her chair, even draping her polka dot towel on it. And, to her surprise, I kissed her oily face. When I ran away, she was still standing there, holding her face, staring after me. I laughed and kept going.

Chicky was going through the garbage pails in broad daylight. I ran to Mitch. "Any bring-backs yet?"

"Yeah," he said, "I put one chair and umbrella aside for you so far." I picked up the chair, but left the umbrella. I couldn't carry them both at the same time yet. I ran to Hudson and Henry.

"This one is for Henry," I told Hudson. I opened it up and grabbed Henry's big hand. "Your throne, Sir."

Henry sat down like a king, the only black person sitting on a chair as far as the eye could see.

When there were two more bring-backs, I set them up for Hudson and Chicky, about twenty-five feet away from the ABC Beach Chair stand. Mitch had thrown me a fifty-cent piece and, with my other tips and Polka Dot's quarter, I had over a dollar and ten cents. I raced under the Boardwalk, where the franks were only seven cents, and got us all franks, orange drinks, and French fries. At nine years of age, I had just provided a real family meal, something that never happened at home.

"Do you want me to get you more mustard, Chicky?"

"Come here, Lady J. Sit on my lap." She took off a tiny ring that seemed so much a part of her finger that it had left a deep groove. "You take this. When someone is doing you a good thing, then you give this ring to them. You hear me?"

My first piece of jewelry. I thought I would keep it forever.

CHAPTER NINETEEN

I Sold My Heart to the Junk Man

I worked seven days a week, except for rainy days. So in a way, 1949 was to be the last year of my childhood.

Papa had a winning streak at pinochle and made it his game of choice for that summer. It was the first time in my life that me and Harvey had money for treats. I gave Papa most of what I earned, and the rest I shared with Harvey, who was still on his Jewish-versus-Catholic kick. This Hebrew School boy, who was studying for his Bar Mitzvah, who had received beating after beating from street toughs for being Jewish and wearing payot, and who had stood his ground and never run (not that he could fight), was sneaking to church and contemplating becoming Catholic.

One Friday morning, I woke at five to a blistering rainstorm. No work. I was looking at the shabby cellar walls when it hit me: my friend Joe Joe worked on the junk cart for old BB. BB got his name from always carrying a BB gun on his junk cart, which he would use if kids tried to swipe anything.

When I was young and unemployed, I used to collect junk for old BB. I had a standing invitation from both BB and Joe Joe to ride the junk cart. Mama had told me more than once, "If I see you on that junk cart, I will break both your legs." Well, I would just make sure Mama wouldn't see me.

I ran to Papa and whispered in his sleeping face that if anyone wanted me, I was out doing a school project. It was summer, but to Papa it was always spring in the alleyway, so it would never occur to him that school was already out.

Joe Joe started at six. It didn't take me long to dress in an old pair of sneakers, shorts, and Harvey's polo shirt and to take a piece of oilcloth from the table to put over my head in the rain. I figured I needed it more than the old wooden table did.

Joe Joe was already walking down the block when I spotted him. He turned when I called. For a moment he looked different: taller, darker, better looking. I felt my heart beating faster.

"What's up? No work today?"

I shook my head. The rain was coming down hard on both of us. I loved it.

"Great," he said, "come on the cart with me and BB." I felt shy for a moment in front of my oldest friend. "What's got into you? You got a stupid grin on your face."

"Fuck off," I replied.

We walked together toward Cropsey Avenue. We had a long walk, about twenty-five blocks or so. "Joe Joe, I just learned a new song, and it's perfect seeing as how you're a junk man now."

"That song's been around for years. My grandma sings it all the time."

"What song?" I asked, embarrassed that I thought the song had just come out.

He turned and looked me in the eye. He was a breath away. The only thing between us two skinny kids was the rain. It seemed that we were the only two people alive. It was 5:45, and the world was still dark and mystical.

"I Sold My Heart to the Junk Man," said Joe Joe. "Now, don't kill it by singing it too loud. It's a love song."

I had never thought of it as that. "I know, Joe Joe, I'm not an asshole."

"No, you're not. You is my woman." Before I could say something smart to my old friend, he kissed me smack on my lips. He puckered up like the child he was, yet it was my first kiss from a boy. I was shocked.

"Whatcha do that for," I said, hitting him hard on the back.

Joe Joe turned. All his feelings were on his face. "I thought you would like it."

"Well, I don't!" I screamed, having loved it and not understanding why. We took hands, reverting back to when we were six and had begun to skip with each other, our hands always together. We were almost at the junkyard, the kiss forgotten, or at least hidden in some secret place.

BB was harnessing Old Mary. He had put plastic on her hat. I went over to her and kissed her.

"You coming with us, Juicey?" BB asked. Georgia's name for me had stuck like glue in the black community. I kinda liked it.

"Yeah, BB, if it's okay."

"Sure is. Joe Joe's been talking a stream about you lately. I'm glad I can see for myself that you ain't put on no airs, at least not yet."

"I ain't got no airs to put on."

"Hop on," he said, after he had settled in the front seat under a jerry-rigged umbrella that covered his side. "Come real close, so you don't get wet."

I cuddled up to the old man. There I felt safe and a lot drier. Joe Joe was next to me. I took some secret delight that he was getting wet. Then I felt bad and pulled him closer to me.

We rode down Cropsey Avenue, the cars beeping at us. When we got to a residential section, I began pulling the bell and screaming like BB taught me to. "We buy junk! We buy anything the ragman buys, and more!"

I felt like a queen riding in her carriage. We kept stopping to collect junk from the old broken houses. Joe Joe kept introducing me as his girl. I blushed for hours.

"Joe Joe, stop that or I'm gonna bust your ass."

A young girl called out, "Junk Man! Junk Man! My granny wants to sell the old bureau. It still got drawers in it." Somehow I knew I shouldn't let Joe Joe go with BB on this one, so I jumped out, telling BB to stay on the cart. I said it was too far up for him to walk, even though the girl was only on the second floor of a two-family house. BB welcomed the break.

We climbed up the stairs. The place was dirty, and there was paper trash all around. The smell of urine greeted us on the second landing. We were wondering which door to knock on when the little girl opened the door on the left side. She had a hundred little braids, all tied up in ribbons. She had clear, olive skin, a little darker than my own, and the most beautiful blue eyes I had ever seen. I turned to see if Joe Joe was looking. Looking wasn't the right word. The boy was downright staring, with his mouth wide open and his eyes as big as golf balls. "I never seen no blue eyes on black folks," said my man, who only five minutes before had been telling the world I was his lady.

"What you got to sell?" I asked her, all business.

We walked in. I pulled Joe Joe by his wet jacket. When we got into the foyer, I was shocked. Her apartment was beautiful. Everything was spotless, and the table was set nice and neat for breakfast. It was set for three. Just then an old lady came out.

"Grandma, here is the people to buy that old set of drawers."

The old lady looked straight at our youth and asked if we would like some fresh-baked cookies. Joe Joe still couldn't speak, and he never stopped staring at the girl.

"Yes, Ma'am," I answered.

Joe Joe and I sat down at the table with the little girl and her grandma.

"Young man," said the old lady, "don't you know it's bad manners to stare at anyone?"

Joe Joe gulped. "Sorry, Ma'am."

"What's your name, honey?" she asked me.

"Juicey…no, Joyce," I answered. My heart was breaking, but not enough to stop me from enjoying my cookies. On the table was a big pitcher of milk. I had never seen anything like that before.

"What is your name, Ma'am?" I asked.

"My name is Evelyn Bell, and this is Louise. Now, how come you two children are working so young?"

Louise Bell piped in. "I want to go to work, too, only my grandma won't let me. I have to stay home and watch my grandpa."

"Where is Grandpa?" I asked innocently.

"In his bedroom. He can't move."

I had never seen anyone that couldn't move, and I certainly wanted to. The old lady took my hand, and we walked into a small room with bright yellow walls and pretty white see-through curtains. On the bed lay a handsome man, just lying there with his eyes staring at the ceiling.

"Abraham, this here is Joyce. She is gonna buy the old bureau from us."

"Good day," I said, talking to the still figure from the doorway.

"Come here, child, don't be afraid," Grandma said.

I came and sat on the bed, somehow wanting to cry.

"Mr. Abraham Bell, I am working for the junk man today. How are you, Sir?" Then something happened. It wasn't much, just a twitch in his right eye, but somehow I knew that he heard me. "Mr. A," I continued, "I really got a better job than Joe Joe. I'm just helping out." I just kept talking on and on about nothing. I knew this old man was listening. I heard Grandma chuckle. "Joyce," she said, "you just stay here with Mr. Abraham. I'm gonna get BB up here to take that bureau out of the back room."

"One second," I said. "I have to get something from the cart." I left my scarf on the bed to show I was coming back and ran past that louse Joe Joe and Louise Bell, who was reading a picture book and wasn't paying a bit of attention to stupid Joe Joe.

When I got to the junk cart, I woke up BB. "Listen, BB, there is an old man upstairs. His name is Abraham Bell, and you gotta give them a good price."

"I know them," he said. "Abraham used to sharpen knives. One day a car just ran him and his cart over and ended his life."

"But he's still alive."

"Yes, but he lost everything."

"Wow," I said, forgetting my worries about Joe Joe. "You're gonna give them a good buck for their bureau, ain't you? See? Here, she gave you cookies."

"Juicey, I am gonna give them what it's worth. Grandma Bell sure enough don't want no handouts. Go on up and spend some time with the old people, and when you're ready, come on down and watch old Mary. Now, go on with you, while I rest my old bones."

I ran back upstairs. Joe Joe was in Mr. Abraham's room over in the corner, afraid to talk. I ran right over to my spot on the bed.

"Mr. A," I began, "would you like to hear a song?"

"He can't hear you none," said Joe Joe.

"How come you ain't with Louise Bell?"

"She already got herself a boyfriend. Come on, Joyce, you is my lady."

"No way. Get your ass out of here."

He walked out of the room. I looked at Mr. Abraham. Grandma was bustling around in the other room.

I began singing: "I Sold My Heart to the Junkman." My voice was shrill, high, and loud. I swear that old man jumped a little and looked toward me. I took his hand. It was cold and dead. I kept singing.

His hand was getting warmer in my hand. I was really getting into it when I felt his hand tighten around mine. It was gray in color and very big. I couldn't believe someone was enjoying my singing. People usually ran away when I sang, given that I can't carry a tune. I just tightened my hold on his hand and belted out the words.

I was standing now, facing my audience of one. His hand began to move up and down. I was thinking, "He is moving with the music." I sang louder.

"Girl," the old man said, "stop that screeching and sit down on this bed."

"That ain't nice to say when I was singing for you."

"Just don't be doing it in my room." He talked low and slurred his words.

I turned to see if anyone had witnessed this embarrassing situation. Grandma Bell was on her knees before a picture of Jesus, and Louise Bell was sobbing. "Why ain't you talked before?" asked Grandma. I thought she was talking to the picture of Christ.

"I ain't had nothing to say," Abraham answered slowly. "Until this child screeched in my ear and made me know, I gotta live."

At that time I understood nothing at all, but I knew I felt good in my heart. I learned a lot that rainy day in 1949, especially don't judge what you don't understand. To this day, I give my time, my love, and, yes, sometimes even a song to those who are in comas or just lying there. I always take their hands in mine. And, every once in a while, I feel a twitch. Yes, doctors say it's just a reflex, but I say it's the Mr. Abraham syndrome.

CHAPTER TWENTY

Pier Moon

The sand felt warm and comforting to my feet. Even at night, the beach was crowded and hot. The moon was hiding behind the Parachute. The big Ferris wheel kept going round and round, the cars swinging out over the sand, and the air was filled with the distant screams of the riders. Lovers under blankets created a motion of their own. The night's scent was filled with salt air, baby oil left over from the day, and barbecued chicken roasting over forbidden fires close to the Boardwalk. Cotton candy still stuck to the faces of lucky kids. Infants were sleeping close to mothers' breasts. Fathers snored loudly into the night.

It was after midnight, yet peddlers were still selling their wares. Late-night fishermen on the pier were keeping sleepy eyes on their lines. Joe Joe and I were enjoying the darkness, hanging out under the big pier. A young couple was making out a few feet away.

I was eating the stale pretzel Hazel had given us as she was packing up her pretzel wagon. I had asked her if it was a safe pretzel or if it was one of the ones she did things to. Grandma had told me in Yiddish how Hazel peed on some of the pretzels, then heated them up and put lots of salt on to hide the taste.

I had never known my grandmother to go too far from home. She went down to Coney Island Avenue only a few times a year, when she would hide her money away from my papa in the big Lincoln Savings Bank. Yet she still knew everything that went on from Coney Island to Manhattan Beach and Sheepshead Bay. It drove my father crazy how the old lady knew everyone and everything.

Hazel had laughed at my question and said, "Joycey, is that grandmother of yours passing rumors again?"

Hazel would give me and Joe Joe a big bag of stale pretzels and some hot coffee from the container that hung on her wagon night and day, where it made a clinking sound as she pushed the heavy load. Hazel always had a pregnant belly. She had about a dozen kids. In winter they ran the streets after school like wild hooligans, but as soon as April came and the weather got a little nicer, her older kids were on the beach or on the boards selling her pretzels.

Joe Joe would watch the couple making out, and then look at me like he was embarrassed. We could hear moaning. "We ought to get us a blanket," he said.

"Shit, what for?"

Hazel turned and grabbed Joe Joe's ear. "Stupid child, what you want to talk like that to Joycey for? Do you want trouble? Let black stay with black and white stay with white. I told Harry to keep an eye on Joyce."

"Hazel," I said, "don't fuck with Joe Joe."

"Keep still and listen. What's different about my little Carl? Both of you tell me."

"Carl be black," said Joe Joe, close to tears.

"That's right. He's my son and he's black and I'm white. So he hurts real bad."

Carl was eight years old and always hid when anyone came near him. I didn't go to the same school as Hazel's kids. They went to PS 100 in Coney Island. Joe Joe and I went to PS 253 in Brighton Beach. I didn't understand what was happening now with Hazel.

"I don't want you kids to be in trouble," she said in a soft voice. "My Carl, he don't know where to put the hurt. You two never want to be under no blanket together, do you hear me?"

"Hey, lady!" interrupted a big soldier. "Are you gonna sell those fuckin' pretzels or just sit on them?"

Hazel's eyes gleamed in the darkness. Joe Joe and I held our breath as she smiled sweetly to the big man. Under the cart she kept a large bag of what she called her "specials." She bent down, holding her big belly, and lifted out the pretzels. "We're having a special. They're two for a dime." Her usual price was five cents a pretzel. Even I could figure this was no bargain.

The soldier asked for ten. His shock of greasy blond hair spilled over one eye as he looked at me and Joe Joe. "Whatcha doing here, boy, with that pretty little white girl?"

"None of your business, mister," I answered before Joe Joe had a chance to speak. I knew that Joe Joe would be mad at me for talking for him; he always hated that.

"Go on with you, handsome, and enjoy your pretzels," Hazel said.

The soldier picked up the stained bag of salty pretzels and walked away, but not before saying to Joe Joe, "Stay away from the white girls, kid."

"Don't worry, kids, he's going to get his as soon as he takes the first bite." Hazel sat her big bulk on the sand. Joe Joe and I sat beside her. "I ain't trying to scare you, but since the war's been over, folks ain't got nothing to gab on about. Now they is gonna start on black and white. You two shouldn't walk the boards where the crowd is different every night. Stay in Brighton where people know you. Okay, kids?" She pulled a pack of Lucky's out of the front of her flowered dress and put two cigarettes in her mouth. Digging deep into her front again, she pulled out a big box of wooden matches. After lighting the cigarettes, she handed me one, saying, "Share."

"I don't smoke," I said, then inhaled deeply and handed the cigarette to Joe Joe.

"I don't smoke either," he said, then, like me, inhaled deeply.

Screams of delight could be heard coming from the streets. The Whip was going round and round at full speed. We could hear the hawkers selling their shows. I sat there next to Hazel, enjoying Joe Joe's presence.

"Now what do you want me and Joe Joe not to do, Hazel?"

Joe Joe poked me in the ribs and said, "End it, Joycey." I turned toward him and saw that Hazel had fallen asleep. The cigarette butt was burning a hole in her dress. I grabbed it and then watched her big belly going up and down with her breath.

It was getting late, and we had two miles to walk to get back to Brighton. Even though Mama would be sleeping and Papa would probably not get home till the morning, why take a chance? I needed to go home.

"We can't leave her if she's sleeping, Joe Joe. What are we gonna do?"

"I don't know," he said staring at the rising and falling belly. "What if the baby slips out?"

"Do you think that Grandma is right and that she really peed on some of her pretzels?"

"I hope so," said Joe Joe, probably thinking of the greasy soldier. "Hey, we got to get out of here. I don't feel good being this far from Brighton."

"Oh, shit, I know everyone. Ain't no one gonna hurt us here."

Hazel started to cough. I put out my cigarette. The big bell rang in the belfry of Our Lady of Solace, announcing to all of Coney Island that it was two in the morning.

"Hazel, wake up. Me and Joe Joe have to get back to Brighton."

Hazel was coughing louder and louder. I looked closely at her and thought I saw some blood at the side of her mouth.

"Hazel, what's happening?" I was scared.

Hazel's eyes flew open. She looked terrible in the moonlight. "Go to the Burst the Balloon stand," she whispered, "and get Eddy. Hurry, get Eddy."

"Joe Joe, you stay here with Hazel."

"Hurry up," he said. Hazel seemed to go back to sleep.

I ran across the wide span of sand until I got to the boards. I ran the boards as I'd never run before. I passed my papa, selling his hot corn, but he didn't see me, thank God. I ran past the Thunderbolt and down the Bowery to the last street before the great Steeplechase.

There, tucked in the corner, was the Burst the Balloons stand. Holding a bunch of darts was Eddy, Hazel's oldest son, a tall redheaded boy of about sixteen. I screamed out to him about his mom. I couldn't catch my breath. A crowd began to form around me.

"Hey, Joycey Babe, whatcha doin'? You wanna do the dart thing?"

I knew Eddy thought I was trying to be a con front by calling attention to the darts and getting him more customers. Us street kids could make a few pennies that way.

"No," I croaked out, "your mama is hurt bad under the big pier."

In two seconds flat, Eddy handed the darts to a friend and jumped over the counter. I held tight to his hand, and we flew past the Bowery. I saw my papa's astonished face as we passed the hot corn stand. I knew I was in for it, but it didn't matter; I had to get back to Hazel and my Joe Joe. We ran and ran. We got to the Boardwalk and ran under the big pier. There I saw the greasy soldier holding onto Joe Joe and punching his face.

"I caught this nigger hitting on the pregnant lady."

I had to get to Joe Joe before Eddy did. Hazel's eldest had a bad temper. "No, Eddy! This is Joe Joe, my best friend."

The soldier was still holding onto Joe Joe, who was punching the big man in the belly. Eddy yanked Joe Joe away from the soldier. "Okay, buddy, the war is over. Get out of here."

Just then Hazel screamed. We stood stock-still. The moon was directly overhead, lighting up everything.

"Eddy, get me to the hospital. Get an ambulance. The baby's coming! Someone call Coney Island Hospital," screamed Hazel.

"It's okay, someone already did. I'm here, Mama."

I heard the fear in Eddy's voice. I was afraid, too. I asked Joe Joe if he was okay. His face was a mess, and there was blood coming from his eye and nose.

"I'm okay. I had that guy under control."

I smiled and took my friend's hand.

"Eddy," screamed out Hazel, "the baby's coming!"

"Get me a blanket, fast, Joycey."

The couple with the blanket were spectators now, and they handed it over. Hazel was breathing hard. The sand around her was soaked with water. She was still bleeding from her mouth, from chewing up her tongue and cheek. Me and Eddy slipped the blanket under her heavy bulk. She wasn't a fat woman, just a thin lady with a big belly.

We heard sirens at the end of the Boardwalk and saw the stretcher coming. Two men arrived, rushed over to Hazel, and said, after examining her, "There's no way we can move her now. The baby's crowning."

Joe Joe came over to me and put his arm around my shoulders.

"Move back everyone, move back." It was O'Brien, the cop. "Let the lady breathe." Behind him, to my surprise, was Papa.

"Oh, shit!" Joe Joe said, his grip on my shoulder getting tighter. A group of people had gathered behind us. The two guys from the ambulance were spreading Hazel's legs apart and holding the baby as it came out of her womb.

"So that's how they come out," said Joe Joe.

"Yeah, and now we got to find out how they get in there," I said.

Everyone burst out laughing, even Hazel, who was asking to see her baby before they cut the cord. There was blood everywhere, including all over the baby. I could see from where I was standing that Hazel had given birth to a baby girl. The two men picked up Hazel and put her on the stretcher. On her belly they placed the new baby girl wrapped in a big blanket. She had chunky cheeks and tight dark curls. The baby could have been Joe Joe's sister; she had dark brown skin, which under the moon looked dark gold. She was so pretty.

"What's her name?" I yelled to Hazel.

"Pier Moon," she called out, "Pier Moon."

I laughed and said the name over and over—Pier Moon. Then I remembered Papa. Me and Joe Joe were just about to make a run for it when I heard his voice.

"Joyce! Joe Joe! Don't even think about running."

"Oh, Papa," I said, and ran to him. Joe Joe followed slowly.

"What the hell happened to you, son?" Papa bent down and stared into Joe Joe's face. He took a hankie out of his pocket and tried to wipe away the blood.

Joe Joe stood there under the moon, the light making his face gray and garish. I started to cry. The whole night went past me in a strange pattern—the soldier, the kids making out under the blanket, the beautiful black baby on top of Hazel's belly, and my friend's face bruised and battered.

Papa took Joe Joe's hand, and we walked down to the ocean. He wet the hankie, getting his shiny shoes soaked in the process. He cleaned up Joe Joe and sat down on the wet sand with Joe Joe and me on either side of him. I was crying softly now, staring into my beloved ocean.

"Why, Papa, why did Joe Joe have to get hurt? Why is the baby black? Why is Hazel always having a baby? Why did Hazel say me and Joe Joe can't be together?"

"What in the name of God are you two kids doing here under the pier at two o'clock in the morning? No, don't answer me. That way you don't have to lie to your papa. You weren't in your beds like children should be, so you're seeing things that adults see. If you play an adult game, your eyes are going to see lots of pain and joy, no matter how old you are. Now Joe, do you want me to take you to the hospital?"

"No," said my friend. "I'm okay. It sure was something to see a baby get born."

"Go on home, kids. Stay on the boards and go straight home. Hold hands and run. Don't cross the street."

"I love you, Papa," I said, as I took Joe Joe's hand.

"Thanks, Harry," said the brave, proud Joe Joe.

On the Boardwalk, we looked back and saw Papa talking to someone at the water's edge. I couldn't make out who it was.

"That's Tirza," said Joe Joe.

"Bullshit," I said, as I stared at my papa's white apron in the moonlight.

"Why is it bullshit?" asked Joe Joe.

"Because why would Tirza be on the beach in the middle of the night? And why would she be with my papa?"

"Oh, don't be a baby, Joycey. Your papa is a good-looking man."

"Fuck off. I would never go under no blanket with you." I ran ahead.

He caught up to me and pulled my braid. I was about to sock him one when his nose began to bleed again. He took off his shirt and pressed it to his nose to stop the bleeding. His thin frame shone black in the moonlight. We kept walking on the boards.

"Pier Moon—what a great name."

"Shit, it ain't a nice name for a black baby. It ain't a nice name for any street kid."

"Why not?"

"Cause no one is gonna understand that she was born under the pier with the moon shining down."

"I think it's a great name."

"If we were to have babies, what would you name them?"

"I ain't never gonna have babies in front of everyone looking at me." We held hands and skipped the boards. Back home, we ran behind my house to where our back windows faced each other. I hit Joe Joe on the shoulder as a sign of affection. He lightly punched my back, and we parted for the night. I climbed into the bathroom window, the name Pier Moon playing in my head.

"She's a special baby," I thought, as I opened the bathroom door and bumped into Grandma, fully dressed, standing by the sink.

"*Ver bist du, Shaindela?*" she asked, using my Yiddish name.

"I was with the little child and her mother."

Grandma grabbed my pigtails and said, "So, *nu*, Hazel had another baby. What is the color?"

I looked at this old lady who hadn't even asked why I was out at three in the morning. "Her color is perfect, Grandma," I answered in Yiddish and again in English just to make sure that she knew that Pier Moon was perfect. I ran past Grandma, past my tired mama asleep on the narrow cot, and threw myself on the bed.

"Her color is perfect," I said again into the dark, "just perfect."

CHAPTER TWENTY-ONE

Illusion and Truth

Tirza was sitting at her dressing table putting on a new purple lipstick. "Kid," she said, "you gotta sneak away tonight and come to the party."

It was the end of the summer. That night there was going to be a Labor Day party for all the Coney Island people. Some of them were heading down to Florida to try their luck selling their wares in flea markets. Others had made enough money to be able to take the winter off. Most were just going to hang around the Island through the fall and winter, praying for nice weekends that would bring folks out to the beach and Boardwalk.

The end of summer meant school and kids who made fun of me because I wore hand-me-downs that never seemed to fit.

"What's the matter?"

"Nah, I'm all right. Can I try on your lipstick?"

"No, you're too young to wear lipstick," replied my friend, who was dressed only in a push-up bra and silk bloomers. "I know what you're thinking. You're thinking that no one is gonna be around here all winter, but I'll be living in Sea Gate with Tony."

I liked Tony. He treated me good even after a whole year of me hanging around. The previous winter, Tirza had gone to Las Vegas, where she was in a show. She stayed for just a month, then came back to Coney Island, where she had a little house right by the beach. Her neighborhood was considered tough, but I loved it. There were people of every color and nationality living together in an area of a few blocks.

"I want you to figure out how you're going to get to my house at two in the morning."

Coney Island parties had to start that late because everything pulled in the bucks till then, especially if it was a warm night. The food for the party would come from all the stands; everyone would bring something to Tirza's. Even Papa had agreed to bring over some corn.

Tirza said, "I want you to be sure that everyone is fed." She lit up a Camel. "You'll figure it out."

"Can I have a cigarette? It will help me think."

She laughed and gave me hers. The tip was covered with her purple lipstick. Neither of us thought to ask Papa to take me to the party. That would be too easy.

"I see how you share everything I give you, even if it's only a bagel. You put everything away for your friends. I know you'll make sure everyone gets enough to eat tonight." She began singing Billie Holiday's hit song, "God Bless the Child."

She put out her cigarette and immediately lit another. Grabbing the ashtray as if I was going to empty it into the garbage, I put the butt into my shorts pocket.

"Throw that butt out, Joyce," she sang out. She was dancing all around the small dressing room. "Look, this is my new grind as I come out of the wine bath."

I followed her step, Da Da *Boom*, Da da *Boom*. We were dancing around the room when she stopped by her dresser.

"Joyce, you want to see me in my new flesh-colored bodysuit?"

"Sure," I said, not knowing what a bodysuit was. She pulled something out of her dresser and went behind the screen.

"Can I have another ciggie?" I asked.

"Okay, but that's the last one you're going to have today."

There were no more in the pack. "There's no more cigarettes!" I yelled at the pretty screen with gold birds on a black background. Tony had bought it for her the year before in a place called Burma.

"Go into my purse and get a new pack."

I grabbed her purse off the dressing table. I was searching for the Camels when, to my surprise, I found a picture of my papa standing behind his hot corn stand, looking as handsome as ever. Just then Tirza danced out wearing her stage costume, just a thin feathered shawl covering her breasts and other private places. This is what she'd wear just before she got into the big see-through tub of red wine. On stage, the lights would dim a little and when they came back up, the audience would see her naked in the bath. I began to blush, forgetting my papa's picture. I said, "I thought you were going to show me a new outfit."

"This is it. Do you like it?"

Now I could see that she was covered in some sort of material. It still looked like she was naked, though.

"What the hell is that for?" I asked, knowing the answer but afraid of the truth.

At my tone of voice, Tirza looked puzzled. She glanced at her open purse and saw the picture of my papa staring back at her. "Is that why you're mad at me?"

I was confused. "I don't care if you have my papa's picture."

"Are you sure? We're just good friends."

I didn't think about that until later. Now I just asked her, "What are you wearing that for?"

"It's my costume for my dance."

"Why do you need it if you're supposed to be naked?" For as long as I could remember, I'd been practicing in our old, filthy bathroom with only the mice as my audience, or an occasional rat, to dance naked just like my idol Tirza. Now I find out that Tirza was a fake? Was I confused!

"Joyce," she said, "please listen."

She took my papa's picture out of her purse and put it on the dressing table. She lit two cigarettes, handing me one. I sat on her footstool and inhaled deeply.

"You know, kid, a dime can buy a lot, but it sure as hell can't buy me."

"What do you mean?" I asked, trying not to cry.

"I ain't no two-bit stripper. I'm a star just doing my shtick."

"But everybody thinks you're naked."

"Come with me," she said, grabbing her bright yellow shorts and her five-inch wedge sandals. She took my hand, and her feather shawl hit me in my face as she led me through the big showroom. We got outside, and the hot end-of-summer air hit us. She pointed to the big marquee. "Can you read that? Read it out loud to me, Joycey girl."

I looked up. I really didn't need to, for I had often asked Papa to read it to me when I was a little girl. I knew it by heart: "Come and See Tirza The Wine Bath Girl! On The Biggest Stage In All Of Coney Island! For One Dime! See Tirza in her Famous Wine Bath!"

"See kid, nowhere does it say that I'm naked."

"She's right," I thought, "she didn't really lie."

We started back inside. Then I saw Tirza motioning to her son, who was setting up the bath for her next show. He was mixing something into the water.

"What the fuck?" I said, as I got closer.

"Hi, Joyce, what's wrong?"

"What is that stuff?" I asked in a harsh voice.

"I'm putting in the food coloring for my mother's show. What bit your ass?"

My mind went completely crazy. "You liar!" I screamed at a stunned Tirza. "That's fake wine! And you can keep my papa's picture. You think I care about anything you do?" I threw down the cigarette butt and ran for the door.

"Joyce, let me explain!" Tirza called after me.

Tony was coming in. "Hey, kid, what's up?"

"Nothing is real," I said, as I passed him into the hot afternoon, crying and running. I thought I would die. In fact I did want to die if everything in the world wasn't real. My braids came loose, and my hair flew in my face as I ran the crowded boards to find my under-the-Boardwalk friends. I wanted my Big Henry in the worst way.

"Feed everyone yourself, you fake Tirza," I cried. "Feed them yourself!"

The tears dried on my face. I ran and ran until I got to the crowd near the Parachute. It was Labor Day weekend, and everyone wanted to get in the last weekend of the summer. I got through the crowd and began to run again, picking up speed. I ran against the warm wind. My shorts and top were soaking wet. I stopped for a drink of water and sat down on a nearby bench. I'd run all the way from Coney Island to Brighton Beach. It was a long run, and my legs were hurting.

Searching my pockets, I found the cigarette butt that I'd put there at Tirza's. The tip still showed her beautiful new purple lipstick. That did it; I started to cry. I reached into my other pocket and found matches. Smoking the remains of the cigarette started calming me down. The scent of the smoke mixed with the strong scent of baby oil and iodine coming from every passing body. The warm air and hot sun lulled me into a gentle space, but the sounds of the ocean and the laughter of children with their parents made me want to weep again.

"Maybe nothing is real," I thought. "Maybe I *am* all alone, maybe no one loves me." I had never felt so bad and lonely in my life. Sleep welcomed me and I went into it.

I awoke with a start. Someone was yelling, "Get away from that child! Police!" I stood up fast, ready to run, a thing all us street kids knew to do at the mention of police. It was too late. Someone had hold of me. I looked up. To my surprise, it was Chicky holding onto my hand.

"Let her go," the cop was saying. "You should be ashamed of yourself trying to rob a little kid. Where is your mother, honey?"

"She is," I said quickly, pointing at Chicky, "and you'd better leave her alone." I had gotten very dark over the summer, and with my pitch-black hair I could have passed for half-black. This wasn't the bay where I usually hung out, so nobody would know me.

There was a crowd around us. I noticed some kids eating ice cream in cones. I was thirsty, tired, and hungry, and I already missed my Tirza. And my thumb hurt where the cigarette had burned it while I slept.

"She's your mother?" asked the stunned cop. It must have been over 90 degrees, and Chicky was dressed in her usual fashion, with about three torn dresses, four sweaters, her army boots, and four different scarves on her head. Scarves were easy to come by on the Boardwalk. The wind always blew them off the folks on the Parachute and onto the beach where the under-the-Boardwalk crew could quickly grab them. Sometimes I would even wait under the Parachute to catch the falling scarves. I noticed that Chicky had on a new purple silk one.

"She was smoking, and her daddy don't want her smoking. Come on, child, let's go."

This was 1949, and black and white didn't mix publicly. Everyone in the crowd appeared stunned that the cop just let us go. After we'd walked a little way, I heard Joe Joe calling me. When he caught up to us, he asked, "Was that you causing all that racket?"

"Yeah."

"I thought you was with Tirza."

Chicky said, "Let her be, boy. Now Joyce, why was you out here smoking for all the world to see?"

"You know what I found out today?" I said, looking from Joe Joe to Chicky.

"Yeah, don't fall asleep when you is smoking," said Chicky.

I looked at the burn on my thumb.

"Come here, child," said Chicky, as we reached the stairs to the beach.

It wasn't our beach, ours was a few bays down. This beach was crowded with white folks trying to get as black as my friends, the people they seemed not to like. Nothing seemed right that Labor Day weekend. Everything was mixed up.

Chicky walked me to the water's edge, where she took off her army boots and told us to take off our shoes. I was wearing my brother's old sneakers. They were too big for me, but you needed something on your feet when you walked the Boardwalk or else you would get big splinters that sometimes got infected. Chicky had me by one hand, and on her other side she held onto Joe Joe.

"Now Lady J, you just go in there and put that thumb in them waves. I'll hold you tight."

"Chicky, I've been swimming forever." Melvin had thrown me in the water when I was really little and made me swim to him.

I remembered at that moment that Chicky had a deep fear of the water and realized that the only reason she was there knee-deep in the waves was for me. She must really love me. "You would never lie to me, would you, Chick?" I asked.

Chicky clutched my hand and proceeded to give me the greatest lesson I ever had. She began, "Lady J, when you is young, you sure think that you know everything. The world is made up in black and white."

Joe Joe laughed. "Ain't that the truth."

I was surprised that he still let Chicky hold his hand.

"Not that kind of black and white, young man. A little kid on her own like Lady J thinks there can only be two ways to life–the truth and the lie. Well, you listen here and keep that thumb in the water. Of course I would lie to you, child, if I was in my drunk spell. I probably would lie to my own mother, if I ever had one."

"Why?" I said, feeling the tears starting to come again.

"Because no one on God's earth is perfect."

"Why?" I asked again. The waves were growing higher. Chicky was getting nervous. I squeezed her hand. "Don't worry, Chicky, me and Joe Joe won't let you drown. Right, Joe Joe?"

"Shut up, Joyce."

Just then a big wave knocked us all down. I heard Chicky screaming. I tried to stand up, but she was on top of me and her weight kept me down. I thought I was going to drown, but at last I was able to get up. We were in about two feet of water. Joe Joe was trying to pull old Chicky up. People were standing all around us. We finally got her up. The whole time she never let us go. My wrist was beginning to hurt.

"My scarf, my new purple scarf!" We just stood there, watching the scarf go out to sea.

Back on the dry sand, I asked again, "Why would you lie to me, Chicky?"

"Child, just love me no matter what I do. Just love everyone no matter what they do."

"Even if they hurt me?" I looked into her eyes, seeing something I'd never seen before. To me her eyes looked like pools of pain, and yet there was love shining in those eyes.

"What the hell, love costs less than hate."

I said the words over and over in my mind. "Love costs less than hate."

We began walking along the water's edge. She said, "Maybe tonight you two kids can come out and teach me how to swim a little."

"Not tonight," I answered.

Joe Joe and Chicky looked shocked. They knew I never refused my friends anything.

"Why not?" Joe Joe asked.

"Cause tonight we're all going to Tirza's party."

"All of us?" asked the startled Chicky.

"Yes," I said, "all of us. I got to make sure everyone's fed."

We walked home. It was starting to get late, yet it was still nice and warm, as if the summer was reluctant to leave. I kept thinking of what my Chicky had said, "Love costs less than hate."

At that moment, she stopped and said, "Not only does it cost a lot less than hate, Lady J, it goes a lot further, too."

I put my arms around my friend and said, "I love you, Chicky." Then I gave Joe Joe a look so he hugged her too, in spite of the heavy wet sweaters that were starting to stink.

"Love costs less than hate," I said, as we kicked the sand and watched the people watching us.

CHAPTER TWENTY-TWO

A Nickel for a Pickle

"Wanna go to Ocean Parkway and see the horses?"

"What for?" was Joe Joe's answer.

"Hey, Brother." I called him that sometimes when I was angry at him. "Hey, Brother," I repeated when I got no reaction, "if you want to sit on this here garbage bin for the rest of your life, it's okay with me, but I'm going to Ocean Parkway and see the horses, and you can sit on your ass here all day if you want."

"Why don't we just go to school today?"

I was shocked at his suggestion. "School?" I said, as if it was a dirty word. "What do you want to do that for? We already went to school three days in a row. Now it's our turn."

The snow had begun to fall again, and I was freezing. I tightened Harvey's scarf around my neck. "What's got into you, Joe Joe?"

He had on Old Joe's heavy army jacket and itchy wool pants. I was wearing my cousin Phyllis's snow pants and black jacket. The pants rode high up on my legs, and the sleeves were too short for my arms. We both wore ski hats that Grandma Georgia had given us.

"Just tell me what you want to go to school for?"

"I want to, that's all. No reason."

I knew something was up, but I didn't know what. "Look," I said, "it's getting late. We almost can't make it to school on time anyway. Why don't we just head over to Ocean Parkway, pick up some butts on the way, and watch the damned horses go by?" The big stable was at Prospect Park, miles from Coney Island or Brighton Beach, but people used to ride along the parkway all the way to Brighton Beach Avenue.

"I don't want to," he said, stubbornly.

"Shit, man, I'm dying for a ciggie, and if we don't move our asses off this garbage bin, we're gonna freeze to death."

I was used to playing hooky with or without Joe Joe. "It doesn't really matter," I said to myself, but I was starting to feel bad in my belly. I thought I'd try one more time to find out what was wrong with him.

"Are you coming or not?"

The snow was falling hard now. Joe Joe looked so handsome in Old Joe's army jacket that my heart skipped a beat when I looked at him. The snow was sticking to his black hat, and he was shivering.

"I'm going," I said getting off the garbage bin.

We had been sitting in the alley behind Joe Joe's house for fifteen minutes trying to figure out what we were going to do that Friday in February. To me, school was out of the question. Three days in a row was enough, and the truant officer wasn't going to bother chasing us for one day a week, although at times he did come after us when we took off the same day every week. We had a plan where we would go to school for two days one week, for three the next, and for four the third week. We had managed to beat the system that way.

"Goodbye, pal," I said, sarcastically. "Don't freeze to death."

I was halfway down the alley when Joe Joe yelled, "I'm hungry, that's why."

I stopped short and turned to my friend, who looked so lost in the snow. His head was hanging down. I ran back to the garbage bin, slipping on the ice. We broke out laughing because my brother's boots with the big buckles were miles too big for me.

"Whatcha talking about, you're hungry?" I said as I got off the ice. My face was freezing cold by now.

"I said I'm hungry, that's all, and I figured if I waited on the line in the cafeteria, they would give me some soup for lunch or something."

"Bullshit, you know you'd have to ask for it or even beg."

If you didn't bring in the twenty-five cents for lunch money each week, they wouldn't give you anything. You could sometimes tell them that you forgot your money, but they'd be looking for you the rest of the week to pay up.

"Shit, girl, I'm really hungry."

"Why ain't you eatin'?" I asked, jumping up and down to keep warm.

"I gave the bread to Sister. She was crying."

This was too much for me to understand. There was always food in Joe Joe's house.

"Grandma went away to Florida for seven days with the Rosens."

I knew Grandma Georgia worked as their maid. "Yeah," I said, "so what?"

"She give Papa Joe the money for the food, and the old man spent it on booze and shit. Now he can't remember what he did with the leftover money. We been searchin' for two days. We only got some bread and some milk, and I gave that to Sister. She ate the rest of the bread, but when she said the milk tasted bad, I hit her."

"What'd you do that for? You never hit Sister."

"I don't know," he answered, looking really down.

"Come on," I said taking his gloveless hand, "let's get out of the cold."

Mama had gone to work already, and Papa was sleeping. Of this I was sure. He would be asleep for a few more hours before waking up and getting ready for the first hand of pinochle in the alleyway. Grandma always seemed to be locked in her little room off the kitchen. She loved being in there cursing Papa all day. My sister Shirley would also be sleeping. Having to work nights kept her asleep most of the morning. My brothers were at school. Mel was already in college at Cooper Union, and Harvey went to the same school as me, PS 253. He was in the last year and always went, which made no sense to me. How could anyone hold all that learning and not burst?

Papa was sleeping on the cot right by the door. We tiptoed past him into the small room with the sink and table, which we called the kitchen. It was either hot as hell or freezing in there. That day, the pipes along the wall and overhead were banging away.

"Give me your jacket," I said to Joe Joe. I draped it over the big hot angry pipe next to mine. You had to be careful not to touch the pipe or you would get burned. We all had burn marks from touching the damned thing. I went into the old icebox. It was as empty as Joe Joe's stomach.

"When did you eat last?" I asked.

"Yesterday morning," he said, mournfully.

"Are you crippled or something? There's always food in the streets."

"Grandma said that if she ever caught me garbage pickin' she'd for sure have to pray my soul out of Hell."

"No shit," I said, touching my heart, wondering who was going to pray my soul out of Hell. I didn't really believe what he was saying. Papa said that if you waited for the sun to shine, you could freeze to death, and if you waited for someone to feed you, you could starve to death. He never said anything about souls.

I opened the closet and watched for a moment as an army of roaches ran around in circles. "Good sign," I thought. Where there were roaches, there was always food. "Look, here's some cornflakes. Let's eat."

It was getting hotter and hotter down there near the furnace. By the time the heat reached the top floor and Mr. Krumpenholtz's apartment, it would be just right. Now it was a burning force.

I got two jelly glasses and filled them with cornflakes.

"Ain't got no milk, Joe," I said as I sat down next to him at the table. "I wonder how it feels," I said, with my mouth full of cornflakes, "to always have food."

"I don't know," answered Joe Joe, "but we do pretty good when Grandma works steady. She is always bringing home some Jewish stuff, like pot roast and shit like that. I ain't never gonna complain again."

"*Vere is dort?*" a voice yelled out in Yiddish. ("Who is there?")

Shit, it was Grandma calling from the other side of the wall. There was a square opening where pipes rested and where I could peek into her room. One thing I have to say is that I never saw Grandma undressed or at least never without a girdle or corset, even in her robe. Grandma came from royalty in Russia, or so she said, and she just couldn't get over that none of her children wanted her except my mama, who was the poorest child she had.

"Who *bist* there?" she yelled out again.

"It's me, Shaindela," I said, using my Hebrew name.

"Who else?" she asked.

"No one," I answered through the wall.

The wet clothes we had hung over the pipes were steaming and starting to smell real bad. I was praying that she wouldn't make a scene until they were dry. Too late—she came storming out the door.

"*Oy vey*," she said, clutching her heart. She had spotted Joe Joe.

"Oh, shit," I thought, "here she goes." To her, if you weren't born in Minsk, even if you were a Russian Jew, you were the devil. When I was younger, she would say to my friends, "Minsk or Pinsk?" They would think it was just a game, but if they answered wrong, they could never come back to our house. It wasn't that she was mean—she was just Grandma.

"Grandma, it's only Joe Joe."

"A black one?" she said in a high voice, then went on from there.

I looked at Joe Joe. He was used to Grandma and didn't pay her much mind, knowing that she had thrown Kathy out of the house for being born in Pinsk—never mind that Kathy was Irish. He sat there eating his cornflakes with his fingers. He must have been pretty hungry to be enjoying them like that.

Finally she said something in Yiddish that was way off, even for Grandma, something that meant "son of a swine and son of a female donkey." I went a little crazy and told her in Yiddish that Joe Joe hadn't eaten for days and that she should go back to Russia or meet up with Hitler's ghost. I was furious, a thing I never was with Grandma. Mama would have killed me if she knew. I went on ranting and raving, and then I noticed that she was just staring at Joe Joe and not saying anything.

"*Kum*," she said, pulling Joe Joe's ear.

I was about to blow a gut when I saw that her face had turned tender. Papa used to call her "SS" or "Gestapo." Here was a tenderness I had never seen before. We followed her into the little closet room, which smelled like Grandma's rose powder. In all the years she lived with us, I can never remember her taking a stranger into her room or, for that matter, my papa or Melvin. Now here we were sitting on her bed, or at least I was. Joe Joe was in Grandma's chair.

She bent down under her bed and pulled out peanut butter and jelly on a wooden tray with pretty napkins, all embroidered, and a knife and a spoon. Well, I tell you, I almost died right there in Grandma's little closet. Next, she pulled out a large loaf of challah bread, as fresh as a spring daisy. It smelled like heaven.

"Here, cut it," she said in Yiddish.

I was too astonished to move. Finally she pulled my ear, so I cut the bread, carefully holding it over the tray even though I doubted that any roaches would dare to go into Grandma's room.

We had taken off our boots and socks. My feet were dry, but the boots had made them black, even through the socks. As I moved my dirty feet off the bed, I noticed Grandma's high rubber boots with the little heels lying there wet in the corner. The old lady who acted like she could hardly move must have gone out by herself to buy the challah.

Joe Joe's mouth was open as Grandma spread large chunks of peanut butter on the bread and then smeared on the jelly. She handed it to me first, then pointed to Joe Joe. I gave him the sandwich and waited for mine.

"I'm dreaming," I said out loud.

Grandma pulled my earlobe hard when she heard me. "Even a *hunt* has to eat." Now she was calling my friend a dog.

I looked at her. She had never looked more beautiful. Her pure white hair was in braids, pinned high on her head. The little pearl earrings she always wore dangled against her jaw. Her eyes, which were growing blind, were glowing in the little cellar light overhead. Her black dress made her look stately.

"Now, why is he hungry?" she asked in Yiddish.

"Because there is no food in the house," I said simply. "His grandpa drank some of the money and can't find the rest."

"Like your papa," she said.

I never saw my papa drunk, but I kept quiet as I stuck a big piece of the yellow challah in my mouth.

"Listen," she said to Joe Joe, as I ate and translated, "there is always food in America. You have to work a little, then always put a few pennies away for a pickle. Never touch those few pennies, even if you're dying, unless there is no food anywhere. Then go and buy a nickel pickle and eat it as slowly as you can. One large whole pickle can keep you from starving all day. One nickel always hold in your secret place."

With these words she lifted up her European pillow with the lace pillowcase, uncovering a large jar of pickles. She opened the jar with her twisted fingers and handed a big pickle to each of us. Then she laughed and laughed.

"Why are you laughing?" I asked.

"Because I make my own music in life. You have to learn to dance."

We finished eating, and I kissed my Bubbie like I'd never kissed her before. Her dry cheeks smelled of rose powder. Joe Joe got up off the chair and kissed the old lady, too.

"*Geyn avek,*" she ordered, "go away," with little force, but making her face stern again.

Joe Joe just smiled and said, "Okay, Grandma, I'll keep a nickel always ready."

"Wait," she said, as we were about to leave the little room. She picked up her black bag with the pretty pearl clasp and took out some change. "Here, a nickel for a pickle." She gave a nickel to Joe Joe, but nothing to me. That was okay.

"Share the pickle and you'll always be friends, and never bring a black one into my house again," she said to me.

We walked out of the room and put on our coats, which were as hot as the pipes. By this time we were sweating.

"Come on, let's go see the horses," said Joe Joe.

"Okay," I said, putting on Harvey's old boots.

Joe Joe was sitting on the floor, putting on his boots, and said, "What do you think she did all that for?"

I couldn't answer.

Papa walked in, looking like a tall, skinny, cuddly dog. "What did the old girl do now?" he asked, as he tapped Joe Joe on the head.

"She gave us a nickel to buy a pickle and to be friends for life."

Papa smiled. "Everyone has to do at least one kind thing in life so someone else can remember them. Now get to school and be careful you don't cross the street."

Me and Joe Joe burst out laughing and went out of the cellar, full and happy. We walked hand in hand down Ocean View Avenue, bravely passing PS 253.

"What do you think they're learning in there today?" Joe Joe asked.

CHAPTER TWENTY-THREE

Chews

My work now takes me to places like Renewal House in South Central Los Angeles, which is a home for mothers and children with AIDS and addictions. One day my chelas and I were on our way to make our rounds of the places that care for the many living and dying with this plague.

"How can I teach detachment if my heart breaks so often?" I asked my beloved guru, my Baba, inside of my being. As always, he answered. "Tears are a true sign of detachment, if one is not attached to one's tears."

On the streets of Los Angeles, I could see children buying and selling crack and heroin. For a moment, the familiar scent of under-the-Boardwalk came to me, and I traveled back in time.

या

Hudson had asked me to find driftwood for the ash can so he could make a big fire. Big Henry had gone somewhere and was coming back with a friend who was "in deep shit," according to Hudson. I had never seen Hudson so serious—and he didn't even look drunk.

Mama and Papa thought I was at Kathy's house. They didn't know that Kathy wasn't allowed to play with me for the rest of her life, which usually meant three days. I was in trouble this time because I had persuaded her to skip church for the first time in her young life.

It was about six in the evening, and in January that meant it was cold at the beach. I had on Harvey's good wool hat and my cousin Phyllis's heavy pea coat, which had come in the mail the day before.

Still, it was cold. I clutched my collar tightly around my neck as I walked to the water's edge searching for driftwood. Despite the cold wind, I felt free and happy.

Hudson called out, "Joyce, does your dad have any wine in the house?"

"No," I answered. Not that Papa didn't like a drink of schnapps once in a while, but he was usually too broke to buy it.

"It's not for me."

"Who's it for?" I asked.

"Chews."

I liked Chews a lot, especially when she and Chicky were together. All they talked about was men and how funny they were, or at least that was what I thought they were laughing about. I knew one thing for sure: Chews wasn't into booze. She used to do something else to make her happy, at least that was what she said. Even so, unless she was with us, she seemed pretty unhappy. I used to see her by herself walking on the Boardwalk, crying.

"Chews needs a drink real bad," Hudson was saying.

I hurried under the Boardwalk. There, stretched out on torn-up pieces of cardboard, was Chews. She was shaking and moaning. I ran to her.

"What is it, Chews?"

"Nothing, darlin', except that I need a fix real bad."

I didn't understand, but I knew I wanted to help her in any way I could.

Hudson and Henry sat down on the sand next to her. She was crying. Every once in a while she would look at me.

Big Henry said, "Joycey, can you get us some wine some place? Chews needs some real bad."

I remembered that my brother Harvey said that Rabbi Rubenstein had lots of wine on the table to welcome in the Sabbath. It was Friday night. If I could figure out how I could get the Sabbath wine to Chews, I knew everything would be all right.

Henry said, "Just don't get caught."

Things must be pretty bad if Henry was going to let me try anything dangerous.

As I was leaving, I heard Chews say, "I don't want her seeing me like this."

Hudson answered, "Maybe if she sees you like this, she won't end up like you."

I didn't like him saying that because I loved Chews, but I kept going until I got to the shul. The rabbi and his family lived above the synagogue. It was way past sunset. I didn't have any idea how I was going to get the wine. I didn't even know which doorway was the rabbi's.

"Juicey, what are you doing out so late?" It was Joe Joe's grandma. I never would lie to Georgia. Mama said she had "the eye" and could see some things no one else saw.

I told her the whole story and then started to cry. Grandma Georgia held me tight and said, "That rabbi ain't gonna give you no wine, darling child. Come with me."

She took my hand and walked me down the dark street, back in the direction where she'd come from. On the corner of Brighton Beach Avenue and Coney Island Avenue there was a great big bank, Lincoln Savings, and in the doorway was a drunk, sleeping. Next to him was a half-full bottle of cheap wine. Grandma took out a quarter and placed it next to the sleeping man. Then she moved his hand over it so no one would steal it from him. She stood up and handed the bottle to me. "Run now, child, run real fast and tell old Chews that Grandma Georgia says hello. Me and that girl go way back."

I ran as fast as I could to the Boardwalk. "Here," I said to Hudson, "here's the wine."

Everyone was looking at Chews. She was just lying there, not moving.

"Chews," I said, "it's me, and I got you some wine."

She focused her black eyes on me. "Hello, child. I sure do appreciate it." She sounded funny, not like my Chews. Her eyes kept rolling up. "Hudson," she said, "come here and push up my sleeve."

He did, and what I saw has stayed with me all my life. Her arms were all purple and yellow. They were terribly swollen, and big abscesses full of pus were everywhere. It looked like little worms were crawling around in them. In the shadows of the fire in the ash can, my Chews' arms looked more like a monster's than a woman's.

I started to cry. "Oh, my Chews, who done that to you?"

Her voice was far away. "I did, baby. I done it to myself. Now you promise me you ain't never gonna stick no shit into your veins."

"I promise," I said. I would have promised anything at that moment.

Hudson said, "Come on, kiss Chews goodbye and run along."

Someone said, "Don't let the kid kiss Chews. She's all full of vomit and piss."

I threw myself down on her thin body. She smelled terrible, but I didn't move.

"You go on, child. You go on and grow up good."

I kissed her paper-thin face and said, "The bottle was from Georgia, Joe Joe's grandma."

Chews smiled and said, "Ain't got no use for drink now."

Big Henry began singing softly as Hudson took my hand. We started to walk away together. The sound of the wind in our ears mixed with Henry's voice in the night. I never saw Chews again. No one would tell me where she was. Hudson would say, "A better place, child, a better place."

मा

Now, here I was, looking at the same scene of heartache and the same stench of living death on my way to Renewal House. "Be with me, Chews," I whispered to my reflection in the car window. "Be with me, girl."

CHAPTER TWENTY-FOUR

Haagen Das

It usually takes a while before a guru gives someone a spiritual name, but when I visited my ashram in West Hollywood, some people got names right away. In walked the most gorgeous man I had ever seen. "I name you 'God'," I said. The name just popped out of my mouth.

"What kind of spiritual name is that?" he asked. "You can't name me God!"

"How much more spiritual do you want than God?" I said. He still looked worried, maybe because he came from a very conservative Christian background, which I didn't know at the time. "OK, I name you Sadhu God."

Later Brian walked in, saying, "I am going to name myself before you do."

"You can't do that Brian, only a guru can name you."

"You said the guru is inside, so I name me Haagen Das."

"You can't name yourself after ice cream!"

"All the other '*Das*' names, they just don't do it for me. At my memorial I want to be Haagen Das."[1] From that day on, that's what we called him.

---

1   "*Das*," or servant, is part of many Indian names. So, for example, *Shiva Das* means "servant of Shiva" or "devotee of Shiva."

When I returned to Los Angeles three months later, purple Kaposi's sarcoma lesions covered one eye and a lot of his face. He had defied all odds just by still being alive.

"Let go, baby," I told him, "you don't have to suffer anymore."

"Ma," he said, "find some humor in all of this."

Death was surrounding him. Everything was shutting down, and he was in a great deal of pain. I kissed him goodbye, thinking it was the last time. So many more were waiting for me back at the Los Angeles ashram, I had to go.

That night found me surrounded by people with HIV or AIDS, all wanting me to teach them about dying. We were sitting in a little room, packed in like sardines in a can.

Someone announced, "Haagen Das is here."

Thinking he meant that Haagen Das had left his body, I said, "His spirit is always with us," which I thought was a good California thing to say. I was hoping this guy would shut up so I could concentrate on the living.

"No," he repeated, "Haagen Das is *here*. This spirit is wearing purple pajamas and getting out of a car."

We jumped up and ran outside. There was Haagen Das, dressed in full purple silk, being helped into the house by his sister and his lover. I put my hands on my hips. "I told you I'm the only queen when I'm in town."

Someone lifted him up and carried him to the bedroom. I lay down next to him. Haagen Das called for a camera and demanded that pictures be taken.

There were quite a few new people there that night. AIDS quickly makes everyone family. They came in small groups to receive *darshan* from the guru in bed with her courageous chela. Later we sent out for—what else?—Häagen-Dazs ice cream and pizza. In his quiet voice, our Haagen Das told us all that it was the best wake anyone could ever have.

CHAPTER TWENTY-FIVE

Rescuing Grandma

I thought Mama would make me go under the turnstile like she usually did to save a few cents. When she put money in the slot instead, I knew that this was not going to be a fun time.

"Joyala, stop talking to yourself and walk."

"Oh, Mama, leave the kid alone," said my twenty-three year old sister. "It's not her fault your brother is a bastard."

I was shocked. It wasn't the first time my sister had stuck up for me, but I never heard her curse. I took hold of my mama's old wool coat that didn't even begin to button, although she did look a little thinner these days. Mama looked like she had been crying. Her face was puffy around the eyes, and there was a light green tint to her skin. It scared me.

"What's up, and why do you look like shit?"

She started to say something just as the train came in. The passing cars made a powerful wind, and the sound drowned out everything else. The train stopped, we got in, and I sat next to my mama. Shirley sat across from us.

"What do you mean I look like shit? And take off that hat in the train. I want to tell you something." The noise from the train was drowning out my mother's words. I moved closer to hear what she had to say. "Remember when Uncle Jack came to get Grandma and take her home with him for a while?"

"Yeah, he said he wanted Grandma to live with him before she died."

She had tears in her eyes.

"Something bad is happening, isn't it, Mama?"

"Yes, honey, I'm dying, and Grandma is in the poorhouse."

"What?" I shrieked.

People stared at us. Shirley pretended she wasn't with us.

"I have cancer," Mama said. "So Grandma needed to live someplace else for a while. Uncle Jack always thought she had money, but when he found out she didn't, he put her in the poorhouse." She continued, "Look, I am not literally dying. The hospital can fix me up. But now we have to get Grandma out of that place. We're gonna take her to Philadelphia to stay with Cousin Sylvia."

"Mama, you don't have cancer for real, do you?"

She looked out the window at the streets going by. I wanted desperately for her to hold me in her arms. She said, "I have the good kind of cancer, and they can get it all out. They are going to remove my breast, and I will get better. You have to be strong for Papa. Now sit and enjoy the ride."

She put her arm around me. I felt the weight of it and was happy for the moment. We changed trains in the city for one that went to the Bronx. By the time the train stopped at the Grand Concourse, Mama looked tired and cold.

We found the address that Mama had written down. She and Shirley went inside and left me sitting outside on the steps. Every once in a while the front door opened, and the smell hit me. Through the open door, I could see into a dark hallway, but no one came in or out. Then the door opened again, and this time someone called, "Girlie, Girlie." There was no one on the steps but me.

"What do you want?" I asked.

"Girlie, come here."

When I stepped through the door, I got the shock of my life, or the first of many shocks. There was an old person tied to a chair with a thick rope like the fishermen use on the boats in Sheepshead Bay. It was wrapped so tightly that all he could move was his right hand, and with that he had been opening and closing the door. Although I couldn't really tell, I assumed the person was a man. He was bald and as skinny as a skeleton. In his face were two round sockets that held two white eyes that seemed to have no color at all. His wrist was black and blue. When I got closer, he smelled like rotten potatoes.

"Girlie," he said, "get me out of here, please."

"How?" I asked.

"I don't know. Can you get me a cigarette?"

Now *that* I could do. I went into the street and looked by the curb. There before me was a fresh butt, only half-smoked. "Mister, open up. I got a butt."

He let me in. "Honey, I'm a woman, and my name is Luchan."

"How did you get bald like a man, Luchan?"

"God knows! Now light that cigarette for me."

"Why don't I untie you?"

She panicked. "No, don't do that! They'll know!"

"Who'll know?"

"Can't you just light it for me? What brand is it?" she asked, staring at the cigarette. I was digging deep in my pockets for the matches I always had on me. I found them and lit the cigarette. It was a Camel, my favorite. I put the cigarette to her lips. They were all caked and dry.

"Who put you in here?" I asked. She looked to be in another world.

"My old man said I was going crazy, because I just wouldn't put up with his shiksa girlfriend."

I looked down the hallway. The floor was sticky and stank of dried piss. A long staircase went up in the middle. Everything was dark and dingy. I was about to ask more questions when I heard a scream. Thinking it was my grandma, I put out the last of the butt under the heel of my shoe and ran up the stairs toward the sound.

I went to a huge door at the head of the stairs. It was made of heavy wood and was hard to open, but when I finally did, the sight before me was something I could never have imagined. In the room were about twenty old people. Most were tied up in their beds, and those that weren't looked to be dead or close to it. The only alive-looking people were two women in dirty white uniforms, having coffee at a desk at the end of the room. I scanned the room quickly, looking for my grandma.

The screaming started again. It sounded like an animal caught in a trap. I ran toward the sound and found a being that didn't resemble anything human in a crib-like bed with high side rails. Still unnoticed by the women in uniforms, I bent down close to the person's face and said, "It's all right, it's all right."

Two eyes looked into mine. The screaming stopped. The person was on his side, staring right into my soul. Never before had I seen such pain and anguish. The sweat was pouring down me. I began to cry. "Who are you?" I asked, still whispering.

"Isaac," said the man, whispering now.

His hands were tied to the bars with thick straps that looked like small belts. He was covered with a sheet and some sort of plastic. I tried to hide my tears as I took off my gloves and unhooked one of the belts. "What is this place?" I asked, wondering if we could kidnap him along with my grandma.

"This is Hell," he answered. I loosened the other belt, but I couldn't get it off. In the next bed was another person, untied yet not moving. I looked over the plastic and his eyes met mine. I smiled, and the person puckered up his lips as if to throw me a kiss.

"Who is in the bed next to you? How come he isn't tied up?"

He didn't say anything for a while. "That is Benjamin," he said finally. "Benjamin plays the game differently from me."

"What game?" I asked, thinking that Isaac's mind had gone.

"The living game. He plays dead and they leave him alone. Me, I play crazy and keep my sanity like that."

"My grandma is in here someplace. We're gonna take her to Philadelphia."

Before I could say anything else, his hand, which resembled a claw, grabbed my wrist. "Get her out of here. If you have a bubbie, get her out!" His accent, which I hadn't noticed before, had gotten thick.

Just then a man came through the door and yelled, "Hey, Gertie, did you see a kid in here?" I ducked. I knew I was in deep shit again, with my mother thinking I was lost, but I sure didn't want to leave Isaac. The man left, but first he told the nurses that there were two fat ladies upstairs, making enough trouble that the supervisor was coming over from the other side of town where he had been at some kind of luncheon for dignitaries.

Isaac put his bony finger to his lips as a signal to keep quiet. "Tell them where you are and, please, little one, come back here."

"I'll try," I told him, looking to see what the ladies were doing. They had gotten donuts from somewhere. The man had said upstairs, so I climbed the stairs to the third floor. This floor had more rooms off each side of the long hall, all with people lying in beds, only here and there were a few folks in old wooden wheelchairs. Everyone was tied up in one way or another.

"Hey, kid, where are you going?"

"I'm looking for my mama," I said in my Brooklyn tough-girl voice.

"You must be the missing kid. Your mama is making a racket on the next floor. Come with me, and I'll show you a shortcut to get to her." He held out his big beefy hand.

It was then that I realized that I had left Harvey's gloves on Isaac's bed.

I wouldn't take the man's hand, afraid he might try to grab me. I just followed him. He took me into a room with about ten bathtubs in it. Three women and a man were washing what seemed to be skeletons, people who looked like the pictures that we'd seen in the papers a few years back when the Americans liberated the concentration camps. The people all had dead eyes and huge sores on their naked bodies. Some people were in tubs, while a few others were on gurneys, waiting to be bathed.

That son of a bitch took me through there to scare me! I was about to say something tough-sounding when my world stood still. There, lying with a sheet covering the lower half of her body, her hands tied together like a pig, and her sagging old breasts hanging out for the world to see, was my sophisticated grandma.

I screamed and called out, "Grandma, it's okay! I'm here!"

The guy freaked and said, "Stay away from her."

I turned like a tiger. "You fucking motherless bastard, come near me and I'll kill you!"

I ran to my grandma and pulled up the dirty sheet to cover her.

"Shaindela," she said, "*vie bist dire gevain, mien kindala? Mien leben iz nicht mehr du!*"[2]

"Grandma," I said in Yiddish, "Mama and Shirley are here looking for you. I'll go get them."

Just then one of the ladies who had been bathing an old man slapped her charge across his thin face. He had just shit in the bathtub, and now he was smiling. He continued to smile even after the lady slapped him. I went crazy when she lifted her hand to hit him again. I ran at her and knocked her down. When she fell, she let go of the old man and now he was sliding under the water. Everybody was screaming and pushing each other out of the way. The water in the bathtub was turning brown. He must have had diarrhea.

Another attendant ran over and pulled him out. Meanwhile the first attendant grabbed me and started to hit me.

All of a sudden there was a loud shriek. It was my mama, who didn't know who to go to first, her mother or her child. She came running. My face was bloody and my clothes were wet. She held me in her arms for a moment.

"Get away from us," she said to the attendants, "and get my mother ready. I want her bathed by a woman and dressed in her own clothes. Do it or I'll have the police here in two minutes."

"Do as she says," came a voice from the other side of the room.

I looked through my tears to see a well-dressed man in a beautiful, expensive-looking suit. Yet, here he was with naked men and women, all Jewish and all reduced to animals. I hated him.

---

2   "Where were you, my child? My life is over."

"Would you please come with me to my office, Mrs. Green, and bring your daughter with you."

"Mama," I said as we were following the nicely dressed man, "I need to go and get Harvey's gloves. I left them with Isaac, and I promised to see him again before we go."

"First let's get you dry and try to find your sister. She's outside looking for you on the street."

Soon, we were sitting in the distinguished gentleman's office, which was another world from where the old people lived. I couldn't believe my eyes. There was a fireplace, thick rugs, and a beautiful light over the big shiny wooden desk.

"Now, Mrs. Green, let's see what we can do for you," said the man.

"There is nothing in the world you can do for me except let me take my mother out of here in dignity and respect. My daughter is hurt. She may have doctor bills. Go sit by the fire, Joyala," she said to me, and continued to talk to Mr. Sumner. "I want to be reimbursed for the expenses of our day, including the cab fare from Brooklyn."

I smiled into the fire. Boy, was my mama a smart one.

"I also want the traveling expenses for the four of us to go to Philadelphia by bus."

"That is impossible, Mrs. Green."

"I am forty-six years old and have breast cancer that is probably not curable. I have no time for a lawsuit. But I'm sure this place is quite a human interest story—especially the part about my ten-year-old daughter saving the life of an old man you were drowning in a bathtub."

Now I was really impressed.

Just then Shirley walked in, crying. She ran to me and pulled my braids. "Where were you? I'm going to kill you." She grabbed me and kissed me all over.

Ugh! I hated it and loved it. "I'm okay," I told her. We were whispering by the fireplace. "And Mama is suing this place, even though she is dying from cancer and all." I thought it was all part of the act. Little did I know how true my mama's words were.

Now she was threatening to call the police and the newspapers, both.

I asked if I could go see my friend Isaac. Mama asked Mr. Sumner to call the ward and tell them to let me in.

"Mrs. Green, I don't think it is wise for your child to wander around this home."

"What is it that you have to hide?" she asked. "Is there more to see?"

My mother took off her old coat. She looked so old in her cotton dress. Her hair was all grey, and she had big bags under her eyes. Still, her hair was set in neat curls, and her fingernails were bright red. Mama had certain standards that may have been weird, but she always had her hair permed and painted her nails, no matter how poor we were. I can remember the cellar, filthy with garbage and stuff all around, and my mama sitting on the couch painting her nails. She would say, "Why not, Joyala? Why not look good in any part of your body that you can?"

Now she was looking at her bright red nails and saying, "Mr. Sumner, I will wait for a little while for my brother, but if he doesn't come soon, I am going out the door with my mother and the funds to get us where we need to go."

A security guard came to get me; his name tag said "Johan." He looked nicer than the other ones. Back in Isaac's room, the two attendants were still sitting where I had last seen them. I ran to Isaac, who was clutching my gloves to his face. "Isaac, I'm here." He looked up, and tears ran down his face at the sight of me. Benjamin in the next bed sat up and looked pleased to see me, too.

I ran back to the attendants, who looked like shocked statues, and said, "Do you have any more donuts?"

The small one said, "Yes, there is a big box on the shelf over there."

Writing on the cover of the box read, "For the patients—enjoy!"

I gave the attendants a look that would kill. Gertie found her tongue and said, "They're not allowed to have solid food."

Ignoring her, I broke the donuts in two. I gave Isaac a piece. Benjamin was already sitting up and holding out his hands. He still had not said a word. I put the other half donut into his waiting hand. Now the smaller nurse started passing out the donuts and loosening the restraints on all the patients so they could eat. Isaac got jelly all over his gown. He didn't seem to care, and neither did I.

I felt more like a grown woman than a ten-year-old kid. I had never seen such pain and desperation, not even under the Boardwalk. No matter how bad things got for my under-the-Boardwalk friends, they always had the freedom to walk to the ocean and smell the sea breeze.

"That's it," I said, "you all need to feel the outside." I grabbed Johan's sleeve and led him to the window. "Come on, Johan, try and open it."

The whole ward became silent and people stopped eating as Johan pushed, but the window was stuck. I could feel the disappointment. But then he pushed on the second window, and it opened! People strained to see, turning and staring as if the Messiah had come.

The window faced another building, but you could still see a little bit of sky. The sun had just come out from behind the clouds. People were crying now, and so was I. From that day on, I never took the outdoors for granted. I knew then that I would be opening windows for everyone all my life.

"What is it, Isaac?" I asked, holding his claw-like hand.

"In a few hours, or sooner, it will all go back to the hell it was, yet you have brought us all hope. We, the lonely and forgotten people, are always."

"Always what?"

But he only said "always" again.

I remembered Henry saying, "Touch someone and it will change everything." I touched Isaac's face ever so gently. "I'll be back," I said.

"No you won't, but that's okay. Go on with your life. We are always. When you get older, take care of us. We are always."

This time, I took Johan's hand to walk up the stairs. There at the top was my bubbie in a wheelchair. Her long white hair was in a beautiful bun. She was wearing her favorite blue dress. She had lost weight, yet she looked regal again. I went to kiss her forehead, and she asked in Yiddish, "Is your father still alive?"

"Yes, Bubbie."

"Too bad."

"Why, Grandma?"

"Your bum of a father put me here."

"Oh Grandma," I said, "it was your—" I stopped, knowing I shouldn't tell her the truth: that her own son had put her in this hellhole.

When we got to the office, my mama was signing papers. Grandma got up and put her old fur coat on, and we all walked out together. I looked into the men's ward as we passed. Everything was the same as before except for one thing—the window was still open.

CHAPTER TWENTY-SIX

Strange Fruit

I hadn't seen Joe Joe for a few days. That was strange in itself, but to make it all the stranger I hadn't seen any of Joe Joe's family on the streets.

Getting out of the cellar window was easy. It was crawling on the ground to go from my backyard into Joe Joe's that was hard. The gravel was digging into my hands. I felt like a soldier and laughed at the thought. After all, I was a young lady now. I had been thinking a lot lately. I was getting older, and certain things weren't making sense anymore, like the strange looks Joe Joe and I got every time we held hands on the Boardwalk.

The night was still. Joe Joe's cellar was dark. I got scared. Their cellar was rarely dark so early in the night. I walked quietly through the alleyway to the front of the house. Everything was silent. I was about to climb the small fence covering the front windows of the cellar so I could peek in, when a great big black car pulled up. I ducked behind the old crooked tree.

A black man, who was as big as a tree, took up the whole passenger seat. He got out of the car, and to this day, I don't think I have ever seen a bigger, darker man in my life. He walked down the stairs to Joe Joe's cellar. Now I was real interested. Suddenly, the outside lights went on, the front door opened, and about fifty people poured out, screaming, "Welcome home, Junior!"

Junior was Joe Joe's daddy, and I knew he had been in jail someplace where they sing a lot. Joe Joe used to say with a lot of pride, "My daddy is in Sing Sing Prison."

I came out from behind my tree and went up on the stoop to watch. Stoops were the living rooms of the streets. From there, the stairs on the left went up into the houses and apartments of the rich people. The stairs to the right of the stoop went down into the cellar people's houses. I was watching the show going on beneath me when I was suddenly lifted off the ground by two big hands underneath my armpits.

"Shit," I said, "put me down."

"Looky here, I caught me a little ragamuffin white kid."

Joe Joe came running out of nowhere. "Put her down, Moe, that's my girlfriend."

All eyes were looking at me now. Grandma Georgia came out of the cellar. "Come in, child. My son's come home."

I went into the hot cellar. The whole place was decorated with streamers and balloons. Junior walked over to me. I expected him to like me the way Papa liked Joe Joe, but now I didn't like the way he was looking at me. Someone said from across the room, "Junior, you behave, you hear me now."

It was Grandpa Joe. But Junior was in front of me now. All noise and laughter stopped. I pulled myself up to my full height. I knew in my heart that Georgia and Grandpa wouldn't let anything happen to me, but they were on the other side of the room.

I looked up at the big man and said, "Welcome home."

"What is a white girl doing with my son?"

I stared into eyes of pure hatred. I tried to keep cool, but I wasn't used to this. I just kept staring into hate, going deeper and deeper into it. He looked as if he wanted me tortured and dead. No one spoke. I said in a low voice that I thought only I could hear, "I ain't doing nothing with your son except to be his friend and play with him since when we were kids. If you want to hate me, go ahead, but you better watch your ass 'cause I got other friends under the Boardwalk, and they will make mincemeat out of you."

No one said anything. Then, suddenly, Junior picked me up and twirled me around. I could hear Joe Joe yelling, "Put her down, put her down!" But it was okay. I could feel the hate fall off this big man, and that this was how he was making things lighter.

Big Joe said, "Let's eat."

Junior put me down and gave me his hand. We linked our pointing fingers together. This was a custom on the streets–when someone is insulted and the one doing the insulting wants to say "sorry" and still save face, then the pointing finger is held up and the one insulted, if he wants, links fingers. All is forgotten. My small finger got lost in his giant one. Everyone was smiling. "I ate the hate," I heard myself say out loud, without understanding the words.

Junior looked stunned, "I guess you did, I guess you did."

"This is Harry's kid," said someone in the crowd.

"Alley Harry?" asked Junior.

"Yeah," I said, liking the term.

Food was being passed around. Someone picked up a guitar, and everyone began to sing.

"Give us a song, Junior, give us a song." The whole room got quiet. Someone got a chair for Junior. Joe Joe and I sat down on the old cement floor at his feet. He began to sway back and forth for a while, his eyes closed. He started to hum a haunting tune. Without his singing a single word, the ladies were already crying quietly. What was going on? I didn't want to ask, yet I thought my heart would break.

The words started to come out, low and husky. It was Billie Holiday's song, "Strange Fruit." I had only heard it a few times before when old Georgia sang it. Junior's eyes were closed, and I saw a tear make a path down his ebony face. Everyone was swaying lightly. I realized that mine was the only white face in the crowd. I had never understood the words when Georgia sang them, but now I knew it was important to listen. Joe Joe took my hand and held on tight. I realized they were singing about lynching, the murder of black people.

I tried to keep still as the song went on. I couldn't catch my breath. My face was wet, and someplace I felt shame. It was shame for the world, though I was too young to know what the world had done. When he finished, there was silence in that cellar. Joe Joe put his thin arm around me.

I heard my father's voice, "Come here, Joyala."

"Papa," I cried out, and before I could reach his open arms and the safety of his embrace, he began to sing and do a soft-shoe: "Sioux City Sue, Sioux City Sue...." I had begun to notice that this was what he did any time he needed to break the tension. Everyone began to laugh and clap their hands. He and I were dancing the steps in perfect time.

"Hey, Harry," called out Junior, "stop that white folk shit and give us a real tune."

I was proud of how my Papa had the ability to make people laugh. But I was stunned that Papa wasn't mad at me. It was way after midnight. Papa stopped dancing and singing. Someone else picked up a guitar and began singing songs I had never heard before. Papa had my hand now and we went over to Junior.

"Welcome home." Papa grabbed the big man by the shoulders.

"Thanks, and thanks for keeping an eye on Joe Joe for me."

I looked at my dad as if to say, "What? You don't even keep an eye on *me*."

Papa just laughed and said, "My pleasure."

"How come you're not mad at me, Papa?" I asked.

"Why? You didn't cross the street."

Grandpa Joe called Papa over to the back bedroom. I saw Papa pull out of his back pocket the ever-waiting pack of cards. "Go on home, Joyala, and be careful you don't wake up your mama or we are both in for it."

I found Georgia in the crowd, her large form stuffed into a frilly red dress. I never saw her more beautiful. "Grandma Georgia, I have to go now. Thank you for letting me be here."

"It was an adult party, but I'm glad you could make it and keep Joe Joe company. Stay his friend, Juicey. It's going to be hard with his daddy home and no mama. After tonight his daddy may not like the idea of Joe Joe hanging out with a white girl, no matter how much he took to you. Don't take it personal because it isn't."

"If it's about me," I thought, "how could it not be personal?"

Joe Joe was waiting for me by the entrance to the cellar stairs. We both looked up at the stone stairs going up into the nice apartments, the real apartments.

"One day, Joyce, me and you are going to walk up the right kind of stairs. We'll go up instead of down."

CHAPTER TWENTY-SEVEN

The Soul's Color

"Whatcha doing out here, child, in the deep dark?"

"Grandma Georgia," I said, "I just wanted to get Joe Joe's attention and not wake Sister."

"Do you know that it is after one o'clock in the morning? What is it you want from Joe Joe?"

Georgia sat down on the old wooden box outside the cellar windows. It was supposed to be for garbage cans, but the rats got so bad that the big box was cleared out and us kids played in it. When I was seven, I used to run and hide there from Shirley when she wanted to brush my hair.

This night the beach and the ocean were calling to me. I could hear the waves in my head and feel the cool night sand on my feet. I wanted desperately to be with Joe Joe under the full moon and feel the warm breeze in our hair. For some reason it felt safe to tell all this to Grandma Georgia. Since I found out that she had known my dead Chews, I felt even closer to this big-hearted woman who had raised my friend Joe Joe.

"Come here, child," she said patting the place next to her on the box. Georgia was a big woman with big breasts who invited children to her. Her eyes were warm, dark, and deep, and you knew that she saw right through you.

It was a hot night. Papa was in Coney Island working at the hot corn stand or gambling at the poker machines at Faber's on Surf Avenue. Papa could always get someone to watch the stand for him so he could get away. I missed him not being in the alley playing cards every night. The old men who kept the game going were bored without him, but, ironically, they kept a better eye on me now that Papa wasn't there all the time. They were always calling to me when I was about to cut through the backyards, leaving on my different adventures. Now I prayed that no one would hear Georgia and me talking under the moonlit sky.

I cuddled next to her and breathed her in. She smelled of bleach.

"Child, don't think that I ain't aware of you two running around." She put her arm around me, and I could hardly hear her words, I felt so warm and comfortable. I felt like crying but I didn't know why. I heard Georgia say, "Soon you and Joe Joe won't be able to run so free together."

"What do you mean? Aren't you going to let Joe Joe hang out with me?"

"Juicey," she said.

Her name for me had always made me smile. Now it just made me mad. "What did I do wrong, Grandma?" I asked, on the edge of tears.

"What's going on out here? You ladies are making more noise than a bullfrog in July." It was Big Joe looking like an old teddy bear. He had sleep in his eyes. His skinny legs stuck out of his cutoff pajamas.

"Grandma said I can't hang out with Joe Joe."

"Whatcha saying that for, Georgia? They still too young to worry about that."

"Oh, shut your mouth, old man. Have you looked at Joe Joe lately? He grew a whole foot this year. Juicey is a big girl, too, for her age."

"Joyce," he said, "all that Grandma is saying is that some folks don't like to see black and white together so much." I knew that. But I still didn't get what they meant.

"What's going on?" It was Joe Joe. "I heard Joyce's voice and came on out to see."

"You came on out," repeated Georgia, "all dressed in your sneakers, shorts, and shirt? Right, young man?"

I watched Joe Joe squirm under the big moon. He shifted from one foot to the other, not saying a word.

"Listen, both of you, you're too old to be holding hands like little children."

"It ain't like that for us," Joe Joe said. "We're just friends."

"Ain't like what?" I asked. I could feel my heart beating fast, remembering the time he kissed me in the rain when we were going to work on the junk wagon. It hadn't happened again, and I had tucked it away in my memory. "Ain't like what?" I repeated.

"Children, listen, some people are already talking. I just don't want trouble here. We're the only black folks on the block."

I had felt the stares when I was under the Boardwalk hanging out with my friends. Even so, I didn't want to believe what Grandma was saying had anything to do with me. Big Joe was looking up at the moon as if he were alone in the yard.

"Grandma, I ain't gonna give up Joyce as a friend." Joe Joe sounded like he was going to cry. I felt like I was going to die.

"You don't know what you're saying. White and black just don't go together. Never go beyond friendship."

"I won't, Grandma," said the handsome Joe Joe.

"I won't either," I said.

She hugged us and said words I would never forget: "God help us all.

I hope the Good Lord protects my children from harm." I realized she was praying for Joe Joe and me. I put my arms around her fleshy neck and kissed her cheek.

"Now you children get back in your houses and let me and my old man enjoy a smoke together."

I ran to our bathroom window and crawled inside. I felt bruised and battered and didn't understand. I peeked out the window to see if the two old ones had left the yard. They were whispering as they passed a cigar back and forth between them. I caught the words that Grandpa said as he exhaled the smoke into the bright night.

"Leave them be, Georgia. We ain't in the South now."

"It's no good, Joe," she said, so low that I could hardly hear her. "It just ain't no good." She crushed out the cigar and stuck it down her dress for later. The two old people looked tired as they got off the box and walked hand in hand out of the alley. I sat on the toilet bowl and laid my head on the windowsill. I must have fallen asleep. I felt someone touching my hand and was about to scream when I saw it was Joe Joe trying to wake me.

"Come on, Joyce, let's go. Me and you gotta talk."

I climbed out the window, ignoring the rats scurrying away. It was a beautiful night, and the boards still had some folks escaping from the heat of their stuffy apartments. We climbed down the stairs to the beach and ran to the water. Joe Joe had to stop to take off his sneakers. Me, I ran right into the water, laughing at the big red moon. Words came to me from the cool waters; the ocean was waveless and smooth as the words hit me hard: "The fight for the soul's freedom is brutal. Fight it well prepared, little one." It was a voice that I heard sometimes in my head, but this time it seemed as if the whole ocean spoke to me. I dove in.

Back on the beach there was only silence. My hair hung wet and loose down to my waist. I could feel Joe Joe behind me. I turned and saw that the moon had worked its magic. My Joe Joe had never looked as handsome or as grown up. The moon was doing strange things to my heart.

"Joe Joe, I would never not be your friend."

We swam for a while and then lay in the sand like two desert rats. When Joe Joe stood up, I realized for the first time that he had grown a few inches; he was now much taller than me. We took hands and ran toward Manhattan Beach.

At the next bay we saw a dark figure lying in the sand. The ocean's gentle waves were touching the body ever so lightly every time they came ashore. I ran over to the person, who resembled a bundle of rags. I was afraid that if he was drunk, he would drown. Then I spotted the crutches and knew it was Old Hudson. He was just lying there; part of his face was in the wet sand. The other part was showing his big brown eye, open and staring. The sight of him reminded me of Chews right before she died. I couldn't imagine my life without Hudson.

"Hudson! Hudson!" I screamed into the bright night.

Joe Joe began to turn him over. All of a sudden a shout came from behind us. It was Chicky coming at us, swinging an empty bottle in her hand.

"That old bastard better be dead, Miss J. Do you hear me, child? He done drank all my Homer's Special."

"Chicky, don't say that. I don't want Hudson dead. I don't want anyone hurt. Please, Chicky, don't let him be dead." I broke down; the whole night was too much. The moon, the sand, the ocean, Big Joe and Grandma Georgia, Chicky swinging an empty bottle, and my friend Hudson dead. I started to cry.

"Hey, little girl, shut up your mouth." It was Hudson.

Suddenly the whole sky was happy. The stars were falling, and the moon was red and beautiful. The ocean was lit up like magic, and Hudson was alive. Joe Joe was pulling Hudson away from the water. Half his face was covered with sand; the other side was clear and black.

"Look," I said, still crying, "Hudson's half-black and half-white!"

"Like me," said my Joe Joe, "like me."

When I heard that, I couldn't move. Everyone kept still. Then Chicky came over to Joe Joe.

"How did you find out, child?" she asked him.

I didn't know what was going on. I knew that Georgia and Chews had once been friends. I didn't know that Chicky knew Joe Joe's life's secrets.

"I overheard Grandma saying it tonight, that my mama was white and that me and Sister ain't got the same mama. That's why she didn't want me and Joyce hangin' out so much now we're older. She didn't want no more trouble between black and white."

"How can someone be white and black?" I asked into the night.

"Listen, girl, and listen well." Hudson was slurring his words, but he wanted us to pay attention. "It don't matter what our mamas and papas are, it only matters what we are inside of ourselves. Now you listen, you black and white children. What me and Chicky and the others are living in is a season in Hell. Don't you two let anyone take away what you have inside of you. That place belongs to you and to you alone."

"Hudson, before, when I was in the ocean, I heard the words: 'The battle for the soul is brutal.' What does that mean?" I asked, in desperation.

"Hey, girl, you just gotta let God come through. That's what that meant."

"Hallelujah!" sang out Chicky.

"Just stay out of a season in Hell like this," said Hudson as he motioned to Joe Joe to pick up his crutches. But one crutch was making its way out to sea like a piece of driftwood. Joe Joe ran into the water. By the time he came back, I was laughing and pointing at the two figures walking hand in hand, Hudson singing and walking with one crutch, Chicky singing way out of tune.

Me and Joe Joe just looked at each other. I was afraid to ask him about his mama. "It's okay if you don't want to talk about it."

"Listen, Joyce, let's become blood brother and sister. This way there will never be any kind of trouble between us."

From his pocket he pulled out the old Swiss Army knife he'd found when he was collecting junk for BB. We sat down on the wet sand. Joe Joe washed the blade off with salt water and then asked me to stick out my hand. I didn't hesitate for a second. He held my hand tight to stop the blood and sliced it a little over the wrist.

At that moment Chicky ran back to us for Hudson's other crutch. I jumped and the knife slipped.

मा

I look down at my wrist as I write these words, and a few tears are born in the deep reaches of my soul. There it is, the scar—the scar of love and the scar of the moon and the ocean, the scar of that night in 1950 when the summer never ended and I became sister to m brother Joe Joe.[3]

मा

"Girl," said Chicky, as she held up my hand in the moonlight, "that there is deep. You may need stitches."

Joe Joe felt so terrible he was speechless. He took out his dirty hankie and pressed it to my wrist.

"Come on, we'll walk over to Coney Island Hospital."

"What will happen if I don't get a stitch, Chicky?"

"Then, beautiful Miss Lady J, you will have a little scar to remember this night forever."

"I vote for that," I said, and took the knife from Joe Joe.

He held out his hand and I gently made the cut over his right wrist. We let my blood drip into his, and we became what we were, two friends for life, brother and sister under the moon of Brighton Beach looking toward the great big ocean.

"Now don't you get no sand in those cuts, do you hear me?" Chicky demanded, as she collected the crutch.

I wrapped Joe Joe's handkerchief tightly around my wrist and took my brother's hand as we ran in the early dawn toward our new tomorrow. I slipped into the bathroom window and looked at my wrist. I was shocked to see so much blood. I put a lot of toilet paper on the cut, thankful to find that one luxury for a change instead of

---

3   This all happened many years before we knew about HIV/AIDS. Please don't ever let anyone do this now.

the paper wrappings from the oranges that the fruit store man gave us cellar kids each evening.

I felt like a woman as I climbed into the cot in the front room, which was mine alone now that Shirley was working nights. I laid my head on the pillow and told Mac that he'd better take care of my new brother. After all, wasn't I the same as Joe Joe now that my blood had mingled with his?

Yet I knew there was a vast difference between the lives of black and white. There were stories in the newspaper about people getting beat up, people being found dead because they were black, not only in the South. And then the song just kept playing over and over in my mind, "Strange Fruit." Even as I promised to be his friend forever, I knew in my heart that soon I would have to listen to Grandma.

Time took its toll, and we drifted apart from each other, not just by accident, but on purpose. Years later I would learn that my Joe Joe died in Vietnam. Perhaps we let go of each other to save whatever joys we could in our memories of the love we had shared—so very innocent, but behind the innocence was the knowledge that the small minds of the few could destroy the big hearts of the many.

CHAPTER TWENTY-EIGHT

Anna's Snowman

As time went on, Mama grew sicker, yet more and more determined for Mel and Harvey to get good educations. She didn't seem to worry about my education. Sometimes I wished she did, but not if it meant going to school every day. Meanwhile my sister Shirley went on with her life, sometimes, I feared, so alone that she would dry up and blow away.

Winter came, and Mama went into the hospital for an operation. Now she was home again, and we were in the middle of the biggest snowstorm in years. This cold morning, I was awakened by the sound of the steam coming up through the pipes. I knew Mama would start yelling as soon as the loud banging began. No one was home but us.

I ran to her. "Mama, isn't it wonderful? We have heat!"

I had heard her tossing and turning in pain all night, but she just smiled at me.

"Do I have to go to school?" I asked. "I hate to leave you alone like this, especially with the steam coming up."

"If you want to stay home, stay home, but don't give me any of that nonsense of wanting to take care of me."

I turned, hurt to the core. I almost made it out of the room, but I couldn't help it; I had to turn around and say something. "For your information, Mama, if I didn't want to go to school, I sure as hell wouldn't have to tell *you* about it."

She called me over to her. I sat on the edge of the hospital bed that the Nurses Aide Society had given to her.

"Joyala," she spoke, softly, "when people are in pain they say things that they don't mean. They look mad, when they're not. You have to understand this. Never judge a person in pain. Stay home if you want to. Put on warm clothes, then go build a snowman right in the alley outside the window, where I can see it. The alley looks clean for once; snow is a good whitewash." The deep snow had pushed the card games out of the alley and into Max's house.

"Aw, Mama, I'm too big to build a snowman."

She grabbed hold of my ear and pulled it hard. "If I had the strength, I would be out there making a snowman, and I'm forty-seven years old. You're never too old to be young."

I got dressed and ran outside to the alley. The cold wind turned my tears to ice, but I kept patting handfuls of snow on top of snow until I had two round lumps. Crying the whole time, I dug big holes for eyes, nose, and mouth. Somehow in my heart I knew Mama wouldn't be home much longer. I got on my knees and looked into the basement window. "Mama, I gotta get something. I'll be right back," I yelled.

Harry had a nice new wool scarf. I grabbed it and ran back to the alleyway and placed it around the neck of my snowman. Through the window, I could see Mama laughing. Next I ran around the corner to Kathy's basement where Aunt Mary kept the coal and stuffed my pockets. I was running around like a chicken without a head, all to please my mama. I put coal pieces in the eyes of the snowman and one big one in the nose, and some twigs to make the mouth. Finally, I took off my own knitted hat and placed it on the snowman's head, and I started to dance around Mr. Snow, with a song in my heart and tears on my face.

Then something went berserk in my brain. I couldn't stop running around the snowman. I kept running, screaming and yelling nonsensical words. People were opening their windows, wondering what the excitement was.

"It's good to be a kid again," I thought as I looked in at my mother.

She looked so fragile, so thin, so beautiful. Perhaps my grey-haired mama was once again a child in her homeland, Russia, where, she used to say, the snow piled as high as the rooftops. For a moment, I could see her there, and we were children together.

When I went back into the house, Mama hugged and kissed me. "I will never forget this moment," she said, "or the snowman we both built."

मा

Now in the present, I think of all who have come over the years to sit before me, many if not most in pain, pain that comes from different places, different sources, different reasons. Nevertheless, pain. And I try to build snowmen for them all—in memory of my mama, who taught me to have patience with people who maybe cannot express the reasons why they yell or are cranky or downright mean.

"Look deep into everyone's heart," I can hear her saying. "Look past everyone's pain...."

CHAPTER TWENTY-NINE

Make Them Laugh

Later that winter, Mama moved into Coney Island Hospital. Cancer had already torn her body apart. Not unlike the little drummer boy who had nothing to bring the Christ Child in the manger, I had nothing to bring my mama in the charity ward. When I told her this, she gave me her usual cuff on the ear, and said, "Joyala, can you smile, can you laugh?"

I said under my breath, "Barely."

"What!" she said. "You know damned well you still have your sense of humor, and if you don't, then you are in worse shape than me."

The lady in the next bed began to cackle. Mama threw her a dirty look. "What are you laughing about?" she asked.

It was Mrs. Rosenberg, the lady without legs. She was to be Mama's friend for the next two years, as both women endured the worst kind of physical pain.

"I'm laughing, Anna, 'cause no one could be in as bad shape as you."

Mama laughed then, too, and threw an orange at Mrs. Mori, the lady in the bed on the other side, who caught it.

"What'd you do that for?" she asked my mama in her thick Italian accent. Mrs. Mori had been in a fire when she was very young and was left with a body and face that were completely scarred. Like everyone on the ward, she had cancer.

"Aren't you in worse shape than me?"

Mrs. Mori thought for a moment and then said, "I don't think so, Anna. I'll probably live longer."

I was beginning to think that I was in the wrong place; the psycho ward was on the top floor. Before I knew it, everyone was joining in, each one saying she was worse off than the other. There were at least eighty patients in the ward.

"Come here," Mama said. I sat on her bed, afraid to touch her anywhere because of all the tubes. "Baby, I haven't been the best mama in the world, but I tried. I want you to look around you and see that if the poor and the sick can laugh as they get ready to die, then the living must laugh too. Never bring a dying person your tears, unless they ask for it. Do you have that?"

I didn't, but I nodded anyway.

"Sometime when I am gone, it will be all right to cry. You are the type of kid who will go into the world and help people, and you will have to cry sometimes."

I didn't have time to think about what Mama was saying. There was too much of a ruckus going on with Mrs. Rosenberg and Mrs. Gould, the lady on the other side of her.

"Joycey, honey," Mrs. Rosenberg was saying, "isn't having no legs worse than being blind?"

"Joyce," said the sightless Mrs. Gould, "tell the truth."

Mama whispered, "Don't you dare!"

"Now listen up," I said. "No one's worse off than anyone else here. Do you know why? Cause I am here, the great Joyce Green, from Brooklyn, New York, and I am gonna sing you a song."

Everyone was silent now, except Mrs. Mori, who said, "Honey, Mrs. Gould may be blind, but she ain't deaf. Can't you read us something instead?" Everyone had heard me sing at one time or another. They knew I loved to sing at the top of my lungs whenever I got a chance. Since my meeting with old Abraham Bell, I knew my voice had some kind of an ability to wake people up—even if I couldn't sing on key. I began, "I'm a little teapot…" and then some of the ladies joined in. I imitated a dancing teapot as I sang, then turned to look at my mama. Tears were running down her face.

"Mama, what is it? I'm sorry."

"No, Joyala, I am happy that we don't scare you, that's all. It's good." I wanted my mama to hold me, something she rarely did, but her words were enough for that day.

CHAPTER THIRTY

Never Ask Why

"Mama, does it hurt to die?"

"No, of course not," she answered.

"Then why are you always in pain?" I asked, really wanting to know.

"Sometimes you cry in pain because the heart hurts so bad you can feel the very inside of you. It's hard, honey, to be such a burden on your family."

"Oh, Mama," I said, "Papa isn't that bad, is he?"

She burst out laughing so hard that I thought the tubes attached to her body would pull out.

The ward was hot and sticky that May morning. It was already over eighty degrees outside, and it seemed even hotter inside. The stench of the ward was unbearable. Mrs. Rosenberg, the legless lady, had soiled her bed, and the nurse and the aide hadn't gotten to her yet. I was trying to ignore the stink, but it was hard; her bed was only a few inches away from Mama's.

"Joyala, I am talking about myself, not Papa." I looked over at Mrs. Rosenberg and saw that the sheet she had put over her head was moving. "Stop laughing," Mama yelled at her.

"Look, Annaka," said the hidden form, "if I can manage to laugh as I lie in my own shit, then what the kid said is funny and true. What are you still doing with that bum of a husband, and where is that *farkakta* aide?"

"I don't know," said Mama, "but if she doesn't come soon, we are all going to croak from the smell instead of from the cancer."

"Stop making her laugh," said Mrs. Mori, on the other side of Mama. "Every time she moves the stink gets worse."

Despite the stench, the spirit of the place was more sacred to me than any temple or church. The months to come would give me the greatest learning experiences of my life. It was alive in that ward even though it was a place of death. Joe Joe and I had taken to talking seriously about what it is to be black and white, sick and healthy, drunk and sober. I wanted some answers, and most of them came from the ward.

One time I asked my mother, "Why you?" I just couldn't get it, why did this good woman have to be in so much pain. Was the world really that unfair?

She called me over to her, and when I bent over the bed, wham! She slapped me hard, with more strength than I thought she had in her bony arm. "Who do you think is gonna give you an answer? You think God is gonna come down and explain it all to you?" I was trying to hold back my tears. "Look," she said, "never ask why, because who is going to answer you? So don't waste your time." She continued, more softly, "You won't get any answers, so just keep going and help who you can."

When Mama was having her last operation, Papa and Shirley went out and got her a plot in Greenwood Cemetery, with time payments. The mail clerk at the hospital screwed up real bad. Instead of giving Shirley the information booklet from the cemetery, he sent it up to Mama on the ward. When Shirley got there, the booklet was being passed around among all the patients, and Mama was crying. Shirley thought she would die right there. Mama looked up, "Shirley, Shirley, see the picture of the cemetery. All the trees!" She yelled to one of the patients to give back the little booklet with the picture.

"Thank you, Shirley."

Shirley was relieved, but when I heard about it, it really scared me. So the next day, I played hooky from school. I was in eighth grade by now and tough as nails. I went up into Mama's ward as bold as can be. "Mama," I said, "you're not dying, because what will I do without you?"

"Listen," she said, "What I feared most was to be buried in potter's field. Now my children have a place to go to remember me. Never let your dead die, Baby, okay?" Her eyes were glazed as if she were already thinking of her new home in Greenwood Cemetery.

She came back for a moment. "Joyala, take care of Harry and Shirley, too."

Well, that was the last straw. I was all of twelve, going on thirteen. Shirley was twenty-six. "Mama," I said, "sure, Mama, sure."

She smiled. "You almost lost it, didn't you?"

"Yeah, but don't worry, I will never let my dead die."

Harry and his second wife lived with me on the ashram for the last ten years of his life. I made sure he always had someone to take him to jai alai or play cards. Shirley was living here with us too, and she took care of a lot of the ashram kids. I loved Papa, I loved Shirley, and I kept my word. Sometimes it's hard to keep one's promises to the dying. But when you do, they never really die.

Very few of the patients had visitors so they welcomed me so much that it sometimes brought tears to my eyes. I would arrive early before school and be there when my mama and the rest of the ward were waking up. If I could get away with not going to school, I would stay there all day. But that only happened when Mama was out of it.

Some of the nurses didn't like me much. One day Miss Terry, the head nurse, called me over. I tucked my polo shirt neatly in the white shorts I had bought with my own money from working the beach chairs on weekends. I was wearing white canvas sneakers I had bought in the five-and-dime. I was proud I could buy my own clothes. Pushing my long black hair back from my face, I walked with a straight back toward the nurses' station. It seemed like the whole ward had woken up at that moment.

"Miss Green," she said as I reached her desk, "why do you come here?"

Before I could answer, I spotted someone in the bed closest to the station, with some curtains separating her from the others. This was where the ladies who were close to death were kept because they needed to be watched. The head of her bed was raised a little, and she was staring right at me. Something in her eyes reminded me of Chews just before she died. It was like her body was there and her mind and heart were somewhere else.

"Who is that?" I asked Miss Terry.

"Who?" she barked, like a drill sergeant.

I was just about to say something when the lady I was looking at called out, "Help, help!"

I ran right to her. She was spitting up blood.

"Get away from that bed," said the angry Miss Terry, as she barked orders to the nurses nearby. But the lady had wrapped her claw-like hand around my wrist and was holding on for dear life. Blood was spilling out of her mouth, and I was terrified.

"I said get away from that bed!"

But I couldn't get the lady to let go of my wrist.

"My name is Brigit," she whispered.

I answered, not even realizing I was talking. "My name is Joyce."

"I just wanted someone to know my name before I died."

She still held my wrist in a vise-like grip. She was staring into my eyes, and I could see fear and pain, but I could also see how much she wanted to tell me something. So I stared right back into Brigit's eyes and waited.

A doctor was standing behind me now, not doing anything but listening. I turned my head to look at him for a moment, and he shook his head as though I was supposed to understand the signal he was giving me. Then I realized he was telling me that the old lady was going to die. What if she died holding my hand? Would I be stuck with her ghost for the rest of my life?

"I'm not afraid," she whispered, "I'm just lonely."

I thought that I should answer her since she was looking straight into my eyes. "Don't be lonely. I won't leave you." I just kept right on talking, although I had nothing to say. "I just got these shorts with my own money," I said. She stared into my eyes more intently, like she was listening to every word and didn't want to miss anything I was saying.

"Brigit is my name," she was repeating, "and I am from Dublin."

"I am Joyce and I am from Brighton Beach, but I work in Coney Island. I work for the beach chairs."

She pulled me toward her. My wrist was killing me. "Please remember me. I have no children to remember me. Please remember me."

"I will," I said, "I promise."

"Thank you, Miss Joyce from Brighton Beach." She smiled and closed her eyes.

I could see her breath slowing down, going in and out, then staying in and finally staying out. I was fascinated and afraid. Her eyes were wide open again, and she was staring at me.

"She's gone, honey." It was the doctor.

"You mean she is dead? Like really dead dead?" I asked, sounding so young even to my own ears.

Then a low moaning came from the other side of the curtains. It was Mrs. Jones singing a gospel song about Jesus in the garden. A few others sang with her. I opened the curtains and yelled out, "Brigit was her name!" Someone picked up the name and sang out that Brigit was in the garden with Jesus. I walked away toward Mama's bed. She was awake and patting the side of her bed for me to sit down. I wished she would hold me in her arms, but I didn't say anything. I just sat down.

"Who bought it now?" Mrs. Gould asked no one in particular.

"A lady named Brigit," I answered, "and she wasn't scared; she was just lonely."

"Aren't we all?" said Mrs. Gould.

I moved closer to Mama. She wasn't an affectionate mother, but I knew she loved me, and I could sometimes feel that love. This was one of those times.

"Did you see her?" she asked.

"She was holding my wrist," I said, trying not to cry.

I looked at my wrist and saw that it was red and sore. I noticed the blood on my clothes and was about to say something when Mama said, "A little cold water will get that out, Joyala. Listen, someday I will be in the same bed as Brigit. We call them the dying beds. I don't want you ever to be afraid of death."

"But, Mama, where will you be?"

"In here." She pointed to her heart and then laid her hand against my chest.

"Oh, all this bullshit is too dramatic for me," said Mrs. Rosenberg. "Come on, Anna, let the kid go to school." I looked at Mrs. Rosenberg with shock in my eyes. "I know, I know," she said, "you want to kill me right now, but it's not good for such a young girl to be hanging around death. So go to school and get some answers."

Once the word "school" was spoken Mama had to make me go, so she kissed me goodbye and told me to go. Just like that, go. Well, I had no intention of going to school. I was going to find my Joe Joe. As if Mama was reading my mind, she said, "And bring Joe Joe around. It's time he gets over his fear and comes to see me. I want to talk to him."

"Okay, Mama."

I ran out of the ward and past the information desk where Shirley worked.

"Is everything okay?" she asked.

"Yeah, Mama is still alive and Brigit is in the garden with Jesus."

I didn't give Shirley a chance to yell or kiss me or whatever she might do. I just kept walking until I was out of the old yellow building, leaving the stench of death behind. Maybe I could catch Joe Joe before he went to school. I ran as fast as I could. My heart was beating fast and my hair was floating behind me as I ran. Somehow I thought that if I was happy, Brigit would be, too.

I finally reached Coney Island Avenue and there was Joe Joe sitting on the steps. His books were in his lap, and he wasn't looking too friendly.

"What's up?" I asked my best friend.

"What's up?" he said mimicking me. "I've been looking all over for you."

"You know that I go see Mama in the mornings."

"Yeah, I know, but I wanted to go with you this morning."

"Why?" I asked.

"Because I miss you."

"Oh, shit, Joe, let's not get all mushy."

"The hell with you," he said, as he got up and began to walk away.

"I need to get my books and then we can walk together to school."

Joe Joe said, "Let's not."

We began to walk in the opposite direction from the school. On the way to the beach, I told him about Brigit. When we reached the sand, we found Big Henry asleep near the water. "Henry!" I shook his big frame to wake him.

"Miss J, why ain't you in school?"

"Because Brigit died, and I need you to spell her name."

Without asking another question, he got up and shook off the sand. We followed him down to the water's edge, where he picked up a Popsicle stick and wrote "Brigit" in the hard sand. Joe Joe knew the whole story by now. Big Henry didn't need me to explain; somehow he knew anyway. The three of us stood there and watched as the water came and claimed its own. The word faded out, leaving just a "B" that could hardly be seen.

I held tight to Joe Joe as I watched the waves coming up the sand and returning. I closed my eyes and could see Brigit's breath coming in and out. I watched her breath go out, and in that moment I breathed in. I looked down, saw the bloodstains on my clothes, and in that moment I knew the world was perfect.

CHAPTER THIRTY-ONE

Stop Praying for Me

The AIDS epidemic is not over, although many seem to have forgotten how it was when AIDS was a death sentence for the young. Meanwhile I kept working with the dying, and when I could, I'd make them laugh. Later, I talked to them about the perfection of the soul and told them again and again not to fear death. And like my own mother, I refused to answer when they asked, "Why me?"

There were still questions, though, including, "Can you help me kill myself?"

"I can't, Janna," I said again to the young woman.

"Why not? I want to be with my babies." All three of her babies had died of AIDS. The pain in her chest had gotten really bad. It was PCP again, the AIDS pneumonia. This was the fourth bout, and we knew it was the last.

Janna had spent most of her adult life on the street turning tricks to support her cocaine habit. She had gotten pregnant by God-only-knows-who, and had had her babies taken away from her one by one—first by the authorities, then by God. Yet she was so pure in that moment that I almost wished I could have assisted her in her passing. Instead, I said something that would get her attention:

"I can't because I already committed murder as a child."

As I expected, this impressed her. She forgot about her agonized breathing for a while, and she tried to sit up in bed. I knew she thought that I was lying, but she didn't want to take a chance in case I wasn't. I must have looked like I was thirteen again, because suddenly that's how I felt.

"Tell me about it, Ma," she said, her voice softening and sounding maternal. This was her chance to mother someone again. I sat back for a second, forgetting my rounds and all the people I had to see. This was Janna's time, or perhaps it was my time.

मा

At first, when Mama was in the hospital, I used to pray and pray for her to get better and come home. "Joyala," she said one summer day, "don't pray."

Just then I was begging God to keep my mama alive and trying so hard for God to hear me, I could hardly hear what my mother was saying. Later she told me that I looked to be in some sort of trance. "Joyala," she repeated, "please don't do that."

"Do what?" I was confused.

"Don't ask God to let me live."

"Do you really think that if I asked God to let you live, that you *would* live?" I was getting excited.

"Of course, God will never refuse you anything. Now listen, I do not want to live like this. I had a good life. Now stop praying."

I looked at my mama and wondered for a moment when she had this good life. All I could remember was her working, coming home, then going to sleep, and back to work again. Where and when was this good life? Just at that moment, a light came into my forehead and I heard the words, "Let her go, little one."

"Bullshit," I cried aloud.

Mama opened her eyes. "Let me go, honey. I can't live like this."

I began to pray even harder, begging, crying, pleading. I felt the strength of my whole healthy young body going into my hands.

I placed them on Mama's chest. She grabbed my hand hard, her bony fingers hurting my small hand. She seemed to grip it tighter and tighter. Mrs. Rosenberg said, "Let her go, Anna. You're hurting her."

With those words, Mama released me. My hand was bruised where her ring had dug into it. There was even a little cut. For spite, I whispered in the air, "God, you better let my mama live."

A cry came from the bed. "Please, Joycey, you don't know who you are. Please let me go. I am in too much pain. I don't want to live. I know that I wasn't that much of a mommy to you, but please let me go." I was shocked to the very core of my being. It was the first time I had felt power over anyone older than me. "Please stop now."

The tingling in my hands began to go away as she drifted off to sleep. I tried to nudge her awake to show her the little cut she had made with her ring. I wanted her to say she was sorry. Bending over the rail, I pushed the button. Down came the bars.

"Mama," I said, "you made me bleed."

She opened her eyes. "If you don't stop praying for me, I will make you dead." With these words we both laughed. "Don't you know that you are a God child? You have the powers and the prayers. It is all in you."

I thought she'd really flipped out. She said, "No more. Do you hear me?" That was the day my prayers ceased. In fact, I stopped praying, period. I didn't want to be no God child.

I watched Mama get worse and worse. Two years passed quickly. Every day I could feel a power rising inside of me. I could feel my hands holding something hot and wonderful. I would put them in cold water every chance I could. I'd still run to my under-the-Boardwalk friends. By now, I didn't bother sneaking out of the cellar window anymore. There was no one around to care, so I just walked out of the house and ran to the beach.

"You better start praying, girl, you hear me?"

"Why, Big Henry?" I asked.

"Cause you need to pray me up a bottle from old Homer's bathtub."

I knew that Henry would get the shakes real bad if he didn't have a drink soon. I looked out at the ocean and said, "Okay, I'm back. I need a few cents for Henry, or maybe for a bottle to fall out of the sky."

Hudson came over. "Hudson, don't say a word. I'm praying."

"Yeah," said Henry, "I gave her a job."

I had made it a point to tell my friends everything about my life, so they knew I had decided not to be a God child.

"Whatcha praying for, sweet thing?" said Hudson.

"I am praying for a bottle for Henry."

"Well, what about that!" said Hudson. From his baggy pants he pulled out some Homer's Special, which Homer made and bottled in any available container. This time it was an old peroxide bottle. Once I saw the guys pouring some Homer's into an old Dixie cup, and it burned right through the cup.

"Shit, girl, you really got the light," said Hudson as he took a drink and passed it to Big Henry.

I got real scared for a moment as my hands felt the tingling. "I'm going," I said.

"Where are you going?" said Big Henry.

"To Coney Island Hospital to see my mama."

"What are you going to do that for?"

It was about two in the morning and the hospital was miles away. Before my two protectors could offer to come with me, I ran to the Boardwalk, and then I ran and ran until I couldn't run anymore. I was going to heal my Mama and get her to come home to me, whether she wanted to or not.

I passed a nightclub at the corner of Ocean Parkway and the Boardwalk. Chicky was outside going through the garbage, looking for booze. "Where the hell are you going, Juicey?" she asked.

"I'm going to see my mama."

"It's the middle of the night. Do you think you'll be able to see her?"

"I don't care. I'm going to heal my mama."

"Oh, shit, kid, are you back to praying again?"

"Yes," I said, looking shy and a little bit ashamed that I'd broken my promise.

I ran down Ocean Parkway. Finally the big old yellow hospital building was in front of me. I went around to the building where they kept the dead bodies. The place didn't scare me, not like when I was a young baby of eight and Shirley had taken me there to show me where she had just gotten a job. For some reason known only to her, she took me into that little building and told me to stand in a certain place and close my eyes. She pulled out a drawer, and I opened my eyes to see my first dead person. I ran, and kept running all around the whole hospital, thinking the dead naked person was running after me.

Now I was in the shadows of the house of death and wasn't afraid one bit, that is, until someone called my name in the dark. Before I could run, I recognized Chicky's voice. She had come on the old bike she sometimes rode, and was all out of breath.

"Chicky," I said, sounding wise, "that is the house of the dead."

"Whatcha talking about, girl?" she asked, looking afraid for a moment.

"That's the morgue. Shirley took me there."

"Let's get now, girlie," she said, as she pedaled past me. I laughed and followed my old friend. I had planned to sneak into the hospital through the laundry entrance in the back. We walked in the door, looking relaxed, as if it was normal to be there. None of the sweating laundry workers stopped us. Now we were looking for the stairs, afraid of getting caught if we went in the elevator together.

Chicky said, "You go on and walk up the stairs, and I'll take the elevator."

"Fifth floor," I told her and ran up the stairs. When I reached the fifth floor, I tiptoed through the big swinging doors to the ward. I was bending low to sneak past the nurses' station when a voice asked, "What's wrong with your back, Joyce Green?" It was Bertha, the ward nurse. I had given up my childhood ambition to be like Tirza, and now the kind Bertha was the person I wanted to be like when I grew up.

"Oh, nothing," I said, as if it was normal to be walking bent over, visiting the ward at three in the morning.

"Where's your papa?"

"I just want to see my mama."

"Your mama took a turn. She's doing poorly and we have her on the night watch."

I had been around the hospital too many nights not to know that the night watch was really the death watch. I rushed to my mama. Now she was the one who'd been moved up front near the nurses' station. She looked so thin and frail. "This is not my mama," I thought, remembering the jolly fat woman who would dance around the cellar with my papa. This was just her shadow.

"Your sister was just here. She went downstairs to say she is taking off the rest of the night to be with your mama," said Bertha.

I put down the bars to the bed, a thing that I did quickly and well.

"Excuse me," said Bertha, "are you supposed to be here?" She was standing over Chicky, who was bending down trying to get herself under the bed to hide.

"She's my aunt," I said.

"On whose side?" The huge black woman eyed the skinny black woman.

"My father's."

"Now, no funny stuff. Your mama has a high fever." She turned away from us. I placed my hands on my mama's hot head and asked Mac to take down her fever and let her live. It felt good to be talking to God again.

Chicky said, "Honey, I think your mama is making ready to die. The angels are gonna come for her, child."

I began to pray harder. I could see a river, and myself sitting on the banks of the flowing waters. It had a wonderful scent, not unlike the smell of my friends under the Boardwalk. It was the smell of life.

"Please, let my mama live." I closed my eyes and pressed Mama's temples hard.

"What the hell are you doing, Joyala?" It was Mama.

"Nothing, Mama." I began to cry.

She looked at me, slurring her words as she spoke. "Joyala, don't you ever bring me back like that again. Do you hear me, child? I told you not to pray for me. I want to die, it's what I want more than anything." She was drifting off again. Chicky was standing in the shadows, quiet and still. Mama never knew she was there. Her slurred whisper sounded just like Chicky on a drunk. "Just remember that I love you enough to not want you to have you take care of me anymore. Forgive me." She drifted into sleep. I felt her head. She was cool. I walked away with Chicky.

As we passed the nurses' station, Bertha called out, "Maybe you'd better stay. We're trying to find your papa."

"Never mind, Bertha. Mama's not going to die right now. Her fever is all gone." Bertha just looked at me. I gave Chicky a dirty look as she tried to swipe some of the nurses' cigarettes left unattended on the desk. "Bertha, please don't tell my sister I was here."

As we were about to go out the swinging doors into the puke-green hallway with the plaster falling from the ceiling and walls, Bertha called, "Does your friend want a cigarette?" She came over to the shocked Chicky and handed her a full pack of Lucky Strikes. We took the elevator down and went out into the parking lot. The moon was high in the sky now.

"Let's light up," I said to Chicky.

She didn't say a word for a change. She took out two whole Luckys, a rare treat. We sat on the curb.

"I am going to let my mama die now, Chicky."

"I know that, honey."

I began to cry and Chicky held me to her bony frame. Mama had lasted for two full agonizing years. Sometimes I thought that she blamed me for her pain and suffering. I knew in my heart that she could have lived even longer than she did, but I kept my prayers and my hands off of her. And so, for many years, I felt that I had killed her.

Then the end came, early on the morning of the Fourth of July. My mama used to say, "They'll all be celebrating when I die." Seeing the fireworks that night, I realized that what she'd said had come true.

I wore a white blouse to the funeral. "*Shanda*," whispered the old people, because it was a shame to wear white to a funeral, but I didn't care. And I refused to look back at the grave. Why should I? I had already seen my mama, whole and laughing, right above the coffin.

Photos 1940-1970

p. 188 (Top) Anna and Harry, 1952. (Bottom Left) Ma's Mother, Anna Green, 1939. (Bottom Right) Baby Joyce with Shirley, Mel & Harvey, 1940.

p. 189 (Top) Ma, 1942. (Bottom) Ma, 1947.

p. 190 On the Beach, 1946.

p. 191 (Top) Ma and Harvey, 1948. (Bottom) Harvey's Bar Mitzvah, 1949.

p. 192 (Top) The Wishing Bench, Brooklyn, 1947. (Bottom) Coney Island, 1950s.

p. 193 (Top Left) Brighton Beach. (Top Right) Tirza the Wine Bath Girl. (Bottom) Harry Playing Cards in the Alley.

p. 194 (Top Left) Ma, 1948. (Top Right) Ma, 1949. (Bottom Left) With Harry, 1947. (Bottom Right) With Harry at the Hot Corn Stand, 1949.

p. 195 Running with the Garrison Gang, 1951.

p. 196 (Top) Telegram from Ann Green on Ma's 12th Birthday. (Bottom) Teenage Ma, 1954.

p. 197 (Top Left) Ma's Russian Maternal Grandmother. (Top Right) At Aunt Lily's Chicken Farm in New Jersey, 1954. (Bottom Left) At Coney Island, 1954. (Bottom Right). Lincoln High School Photo, June 1954.

p. 198 (Top Left) With Harry, 1950s. (Top Right) Ma with Denise and Jimmy, 1960s. (Bottom) Ma with Baby Denise, 1957.

HOW GOD FOUND ME

MA JAYA SATI BHAGAVATI

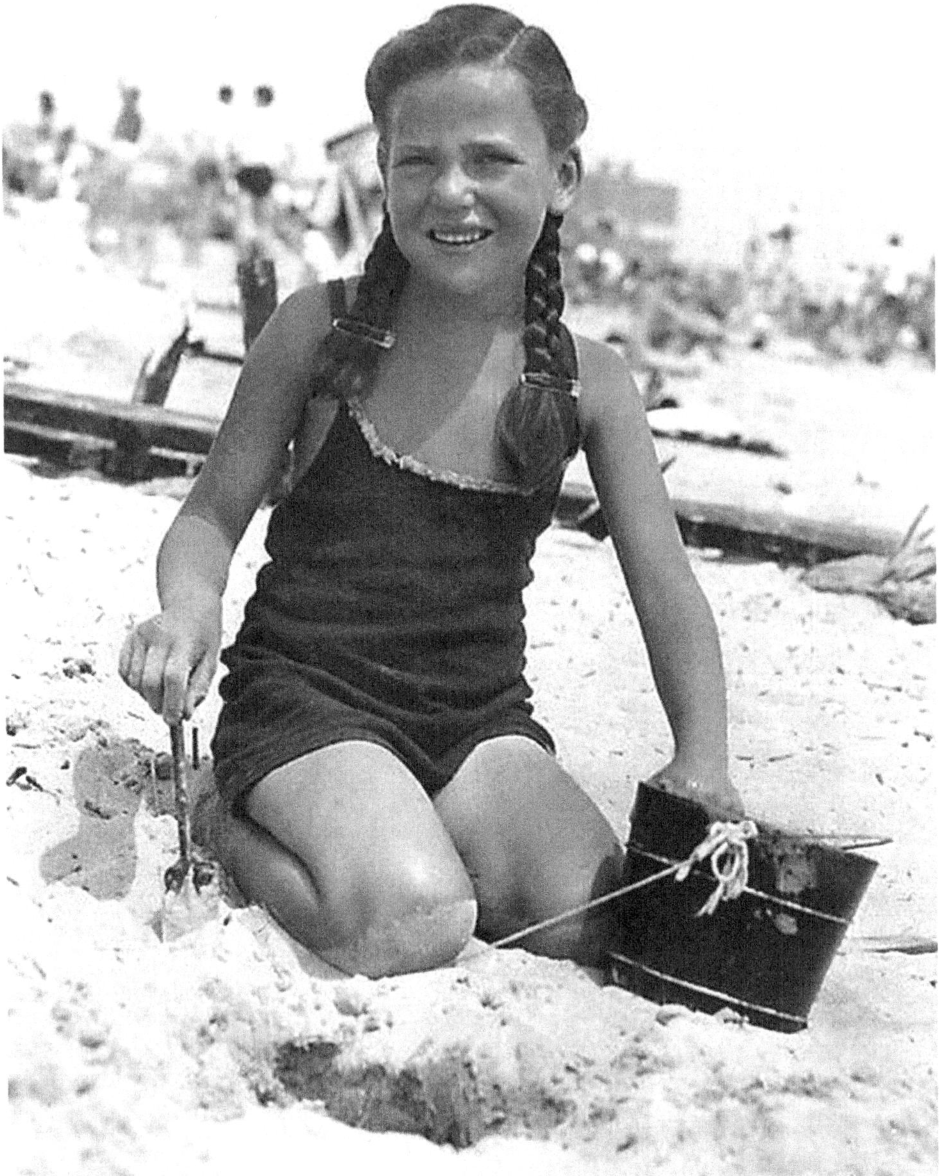

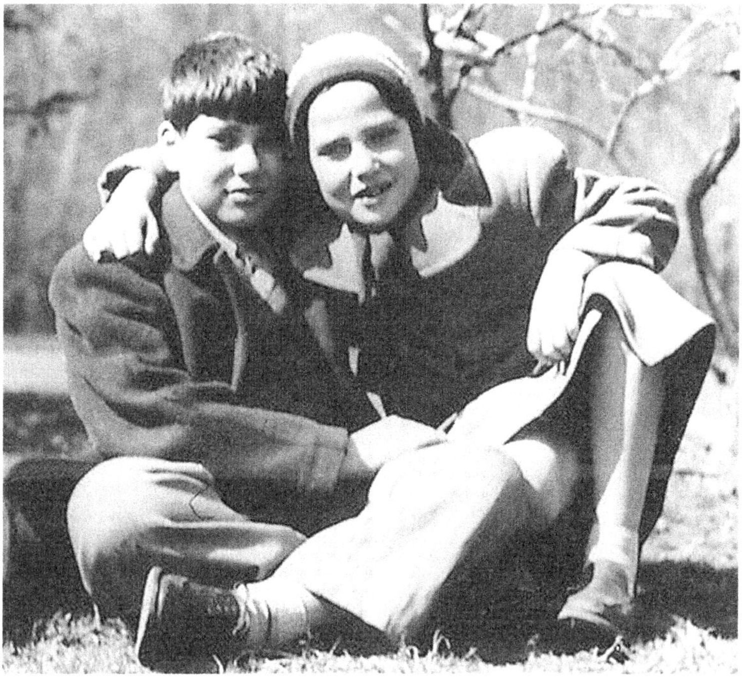

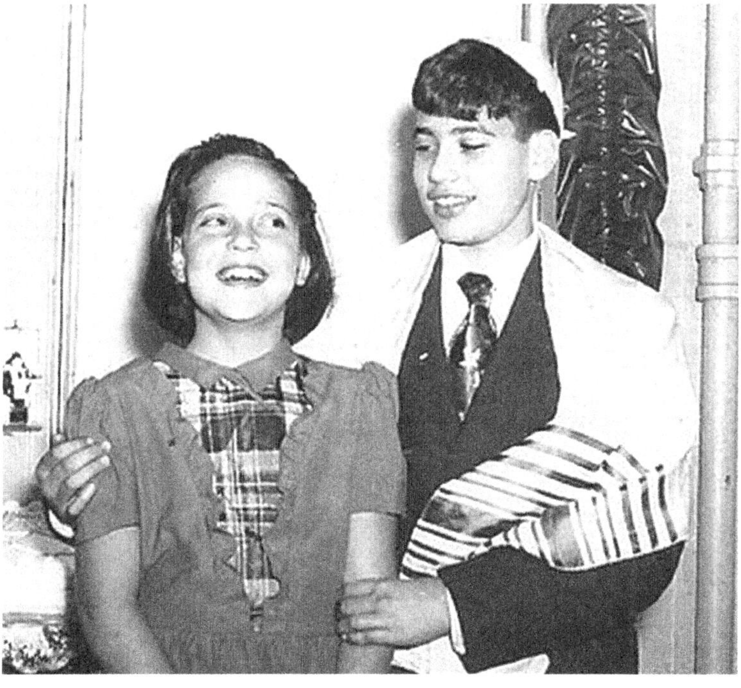

HOW GOD FOUND ME

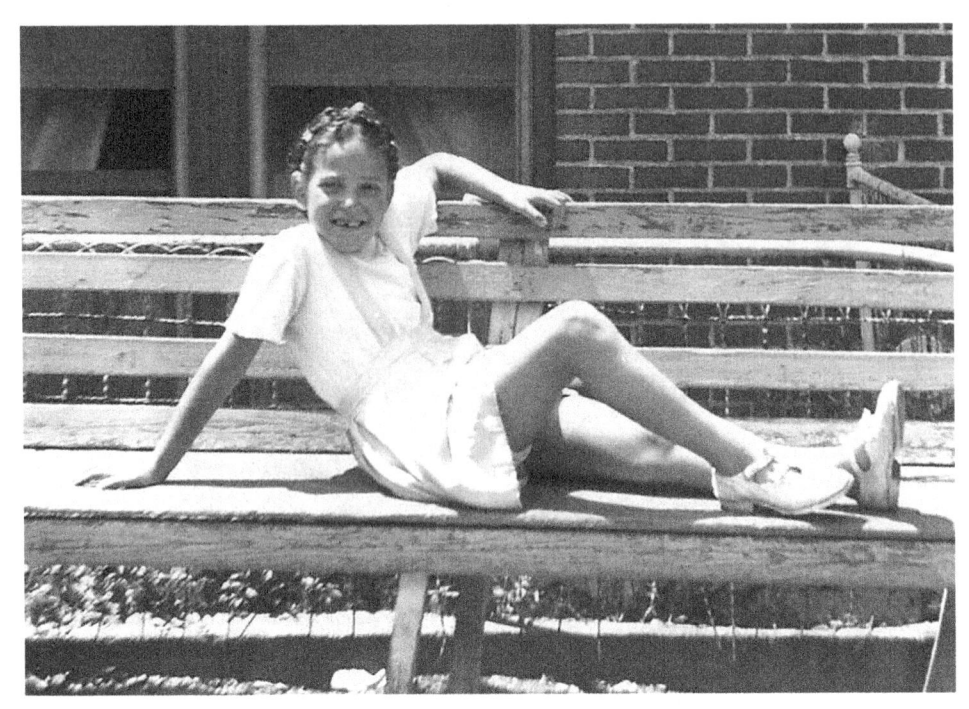

MA JAYA SATI BHAGAVATI

HOW GOD FOUND ME

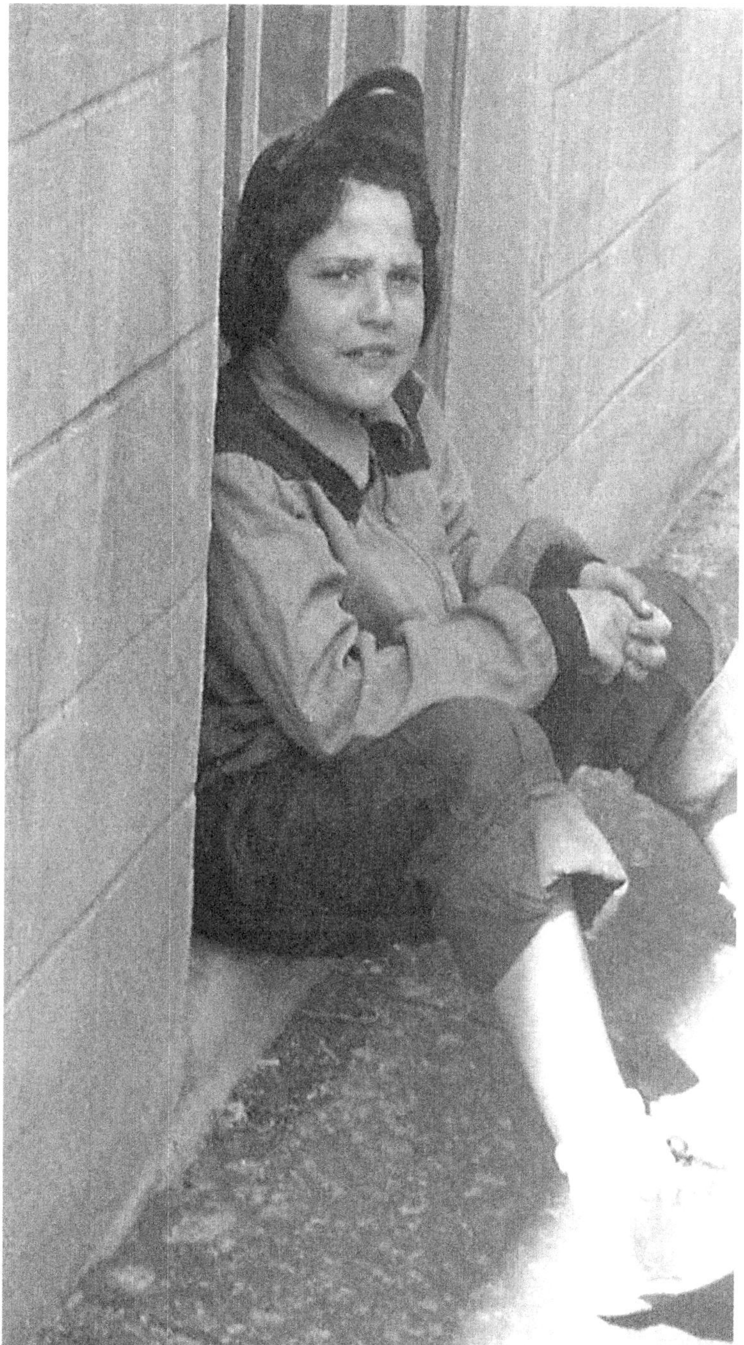

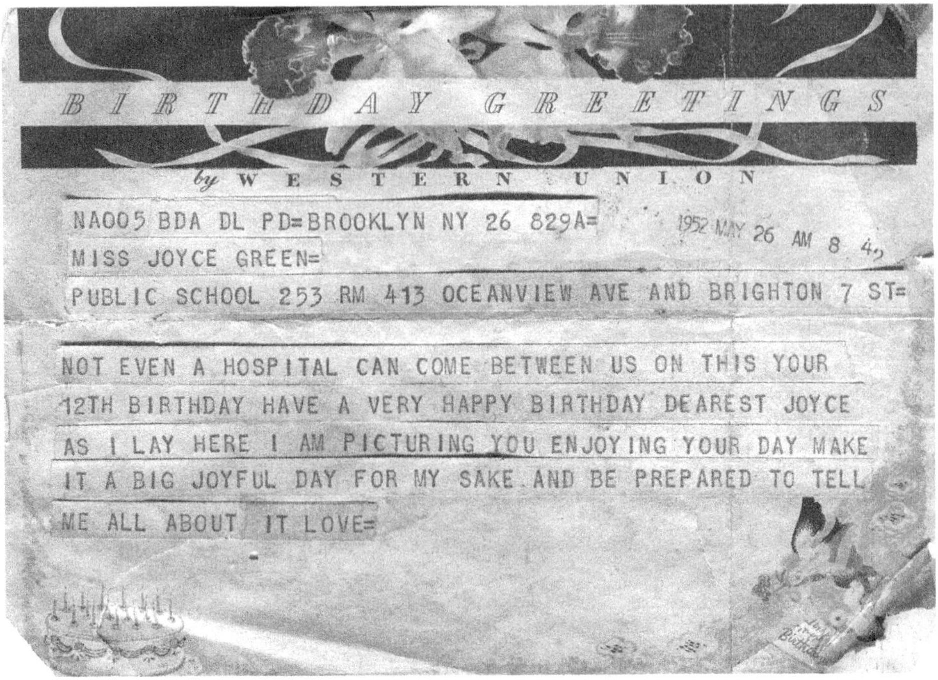

BIRTHDAY GREETINGS
by WESTERN UNION

NA005 BDA DL PD=BROOKLYN NY 26 829A= 1952 MAY 26 AM 8 42
MISS JOYCE GREEN=
PUBLIC SCHOOL 253 RM 413 OCEANVIEW AVE AND BRIGHTON 7 ST=

NOT EVEN A HOSPITAL CAN COME BETWEEN US ON THIS YOUR 12TH BIRTHDAY HAVE A VERY HAPPY BIRTHDAY DEAREST JOYCE AS I LAY HERE I AM PICTURING YOU ENJOYING YOUR DAY MAKE IT A BIG JOYFUL DAY FOR MY SAKE AND BE PREPARED TO TELL ME ALL ABOUT IT LOVE=

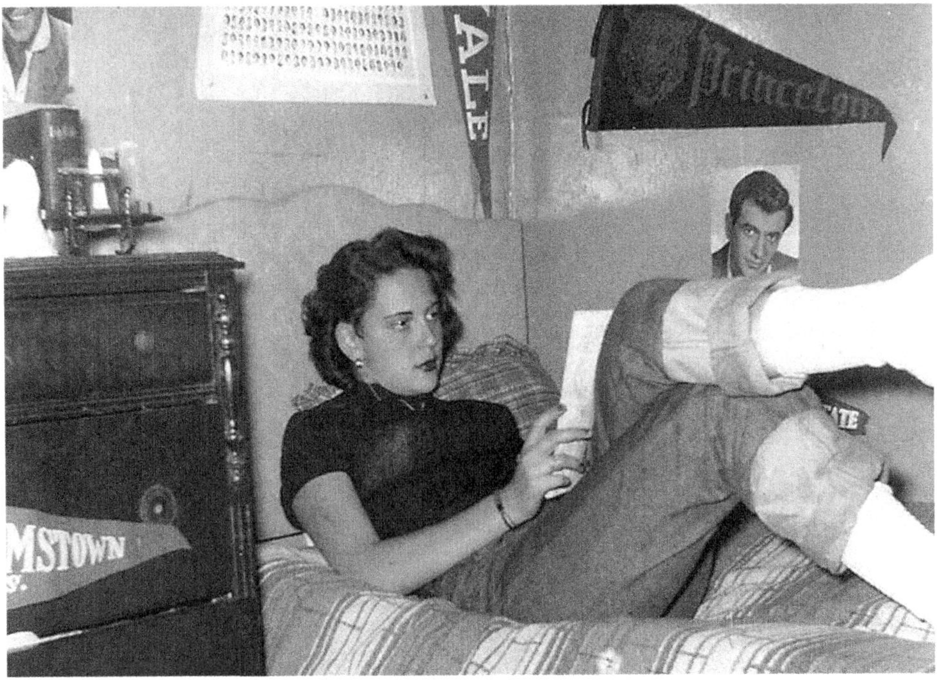

MA JAYA SATI BHAGAVATI

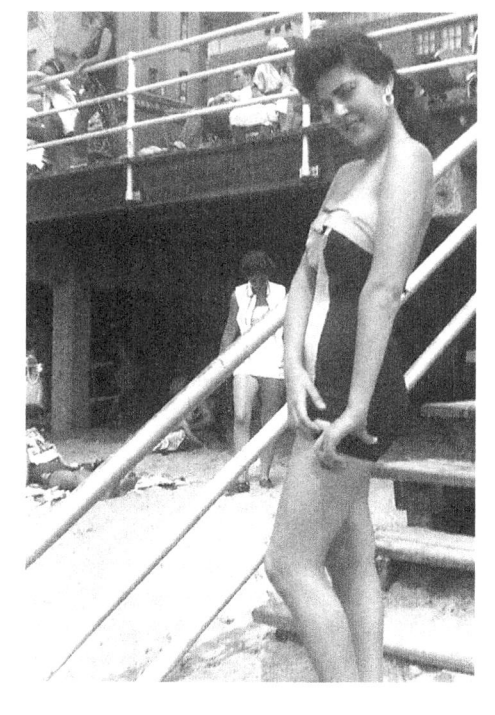

HOW GOD FOUND ME

CHAPTER THIRTY-TWO

Aunt Lily's Chicken Farm

Mama had been dead six months, and I was spending the Christmas holidays on Aunt Lily's chicken farm in New Jersey. I had started going there since Mama was in the hospital, taking the bus out of the Port Authority terminal by myself. I was losing touch with my old friends now. This would be the first Christmas that I didn't go to Mass with Kathy. Meanwhile Joe Joe had started drifting away from his family, and that included me.

We were down in the cellar cleaning the shit off the eggs, just me and Aunt Lily. I held an egg gently in my fingers of my left hand, a wire brush in my right, the way Aunt Lily had showed me. Aunt Lily told me one time that the eggs were like the soul—you just have to clean the shit off to let them shine through.

"You miss your mama, don't you, honey?"

I looked up, shocked. She rarely spoke to me like that. The egg broke, its yellow bounty gushing out all over my hands.

"What's the matter with you?" Aunt Lily asked, not so nicely.

"I just got surprised you called me 'honey,' that's all. I'm sorry," I said, getting up to go to the small rusty sink in the corner.

"You've really had it hard. I know that your bum of a father didn't do nice by you." She sounded like my grandma. I washed off the goo on my hand and took my seat. In the dim light, Aunt Lily looked just like my mama.

"Hold the brush lightly and firmly," she said. "Make believe the egg is a baby and you are cleaning his bottom gently with the wire brush."

I had to laugh at that one. I had been babysitting neighborhood kids now and then.

"Your mama was so in love with your papa that she had no time for anyone. She had no time for life."

"She was happy," I said, thinking that the one thing that Mama did a lot was smile. Aunt Lily didn't smile much, but I loved this little tough lady in her farm dungarees and her dead husband's shirt.

"I am here for you if you want to work for me in the summers. Phyllis is planning to go to college, and I'll need all the help I can get."

I thought for a moment and said, "You know, I have to take care of Shirley. She hasn't been doing so good since Mama died."

"The sins of the parents falling on the children."

Just then, the man-eating dog, Fin, started to bark. Aunt Lily grabbed hold of a big loose pipe in the corner. It was bigger than her. I took the pipe from her and climbed out of the trapdoor into the night. Fin was foaming at the mouth, barking and barking. I went up to the huge mutt, loving the craziness of him, and started to unhook his collar.

"What are you, nuts?" a voice called out from nearby.

"Jack, is that you?"

"Who else would it be?"

Aunt Lily came up the stairs and said, "Who are you, and how do you know my niece?"

"Aunt Lily, Jack is in trouble. Can he come in for a moment and have a cup of coffee?"

"How do you know this boy?" she asked me. I explained that I had met him last summer at the flea market. I didn't mention that I had caught him trying to steal from our booth or that he was already hooked on heroin at the age of sixteen.

"Okay. I can use a cup myself. First feed the dog."

"Come on," I said. We walked out to the barn where Fin lived. I turned on the light just as Jack was saying, "Leave it dark." I saw the bruises all over his face. Under his eye was a fresh cut.

"I was looking for a fix, and I got beat up." He began to tremble.

"Joyce, are you coming in? What are you doing out there?"

We went into the house, where the smell of coffee filled the small kitchen. Jack looked like a skinny lost puppy, a mutt, alone in the night. I glanced at the clock; it was midnight. We had been cleaning the eggs since nine. "Aunt Lily, can Jack sleep here tonight?"

"Definitely not!"

But I remembered my mama's words. "Joyala, there are no throwaway people." Now I repeated them: "Aunt Lily, there are no throwaway people."

"All right," she said. "He can sleep in the barn with the dog. I'll get some blankets."

I sat with Jack. "I got beat up cuz I couldn't pay for the stuff," he told me. "I got to get out of here. I got to have it, and I got to get some money, or I'll do something bad." Just then Aunt Lily came in. Her hands were empty.

"Where's his bedding?" I asked.

"He don't want to stay here tonight. Isn't that so, Jack?"

By now he was trembling badly. "Right Ma'am," he said.

"Here," she said as she dug into her dungaree pocket. She came up with a ten-dollar bill. In 1953 that was a lot of money. "You take this and get yourself a good meal."

I walked out into the night with him. It was snowing hard now. Jack was shivering, not from the cold, but from the need for a fix. He closed the top button on his worn-out jacket that was much too big for him. Yet then again, all of life was too big for my friend. He walked out onto the road and out of my life. I never saw him again.

Back in the kitchen, Aunt Lily was cleaning up. "This night is just between us," she said. It was just her and me and old Fin and the memory of one lost sixteen-year-old boy walking in the snow alone. She knew that Jack couldn't stay or he would have done something that would have hurt him and us. Yet he had a moment of love sitting there in the kitchen.

"That's how you clean the eggs with a wire brush," she continued. "Gently and firm."

CHAPTER THIRTY-THREE

Vinny's Lesson

Mama had been dead a year, and I was pretty much on my own, same as always, except for the empty space in my heart that Mama used to fill. I missed her, but I was learning about reality fast. Meanwhile, Harvey was growing more and more distant, seeking more and more religion, and learning more and more languages. Melvin didn't come around much. He was one of the first Jewish boys to graduate from Cooper Union, and he'd already gotten married.

Shirley became very depressed after Mama died. In the next few years, she was hospitalized in King's County, Hillside, and Saint Vincent's for severe nervous breakdowns. All of us kids, all our troubles, and all the horrors lay heavily on her shoulders.

I stayed for a while with Aunt Lily and for a while with my other aunt in Philadelphia, who had a beautiful home and promised me a bright future if I wanted one. But I always went back to Brighton 8th Street.

After Mama died, Harry became very attentive, most likely out of guilt, and he demanded one thing of me: to be home by 9:30 p.m. if I went out with boys. I bowed to this rule because somehow I understood that Harry, in his old age, wanted to become a father.

At fourteen I was gorgeous and could have any boy I wanted. One day I was walking home on Coney Island Avenue from the corner of Avenue X, where I used to hang out with the Garrisons when I wasn't working. I had on dungarees, a tight black shirt, and the big, thick, studded garrison belt that I had dreamed of having since I was little. Finally a member of the Garrisons, I loved the feel of belonging to a gang.

Gangs then weren't like gangs today. It was more like a bunch of kids protecting their own territory. Our territory ended at West 10th Street, the street of the Cyclone. Nobody messed with us.

But this day, a young man started to walk alongside of me. He told me, "My name is Vinny."

"Get lost."

"I've seen you around here. What are you doing with that gang?"

I told him to fuck off, yet I couldn't avoid noticing his big, brown, bedroom eyes. There was something in those eyes that said I could trust him. He was very handsome. About nineteen, he was over six feet tall, with wavy hair in a high pompadour. He wore black peg pants and a black silk shirt.

"I run the supermarket on Avenue X. I know a lot of your friends. Come on, let's go for a soda."

I figured he was safe enough, and besides, no one messed with the Garrisons. We went into the candy store, the same one I used to hang out in.

"I've been watching you for a long time, and I'd like to go out with you."

I told him I always had to be home by 9:30.

"Whatever you want," he said.

We made a date for the next night. We went to Lundy's, a big restaurant on the water in Sheepshead Bay. When I was little and very hungry, hanging around the docks with my brothers to see if anyone had an extra fish they wanted to give away, it was my dream to go to Lundy's. In those days, it seemed like it was in another country from the one I lived in. Now every time Vinny and I went out on a date, we would eat there.

One day Vinny said, "I'd like to talk to your father."

Now, my papa didn't care if I went out with boys, as long as they were Jewish. He used to say, "I never want you to go out with an Italian boy. They don't know how to treat a woman."

Ever since he had mentioned that, I noticed Italian boys everywhere. Italian groceries, Italian bakeries, any place I went, I would ask, "Are you Italian?" If the boy said, "yes," I would talk to him.

So now here was this boy wanting to talk to my papa.

"About what?" I asked.

He quietly said, "I want to marry you."

I got such a kick out of that, but I didn't take it real seriously. At fourteen, marriage was the furthest thing from my mind. I thought that marriage was another woman's grief, not mine. I had seen enough with my papa and my mama to know that marriage meant a woman had to give up her life to a man, or so I thought.

The next night after work, Vinny was waiting for me in front of GMC, where I was selling clothes. All the girls who worked there were oohing and ahhing. They thought he was sooo handsome. He took my hand, and we crossed the street together. When we got to Brighton 8th Street, Papa was in the alleyway as usual.

"Papa," I said, "someone here needs to speak to you."

"Joyala, you see I'm busy. I have a good hand."

"When you finish losing, come talk."

He looked at me and thought I was serious. I really wasn't. I liked Vinny well enough, but not enough to get married. I was just curious to see what Papa would do. Papa came out of the alley, looking not so happy; he must have lost his good hand. Vinny and I were sitting on the bench next door to my house—the one I had called my wishing bench when I was a little kid.

Vinny stood up as Papa approached. "Thank you for seeing me, Mr. Green. My name is Vinny Puglisi."

He held out his hand for my father to shake. Papa ignored it and said, "I told you, I don't want you to go out with Italian boys." He said that right to Vinny's face.

Vinny was calm, and said, "Sir, I am not Italian. I am Sicilian."

Papa got confused a little bit. At that moment, Vinny pulled out a small jewelry box. Papa's eyes lit up. "I would like to have you hold this ring for me, Sir. It's for your daughter, and I'm willing to wait for her, however long it takes."

I was in shock. "What's that ring for?"

"Joyce, I'm in love with you and want to make you my wife."

The ring was a one-carat round diamond with a little baguette on each side of it. Papa's eyes were as big as golf balls. He looked at me. He looked at Vinny. He looked at the ring in Vinny's hand. Then he said, loud and clear for the whole world to hear, "Joyala, you are engaged!"

"Papala, I am not."

"It's fine, trust me. You could be engaged for five years." He turned to Vinny. "I'll hold the ring till she's nineteen."

I said, "Vincent, you're making a big mistake."

He said, "Will you marry me?"

"You know what? If you can put that same ring on my finger in one year—and it has to be that ring in that box—I will marry you."

"Can you make it six months?" Vinny asked.

"Deal," I said, knowing my papa very well.

"No, when she's nineteen," said Papa, with a little twinge of conscience.

I had to laugh. "We're going out, Papa. We're going to Lundy's."

"Bring me back something."

"What," I asked, "another ring?"

"No, just some French fries. Don't eat anything other than French fries; the place isn't kosher."

"Oh, Papa, sure it is. Every Jewish person in the neighborhood eats there."

"It's not kosher, Joyala."

Another illusion fell. I turned to Vinny. "Come on, let's go to Nathan's."

We took hands and walked to the Boardwalk. The ocean was beautiful. The stars were out and dancing in the sky, the moon was full, and I was with this very handsome boy. I didn't love him, but I liked his kindness.

"You know, we're engaged," he said.

"You're nineteen years old, and you're too trusting."

"What gives you the right to say that, Joyce?"

I said, "I know not to give my Papa a diamond ring. Vinny, you're a good guy, but I don't love you."

"I know," he said, "but you will." We continued to walk beneath the full moon, listening to the sound of the waves.

Vinny and I became good friends, but I still wasn't in love with him. We kissed only once or twice. My knowledge of sex was zero. I looked like I knew it all, but in reality, I didn't know a thing. Meanwhile, I would look at Vinny and think, "Boy, is my papa going to teach him a good lesson."

Six months later, Vinny said, "It's time to talk to your dad."

He came over that night. Harry was in his usual place in the alley, where he conducted all the business of his life, and mine, too.

"Harry, can I have the diamond ring back? I would like to present it to your daughter."

Harry never lifted his eyes off the cards. He replied, "She's too young. Trust me, Vinny. She can't get married, she can't get engaged, she just turned fifteen."

I laughed and said, "Vinny, you're never going to see that ring again, and my father is an old man. What are you going to do?"

"Are you kidding, Joyce? I'll have him put in cement boots."

I really began to laugh. "Papa, you got yourself into deep shit now." He was still playing cards, but I could tell his mind wasn't on his hand.

He looked Vinny straight in his eye and said, "Look here, son, why don't you wait three more months? Joyce will be a little older."

Vinny said, "Harry, where is the ring?"

Harry repeated, "Give me three more months, and I will let you give it to her."

I said to Vinny, "My father sold me to you for a diamond ring. Do you think I come that cheap?"

Vinny just walked away.

"Harry!" I said, sharply.

"Don't call me 'Harry.' I am your papa!"

"How much did you get for the ring?"

"I have to tell you something. I needed to teach that boy."

I stopped him short. "Harry?"

"Six hundred dollars. Now there are no more problems in our life. I paid off all of our debts."

"Oh, Papa, Papa." I walked away to follow Vinny. It felt as if I was walking away from a naughty child. I figured I would pay Vinny off slowly for the ring. Even though I had warned him about my papa, it wasn't fair.

I began to hum "Sioux City Sue," trying to bring back the memories of a lost youth that I'd never had in the first place, trying to remember my papa shuffling with me, doing the soft-shoe, and Mama laughing. I stopped for a moment and said to Mac, "I need to get out of here or my life will be that alleyway and all it represents. I need to get away from it all. I need to make my own life."

The episode with Vinny left me shaken. He came around again soon, and said, "You know, Joyce, I was taken by an old man. Your father took Vinny Puglisi. I have to appreciate your dad for that. It taught me a good lesson."

"What lesson?"

"Well, one thing is that you can't buy love, and the other thing is that I can't buy you."

"Vinny, I'll pay off the ring."

"Where is it?" he asked.

"My papa sold it for $600."

"I paid $2,000 for it. It was a perfect diamond." I almost passed out. After that I started paying Vinny, bit by bit, until he said, "Don't worry about it. Let's just you and me just become friends."

We hung out together a lot over the next year. Just friends. We took in a movie once in a while, we held hands and talked about our dreams. He never said anything else to Papa about cement boots. Vinny resigned himself to us being only buddies. I liked him a lot for the way he respected Harry, even though I was losing what respect I had left for my papa. I didn't think it was funny about the ring and constantly told Papa how I felt. Papa just shrugged and said it was a good lesson for Vinny. No matter how many times I told him that he was almost swimming with the fishes, he didn't believe me.

CHAPTER THIRTY-FOUR

Frankie Boy

It was a warm June night. I was working late under the Boardwalk, taking money and giving change for the beach chairs and umbrellas. At fifteen, I was the senior employee. After all, I'd worked for ABC Beach Chairs since I was nine years old.

For some reason unknown to any of us, the money for the day's rentals had to be taken back to the office at the corner of West 10th Street and the Boardwalk in a money bag that had a big dollar sign on it. One evening, Vinny helped me close up the dank smelling shop under the Boardwalk. As we reached the street, we heard the familiar sound of a police siren quite near.

"Let's go," I shouted to Vinny, who was carrying the money bag for me.

"Are you crazy? Let's get this money back to old pig head." He was referring to the boss's son, whose head really did look like a stuffed pig's.

"No time, Vinny," I shouted, "I don't feel right." We ran until we saw a crowd. I ran right through them with the authority that only the young possess. I reached the corner, and there were the cops, holding three guys against the cotton candy stall.

"Nacko, what's up?" I asked the owner.

"Don't go no closer, Joycey. Someone is hurt real bad."

I looked again and saw a bundle on the street. For some reason, I ran to the bundle and, to my shock, saw that it was Vinny's brother, Frankie Boy. I felt the ground drop away.

"Vinny!" I screamed.

To my horror, I saw that a big cop we all called Hitler was holding Vinny.

"Hey," I yelled, "let him go. That's his brother on the ground."

"What did you say, Joyce?" Vinny screamed.

Then I saw what the cop was holding Vinny for. In his hand was the stupid money bag. "Sir," I yelled, in all the confusion, "I work for ABC Beach Chairs. You know me."

He popped Vinny one on his cheek with his nightstick and said, "Give her the bag and get lost."

I ran to Vinny and took his arm, urging him to let it be. "Vinny, it's Frankie Boy on the ground."

We pushed through the crowd. There was blood everywhere. Frankie Boy was unconscious. His neck looked funny, like it wasn't connected to his body. His leather jacket was ripped down the front. His face and chest were bright red and brown in places where the blood was drying in the hot night.

"Oh, my God, Joyce, do something."

"How do I fix him?" I thought. "Only God can do that." I looked up and saw Nacko looking at me. He looked so sad and old. "Nacko, why isn't the ambulance here yet?" Someone had covered Frankie Boy with an old beach blanket, the sand still on it.

Frankie was Vinny's younger brother. He was only seventeen, but unlike Vinny, he was always in trouble. Nacko was saying something about a fire on Ocean Parkway and that the ambulances were all busy. I touched Frankie's chest. My finger felt a hole. "Oh, fucking shit!" I said. "He's been shot!"

One of the cops came over to me and said, "It was a zip gun. Is he your boyfriend?"

"No, he's Vinny's brother." I looked at Vinny, who was staring at his little brother with tears running down his face. "We got to get him to the hospital."

The cop said, "Honey, he can't be moved."

"For fuck's sake," I said, "take him yourself if the ambulances are busy." There were eight or nine police cars there, but still no ambulance in sight.

"Okay," he finally said. "Get your boyfriend and get him into the patrol car."

In the back of the police car, Frankie's head was in my lap. I felt faint and nauseous. "Please, dear God, let this boy live." We got to the hospital within minutes. It struck me odd, riding in that patrol car with the lights and siren on and death so close at hand, while Coney Island just kept going on living and breathing with its laughter and rides and food stands.

"Do you believe in God?" asked the cop, after the orderlies had Frankie on a gurney. "Start praying 'cause that kid ain't gonna make it unless there's a miracle."

Vinny choked at those words. "Joyce, fix him, please."

I took Vinny's hand and led him into the small waiting room. "I'm Shirley Green's sister," I said to the elderly lady I recognized from Information. She used to visit Shirley, who at the time was living in a cottage at Hillside Mental Hospital, which was much nicer than our cellar.

"Were you in an accident?" she asked, looking at my blouse all stained with Frankie's blood.

"No, it is my friend's brother. I need to know how he is."

"Since you're Shirley's sister, I can tell you what I heard the intern say: 'This one ain't gonna make it'."

I walked straight into the operating room without even saying goodbye to her or Vinny and went right over to the table where they were working on Frankie. No one even noticed me, and to this day I can't say why. I opened my heart and looked up at the fluorescent lights overhead. I remembered feeling as if I wasn't there. I went into the place in my heart that still missed my mama. A white light came in over my head and touched the still form of Frankie Boy. I watched the light, which was almost transparent.

"He's coming back," I heard someone say.

I ran out and found Vinny. "Vinny, he's gonna live."

Vinny lifted his head and gave me a smile that I remember to this day. "You fixed it, Joyce. You did it."

"No, I didn't do shit. It was the light."

A young doctor came over to us and held out his hand. Vinny took it. "Your brother will live." He explained Frankie's injuries, and then he turned to me. "And you, young lady, stay out of the operating room." He gave me a big smile. "Unless it's me on that table."

Vinny couldn't speak. The tears were running down his face as he embraced me. "I asked you to fix it, and you did."

"Bullshit, Vinny," I said aloud, and inside my heart I said, "Thank you, Mac."

मा

I write this chapter on my porch, with Christmas music coming through my new speakers. The morning is cold. The sun is trying to peek out from behind the clouds that are taking over the sky. Neil Diamond sings, "Fall on your knees...."

I fall on my knees every day of my life in gratitude that I am allowed to serve the beautiful souls of the world. The last I heard, which is about thirty years ago, Frankie went on to become a priest. He wanted to be a cop, but he lost his leg in a motorcycle accident about two years after the Coney Island shooting.

CHAPTER THIRTY-FIVE

Take Me to Kashi to Die

"Take me home to Kashi to die, please, Ma," said the blind man in the wheelchair.

It was 1992, the AIDS Memorial Quilt had come to West Palm Beach, and we at Kashi were asked to participate in the reading of names and the unfolding of the panels. Now it was time to present new panels in memory of people who had died of AIDS. There were at least a hundred new panels added to the quilt that day, just from our part of Florida.

Waiting in line, I was holding one corner of the quilt panel that my chelas had made to represent the people of the County Home. I held tight to my corner, happy for a moment to be told what to do. It felt right that all my people who had died there, the forgotten and the lonely, should be in my arms again, even symbolically. Now they were all together, holding and loving one another in death's realm. Behind us were hundreds of grieving people holding tight to their own quilts. I could feel the tears beginning to fall.

"Ma, Ma," someone called my name.

I almost wanted to pull the quilt over my head so I could hide from life and receive comfort from the dead. Instead I called out, "Over here, I am here near the beginning of the line." I heard the tension in my voice and was ashamed.

I saw my Randy, thirty-four years old, sitting slumped over in his wheelchair. AIDS had struck him blind in two weeks. Totally blind. I ran over to him. His brother, Roger, who was also HIV-positive, had gotten him out of bed to be there when they presented a quilt panel for Randy's lover Danny.

या

That day is fresh in my mind as I sit here on my porch, writing and watching the sun come up. I can't believe that I have lost so many. Every day another one is struck down, another tear shed, another panel made for the quilt. I can hear my Baba saying, "Go on with the story. Let the world know the truth." I will try, but never have I written with the blood of my children so fresh on my heart.

या

Ma," said the handsome young man, slumped in his chair, "I'm blind now."

"I know." I said, "I'm here for you." In my passion for this child, I didn't remember that there were hundreds of people behind us holding their quilt panels and watching the whole scene unfold. I could hear weeping, yet I was concerned at that moment only for Randy. "Randy," I said, "do you want to go on?"

"No!"

"But Randy, I can still see life in you."

"No, Ma! I don't want to fight the darkness, I want to go into it."

"Okay, son," I said.

When a dying person, near the end, wants to fight for life, I will help him, support him, give him strength to live fully every moment. But when he chooses to let go, I will honor and respect that choice, too.

He smiled. I bent to kiss his blind eyes when he lifted up his hand and caressed my face. "Eye to eye," he said, "I see you."

I lost it, remembering Paul Monette's book, *Borrowed Time*, and the part when he and his lover, who was suffering from AIDS, were climbing up a hill in Los Angeles. He said to Paul, "I see you." Those three words meant everything to Paul, and now meant everything to me.

"No, I really mean it," said Randy, "I can see you."

"I know, darling. I can see you, too," I replied.

Randy would insist right up until he died five days later that at that moment he indeed had been able to see me.

या

Tears shed, hugs given, songs sung, and the quilt ceremony was over. The tears dried, and I bid my people farewell. Many came for a hug. I must admit that, if I didn't know how to drink from my own river, I would have dried up right there and gone to sleep forever under my own quilt. But I had agreed to emcee a drag queen show that night to raise money for Mother's Cupboard, an organization in West Palm Beach that fed many people with AIDS.

Mother, the drag queen who started the benefit, came over to me. She and I were to co-host the show that night at the Heartbreaker bar. I could see her holding back tears as she embraced me. She had just presented a panel for a friend. I held on tight to her arms. "Getting ready for tonight?" I asked.

"Oh, darling, you know it."

We were on our way, a caravan of many carloads of yogis going to a gay bar in the late night. "What a teaching, Baba," I thought.

We finally pulled up in front of the bar. I could see Agni waiting for me. He was dressed in his macho leather outfit and insisted on being my escort. I had on a chartreuse sari and a purple leotard. My hair was wild, or at least what I thought was wild.

I was led to the dressing room. These were my people, the courageous drag queens who have done so much for people with AIDS. Here they were, gathered together in all states of dress and undress. No matter what they wore, I could look right through them and see their hearts. Some of them didn't know me and couldn't figure out what the hell I was doing there. I saw the confusion. I decided to go for it. I walked boldly up to a young man who was styling the hair of some of the queens.

"Darling, I said, "could you do me?"

The whole dressing room got quiet, until I heard someone whisper, "Shawn does *not* do women."

"Shut up," someone else answered. "That's not a woman, that is Ma."

"Well, Shawn, I have to go on stage with Mother and you know her wigs could put me to shame," I said.

Shawn thought for a moment and then said, "I would be honored." He started with my hair. When I sneaked a look in the mirror, I gasped. I was two feet taller! Shawn had teased my hair so high that I thought he had slipped a wig on my head. Everyone was admiring his handiwork, when he said, "Now a little makeup, darling." In for a penny and in for a pound, as my mama would say.

"Sure," I said, and then whispered, "This is for you, my Randy."

When he was done, I looked in the mirror. Wow, one beautiful guru stared back at me! The large red dot on my forehead stood out proudly beneath tons of hair. I was almost eight feet tall.

The show began. Once I got hold of the mic, I had a hard time letting it go. It was a tough crowd, but they didn't know that I had grown up in the streets of Brooklyn. I kept thinking of Randy and the stories I would tell him.

I could feel the disease floating around the bar, and I was saddened. Some of the queens were on AZT or other medications that made their mouths dry, and some were fatigued after their numbers, yet the show went on. Near the end, to raise a few more dollars, I changed into skintight pants, a red leotard, a black leather jacket, and high black cowboy boots. The crowd went wild. They couldn't stop clapping and went even more crazy when Mother came out with my sari on.

They asked me to get the place silent for a moment in honor of the dead. I got them quiet, all right. The gay bar became as sacred and holy as any temple or church I have ever been in.

The night came to an end. We had raised over $5,000. I couldn't stop crying. I was so proud of these men who dressed as women for their brothers and sisters in the war.

मा

Less than a week later, we were standing in the cool night air of my ashram, and the funeral people were taking my Randy away. Randy had made his death wish clear: to die at Kashi. Joe, his nurse, along with Roger, his brother, had planned to make sure that his wish was fulfilled, but in spite of their plans Randy had died in his apartment in Fort Lauderdale. So they took matters into their own hands.

Once they got the hospice nurse to leave, Roger and Joe had carried Randy's body out to the waiting van to bring him to Kashi. One of the neighbors saw them taking the body out and called the police. Before anyone knew anything, there was a state-wide alarm.

The cops came to the ashram to look for the body. They went away, satisfied that it wasn't there, but we knew Joe was in big trouble. When he called in on the car phone, we told them about the cops. Joe and Roger decided to call the police, who told them in no uncertain terms to get the body back to the medical examiner in Fort

Lauderdale. When they got there, they faced intense questioning. The authorities were trying to determine if this had been a mercy killing. Then they insisted on an autopsy before releasing the body.

Danny and Randy used to like to camp in their van in a wooded part of the ashram, so that's where Joe parked. I went right out to meet them. As soon as I climbed into the van, I saw that whoever had done the autopsy hadn't sewn my Randy back up as they should have.

Some of my chelas who are nurses donned rubber gloves and started to dress their friend, first putting on his favorite tape, Paul Simon's "Graceland." A holy *Ram* shawl was placed around his torn-up head, and any other scars were hidden beneath flowers and sacred cloths. Once his body was properly laid out in the van, my chelas came to pay their respects, including a bunch of teenagers all dressed up for a Christmas dance. I sat in the corner near my Randy, as my chelas passed by, one by one, amazed at their strength and love.

The cops came again, and why not? We had a van holding a dead body in the middle of the dark woods, with candles lighting the path and a lot of people dressed for a party. "We honor our dead differently here," I told them.

"I can see that, Ma'am," the younger one said, touching his gun. We persuaded them to eat a few cookies, and they went outside to wait for the hearse to arrive.

After they left, Joe still needed to show someone what had been done to Randy, and he unwrapped the shawl from his head. There for the whole world to see was the deep hole made to remove his brain. I kissed his head tenderly as if to kiss a little boy's boo-boo. Randy wasn't there. I felt his hand on my shoulder and heard the words, "I see you."

I felt empty and alone when the funeral home people finally took Randy away. I hugged Roger to my breast. He, too, had to fight this virus.

I see you, my darling. I see you forever and ever. I see you in the hearts of everyone who is touched by AIDS. I see you in the children who kissed you farewell. I see you always as you first came to me, laughing and holding your lover's hand outside by my pond. Another chela lost to AIDS and found again in my heart.

I see you.

CHAPTER THIRTY-SIX

Sal

The summer of 1955 I held two jobs, one at the GMC clothing store and the other at ABC Beach Chairs. I was making out okay in the money department and was trying to save up for some clothes for high school and to help out with the rent, although I knew never to give all my money directly to Papa, like Shirley did. He would always ask for my paycheck, and I would have to hand over some cash. But I wouldn't give him all of it because someone had to make sure there was food in the house.

I was walking home from my beach chair job. It was my weekend job until school was out; after that it was full-time. It was a rainy Saturday, but they liked us to "shape up" anyway, in case it got sunny out. Even an old timer like me had to check in, rain or not. I was walking on the beach with my girlfriend, Marlene Goldstein. The rain slowed to a drizzle. We had walked from our bay near the Cyclone to Brighton Beach, where we would get off the beach to go home. The rain and the ocean made me feel clean and whole. Someone called out, "Hey, babe."

I had noticed that two boys had followed us from Coney Island all the way to Brighton Beach, which was about three miles.

"Hey, babe," he called again.

"Screw you," I said, and kept walking. I was gorgeous in my bathing suit and my friend Joan Katz's old jacket. I didn't like boys who called out names at girls, no matter how cute the boys were. I turned, intending to tell him so in no uncertain terms, but there in front of me was the best-looking guy I had ever seen. His hair was pitch black and thick, and his eyes were black, too. He was wearing a bright orange shirt. In those days we all wore bright orange and fuchsia; anything fluorescent was in. This guy was very masculine, with his peg pants, black as night, with gray pegs going up and down his legs. Vinny was a thin kind of good-looking. This boy was built—big and muscular.

"My name is Salvatore, babe, what's yours?"

"I am not your babe. Get that straight."

"How much you want to bet?" he said. Years later, he told me that he knew right then and there that he was going to marry me. "Look, I'm sorry if I insulted you. Let's start over."

Marlene was falling all over herself. Her mama once said in front of me that if Marlene ever went out with a *goy*, she would *sit shivah* for her as if she had died. Marlene didn't look like she heard her mama too well—she couldn't keep her eyes off the boys.

"Can I see you tonight?" Salvatore asked me.

"You don't even know my name."

"What is your name, if it's not Babe?"

"Joyce."

"Look, Joyce, I'll tell you what. I'm going to let you borrow this shirt to wear over your bathing suit, and I'll take your jacket. Then we can exchange everything tonight."

I had to admit I liked his style, and his shirt was gorgeous. I took off the old jacket. Joan Katz was looking to throw it away anyway. Salvatore put his shirt on me. It smelled of aftershave lotion. He took the jacket, and I gave him my address. It was all a game, a joke. I was wild. I was young. I was street smart. I was tough, and I was beautiful. The interchange between jacket and shirt, between a good-looking guy and a good-looking girl, was part of the everyday game of growing up. I made a date with him for that night, not even thinking twice, never imagining that this was the boy I would end up marrying.

I had already made a date with Vinny for that night. I left Sal's shirt with the people across the street, just in case he really showed up. He'd told me he lived in Red Hook, so I figured he wouldn't go all that way two times in one day. I thought he would call the next day or so for his shirt. Well, he certainly did show and was he ever pissed! The Morellis told him that my aunt had died, a tale he didn't believe for one minute.

He called the next day. His first words were, "Look, Joyce, I want to go steady with you or else it doesn't pay to come down to Brighton Beach from Red Hook." I was intrigued with his thinking and agreed to go steady. It didn't matter to me. After all, I had to be home by 9:30 anyway.

He came down the next night and asked to see my papa. "I need to see if it's worth my while to take the three trains from Red Hook. You see, Joyce, I fell in love with you."

"Salvatore, I don't even know you."

"Just let me talk to your father."

He knocked on the door of the cellar. Papa wasn't in his usual place in the alley. He must have gotten hungry.

Papa answered the door as if he was lord of the manor. "Can I help you, young man?"

Sal looked at him in amazement. Behind my papa were these ugly pipes and there were no drapes on the cellar windows. Papa wasn't a bit ashamed, and neither was I, though I must admit I was curious to see if Sal was going to bolt after he saw how I lived.

"Sir, I came here to ask if it was okay for your daughter to go steady with me."

I gulped.

Papa asked his favorite question. "Are you Italian?"

"No," answered the very Italian Sal. "I am Sicilian." That seemed to be the standard joke among Italians, only it looked like Sal took it seriously.

"How much do you have in the bank?" asked Papa.

"Papa! Let's cut it out right now."

"Do you have a bankbook worthy of my daughter?"

"No," he answered, "but I have love worthy of your daughter. I love and respect your daughter."

"How long do you know my daughter?" asked Harry, acting like a concerned father.

"Two days, Sir."

Well, my papa really went insane. "Joyce!" he yelled in my face. "You will not go out with any *goyim*, do you hear me? No one that is not Jewish!"

"Don't you mean, Papa, no one that is not Jewish and doesn't have a fat bank account? Isn't that what you mean?"

"You break up with him, do you hear me?"

"Papa, I wasn't going with him until this moment."

"What does that mean?" he asked.

"I'll wait outside," Sal said. He looked confused.

"Papa, I'm going to talk to Salvatore."

"Hurry up," he said, "I'm waiting for you."

I found Sal sitting on my wishing bench. I sat next to him, looked into his eyes, and right then I knew that this was the boy I wanted to spend my life with. I said, "I will meet you in half an hour on Brighton Beach Avenue." I had never defied my papa like this before, but there was no choice. I was in love.

या

Sal and I went out for almost a year. Each time we saw each other, our love grew deeper and deeper. It was a wonderful time to be going steady. There were the Penguins singing "Earth Angel," and "Sincerely" was number one on the charts. Johnny Ace singing "Pledging My Love" became our song.

If Papa had left us alone, I would never have gotten married so early in life. I would have graduated high school first. I told him I was going out with a Jewish boy, Wally, who wasn't Jewish at all, just a friend of Sal's. He was going out with an Italian girl, Marie, from Avenue K, who had the same problem as me. Salvatore would pick Marie up, and Wally would pick me up. Papa wasn't the least bit suspicious, but I couldn't stand the lying and the tension of maybe getting caught. When Papa began asking Wally how much he had in the bank, I knew it was time for something else. Sal was already asking when we were going to get married. Marie's parents were asking him what his intentions were toward their daughter. Sal had told his family about me, and they were none too pleased. We decided to get married as soon as possible.

Sal had already graduated high school and was working on the docks, working the bull lines down in the holds of the ships. He was trying to save up enough money for our marriage. In those days, you had to be twenty-one to marry without permission, but we heard that if you had a birth certificate, you could get married at City Hall, and they didn't check up on you.

We took the birth certificates of everyone in our two families and went to Greenpoint, at the far end of Brooklyn, where you can't go any further. It was deserted. It was a chilly night for April. We had brought hubcaps with us and a big bottle of bleach. Sal filled the hubcaps with the bleach, and I put the papers in them, one by one. The handwriting of the different names and ages disappeared in the bleach. Now we had about eight different blank birth certificates, all soaking wet. We wanted to make sure we had enough in case we made a mistake.

We got into Sal's father's Ford and headed back to his Aunt Jenny's house. When we arrived, we hung the birth certificates on the clothesline to dry in the night air. That worked okay; they came out wrinkled but dry. They just looked like they had been used a lot.

Papa thought I was sleeping over at Joan Katz's house, so I was okay for time. (I had stuck to his 9:30 rule the whole year.) The three of us sat around Aunt Jenny's kitchen table, testing to see who had the best penmanship. It certainly wasn't me. We were hiding out from Sal's mother and father, who had no idea that we were across the street.

When the ink dried, Sal and I borrowed some money from Uncle Phil for gas and headed for Coney Island. I had never been out so late at night with a boy, and I was a little frightened. So I said, "Let's go eat at Nathan's."

"How can you want to eat at a time like this?"

"I'm hungry. Let's go!"

On the Boardwalk, I looked toward the sky. My favorite stars looked back at me, the ones that made their home over my ocean. I was only fifteen, yet I had tasted life in a very different way than the average teenager. A thought came to me, and all of a sudden I missed my papa's alley; in that moment I knew my papa loved me. I began to cry. Sal held me tight. We were all alone with the ocean and the stars. Then hand-in-hand we walked toward the car with our forged birth certificates, the passports to our new life.

"Good night, Mac. Take care of my papa and give him some good hands."

I skipped school the next day. Sal picked me up, and off we went to a weird doctor on Columbia Street behind a butcher store to get our blood tests. A few days later we went to downtown Brooklyn. Blood test papers and forged birth certificates in hand, we waited on line for our license.

While Sal was signing papers, I spotted a sign that read, "All forgeries will be prosecuted to the full extent of the law." I whispered in my fiancé's ear, "I'm out of here," and I took off. I was streetwise enough to know that I didn't want a prosecution for a phony birth certificate, or eight of them.

Sal looked so stunned that the clerk said, "You better catch that good-looking bride of yours," and he burst out laughing.

And that was how we ended up in Elkton, Maryland, where marriage was their business and phony papers were their way of life. Sal's boss told him, "You go to Elkton, Maryland, you get married onetwothree." So we hocked Shirley's saxophone to pay for the bus, and I left my father a beautiful letter, explaining everything. It was about twenty-five pages long. I figured by the time he read from the beginning of the first page to the last page, I'd be married already.

They had a whole deal in Elkton, Maryland. You get off the bus, and there's a cabdriver whose cousin is a minister, another cousin owns the motel, and all you do is raise your hand and say, "I do."

But first you had to have a three-day residence. We got to the motel, and there was this rusty bed, like in *Bonnie and Clyde*. It was terrible.

I said, "Where's the priest, or the minister, or somebody or other?"

Sal told me then about the three days. That was the first I'd heard about that part of the deal. "You can go live with your mother," I told him and I got right back on the bus. He had to pay for the motel room for a whole week so we could be residents by the next Saturday.

I snuck back into the house, got the letter before my papa found it, made normal, and then the next weekend we went away again and got married.

मा

When we got back, we presented ourselves to Sal's mother, who had been looking for us. Plus my father had police out after us. Then Sal's grandmother, Sadie, came in, and the first thing she ever said to me was, "Are you knocked up?"

I didn't know what "knocked up" meant. I thought she was talking about fighting, so I said, "Anybody touches me, I'll knock their fucking head off." We got along fine after that.

We moved in with Sal's other grandfather in Red Hook. The first night, we were lying there in bed (I'm a Jewish girl from Brooklyn, remember), and the grandfather came into the bedroom and made the sign of the cross over the bed. Then the grandmother came in. She called me Josie; she still didn't know I was Jewish. "In the name of the Father, the Son, and the Holy Ghost," she said, also making the sign of the cross. Then a little bit later in came an old-maid aunt with a big red candle. She went around the bed making the sign of the cross.

There was no sex involved. There couldn't be; people kept on coming into the room. Then finally Sadie came in, with strings of garlic hanging from her hands like garlands, just like you see in vampire movies. (This was to make sure I would have a son.) I ran screaming from the room in my nightgown, out into the Italian streets of Red Hook. I was hysterical. Poor Sal had to run after me and convince me to come back home.

And so we were married.

CHAPTER THIRTY-SEVEN

Jimmy Has Tits!

I am listening intently to the words of the young woman in front of me. Her hair is jet black and comes to her chin line. She is wearing a black shawl over her black blouse which is tucked into a flowing skirt. Long earrings move back and forth gently as she speaks. Michelle was once Michael. Michelle was once a man.

I am looking into the face of love.

All of a sudden I begin to cry, and I have never cried in front of any visitor who came to me for help. Her pain touched me so deeply, her pain of childhood when no one knew if she was a boy or a girl; the pain of being molested by her father time after time; and now the pain of AIDS and the rejection from a lover who couldn't stand the fact that he had infected her with the virus.

I embrace her. I want to hold her in my arms forever and protect her from all of life. I can feel my mind going back, back into another time and place, where I am holding a handsome young boy in my arms. He is tall, strong, muscular, and very handsome. The year is 1955. His name is Jimmy, and he is a woman.

मा

Sal and I came back from Maryland without a penny between us. Sal was working down the docks trying to put a few dollars together so we could get an apartment near his family in Red Hook. Meanwhile, we were living in a furnished room in a large brownstone in the Park Slope area of Brooklyn. The owners offered us a job running a fruit store in Rockaway.

I never had much contact with fresh fruit in my life and couldn't tell a grapefruit from an orange. Yet we lied through our young teeth and took over the fruit store, traveling for over an hour every day from Brooklyn to Rockaway. Sal quit the docks, and we became fruit vendors.

Coming home one night late, we met the young couple who had a room on the floor below us. Jimmy was in his twenties and very good-looking, and his wife Milly was just as beautiful. Her light brown hair was full and wavy and reached down to the back of her knees. I was thrilled to have another young couple living in the same house. We became friends although there wasn't much time to hang out. They worked in some club in Greenwich Village most of the night, and Sal and I worked all day in Rockaway.

One Thursday, I had gotten very sick and Sal made me take the day off. We had no money for a doctor, so I just took aspirins and stayed in bed.

I was walking, wobbly, in the hallway going to the bathroom we shared with another tenant on our floor. I heard a noise below. Thinking it was Jimmy or Milly, I looked over the banister and saw indeed it was my new friend, the handsome Jim.

"Hi, Jim, I'm home sick." Jimmy turned away from me fast and faced the wall. "Jim," I said, "what is it?" Just then Milly came out of the door to hand her husband a towel. As he turned toward her, I saw he was wearing a guinea shirt and had the biggest, highest, fullest breasts I have ever seen on a woman, never mind a man.

I felt dizzy and confused. All I could think of was that Jimmy had tits. I went a little bit insane. I had been lied to, betrayed by the first friends that we had made in Park Slope. All I could say was the word "freak," a word I would regret. I ran into my room and slammed the door.

All day I wouldn't even go out to the bathroom. I felt alone and betrayed. My fever was rising. Finally I heard Sal's key in the door. I jumped out of bed and ran into my young lover's arms. "Sal, Jimmy has tits! Sal, Jimmy has tits!" Sal thought I was delirious.

When I told him the story, he went down the stairs to talk to Jimmy. She told him that they were a lesbian couple. They never meant to betray me, they just didn't want to confuse me.

Sal related this to me, but I didn't buy it. I still felt betrayed and hurt. What I felt most was confusion. Sal had used a strange word, lesbian. So how could I love them both? I didn't know if they were going after me or my husband, never thinking for a moment that all they wanted was our friendship. I put up my guard and watched every move they made.

One day a friend of theirs invited a bunch of people to the house. Milly had given him the key while she was at work, although I don't think she expected a party. When Sal and I came home from work, a whole lot of people were drinking and spilling out of the rented room and into the hallways. They assumed Sal and I were friends, but I thought they were trying to come on to us. Sal just pushed through and made a path to get us in our room.

I was furious.

Later we could hear Jimmy and Milly come home and begin to yell at the young man who hosted the party. They called him Roberta, and that really confused me.

About three days later it was rent day. I went into the big downstairs kitchen that the landlords always kept open for their kids. They had four kids who ran through the whole house like crazy people. I, at fifteen, used to run with them, but not lately because I was afraid of bumping into the strangers that Jimmy and Milly had become.

I walked into the kitchen while Sal was parking the truck, and I found myself alone with Jimmy, who was sitting at the big table with Josie, the landlord's youngest child, on his lap. I thought the kid was in danger so I said, "Listen up, fuck, don't you and your whore of a woman ever go near my husband or these kids again."

Jimmy put the child down and raised himself to his full 6 foot 3 height.

"What did you call Milly?"

I was afraid, yet not scared enough to stop. "She's a whore, and you're a freak." Without thinking, I went to give him a punch to the balls, like my dad had taught me. All of a sudden Jimmy punched me hard in the side of my face, connecting his fist to my ear drum. The last thing I remember was Milly and Sal running into the kitchen, and then I passed out.

I woke up in a strange bed in the hospital. Not only was my eardrum punctured, but I had stitches behind my ear where Jimmy's ring had left its mark.

I had heard footsteps. Those lesbians were trying to get me! I pretended to be asleep.

It was Jimmy. I could smell the Old Spice. I lay there scared and alone. He—or should I say she—sat on my bed. Where the hell was Sal?

Jimmy began talking softly telling me about all the pain in her life, in Milly's life, in the lives of her friends. "I'm sorry kid. I never hurt anyone in my life."

I opened my eyes. Now I was crying, too. My head felt like a large ball just shot out of a cannon. To my surprise, the room was filled with Jimmy's and Milly's friends, in all different kinds of costumes and dress. I couldn't tell who was a woman and who was a man, and to my astonishment I didn't care. They were just friends that came to see me in the hospital. I could only look around and say, "I am so sorry, so very sorry."

We stayed there for what seemed like hours, and I heard many stories and saw many tears. The nurses left us alone, I guess because we all looked too strange.

"What the hell is going on here?" It was Sal in the doorway looking like he was in a state of shock.

Behind him was a policeman. "Are these the people you want to press charges against?"

"No," I said, "these are my friends."

"Is the man who hit you here in this room?"

"I didn't get hit, officer," I said in my best grown-up voice. "I fell down the steps."

Sal had spent the day at the police station trying to press charges, so of course he was furious. I knew I didn't have long to live in those furnished rooms. In fact, he had us living in Red Hook one week later. He went back to working the bull lines, and I got a job in A&S, the department store in downtown Brooklyn.

Living in Red Hook made it hard for my new friends to visit me. It was too dangerous for them to be there. There was a lot of gay bashing going on then, only they called it queer hunting. I remember sitting down with Sal's grandfather and asking if he could arrange some protection for my friends to visit me, but that is another story.

CHAPTER THIRTY-EIGHT

Cooking Italian

When I was growing up, we never sat down to a meal. Whatever you grabbed, you ate. Whatever you ate, you grabbed. That's just how it was. Then all of a sudden I was married to this big Italian man, who wanted to eat. Sal said, "You gotta learn to cook Italian."

The landlord's wife Gina offered to teach me, but instead I got a book. It didn't have a lot of Italian recipes, but I told Sal, "I'm gonna make you Spanish rice." Spain is close to Italy, right?

I never was much good at directions, or measuring, so I put in ten times as much rice in the pot. The pot bubbled over, just kept on bubbling over, pouring out rice all over the floor. The directions said you have to color it yellow, so now I was going to follow the recipe and I started mixing the food coloring in, while the pot was still overflowing. That's when Sal came in and found me.

After that I used to go down to Gina's kitchen when I got home from work, and I learned to cook like that.

Back upstairs, I would start with what Gina said and then I added whatever I had, anything I could find in the kitchen, I threw in my gravy. It never tasted the same because I never had the same ingredients, and no pot was ever big enough. I didn't care, as long as everything was abundant. Then people began to drop in at dinner time. It reminded me of what my mother said, "Somebody gives you a half an ounce of knowledge, you make fifty pounds from it and they think you know what you're talking about. Keep it up, you're gonna get yourself in a lot of trouble." She was right. When I started teaching, I had no knowledge and no wisdom, all I had was the passionate heart of the Mother.

After we moved back to Red Hook, it was time to invite my father and his new wife, Rae, over for dinner. They weren't too happy about me living in Italian Red Hook, and meanwhile some of the old Italian women were literally trying to cast evil-eye spells on me for being Jewish. That never bothered me, but I wanted Papa to love me in spite of everything, and most of all I wanted him to love Sal. I remembered how Vinny had tried to buy me with a ring, so I thought maybe it would work again. I went to the five-and-dime and got myself a diamond ring, just so I could wave it around and say, "Look what Sal gave me!" I was happily married, I had my diamond, and that was that.

Nothing exploded on the stove, the food was delicious, and everything went great right up until it came time to wash the dishes. I looked down at my hands in the hot water and there was no diamond! It had melted right out of the setting! It took me less than a split second to start yelling—"The diamond! It went down the sink!"

Harry jumped right up. I never saw this old man move so fast, like he was going to rip open the pipes with his bare hands. Pretty soon the neighbors were banging on the door, and Rae was screaming almost as loud as me. Harry found a wrench someplace, and he made poor Sal open up the pipes. Next he wanted to call the plumbers to dig up the basement. It was awful! Yet in the middle of all the screaming and carrying on, at least I knew my dad loved me. Or did he love the ring?

CHAPTER THIRTY-NINE

Professional Mourner

Dr. Consentino came out of his office into the waiting room, looking as if he was about to become a mother himself, exclaiming, "Well, Joycey, we are pregnant!"

I was seriously in ecstasy.

We were living between Clinton and Court streets in Red Hook, that tough Italian section of Brooklyn. Aside from the store owners, I was the only Jew for miles around.

A&S Department Store would enjoy my services only until I was late in the ninth month. Then I wanted to take care of my baby. A baby, my sixteen-year-old mind was telling me, will make me like all the other mamas, no matter what age. I actually ached to hold my own baby in my arms.

Sal was looking very pleased and very afraid. "How are we gonna do this, Babe?" he would ask, his handsome face in a frown. Sal was always willing to work, and he took work where he could get it. In Red Hook, the docks were a sure thing, especially if you were willing to work down in the hold of the ship. Men got paid overtime there, but got old quickly in the cramped space where they lifted constantly and drank out of a dirty pail dropped down by their supervisor. Sal had been working on the bull lines since he was about thirteen. But now, with my belly growing, he got a good job driving a truck at Coca-Cola.

मा

Now I was in my eighth month. "Listen," Grandma Sadie said to me, "how about we two make good use out of that belly of yours?" I wouldn't know what she meant until the following day.

"Grandma," I answered, "the last time you touched my belly I stunk for a week."

About a month before, Grandma Sadie and her friend of fifty years, Grandma Flo, had cornered me in Granny's basement kitchen on Clinton Street. "Judatz, let's make sure we get a healthy baby boy." They began rubbing my belly with the juice of fresh-squeezed garlic cloves.

"What the hell are you two doing?" asked Grandpa Steve. He and Grandma Sadie had taken me under their wing as soon as Sal brought me around, an unheard of thing in an Italian neighborhood where people still draped their houses in black when a son or daughter intermarried.

Grandpa continued, "What's that stink? Sadie, you stop that right now. Come here, Joyce." I lowered my new maternity top. Sal had hocked his graduation ring to buy new outfits for me. "It smells real bad here," Grandpa said, and he gave me a five-dollar bill. "Go out and buy yourself another top, and stay away from those two old bags."

"You wanna double that five dollars?" Sadie asked.

"No thank you, Grandma." I had been well trained by my papa.

I walked out, smelling like a huge garlic, and went straight to the store on Court Street. When I walked in, everyone stared at me. The owner, Sammy, an old Jewish man, said, "Did Sadie put garlic all over you?"

"Yeah, she wants a grandson."

"I knew. She was in here taking bets it would be a boy."

To this day, the scent of garlic reminds me of Grandma Sadie.

This next morning, I heard, "Joycey, Joycey! Wake up!" It was Grandma Sadie, screaming at the top of her lungs in my hallway. "Judatz, wake up!"

I had been hanging clothes from my window to dry. Sal had gone to his mother's to take a shower, as we didn't have a shower or bathtub. It was about seven in the morning.

Fat Mary, who lived right under me, opened her door, and called up, "Joyce, are you okay?" We both did piecework at home, sewing the straps onto bras, and she kind of kept an eye on me.

"Yeah," I answered, dragging Grandma into my rooms.

"Joycey, we are going to make a lot of money this week. You know Baldoni's Uncle Giorgio died last night. He is going to be laid out in Anthony's Funeral Parlor. Now, listen up. This morning old Mario dropped dead, and he is laid out at Anthony's also."

"Grandma, why are you so happy?"

Just then Sal came through the door. "Grandma!" He was her favorite. "What are you talking about with my wife?"

"Old Mario died this morning and, being it was Joyce's day off, I thought she would come with me to pay our respects."

"Grandma, you never liked old Mario."

"Well, I thought I would go see Baldoni's Uncle Giorgio. He will be laid out in the same funeral parlor."

"Grandma, don't you dare make my wife into a professional mourner."

"What the hell is a professional mourner?" I asked.

Grandma asked innocently, "Salvatore, would I do a thing like that?"

He looked her straight in the eye. "Yes."

She put her hand over her heart and said, "I never thought I would live to see a grandson of mine not trust me." We all laughed at that, even Grandma.

"Grandma, I mean it. I am going to take my wife and baby out of the neighborhood if you two keep getting in trouble."

Now it was my turn to look shocked, only mine was real. "Salvatore, I would never move from the neighborhood." The neighborhood meant everything to me. For the first time in my life, I had a family. As crazy as it was, it was still family. I wanted my baby to grow up among his own people. No way was I gonna move. I kissed my Sally goodbye, promising to stay out of trouble. After all, how much damage could one old lady and one pregnant teenager do?

As Sal was walking out, he said, "Sadie, put some clothes on." She laughed and looked down at her slip and Grandpa's shirt. On her feet were the old pair of basketball sneakers that I swear she must have found in the gutter.

As soon as Sal shut the door, Sadie got real animated. "Joycey, all you got to do for five dollars an hour is wail in the front of the casket, then again in back of the room. For an extra two dollars, you kiss the body."

"Grandma, what are you talking about?"

She just kept on going. "Now, on the other hand, you're pregnant, so you can come home with seven dollars an hour, plus more for kissing the corpse. I can only make five bucks an hour."

"Are you saying if we stay for two hours, I can make fourteen dollars?" In 1956, this was big bucks. I was only taking home about thirty dollars a week working at A&S. "Is this legal?"

"Of course. Everyone knows you're not related. It just looks good for the family that comes from out of town. Now, Joycey, I left the best part out. If you can pretend you're leaving to go out to the bathroom, you can work both funerals and come home with twenty-eight dollars! We start where Uncle Giorgio is laid out and then we go to old Mario. And they'll be laid out for five days, at least."

I couldn't believe my ears. "Let me get dressed."

"Do you have a black maternity?"

"No, of course not."

Out of her shopping bag she took a big black dress that stank of mothballs.

"Grandma, I am not gonna wear that rag."

"For twenty-eight dollars, you are. Go on, get dressed. I'll finish hanging out the wash."

When I was dressed I looked in the mirror. I looked like something out of an Italian movie. I could have played an old pregnant grandma.

Grandma was saying, "Honey, it's late."

"Sadie, you know the parlors don't open till 10:30. It's only 7:45."

"Judatz, we have to make some stops first. I just have to place a few numbers." Sadie always had a lot of mysterious errands on the streets of Red Hook. I knew not to ask too many questions. "You're making memories," she said. That was the same thing my papa always used to say when there was no food in the house. "Now, come on. Let's place our numbers and go to the church."

"Why, may I ask, are we going to church?"

"After we place the numbers, we have to go to Saint Stephen's to pray we hit them tonight. Do you have five dollars? I'll pay you back after we wail."

"No, Grandma, that's why I'm gonna wail."

"Now you're learning, kid."

We took hands and walked down the busy street. Grandma stopped on Columbia Street and said, "Look at us. You look like an old widow with a pillow under her dress, and I forgot to put on my skirt over my slip. You know, Judatz, I am glad you married my grandson."

I kissed her withered cheek. "So am I, Grandma Sadie, so am I."

CHAPTER FORTY

Hot Goods

Sal kept working for Coca-Cola, and after a few years we moved to a tenement on Quentin Road to have more room for the kids—Denise, Jimmy, and finally the baby Desiree. We were three rooms, three kids, and a German shepherd until we saved $5,000 to put down on a big split-level house with a good-sized yard for the kids in a new part of Brooklyn.

Sal was a hard-working man, up every day at 4:30 in the morning to go on his route. He was the first grandson in a large Italian family, and he wanted his wife barefoot and pregnant in the kitchen. That was okay with me; I never wore shoes, loved being pregnant, and by now cooking was my way of life. I managed to keep a clean house and run a good business selling closeout goods to all my friends.

My business started when Sal's friend Joey brought over a whole load of bead necklaces. "Hey, Joyce, why don't you sell this stuff and make us all rich?"

"With beads? Are you kidding? Okay, give them to me on consignment."

"You got it."

That night Sal and I were delivering Coca-Cola to Elaine Powers, a women's gym in Brooklyn. I had gotten him the account. While he was filling the soda machine, I went into the locker room.

"Hey," I said to the women in the locker room, holding up the necklaces. No one answered. "Hey," I tried again, "they're red hot," not knowing if it was true or not. I thought I would give it a try.

A few women came over. "How much?"

Joey wanted twenty-five cents each. "Give me a buck," I said.

They started to fly out of my hands. Before I knew it, I was sold out. I came out of the locker room with a big grin on my face.

Sal said, "Hey, Babe, how much did we make?"

"Whatever it was, one third is going to Deborah Heart Hospital."

"Come on, Joyce, that was eleven years ago."

"No way out. I gave my word."

When I was having my first child, I went to a maternity clinic where they treated everyone like cattle. By the time I gave birth, all the women having babies had gotten pretty friendly. A young woman named Tina who was in the ward with me gave birth to a baby with a heart defect that no doctor could treat—that is, no doctor who took care of the poor. She made an appointment with a famous heart specialist who told her that unless she had insurance, he couldn't take her baby's case.

Over the years, Tina and I stayed in touch. Although our babies were the same age, her little one, Jenny, was half Denise's size, and she seemed to be getting sicker. She would die before she grew up unless something was done. Then I heard about a hospital in New Jersey where they took in anyone. Only a donation was needed if one had the money, and if not, it was free. We took the bus to Jersey, and they accepted Jenny as a patient. On the way there, I kept promising God that if Jenny lived I would give one third of any money I ever made to the hospital until she was twenty-one years old. She lived, and I kept my word.

So now my husband was saying, "Come on, kick in the bread."

"No way! One third goes to the hospital."

He finally gave in. It was hard in those days to make ends meet, especially if you had a wife who gave away a third of her income and fed a whole bunch of extra kids every night. My front door and my refrigerator were always open for any kid in the neighborhood. There were my kids' friends, and my friends' kids and their friends, and sometimes a young helper from Sal's route. It didn't matter, everybody was welcome.

या

The beads started me on a business adventure that would last a long time. One day our neighbor Jay came over to the house. He lived down the block at the corner and ran a cosmetics company. "Joyce," he said, "I'll give you Intoxication perfume for $3. It's in Thriftway right now for $24."

"Bullshit," I said. I was making the sauce and was in no mood for stupidity.

"Go check," he said.

"Sal, I'll be right back. Stir the pot."

Off I went. In those days, I didn't drive. Sal didn't believe in women drivers, and I was content staying home, taking care of my babies, keeping house, and selling beads. Just putting the white shoe polish on my babies' shoes would put me into ecstasy.

Sure enough, in Thriftway on Ralph Avenue, there it was: Intoxication perfume for $24.95. As soon as I got home, I asked Jay, "How hot is the stuff?"

"Not hot, Joyce, but closed out."

"Give me ten bottles on consignment."

We had a deal. That night Florie from Sanitary Butchers came over to the house. She couldn't believe it. "How hot is it?"

"Wow!" I answered, avoiding her question. She took all ten bottles. I called Jay and ordered more. Later that night, after I fed the family, I was cleaning up when the phone rang.

"Joyce, can I sell the perfume for twelve dollars a bottle?" asked Betty, who lived around the corner.

"Sure, go ahead."

That's how I ended up with forty-two girls working for me, and how I opened my first store out of my garage, elegantly named "Joyce's Joint." I sold everything from televisions to closeout jackets, all on consignment. One time Sal got home from work to find that I had taken delivery of a hundred toilets, which were arranged around the front yard. I had receipts for everything, even though I let people think it was all hot. I never laid out a penny of my own. Meanwhile, Deborah Heart Hospital did good by little Jenny. Last I heard, she has children of her own and is living in Nevada.

CHAPTER FORTY-ONE

The Cord Replica

Sal said, "How about we take our new car over to Coney Island and get some hot dogs at Nathan's?"

I looked at my children in our first brand-new car, a 1969 Oldsmobile Toronado. The three of them were cuddled in the backseat. Sal, of course, was driving. The car was maroon and black with black leather seats.

Things were looking up with both of us working, Sal with Coca-Cola and me in my store, which I had changed from "Joyce's Joint" to "Joyce's Marché." My accountant said I had to have more class now that he'd made me a legitimate businesswoman. I really liked "Joyce's Joint" better, but who cared, as long as I could make enough to feed all the extra mouths each night. I figured that all the neighborhood kids I invited over were my responsibility, along with my children's friends who seemed to hang out in our house.

The kids were thrilled to be going to Nathan's. We were on the Belt Parkway heading toward Coney Island, and we could see the Ferris wheel in the distance. Suddenly, and at the same moment, Sal and I saw this terrific looking little red car heading in the other direction. We were into cars and pretty much knew all of them. This one was different; it was sleek and close to the ground, with beautiful lines. Sal looked at me.

"Go for it, Sal. Let's find out what it is," I said.

Denise said, "I knew it was too good to be true."

Sal was busy trying to make a U-turn on the Belt Parkway. I calmly turned and asked my twelve-year-old daughter what was too good to be true.

"Having this normal new car."

"What are you talking about?" I asked.

All the other cars were at a standstill and beeping their horns as only Brooklynites can. I kept talking as if nothing strange was happening in the middle of the busiest parkway in Brooklyn.

"Denisey, of course we are keeping this beautiful new car. We wouldn't think of getting something small like that, even if we knew what it was." I turned to Sal and said, "Floor it, Babe, he's getting away."

Sal was hitting seventy when the little sports car made a quick turn at the Flatbush Avenue exit. Sal jammed on the brakes and followed him. We had to find out what that car was! We drove down a few blocks, our car starting to smoke. In the chase both of us had forgotten that we weren't supposed to drive the Toronado fast for the first thousand miles.

We spotted the little red car parked outside a two-family house. The door was open on the driver's side as if the driver had just run away.

"Strange," I said, "why would he leave the car unlocked?"

"Especially with two maniacs following him," said Denise.

"Watch the children, Denise. We'll be right back."

Just then two huge men came out of the house. One had a pipe in his hand; the other held a baseball bat. "Get away from that car!" shouted the smaller of the two, who was probably about six-foot-two and three hundred pounds.

"What kind is it?" I asked.

"Are you nuts, lady? You scare my nephew half to death, and I'm facing you with a bat in my hand, and you have the balls to ask what kind of car it is?"

"Well," Salvatore asked, "what is it?"

"Are you interested in buying the car?"

I looked at Sal, and we turned at the same time to look at our shiny new Toronado, which we'd possessed for two whole days. We answered together, "Yes."

Everything changed. "Get the kids and come in," he said sweetly.

I went to tell Denise to bring the kids in. She just looked at me and said, "I prefer to stay right here, if it's all right."

"Denise," I said, just as politely, "get your ass out of there immediately. That is the car of our dreams."

"Mama, you do have three children."

"Don't worry, Denise. We'll make room."

Denise got her brother and sister out of the car. As she walked past the red car, she said to no one in particular, "Oh, yes, there's plenty of space on the roof."

By the time I got the kids into the house, the wife had trays of cookies and cakes ready on the table. If we weren't so blinded by love, we might have been on the ball and noticed how well these people were treating the same people they'd wanted to kill five minutes earlier. Somehow arrangements for the sale of the Toronado and purchase of the red car were made. The price they were asking was about $3,000 more than we'd paid for the Toronado, but wise Sal and his smart wife talked them down to the lower price.

Before we signed on the bottom line, the big man asked, "Are you sure you two want to go through with this?"

We both said "Yes" rather quickly. We were afraid he was going to change his mind. I must say, he did give us a chance to back down.

As Sal was signing the papers, the wife came over to us and asked the same question, "Are you sure you want to go through with this?" She was looking at my Denisey as if the kid was the mother.

Denise just as politely said, "They're sure, believe me."

The car was a replica of a 1937 Cord, built from a kit. Later we found out that there were only four in all of New York City. Outside, the owners gave us two boxes of parts for the car, which we naturally assumed were spare parts. Sal and I walked toward our shiny new Cord. After taking our things out of our "old" car, we stuffed Denise and her brother into the jump seat. I put the baby on my lap, and we were off, everyone waving and smiling. As we pulled out of the driveway, I saw the wife making the sign of the cross.

"You know, Babe, I feel like we stole this beauty from those people."

"I know, Sal. We'll send them a basket of fruit tomorrow."

That was the last nice thing either one of us would ever say about the previous owners of our spectacular 1937 Cord. Near the corner of Ralph and Flatbush Avenues we heard something hard fall to the pavement. Whatever it was, we were dragging it. Sal stopped the car.

"Holy shit!" he said. "We just lost the axle."

Denisey commented from the jump seat, "Never a dull moment in this household—or car."

We all started to laugh, a good thing because I think if we hadn't, we would have thrown ourselves in front of the traffic coming and going on Ralph Avenue. Instead we just waved at the people who were giving us the high sign, impressed by the beauty of our car. Sal called a tow truck, a call that we would repeat frequently over the next twelve months.

After the car was towed away and we were dropped off at our house, Sal, the kids, and I sat in the kitchen and ate everything in sight. I kept giving Denise dirty looks as if to say, "Open your mouth and I'll kill you." We started writing an ad to put in the car section of *The New York Times*.

As we were looking through the *Times*, we spotted three other Cords for sale. Sal and I just looked at each other, and I took out the frozen éclairs I'd been saving for Sunday. At least Salvatore waited for the éclairs to defrost; I just chewed on mine, frozen and all.

Thank God the next day was Saturday, and Sal didn't have to go to work. He went to pick up our car. The guys at the gas station were in love with it. Sal immediately asked if they wanted to buy it.

The mechanic said, "No way, that's a rich man's car." After he gave Sal the bill, my poor husband saw what he meant. Of course we raided the fridge again. The goddamned car was gonna make me gain weight. I knew it in my bones as I brought out the ice cream and chocolate syrup.

Our ad came out the next day in the Sunday paper. At 7 a.m. the phone rang. I picked up the receiver. A man on the other end said, "Do you have a '37 Cord for sale?"

"To tell you the truth," I answered, in my most sophisticated voice, "my husband does have a Cord, and I'm sick at the thought of selling the car. But you see, we have three children, and the little beauty is much too small for us."

The man began to laugh. "Lady," he said, "you need to get another line if you want to sell that bomb."

"Fuck you, buster," I said, and was about to hang up when I heard him yell, "Hey, I have the same one, only in silver!"

"What?"

"Yes," he said, "and I've been trying to get rid of it for a year." He continued speaking fast, as if he knew that I was going to hang up any second. "My friend has one too, a yellow one. Yesterday he lost the front fender; it just blew right off in the middle of Manhattan. How about we all get together and have some fun with the cars?"

Sal had come down, and he took the phone. The two men made arrangements to meet the next week. They planned to drive slowly all around Brooklyn, waving to the people on the sidewalk as they gaped to see three Cords and their proud owners. I made sure Coney Island and Brighton Beach would be included, thinking back to the day Tirza and I went to Nathan's in a Bentley.

Of course no one could know that Sal's appendix would burst that afternoon and that I would have to drive him to the hospital because the ambulance never showed up at the house. In the middle of King's Highway, with Sal moaning and groaning, the steering wheel came right off in my hands. It was just like in the movies. One second I was saying, "We're almost there," as I looked over at him to see if he was still alive. At the same time, I was making the last turn toward the hospital. The next second, only me and the steering wheel turned, not the car. Sal screamed, "Hit the brake!" I did, and we both went flying. Thank God we were in front of the hospital. The attendants took Salvatore inside, leaving me on the sidewalk with a steering wheel in my hand and a beautiful replica of a 1937 Cord.

He was in the hospital with peritonitis for a long time. Finally I went to bring him home. I had had the car washed, and it looked gorgeous on that bright fall day. We were about two blocks from our house when without warning we were in the middle of a heavy rain shower.

"Put on the windshield wipers!"

"I did already, they fell off!"

We both started laughing.

"Stop," said Sal, "or I'll have to go back into the hospital." We arrived home nice and safe. As soon as he got settled, he asked me to call that guy Richie about the Cord. The next afternoon Richie came over, driving his silver nightmare, his own Cord. With him was his wife, Franny. That day marked the beginning of a friendship between me and Franny that would last a lifetime. Later, I gave her the spiritual name "Bina." After that very first meeting of the red and silver Cords and their crazy owners, she would stay right by my side.

CHAPTER FORTY-TWO

Why Don't You Eat A Little?

"Go downstairs," I told my handsome husband. "Watch TV with the kids."

"That was a great meal, Babe. But why didn't you eat?"

"Sal, I'm never very hungry," I said, coyly, looking him straight in the eye the way my mama had taught me to do whenever the truth had to be stretched ever so slightly.

My heart was beating fast in my 250-pound frame.

"Denise," he yelled downstairs, "help your mother do the dishes."

My mind was on the upstairs bathroom. Stashed behind the toilet were two loaves of fresh Italian bread. The leftover salad had my name written all over it, beckoning the hidden Italian bread to merge with its dripping thick olive oil. I was dizzy from the anticipation, and this guy wanted Dee to do the dishes—Little Miss Perfect, who, when she was five, claimed to do dishes and clean house better than me. I did not want her in my kitchen just then!

"No," I anxiously said, "go watch TV." He grabbed a canoli, the last one. "Never mind," I told myself. "What you want is waiting like a lover."

No one made a salad like me. I used plenty of olive oil, saturating every piece of lettuce, tomato, celery, garlic, cheese, cucumber, day-old bread saved just for the salad and cut into cubes, olives, chives, bread crumbs, onions, bacon bits, salami, provolone, and red-hot sausage—it was all swimming in oil and the little vinegar I daintily added just for show. My salads were a work of art, and I always made too much so there would be some left over to dunk my Italian bread in.

Jimmy Boy and a friend appeared in the kitchen. "Mama, can Johnny and I go outside and play around with our bikes?"

"No!" I yelled, noticing that their hands were already greasy from their bikes. "Go wash your hands or I'll break both your legs!"

All of a sudden it hit me. "Wait!" I yelled at the top of my voice. "One minute!" Johnny was about to enter the bathroom where my bread was hidden. Both these boys always missed the bowl when they peed. I ran up the stairs with an empty garbage bag, just as he was about to enter.

"Okay, okay, Aunt Joyce!"

I slammed the door behind me, grabbed the bread, and walked out with my loot safely in the bag. "Just getting the garbage," I said, in a very adult way.

As I was walking down the steps, Jim, the beast, said, "Mama always hides the bread behind the toilet."

Johnny said, "Oh," as if this was the most normal thing in the world to do.

"Screw them," I thought. I sat down with the bread and salad and began to enjoy myself immensely.

I didn't hear Salvatore coming up the stairs. He must have been standing there for a while, when he said quietly, "Why don't you eat a little, Babe?"

"*Excuse* me," I muttered. "Did you say something?" The oil was dripping down my chin.

"Why don't you eat a little?" he repeated.

Those words changed my life. I just sat there stunned. Right then and there I decided to lose weight. I started immediately. "Denisey,"

I sweetly called, "come here. Mommy wants to talk to you."

"Ma, are you finished with your salad?"

I thought, "Isn't anything sacred around here?"

"As a matter of fact, I wasn't planning on finishing it. Now, come here."

The week before I had heard of a place that wrapped you up like a mummy so you would lose lots of weight and inches. I had paid little attention to it. I thought Salvatore liked me the way I was. Now I was trying to remember all the things I had ever heard about losing weight.

"Denisey, how would you like to get rid of your fat?"

My sixteen-year-old daughter looked at me, shocked to the core of her being. "Mommy, am I fat?" She ran to the nearest mirror. She actually had a perfect shape.

"No, silly, but this will stop you from getting fat," I whispered.

"Salvatore!" I yelled down to my husband, who had returned to the TV room. "Denise and I are going for a walk. We need to walk off what we ate."

"We are?"

"Come, sweetheart."

Sal came sheepishly up the stairs. "Listen, Babe, I was only teasing you. You look fine."

"Excuse me," I said, "I have to put on my eyelashes."

"To go around the block with your daughter?"

"You never know who you might meet."

Denise and I walked out the door, me in a huff, giving Salvatore a good last dirty look, and Denise in confusion.

As we walked out, we saw my friend Anita's car slowing down in front of our house. She saw us and called us over. "Joyce," she said, all excited, "you gotta go to this gym on Flatbush Avenue. It's called Jack LaLanne's."

"Whatever for?" I asked my beautiful blond friend, who also had a weight problem. The difference was, she admitted it.

"They got this yoga teacher. She teaches you a breath to lose weight."

"What?" I yelled.

"Mommy," Denise said, "I thought we were going to that place to get wrapped."

"Listen," I said to Anita, "you go check out this yoga, and we'll check out the other thing. Then we'll meet and compare notes."

"Deal," said my tough Italian friend.

We went the next day. I said to the very thin lady behind the desk. "Me and the kid want to get wrapped. The kid will go first."

She gave us the price and asked if we wanted the tour before we got started. I couldn't move, not with those prices. I believe it was twenty-five dollars a session. For the two of us, that made fifty bucks a week. This was 1971, a time when folks made $100 to $150 a week.

"Dolores," I said sweetly, reading her name tag, "I just happen to have in my car some Geoffrey Beene dresses that fell off a truck."

Her eyes lit up. She followed me to the car, asking Denise to please answer the phone. When we got to the car, I popped the trunk and Dolores' eyes went crazy. She was in my territory now. I started my spiel. Soon she was taking two gowns, worth a thousand bucks.

Little did she know that they were a two-year-old style, as hot as Alaska in winter. We made a deal. In exchange for the gowns, Denise and I could take the treatments for however long it took.

Back inside, we proceeded to strip naked, stand in a shower, and get wrapped by two size-three young women. Then these sweet little things politely supported us while we took baby steps into a special room where twelve other mummies lay, each for twenty-five dollars a session, three times a week. Then the tiny young women laid us down and poured a thick gooey substance over our bandages. All eyes were on the new kids on the block.

I quickly said, loud enough to wake the dead, "Does this stuff rinse off the body nicely? I have to try on a whole load of Geoffrey Beene gowns when I get home. I wouldn't want to stain them. I do hope I can lose a few inches." I spoke to my silent daughter who, if looks could kill, would have become half an orphan right there. "It's a good thing, Denise, that they come in all sizes. I guess if you lost a few inches, your size might change."

"Excuse me," said a white-haired mummy. "You did say 'Geoffrey Beene'?"

"Oh, yes. Am I disturbing you?"

"No, on the contrary. I was looking for a gown."

"Well," I said calmly, looking at the six-carat diamond on the only flesh that was exposed except for her face. "If you want, why don't you wait for me. I'll be only a little longer than you."

A few of the other mummies wanted to do the same. That was the beginning of my new career selling clothes in weight-loss places all over Brooklyn.

It was also the beginning of my journey, believe it or not, to meet my Christ.

CHAPTER FORTY-THREE

Jack LaLanne's

After a while it became clear that the wrapping system didn't really take off the weight for me and Denise, it just moved it around. We did lose inches around the middle, but we developed wings of fat up around our armpits. Then I tried another treatment that involved getting shots that were made from the pee of pregnant women, and this time I paid with some I. Miller shoes for the nurse in the unsuspecting doctor's office. That diet required us to eat about zero calories, no more olive oil, no more mozzarella. Meanwhile, Anita and the girls were losing weight, taking that weird yoga course at Jack LaLanne's. I still hadn't forgiven Salvatore, so I decided yoga was next.

I walked into the gym and straight up to the front desk. "I wanna try out the yoga class," I said to a lady wearing a label that said, "Hi, I'm Tina."

"You can't just take the yoga class. You have to be a guest."

"Listen, Tina, I can't sell you a pure mohair sweater set with the label cut out—if you get my drift—unless you see it first."

"Mohair!" Tina exclaimed. "What colors?"

"Why, of course, all colors, all sizes, and what I don't have I can get." I began opening my suitcase. It was early in the morning. The main part of the gym was still being opened. Tina had let us into the office waiting room to get us out of the cold. As I was speaking, a woman was doing her exercise right there in the waiting room.

"Listen!" I shouted to her. "You wanna stop for a minute? I'm talking to Tina."

She looked scared out of her mind. I instantly felt bad.

She took in my 250-pound frame in my red one-piece leotard, my made-up face, and my three pairs of eyelashes. She stood stark still. I looked in her eyes. She turned away. Something was happening in my heart. As it turned out, I was looking into the face of the first person, after Franny, who would one day become my chela.

"What's your name?" I asked sweetly, not understanding what was going on.

"Linda," she answered and walked away. She couldn't walk far; the room was too small.

The main door opened and in came everyone, like at a half-price sale at Macy's.

I asked Tina, "What are they all running to?"

"The yoga class," she answered, focusing on the sweaters. "The teacher's name is Donna, and the ladies are losing weight from the breathing exercises."

"Where do I sign up?" I asked. Tina was too busy picking out her sweater set to answer. It sounded like the yoga class might start without me if I didn't hurry. "Tina, I'm going in. You watch my suitcase, and if anyone is interested, just tell them they're $14.95 and sell in the store for $39.95."

Tina said, "Thank you so much. By the way, what is your name?"

I began to answer, but I couldn't. The word "Ma" was banging against my brain, holding my tongue from saying my name. I almost said "Ma" in order to stop myself from going crazy and to release the pressure in my head. I finally sputtered, "Joyce."

I walked into the yoga room. On the stage, lit by a couple of candles, was a little girl no bigger than a size zero. I guessed she was Donna.

"Is this the yoga place?" I inquired.

The room was dark. I couldn't see anyone, but I sure did hear this moaning sound coming from the floor. You could make out the shadows of figures lying there.

"Yes," said the skinny girl on the stage, "would you like to join us?"

Just then someone said, "Joyce, shut up. Ain't you got no class? We are Oming." It was Mary Lou, one of the tough girls from Avenue U.

"Where the hell are you?" I asked. I reached for the switch on the right side of the wall, where there was a little nightlight plugged in. The light went on, and everyone began yelling. I was shocked! There on the floor, in every size and shape and dress, were my friends and a lot of the ladies who worked for me, too. I couldn't believe it. They were all yelling at me, telling me to shut off the fucking light.

There was Sonya, all 350 pounds of her, in a red leotard, lying on the floor, yelling the loudest. "Shut the fucking light!" For a moment I was sorry that I had also worn red. Yet I was a hundred pounds thinner than her, which didn't exactly make me Twiggy, but I wasn't as big as Sonya.

The little girl on the stage looked like she was going to cry. "Please join us or leave."

"Just give me the breath, and I will get out of here."

She bravely said, "You must join the class."

"What for?"

"The breath is not only about losing weight," said the feather on the stage. "Yoga is about God."

"Why do you want to bring God into this?" I rudely asked. "God isn't bothering you." Before I gave her a chance to answer, I lay down next to my friend Josie from Nostrand Avenue. The girl shut the lights, and everyone settled down.

I whispered to Josie, "Does this shit really work?"

She hissed back, "Better than what you've been trying."

"Can't you see I lost weight?" I said, lying.

"No, Joyce, to tell you the truth. Sammy saw you eating cheesecake in Waldbaums's parking lot."

"He didn't only see me; I shared the cake with him."

"I'm gonna kill him," she said. "He's supposed to be on a diet."

I felt bad that I had ratted out her husband. He was a great guy.

"Shut up, Joyce!" Sonya was yelling again.

"Sonya, if you don't stop telling me to shut up, you won't get any of the load of jewelry that just came in."

"What jewelry?" a voice asked from the back of the room. It was too dark to see.

"The 14-carat gold jewelry," I answered in the blackness. Joanie crawled over to me. Even Sonya was at my side. All of a sudden the lights went on. I was really getting comfortable in the dark.

"Please, ladies, I will lose my job if I can't teach yoga."

Now I was feeling bad. "Okay, go on. All you ladies, shut up now."

Donna said something about relaxing, and when the room got quiet she came over to me and sat down. "I will give you the breath and then you must leave."

"Sure thing," I answered, not feeling a bit offended. This wasn't my cup of tea.

She proceeded to give me the breath. I breathed in and out the way she showed me. When she was finished, my heart was beating fast. I had no idea why. I thanked her and asked if she wanted anything from my store.

"No, thank you," she said politely. She hesitated for a moment. "Did you ever take yoga before?"

"No, sweetheart," I answered kindly.

"Your eyes are something else."

"Well, thank you," I said, not knowing if it was a compliment or not. I got up to leave, and the class began that strange sound again. It vibrated in my head as I got into the car. The sound was in my head, the sound of *Om*. "Great," I thought. "Another sound running around in my brain." I had finally made peace with the sound of "Ma."

CHAPTER FORTY-FOUR

I'm Jewish—You Got the Wrong House

When I got home from Jack LaLanne's that day, I went right into the kitchen and started cutting up my already-cooked potatoes. I had started cooking at five that morning, making my potatoes and sauce. There was always some sort of music going on in our house. The radio was blasting a song from *Jesus Christ Superstar*. I stopped a moment. A woman was singing "I Don't Know How to Love Him." I understood that she must have been singing about Jesus.

"Just love him," I thought. Then my heart started beating fast. I shut off the radio and put on good old Dinah Washington. I sang along with "Say It Isn't So" as I started to mash the potatoes with my hands. (I wouldn't think of using a potato masher.) The other song was still in my head, and I kept saying, "Just love him." If he was mine, which he wasn't, I would love him to death. "Oh, Joyce," I told myself "get that song out of your head." I blasted Dinah even louder.

I proceeded to add the ten sticks of butter to the mashed potatoes, thinking, "No wonder I have to work. This butter is expensive." I never thought for a moment that if I weren't feeding all the kids in the neighborhood perhaps things would be a little less expensive. I got out the perfectly chilled heavy cream, added my own bacon bits that I'd cut up earlier, put in some onions and parsley, some shredded mozzarella cheese, some cheddar cheese, and a whole load of bread crumbs. I never measured anything. I mixed it all together and rolled it all up in big balls. Oil was heating on the stove. I put my potato balls in the oil, one by one, frying them to perfection.

As I was making my special Joyce salad, I began to think about loving Christ. "I guess that would be nice," I thought. "He looks like a good guy."

Denise said, "Mommy, why do you look funny, kinda like thoughtful?"

"I don't know, baby, maybe it was the yoga class."

"Did you behave yourself there, Mom?"

"Well, kinda," I answered.

"Mom, tell me."

"Well, it was dark, and the girls were making strange noises. I just opened the lights. Boy, you should have seen big Sonya."

"You are bad, and you better not get hooked on yoga."

"No way. I am just gonna do the breath and lose the weight."

Donna had told us, "You do this breath for fifteen minutes a day, and you'll lose five pounds in a week." So I immediately think, fifteen minutes, five pounds, that's twenty pounds in an hour. Why, I could lose the whole hundred pounds in one night! And when Sal gets up in the morning there I'll be at the foot of the stairs like a toothpick, a skinny toothpick like Donna.

I couldn't wait to get started, but of course there was the family to take care of first. That night, as my family was eating my cooking, I looked at them, almost like I was taking a picture with my mind's eye. There were Jonesy's kids; Vincent and Johnny Boy; Debby and her boyfriend; Darleen's two daughters from next door; the upstairs tenants' son; Chris, my friend Jeannie's son; and Sal's friend Stevie.

No one could stop talking about my veal parmesan and potatoes and the hot corn I had rolled in butter and heavy cream and then put in the oven for a few minutes. "Great meal, Babe," said my husband.

He was about to go downstairs with Stevie, who was rubbing his stomach and making noises to compliment my cooking.

"Stay a minute, Salvatore," I said.

He looked suspicious. "What's up?"

"Honey," I said, surprising him, since I had been cold since he'd told me to eat a little, "I want time to do a yoga breath when you and the kids are in bed tonight."

"A what?"

"A yoga breath to lose weight."

Weight was a subject he didn't want to touch, but he said, "What do you want to fuck around with yoga for?"

"Look, Sal, I am just doing a breath I learned today in yoga class."

"Were there men there?" he asked softly, with a lot of meaning.

"Of course not," I answered, "only ladies. Sonya was there in her red tights."

He laughed at that, but not too much. After all, I was still in my own red tights under my pants, the top of the leotard skintight over my bust.

"Okay, but don't be too long." He grabbed me and held me tight. "I love you, Babe. Please don't get involved in yoga."

"Sal, I love you, too, and don't worry, it's all too weird for me."

After a while, everyone left. Denise helped me clean up. I put Desiree to bed and told the kids who were sleeping over to go right to bed. Around midnight, I came downstairs into the living room and sat in the full lotus, like I had seen skinny Donna do. Believe me, this was no easy feat at 250 pounds. I started to breathe in and out in the pattern she had showed me.

In yoga there are many forms of breathing exercise, or *pranayama*, and this was a very simple one. The trick of it is to curl the tongue into a shape like a trough and stick it out of your mouth a little bit, so that when you breathe in it feels like you're drinking through a straw. Sit comfortably, but with a straight back. Take a slow deep breath in and visualize that the breath is all going into your head, as if your head is filling up like a balloon. Hold the breath as long as it's comfortable, and then breathe out imagining that the breath leaves through the top of the head. (You can relax the tongue except while you breathe in.) Breathe in again, but this time fill your belly until you feel like you just ate a big meal. Hold it as long as you're comfortable, and then breathe out the top of the head. And keep going, one breath in the head, one breath in the belly. Just remember to always curl the tongue when you breathe in, and always breathe out the top of the head.

Of course you were only supposed to do this for a few minutes, but I overdo everything. I did it for an hour and said, "God, Mac, if you got anything to do with this yoga stuff, then take a few pounds off me while I sleep." Then I did the breath a little longer.

"See you later, Mac," I said to God, as I got ready for bed. Of course, I said good night to the scale, a thing I was superstitious about doing religiously.

The next morning I was up at five and on the scale one minute after. I had lost three pounds! After that, the days went quickly. I couldn't wait for the nights and my breath. I did the breath for three days and lost seven pounds. I was beside myself. This was great.

That night at dinner, Sal said, "Babe, I really don't like you fooling around with that yoga stuff. It's all too strange."

"Sal, just let me do it for a little while until I lose the weight."

"I really don't like it. But I guess it's not taking anything away from me and the kids."

I thought about that for a while. Was it taking anything away from my family? I wouldn't do anything that would hurt them or anyone. I decided that if I lost weight, it would be good for all of us. I knew I had to do this thing. Something inside of me knew this to be true.

मा

The house was three levels. There was a foyer just inside the front door. From there, you could go down to the TV room in the basement, or up an open stairway to the living room and kitchen level, or up more steps to the bedrooms. After the house was quiet and the kids were asleep, I lit candles and incense and sat down in the living room. "Wow," I thought, "I am really getting into this."

I breathed for an hour. Then two, then three. It felt good. It felt like God was there with me. Or maybe it was just the incense. I couldn't explain it, even to myself.

My heart began to pound. I was getting a floating sensation. "Oh, I'm just hungry," I thought. A breeze gently touched my feet. Someone must have left a window open. I wasn't getting out of the lotus position to shut any window; it took me too long to get into it. Anyway, I thought if I moved, I wouldn't lose as much weight. Then I thought I heard a sound coming from the foyer, but my eyes were shut and I ignored it. I just kept breathing in and out. I realized I was breathing to the word "Ma." "Ma" in and "Ma" out. Oh well, I figured, anything to lose weight.

The noise got louder, like someone walking.

"Who is it?" I asked, now struggling to get quickly out of the position. "Who is it?" I heard a dragging sound. "Sal!" I cried out. He was upstairs waiting for me in bed. The TV was blasting in the bedroom so he couldn't hear me. "Dee! Jimmy Boy!"

No one answered. Still stuck in the lotus position, I opened my eyes and looked down through the railing. I see a man coming up the few stairs from the front door, and I think, "Oh, shit!" He's wearing a white robe and carrying a cross. He has black hair, a black beard, black eyes, his skin is darker than mine, and he's wearing sandals.

I never in my life knew fear like that. I began to yell. "Someone, help me, please! I'm stuck!" Yet, my voice had left me and no sound came out. I was sweating profusely.

I said in a whisper, "I'm Jewish, you got the wrong house." My voice was shaking, I heard my voice shaking from a thousand miles away. The house was very dark, but inside the dark was this very bright brightness, and his eyes, black eyes, and so much love I couldn't even tell if it was love. I wouldn't know what to call it, there was so much. I'm not scared even though I'm trembling, and at the same time I'm really completely terrified.

He smiled and held out his arms to me. That did it. I started to climb the stairs away from him, still in a full lotus, using my knees to get myself onto the stairs. By the time I got to the bedroom, I was incoherent.

Sal had fallen asleep. "Joyce," he called out, "what are you doing on the floor like that?"

"Sal," I said. "Sal…Sal." I found I couldn't talk.

"What is it, Babe?" He was fully awake now. He jumped out of bed and began to unfold me.

"Wait! Jesus Christ is downstairs."

"What! Are you crazy? Don't fuck around like that."

"Salvatore," I said, choking on my own words, "the Christ is in our living room, and he sure as hell does not want *me*!" After all, it was

Sal who was Catholic. I made him go get the three kids and the three dogs. I wanted everybody together in the bed.

"Mommy, what is it?" Denise asked.

"Nothing," answered her frightened father, "only that your mother brought God down upon us with that stupid yoga." He had started to make the sign of the cross when I first mentioned Christ and he kept doing it over and over. His hand looked like it had a mind of its own. "But, don't worry, tomorrow we'll get the priest to come." His voice was shaking.

I finally found my voice. "Why you are going to get a priest when the main man is downstairs?"

No one spoke. I thought they were all in shock. I turned and saw that my three babies and even the dogs were all asleep. Only my wide-eyed husband and I were awake.

"You did it now, Babe. You did it now," said my frightened husband. "I told you not to fuck around with yoga. Now God's here."

"Well, I'm Jewish, and you can go right down and tell him so."

"Are you crazy? It's you he wants."

Denise woke up and said, "You know something? You two are the weirdest parents any kid could have. Good night, Mama. Good night, Dad. Good night, Jesus," and she went back to her own bed, leaving us with each other and the two little ones. The dogs were having a great time on the bed.

CHAPTER FORTY-FIVE

Yearning and Terror

After the Christ came, I walked around in shock. Sal walked around crossing himself. Denise walked around saying her parents were nuts. The little ones were oblivious to it all. The next day, first thing on the way to work, Sal stopped by Mary Queen of Heaven and had them send a priest over. After breakfast, I opened the door and there was Father, who started right in flinging holy water all over the place. "Not on the wood floors, Father!" I said. "He only walked a little bit over there." I had just got through polishing the fucking floor, and I was in no mood for this.

The priest was shaking. He probably never would have believed this tale from me, but nice, calm, reasonable Catholic Sal—well, that was another story. "Father, you are staining my floors. Anyway, Christ is already blessed. Why would you want to bless God?"

"How do you know it was Christ?"

I looked very close into his face. "How many guys do you know who would be willing to drag around a cross? Moses, at least, *carried* the Ten Commandments. He didn't have to drag them anywhere."

He started throwing his holy water at an even more frantic pace. "Did Moses come also, Ma'am?"

I had known this priest for many years. He'd always called me Joyce. Now, all of a sudden, he was calling me Ma'am. It was my first lesson in the aloneness of loving God. Why did the thought of God put distance between people?

After he left, I had to polish my floors all over again to get out the holy water stains. I was pissed and confused. On my hands and knees, I began to think about Christ. His dark beauty had stunned me. Even in my fear, I had seen the serenity in his face and hands. Somehow, kneeling there on my floors, a yearning began, a yearning that would not leave until my Christ was with me always.

It was yearning and terror at the same time. For a while, fear won out. The seven pounds I'd lost from the yogic breath came back, plus one more. Now I was in a quandary. Do I stay fat without Christ, or do I do the breath and take the chance that Christ might come back? Meanwhile Sal kept warning me, "Don't fuck around with that yoga." And almost every day I would polish those same wood floors, the place where I had seen him.

"I want him back," I said one day. I said it out loud to no one, in the silence of my empty house, quietly at first, then louder. "I want him back!" I screamed. "I want Christ back in my home and heart!" I kept polishing the wooden floors. They never looked so shiny. "Mac, I promise I won't convert," (a promise I've kept all these years), "but I want him."

I began searching for my tape of *Jesus Christ Superstar*. I was a madwoman. I ran to my friend, Maureen, who lived two doors down. Her son had a tape recorder. "Maureen! Maureen! Just tape this one song, so it plays over and over for me." I had my hair tied up in a scarf, and Sal's old Coke shirt hung to my knees. My jeans were torn, and I was barefoot.

"Joyce, are you nuts?"

"Please, just do this for me."

I left the tape and ran home. I ran the bath, adding half a bottle of scented oil that I had been saving for our anniversary. After bathing, I dressed in my best slacks and blouse, and brushed my long black hair till it shone like my newly polished floors, then pushed it back and to the side with a rhinestone pin. I was ready when Maureen rang the doorbell.

"Joyce, why are you dressed like that at two in the afternoon?"

I looked at her through my three pairs of eyelashes and thick blue eye shadow. "Like what?" I asked, innocently.

"You look like you're either going out on the town or wanting to get laid." Everyone knew that my Sal was home about 1:30 every afternoon. But today he would be late because he was setting up a new account.

"I am going to have Christ come to me."

"Sure, Joyce. What time?" My good friend looked anxious for me.

"Don't worry. I'm not cracking up. I'm in love with another man, and his name is Jesus. Now, I don't think he's God or anything like that. I just love him."

"Joyce, you mean it!"

"I certainly do."

"Are you gonna convert?"

"Convert to what? To Christ? I just want to see him, not marry him." This was too much for my Catholic friend. "Joyce, you really are nuts," she said, and left after giving me back my tape and the one she'd made for me.

I put the tape on the machine. The words of the song hit me. I began to cry. I wanted him back.

Even so, I needed to get supper ready. For the first time, I worked in my kitchen unaware of what my hands were doing. All the time I was cooking, I was asking Mac to send me Christ. To myself I said it was just about losing weight, yet Mac and I both knew the truth. I wanted my Christ. Oh, did I ever want my Christ.

CHAPTER FORTY-SIX

Teach All Ways

The night at Kashi was dressed in the spirit of Christmas. As I began to walk around the pond in my usual fashion, I saw reflected against the sky two hundred candles. It was Christmas Eve, and my chelas were singing "Silent Night" out there in the cool December air. I walked toward my own, my heart bursting with pride. The children's faces were radiant. At the head of the pond, I came to the Hanuman temple with three rings of seats for my chelas.

First, I knelt before the burning fire or *dhuni*, representing the eternal flame of God. Next, I entered into the Hanuman temple—Hanuman, the god of service, the god I worship, the god I believe in. Service is the saving factor of mankind. As I walked back down the temple stairs, I heard my chelas still singing "Silent Night." With all the feeling of the evening, I yelled into the night, "Merry Christmas!" and *"Namaste!"*

"Merry Christmas, Ma!" Their voices echoed around the pond and to every corner of the ashram.

I looked toward the two trees on either side of the temple. We call them our Memory Trees. I remember when there were just a few names on the branches. Now, with the plague of AIDS always with us, the trees bear their burden. Their branches droop like rain-soaked honeysuckle. Each tree has become a collector of names, a sort of shepherd watching over the dead.

The leaves were dancing slightly in the wind. I had a floating sensation; I could feel the spirit of those who had gone on. So young, so brilliant, so vibrant—they were there with me. The candles flickered in the nighttime wind; the dark had its own light. I was in bliss. My dead were alive. The spirit became reality. I found out the dead can even laugh. Christmas Eve, and the pond was lit with floating candles while each chela held a flickering light. I said "Welcome" to my dead, and waves of ecstasy rippled through me.

Welcome, all of you. AIDS had thought it was the victor. Yet, you are still here, wandering around my ashram, coming through from the dead side of life. I shall always walk with my dead. Christmas Eve, I bow to the dead, the ash and bone, and I speak of Christ, the Christ who told me the worst thing that can happen to a human being is to have a dry heart.

मा

Thoughts of Christ bring me back to that day at the end of 1972, to that day in Brooklyn. As my husband went to sleep upstairs, I sat in the living room and began to do the breath I had learned at Jack Lalanne's. I was wearing four different sizes of Jewish stars around my neck. I didn't care; I wasn't taking any chances. I had turned every light on, including five extra tensor lamps, which I begged, borrowed, and stole. A sound startled me. I was frozen to the spot. I was sitting there in a full lotus, trembling. The sound became louder. I was ready to bolt, the same as when he came the first time, when a gentle voice said, "Stop. If you run from me now, you will never know." And suddenly, there he was, carrying his cross. He told me not to be afraid.

"Hey, who's afraid?" I said, but to the root of my being I was trembling. My hair stood on end. Everything in me became jelly.

"If you run from me now, you will never know." There was nothing I wanted to know. Oh, but what a curious woman I was, and my curiosity would get me in trouble again and again. "What will I never know?" I asked, my first real words to the Christ, and I was hooked. I was hooked for life. Or was I hooked long before that?

"If you want to go, you go. If you want to stay, you stay," said the Christ. "I am here for you now and in the heart of my mother, Mary. I am the secret of the universe."

If I allowed myself to think that I was sitting in front of God, I probably would have gone insane and run up the stairs in the full lotus again—there was no way I could have untangled my legs at that moment. So I listened intently to hear that secret, though I was shaking and deathly afraid.

He said, very softly, so softly I could hardly hear him, "The secret of the universe is love."

"Bullshit," I thought. This seemed like a cliché, some flower-child thing, and I was a tough chick from Brooklyn. There had to be another answer. I begged for another answer. I searched for another answer. But there was none. The secret of the universe is love.

I was afraid because I knew he was *real* and because of how much I loved him. I was terrified of the love I felt. I never knew there could be such love. He was inside my head, in my teeth, in my eyes, and in the roots of my hair. He was even in my breath—I was breathing him in and out.

That first night he told me that I must teach. Teach what? But that is what he said: "Teach all ways, for all ways are mine."

"I am Jewish," I said, becoming defiant from fear. "Why are all ways yours?" But even in my confusion, something in me felt the reason for his words. And then I saw he had a thumb missing, his right thumb, and I said, "This is because I'm Jewish, right, that you come to me with a piece of you missing?"

"I'm Jewish too!"

"And we're the chosen people, I suppose!" I was so scared I was shaking, and that's why I talked fresh to him like that.

He said very quietly, "I was chosen. You are chosen. Everyone is chosen. No one is ever left out."

He had walked up the few steps to where I was, cross and all. I wanted to see what was wrong with his hand, that's where I got the courage to touch him. Then I started poking him in the arm, in the shoulder. You see, he wasn't a *vision*. He was solid, he was flesh. And every time I poked him, he would crack up. Like everything was a big joke.

But what did he mean, I should *teach*?

"Teach all ways, for all ways are mine," he said, getting serious again. "As long as you can light a candle with your hands, with your eyes, with your heart, with your mind, I will be there for you and for those you teach. And, when you learn to keep that candle in the eye and can only see the sight of God, we will never be apart. For, if thine eye be single, thy body be filled with light."

I kept asking questions, asking all about his broken thumb, asking all about his life. One of the first things he said to me was to follow the story of Luke. The facts of his life had been distorted, but it was Luke who touched the heart. "Follow Luke." What did I know from Luke? When I was younger, I wasn't even allowed to look at the New Testament. "Who are you talking about?" I asked.

He had to explain. "There were four who carried my words. They were all beautiful, yet Luke has the closest word to the truth."

I didn't want to hear about Luke; I wanted to hear about him. I wanted to love him. I wanted to be his mother, his woman, his daughter. I wanted to *know* him.

"You cannot claim to know me, for I do not exist where the mind dwells. You cannot claim to know me if you cannot see me in another human being. I am not half a man, nor am I half a son to my father. You cannot see me on the left and ignore me on the right.

You cannot say I stand in front of you and say, 'My God, where is he? Not behind me?' You must know that I am all around, and you shall know my father and my mother who birthed me. For if I am all around, what must the Kingdom of Heaven be? This, here, is Heaven and Hell. Do you think these hands raised the dead or healed the sick? In my covering of flesh and skin and bone and blood, I am nothing but a son, and each day of your life you will do honor to who I have become to you: your friend, your father, your sister, your brother, your child."

"Wait a minute. Why are you with me? What strange thing called you to me? I only wanted to lose weight. I didn't want a whole course in theology." I lied. I lied. I wanted it all. My God, I wanted it all. I was in love, madly in love—every kind of love belonged to me in that moment.

"You must teach," he said again.

"Hey, I teach and I end up like you, dead and dragging a cross? And, anyway, didn't you say to your father, 'Why have you forsaken me?' when you were on the cross? Are you going to forsake me, Christ?"

"Why do you forsake me?" he answered, and as he said those words, I knew I was not forsaken. "As I was not forsaken, so shall I never forsake you." He explained it to me. When he said those words on the cross, he was afraid that people would glorify him because of the crucifixion—that it would be us that forsake him, not God, when we focus on the blood and forget about raising the level of our consciousness.

He talked clearly and beautifully, and didn't sound at all like me. "I guess you don't come from Brooklyn, do you?"

He laughed and continued: "To come to me in the clearness and the beauty of love, you must honor my mother, and this you must teach. And many will scorn you and cut you down, and say, 'This could not be, a child could not be born from a virgin.' You must teach that it could not be any other way. Books shall be written in your lifetime, and great philosophers will state it could not be; it is a scientific matter. The star that represents my birth cannot be, they will say, but you shall know, for doubt shall always come to the worthy, and the worthy will understand eventually, and doubts will always disappear from the worthy. But you must be careful that you do not teach of my mother to those who cannot hear."

I said, "I don't know your mother."

"How can a child say that she does not know her own mother? Your heart will be torn like a child left alone, if you do not acknowledge your mother."

His words ripped me open. I need to acknowledge his mother. How will I do that? I never knew the kind of mother's love I thought I needed. How do I trust his words?

He told me I would lose my family and all that I loved in the world, lose it and find it again. I knew in my heart and in the deepest place of my being that I would lose it all. I also knew that I wouldn't give up my family without a fight. Thinking of suffering, I asked him, "Why, then, do you come with a cross?"

"How then, would you, a mere child, recognize me?"

"I am not a child," I answered, boldly. "I am a woman, though I must admit I am very frightened of you."

And then he was real quiet, and it was very bright. I had every light blazing, but they were like nothing in his light. For a long time, we were just sitting there together, and I could feel my fear going away when I looked into his eyes. He was eating all my fear.

Then he said, "I shall come four times, and the fourth time I shall not be on a cross, but inside your heart. Then I shall not return to you until you become who you are. You will be able to teach the little that you know in every way that there is. You must honor the Buddha. You must honor the Hindu gods, and you must represent the Mother in all her forms. And they will stone you, and they will crucify you, but you will remember this moment and the love flowing between us, and when they ask for their own personal blessing, you will not speak of me. You will not give pearls to the swine. But, one day, they will ask for humanity, and in that same name of humanity, will you speak, and in the name of God will they understand."

I closed my eyes and listened with all my power of concentration. Time had no meaning. Then he said, "Your family will be stirring soon. Is there a place where we can go where it's quiet and private?"

I gradually unfolded my legs. One foot after the other, I got out of the lotus. Hanging onto the banister, I went up the stairs and entered the bathroom, which was the only room with a lock. The Christ followed me in. The cross always remained near him or on his shoulder because, symbolic cross or real, he carried the cross so we didn't have to.

There, in that bathroom on a cold December night, the Christ continued his teaching of life and death, joy and sorrow, happiness and fear. He said that's the main thing separating God and man—fear. And he told me about his mother. He talked a lot about Mary and how he loved her. I sat with my eyes closed and listened. He spoke and spoke, and his gentle voice soothed every part of my being. I thought we were together for about an hour. I opened my eyes and night had turned into morning. I couldn't believe it.

"What trick did you play on me?"

"Not a trick, child," he said, "but love."

It was about ten at night when he came. Now, in what seemed a blink of an eye, it was six in the morning. When I went back downstairs, I could see through the sliding glass doors that dawn was coming into the backyard. When he was gone, I still felt him in my blood and my bones like I had never felt anything before. And I was burning up like a mad woman, I loved him so much.

I had met Christ. I had met my Love.

या

Back at the temple at Kashi on Christmas Eve, I thought about all that happened in 1972, and time went like a blink of an eye again. I walked with my living chelas around my pond. I looked back and saw the dead also following me. After touching each *murti* in every temple, I stopped finally in the garden of my Christ, where his statue is protected on three sides by the tallest bamboo. I gathered my chelas, the dead and the living, and we sang "O Holy Night." We were together deep in this moment. But what moment? Aren't all moments the same? Love equalizes time.

या

As Christ had promised me, he came to me four times. The third time was right after Christmas, and I asked him, "So, what's it like being born in a manger?"

He answered me, "So what's it like being born and laid in a drawer in Brighton Beach?" What could I say? Then he told me stories of his life, and my life, the life of yesterday, and the life that would come. He started talking to me about my kids, and I realized he knew everything, including how I had bribed the nuns with "hot" gold crosses to get my kids into Catholic school.

I said, "You're Catholic, aren't you?" That's really all I knew, from going to church first with my friend Kathy and later with Sal and the family.

He just started laughing at that. "I'm not a Catholic—I'm not even a Christian. I'm not an anything. I'm everything. I'm all paths." Then he said it again, "Teach all ways for all ways are mine." I saw that he represented all paths, all ways; he represented all religions; he represented all men, all women, all children. But what did I have to teach? That's when I asked him, "What's the worst thing that can happen to a human being?"

"A dry heart," he said. "The worst thing that can happen is to have a dry heart."

When he came for the fourth time, he was very quiet and very serious. I tried to kid around, but he said, "Cut it out, Ma." That's right, he called me Ma. He talked to me about love, how much I loved him, and how much he loved me. But he said for love like this, you have to give up everything. I knew, looking at him, that nothing else in my life mattered. It was like I was looking at the whole universe. All I needed was God and my family.

He heard my thoughts. "Not now, but one day, next year or the next, you will have to walk away from your family because they do not understand." That was ridiculous. I couldn't imagine leaving my family, and yet I knew everything he told me was truth.

"Now I have to leave you," he said.

"What, you got someone else to call on?" Then his words began to sink in. "How can you leave me now?"

He said, "You have me. You will always have me. I have taken everything from you, and I have given you myself." And then he was gone! Just got up and walked out on me.

CHAPTER FORTY-SEVEN

Mount Manresa

I felt such pain, because I was in love with Christ every way a woman could be in love. And now he was gone. He had said he would return when I became who I truly was, but who was I? Before he came to me, I would have said that I was a wife, a mother, a businesswoman. But who was I now?

One day Denise came home complaining about the Catholic school retreat she had been on, a boring weekend at some monastery. As soon as she described it, I had a terrible urge to go see the place. It was Mount Manresa, a Jesuit retreat house on Staten Island. I asked her to watch the younger children, and I was off to find my Christ.

I rarely left Brooklyn in those days, but there I was, out alone in the car. I took the first right turn off the Verrazano Bridge, then a left up a long hill, the driveway to Mount Manresa. I was very frightened. I knew that something was going to happen, something that would change my life forever, and yet, why was I here if not to have something happen?

At the top of the hill, I went into the rectory and looked for a priest. I knocked on the door of the head Jesuit, Father Atherton. Here was this old priest, very tall and thin. I was very innocent. I was lost, and I was in love. "Is Christ here?" I asked.

"No," he answered, looking surprised.

That kind of shocked me, but I said, "Could I stay here? I'm looking for my Christ."

"This monastery is yours," he kindly said. I was welcome to walk around on the grounds. I went down the hill, walked along a path, and came to an arch, my heart pounding. I walked slowly through the arch, trembling and scared and alone, and there was the Christ, made of white stone. I couldn't move. What if he spoke? Then I saw his hand. His thumb was broken. It was my imperfect Christ the way he had come to me. It was my clue, my sign, my breath of spring.

I fell to my knees. The day passed into the night. I had no children, no husband, no mother, no father. I was never born, I'd never die, I couldn't walk, I couldn't fly. It didn't matter. One finger was missing from the Christ. He was real, and so my search was true.

Before I knew it, there were police behind me. Salvatore had been looking for me. I was never late in cooking dinner, and it was very late. I thought I had been kneeling there for five minutes.

I kept going back to Mount Manresa to kneel before Christ on the stones until my legs were scarred from the pebbles. I wouldn't move, as hours and hours passed. There was my Christ and there was nothing else.

The priests began to teach me about Christ because I begged to learn. I didn't want to convert; I was already in love. Then it came out that I had seen the Christ. They told me it had been a vision, and I replied, "No, I could touch him. That's why I was so scared."

They'd all talk and discuss. They would quote the Bible, and I would quote the Christ. One of the first times I was there with the priests, I remembered something Christ had told me, and I started telling them what he said. I sat there, watching myself talk. With this unbelievable Brooklyn accent, I began to spiel, and the words just kept coming from me.

I don't remember it all now, but it was about these demons inside of us that are not demons at all, but our own fears of the dark side of our lives. The demons, Christ taught me, are the fear in the human mind. So you could project something that is so small but eats away at you and becomes so big that the dark side of you projects much more darkness than the light side can project light. Evil does exist, but it exists only in the mind as negativity.

If you overcome your fear, that means you have total faith in God and there is no dark side. The dark side is created by fear, and fear comes from the dark side; it goes round and round. Faith is what sets you free. Though the demons of the mind exist, you always have the protection of Christ.

That was the first thing that the Christ had taught me, that there is no true path to him except through the heart. He also taught me how he protects us. Whenever anything scares you, he said, especially something in a vision or a dream, some presence that terrifies you, point your finger and say, "In the name of Christ, who are you?" If the apparition is not real, or if it would hurt you, it will disappear, because the power of Christ is so strong that it brings a warmth to the naked heart. If you remember that always, you need never be afraid.

I'm sure the Jesuits wondered how I, with so little education, would know how to speak such words, or how I dared to claim that they were the words of Christ. "They are not my words but those of the Christ," I would tell them.

I had touched the hem of his robe, I had felt the softness of his hands, I had heard him speak. When I would speak of Christ, these learned Jesuits could feel something. They knew, against all logic and learning, that I had seen him, because they could feel it. And they saw that I had nothing to gain by saying these words; I wanted no money, I wanted no fame, I wanted nothing but to learn where the Christ was.

Eventually they started sitting around me and asking me questions. That's how I began to teach. Sometimes they were embarrassed by my love for God. When I would go to the Stations of the Cross, I would feel each one, feel the pain of each one. Or if I went into a Protestant church, I could feel the clean emptiness of it and love that too. Or I would go into a synagogue and feel the beauty and depth of an ancient religion into which I had been born. I didn't know how to put a polite face on love. I would speak of God with tears flowing down my face, still not really knowing how to express what I felt. It was greater than having a lover, greater than putting a child to my breast, it was the greatest feeling of them all.

Catholicism brings a lot of guilt, the same as Judaism, because it is thought that only the perfect can know God. It is said in the Old Testament, "No man shall see the face of the Lord God." But many a man has seen the face of Jesus, yet did not know him to be God. My learned Jesuits had forgotten the simple stories of Christ. Why would a child so young go into the temple to discuss God with the rabbis? There they were, looking at the face of God. If they were already perfect, would he need to teach them? If they were perfect, they would not need to see him. It is the scoundrels, the sinners and the whores, who know God, and they are perfect because they are human. We are born perfect and forget our perfection. Anyone who is put upon this Earth in human form can know God, personally.

I would speak in this way to the priests. Later, I went with them into the cellars of the monastery, which were like catacombs, and they showed me some of the things that usually only Jesuits are allowed to learn. Why would they share that with me—a stranger, a woman, a Jew? Simply because they felt Christ through me when I talked of him. I just talked of my own experiences and they gathered around.

They said, "Just talk to us, speak to us, for we are willing to listen."

"And willing to deny that you listened," I said. I knew that was to be true, for the Christ had told me so. But that didn't happen until later, after I began to teach all ways.

CHAPTER FORTY-EIGHT

The Joy of God

Before finding God, I had tasted the love of a husband and the love of my children. I used to always say that I could die tomorrow and I would have had it all. There was never a happier woman in this world than I was, but from the very second that I met the Christ, I knew I had had no joy whatsoever before. There was no comparison. It was worlds and worlds and worlds apart. Now there was no satisfaction in my life. I, who had been so content with just breathing, now could barely live without him.

The joy of God can fill you, can erase all sorrows, and can erase all earthly joys. It is through God that the world becomes profoundly beautiful. One begins to see God in all things, in the pain as well as the joy. Tears of sorrow become God's tears.

The joy of God eases the way. It protects, it fulfills. From the very first intimate moment of God and me, when the fear was so great, the sweat was pouring down, and the heart was beating like drums, I felt the joy of God. And nothing remained the same, for all the Earth became the joy of God.

Before Christ could stay with me, I would go through the depths of pain, pain beyond anything I had ever known. Although I make light of the hardships in my life, if you read between the lines, it is clear that I knew pain in my childhood and youth. There was pain and there was joy, both in the fullest degree. But now I knew that everything else in my life—all joy, all pain—was nothing compared to the joy of finding my Christ, and the agony of losing him.

Why did he go? I had never yearned for anything, because I had everything. Even as a starving child, I had it all. So I needed to yearn, to want something deeply. I needed to understand what it is to be away from God, in order to teach of yearning. The only time I ever truly suffered was when I was looking for my Christ, after he left me. Then, for the first time, I knew what it was to be away from God. There was nothing, not my children, not my husband, no happiness, nothing that took away the sorrow of losing Christ.

Pain is separation from God. Ecstasy is not to be separated from God. He had to leave me so I could know this.

All I wanted was to find my Christ, my lover. I didn't want to do anything. I didn't want to cook, I didn't want to sleep, I didn't want to eat. I only wanted Christ. I started to go to every monastery and every church, asking, "Where's Christ, where's Christ, where's Christ?" I kept on knocking on church doors, asking if Christ lived there. One church, they told me right away, "No, but we have bingo." Or I would ask them when was the last time they had seen Christ in their church. They thought I was crazy. I remember one priest, he said, "What do you mean, do I ever *see* Christ?"

"Can you see Christ? Can you touch his flesh? Can you feel his breath upon your neck?"

"Lady, if that ever happened I'd quit in a minute," he said.

How could this be? My search became more desperate, and I would sneak out alone in our big black Cadillac and drive all around Brooklyn looking for Christ.

या

I had no control. I'd go into ecstasy and just fall down where I stood. It was the world that was twirling, twirling, and twirling. One day, I fell down on the street, with the keys in my hand and the car parked a little ways away. A big black guy came over and picked me up in his arms. The cops came over and asked him what I was on, because what could I possibly be doing there? Was I a whore? A junkie? They grabbed my arms to search for track marks. They were ready to lock me up. But this man told them, "Oh no, she's just sick. She was coming here to our meeting," and he carried me into a storefront church. That's how I went to my first revival meeting.

From having been with Christ, I had all the power of God running through me, all the power of *shakti* in my hands, all this love for humanity, and all these soapboxes to stand on. And I couldn't handle it—it was so powerful and so sudden.

So here I was in some place that used to be a laundromat. There was a big mother of a bathtub on a platform where the dryers used to be, and they were baptizing people. "Do you take the Lord Jesus in your heart and your soul?"

The man who saved me from the police said, "Come up, child. Come up, child."

I went up there on the platform, and he asked, "What are you doing here?"

I said, "I don't know. All I know is that I'm looking for Christ."

This one woman they called Mama, the leader of the choir, said, "Listen to me sing. When you sing, God listens. Do you think the Lord only listens to those that are pure? Do you think that the Lord Jesus never looks at the sinners? One day your hands will have the power to bless, for you have touched Christ in a way none of us have."

"How did you know?" I asked.

"Cause you're still carrying your purse, and you're here in one piece. Now sing, child."

I didn't know what to sing. I didn't know where to begin. I'd been Jewish all my life, and I knew the Catholic church, but nobody ever once asked me to stand up on a stage and sing to God.

She said, "Belt it out—belt out what you feel."

I looked around me, and I just saw people looking for the same Christ that I was looking for. And I sang:

> *Why did you come to me my lord just four times?*
> *Didn't you know that I was yours and you were mine?*

Pretty soon we were all singing to my Christ, just singing and stomping and carrying on, and for a few hours I could stop my crazy searching. He was more in that storefront than in all those churches I had been running to, running here and there so desperate to find my Christ.

People were leaving. The man who found me said, "Time to go home. I'll walk you to your car."

I got into that big black Cadillac. He said, "Thank you, child."

"You saved my life," I said. "You saved me from a call to my husband to come get me out of jail."

"You know the 'Jailhouse Blues'?"

"I was brought up on them."

"Well, sing it on your way home."

And I hummed the blues all the way home. There was Salvatore, waiting at the front door. My face was streaked, for I was crying. Not for one second did this jealous Italian think I was with another man, for he knew that I was out looking for God any place I could find him.

CHAPTER FORTY-NINE

Swami Bhagawan Nityananda

My statue at Mount Manresa was the closest I had come in my search for Christ, and for a while it helped the ache in my heart. I was still begging for Christ, even as I knelt before him. I was still searching. Where was the man himself, my God, my friend, my lover? He had promised to return, but when?

At Mount Manresa, I would climb the steps to the belfry looking for solitude, looking for my Christ. The lower steps were in darkness, with a spiral staircase going up. I shut the door so no one could know I was in that small space, all alone in the dark with my racing heart. At the top, where the bells were, it was light, and I could see the birds fly in and out. I began to climb, with a prayer on every step. On my first step, I would pray, "God, be here." The second step, I'd say, "God, please don't be here." Then "God, be here." Then "God, don't be here." All the way up to the tower. See, I know the game, because I played it myself. You want it and you don't want it. We've all said it: "Touch me, God, but not too hard."

Winter became spring, and where was my Christ? I wanted him desperately. Christ had told me, "I will only come to you four times, and then I will not come to you until you become who you are." When he didn't come again, I cried as if I had lost a child; I cried as if my fingers were cut off. He said I must teach, but I didn't know what to teach, or to whom. I didn't know what to do. "Where are you? Where are you?" I was out of my head. Where was my lover? He was my lover, he was everything to me, and he had disappeared.

As months went by, I started getting very sick. My heart was very sick. The only thing I knew was the breath I had learned at Jack Lalanne's. I would go in the bathroom, the only place I could lock the door, and I would do that breath, sometimes all night. All this time I had kept up with the yoga. Donna let me back into class, and I just never mentioned it to Sal. I even had Donna giving classes at my house for my friends, and then I would sell them clothes. After a while I started making up my own asanas, although I wasn't really making them up. They just seemed to come to me, I had no idea from where.

I started sitting in the bathtub to meditate because, even though I kept the house spotless, sometimes there were water bugs on the floor. They came in through the air conditioner. Grandma Sadie had warned me, "If a water bug goes up your tomato you could get pregnant." So really the bathtub was nothing esoteric, just a little memory of Grandma Sadie and Red Hook. I would fill up the tub with warm water to be nice and comfortable, and I would sit in full lotus.

I would sit in the tub for hours, and when I tried to get out, I couldn't move my legs from sitting so long in the lotus posture. So I would slip my hands to the top of the bathtub, lift myself out, and crawl into the bed on my hands and knees. Gradually during the night the muscles would relax, and I would get possibly an hour's sleep.

I wanted God. And when he didn't come after teasing me with four visits, I screamed out in the agony of the garden, "Know me, God. Know me because I deserve for you to know me. Know me, my God. Do not let another day pass without touching my soul." I was mad for God, wild with hunger for something that was deep inside me.

I demanded God, twenty-four hours a day. I wanted it all. I neglected three children and a husband. I only wanted God, with every living breath. What is there, more than God? But for most people you want more than God. You want peace, you want comfort, you want joy, you want eternal life, you want all these fringe benefits. And so you make the desire for God less. You say, "I want God so I can be happy." I did not think about happiness. I WAS happy; I had a beautiful home, a good business, three children, a good-looking husband who was madly in love with me and I with him. I had what so many other women wanted. I wasn't disturbed. I wasn't neurotic. I wanted no fringe benefits; I wanted God. I had always wanted God, but did not know it.

As a child who was brought up in a cellar with pipes overhead, or married with three kids in three rooms, I still wanted God. I just didn't know what to call it. Finally I felt him—I felt God. It wasn't happiness; it wasn't anything I'd ever known. I wanted God just for God's sake, just for that which was. I wanted God.

I threatened him, I begged him, I crawled in the backyard on my hands and knees until my knees bled. I did that breath eight hours a night for months and months, until my throat was so bad one doctor told me I had throat cancer. Another one looked at my nose and thought I had a cocaine habit because the membranes were so burned just from doing that breath night after night.

After a while, Sal wanted to commit me for my own protection. He thought I was crazy. What else could he think? I didn't care what anyone thought because nothing mattered to me but God. I would scream out in that backyard in Brooklyn, "Touch me and take me. Strip me of pride, strip me of ego, and even, if you must, strip me of God." I didn't even know what I was saying; the words would just come. Imagine, a beautiful woman yelling like that: "Strip me, strip me." We had this neighbor who would lean out his window. "I'll strip ya," he'd go. Sal would come and yell at me, "Get in the house!"

How many of you, sitting in your home with three children and a husband, would say, "Take me God, at any cost?" I don't think you would, if you really believed, as I did, that God heard you. But I did that—I screamed it loud, and I screamed it clear. No price was too great to pay, no price was too heavy. And believe me, the price was very heavy. Eventually, I would lose everything.

One day I decided that if God would not come to me, I would go to him. I decided I was going to die, but first I ironed all the kids' clothes and put a week's worth of dinner in the freezer. I went into my bathroom at eight o'clock at night. I knew I would not come out until I saw God.

I did the breath I learned at Jack Lalanne's because that was still all I knew—breathing in and breathing out, until there was no breath at all. At about one in the morning, Swami Nityananda came to me, a huge man with a big belly and round head, naked except for a little loincloth. When I opened my eyes he was sitting before me on the toilet bowl, with the lid down. I shut my eyes fast, but he was still there. This was not possible. Was I ready for Bellevue? Was I dying? How fast could I get out of that bathtub?

When Christ was before me, he had told me that many others would come and that they would be from different religions and different ways of life. He even described Swami to me and told me that he, too, would be God. But when Swami came to me, I just wanted him gone.

"What are you doing here? You don't belong here. I want Christ. You're not here. You don't exist." I went to push him out and there was flesh! I was petrified. I was in a state of absolute horror, for I wanted my Christ, my lover, not some fat man wearing a little cloth like a diaper. I had no knowledge of this man. "Where are your clothes? What are you doing here? I asked for Jesus, and this is what I get?"

He wouldn't talk. So finally I said, "Can you bring my Christ to me?"

He replied, "This one cannot bring the Christ to you, but this one can bring you to the Christ."

That was all he would say, but that was all I needed to hear. (Whenever Swami spoke to me, he spoke in the third person, calling himself "this one.")

The next day I started to get my health back. The bags under my eyes began to lessen, and I had some strength that I hadn't had for a long time. Swami had started to bring health back into my body and prepare me for *samadhi*.

In the bathroom the next night, I said, "Okay, speak to me." But he didn't speak. I begged him to speak, I insulted him, I called him fat, I tried to make him go away. But I began to wait for nighttime to come so I would see him. If I had to go crazy, let me go crazy with someone as kind and stern-looking as this man. But except for that one night, he didn't speak a word. He just taught me by his presence and his silence, night after night.

I went through the days like one who is blind and knows not what she does. I told the girls to take any merchandise they wanted from the store. I was steadily losing a hundred dollars a day. Nothing mattered.

I knew nothing and I was petrified. If anyone who is truly on the path to God tells you that they're not afraid, they're lying. But though my fear was great, my curiosity was greater. It's only curiosity and the longing for God that keeps you going no matter what.

CHAPTER FIFTY

Nothing but Ash

I was completely alone. I had no teacher that anyone would call alive. I had lost most of my old friends by now. The only person who stayed by me through everything was my friend Fran, who I had first met when Sal and I were trying to get rid of our Cord.

I went into the bathroom each night, and Swami would come at 9:30. He didn't speak, but he trained me to be able to sit straight for hours. When one sits in samadhi, the body must be straight but not rigid. He wouldn't even look at me unless I sat up straight. That was really my first teaching. He trained me like that for months. He showed me that if we sit stooped over we are not being humble, we are just letting ourselves be defeated by the weight of the world. But if we extend ourselves to our full height, with a straight back, we can carry the world upon our shoulders.

I had to be trained hard like that to be able to handle what was happening to me. Like Saint Teresa of Avila, when she would float to the ceiling with her love of God, I didn't know what was happening to me. And as I had no teacher to reassure me, I thought I had gone crazy. Yet, there was no place else I could be except right there in my bathroom.

But if my Swami was real, he must speak to me. Night after night, I would beg him to talk. He would sit so silent and straight, sometimes playing with his own toes, but not speaking a word. I cried, I whimpered, I begged, I screamed out in despair. I didn't exactly want to hear what he had to say, but I didn't understand the silence.

In the beginning, when I said, "Talk, talk," and reached out to touch him, sometimes my hands went right through him. Other times I would go to touch him and find that there was something to touch, that this was a man of flesh and blood sitting in my bathroom.

My fear was not of the unknown, for the unknown had no meaning to me by that time. My greatest fear was that one day he would not be there.

Finally, one night he said to me, "If this one speaks to you, you must heed his words."

That should have slowed me down, but I said, "Speak, speak—anything!"

He told me I must become celibate. I laughed in his face, but I knew I would do what he said. Whether he was a piece of my imagination coming forth to torture me, or whether he was God himself, I didn't care. I knew he could take me to my Christ.

"Then show me the universe," I said, thinking I was cute. I had read that someplace, in the *Bhagavad Gita*, I think. I had never gone to school, but Franny and I were reading books now, trying to understand what was happening to me.

Swami said, "Let me show you a hundred years from now what will be," and he took me to the rooms in which my three children and my husband were sleeping. On each bed was nothing but dust, little piles of dust. And I knew in that moment that life was nothing without God, that in reality we will return to ash. He showed me the nothingness of the body and the perfection of the soul. There was truly nothing more that I had to grasp. I knew I belonged no place but in the arms of God.

Oh, but first I freaked completely! These were my babies! I screamed, "Bring them back! Bring them back!" Then he brought them back. But even as I freaked, I understood.

He said, "This one is asking you to give up this, the body."

It was nothing to give up, because it was everything to give up. Because the body is so full and wonderful, it was a magnificent gift to give the gods. You can't give a hollow gift. You must give up the fullness of life, and then you receive the fullness of life.

Why did I do as he told me? Everything was slipping. I had lost my business. My husband thought I was crazy. I was neglecting the house. I was no longer who I had been. I couldn't go back, but I couldn't go forward without a teacher. So I had to do what he said because I had no other choice. Once I had seen Christ, once I had seen God, there was no way to go back to my normal way of living, so I had to go on.

So when Swami would ask, "Is this one scaring you?" I would say "No." No matter how scared I was, there was always the worse fear that he would stop. Meanwhile, the terrible fear of learning was tearing me apart, so I was torn from one fear to another. The fear of learning is that once you hear wisdom, it can't be ripped down or thrown away. Fear enters the heart like a tornado because you can't go back to what you were a second before. That's what Swami meant when he said, "If this one speaks to you, you must heed his words."

It was such a crazy time, I had all this power of God in my hands from being with the Christ, and I didn't know what God intended me to do with all the power. I thought I had heard Christ say to me, "Teach always," so I did. I would go see my tough Italian friends and tell them about God. I lost a lot of friends like that, but I was in search of Christ, and that's all I knew.

I also knew I had to touch people, I had to use this thing that was happening to me. I had no interest in possessing this power. I was trying all day to give it away to whoever would take it. People aren't used to that so I was always making trouble, wherever I went.

Finally, I was introduced to a wonderful priest who took me to a hospital where I began working with children who had leukemia. In those days, these children had almost no hope. A child would die, and the nurse would come around and say to the other children, "Oh, Johnny went home." I kind of went along with this for a while until one little girl said to me, "We know they're lying." She was really little. "Johnny would never go home and leave his favorite blanket and his teddy bear," she said. "We all know we're gonna die."

These kids taught me never to lie to the dying, no matter how young. The dying know. Trust the dying person, and if they want you there, be there with your whole being. Give them love, give them yourself, and just by being there you will help them go ever so gently into the arms of death.

I got in trouble after that, because I began to talk straight to these kids and tell them where Johnny did go. Explaining to them that hope was always there brought tears to their eyes and my own. To the really little ones, I would say, "Sweetheart, God loves you, and you're special." And I always made sure to tell them all that the sickness wasn't their fault in any way, that it wasn't a punishment, because young children will sometimes think like that.

We didn't talk about death all the time, just when they asked. Most of the time we played and laughed. I found that these kids had learned for themselves how to make the most of every moment of their short lives. Finally I was thrown out, literally, by the security guards, for bringing too many cookies and toys and breaking the rules. They said I was spoiling the kids! But that was after a long time. I'll never forget those children making the most of their days looking out a hospital window. How can you spoil such sick kids? Though the pain was great, their love of life was even greater.

CHAPTER FIFTY-ONE

Not a Kiddy Pool

The posters read, "Ma Jaya: Initiation into Shakti." It was 1992 and I had been traveling in my bus all over the country to teach, but for a moment I wondered how I would teach about shakti to people unfamiliar with the idea. My mind raced back to Swami, telling me that I held inside of me the renewal of shakti here in the West. Who knew from strange words from strange lands? Remember, I quit school when I was fourteen. Riding in my bus, I remembered how I became aware of shakti, this flowing essence of God.

मा

One hot day in Brooklyn, back when my life was normal, I told Sal I'd like a pool for the kids, not just my kids, but for all the kids in the neighborhood. There were never less than ten kids sitting at my table. He said, "No."

I just kept talking. "An over-the-ground pool, you know, like for kids."

"Well," he finally said, "okay, a little wading pool."

"An over-the-ground pool. You're saying I can buy an over-the-ground pool?"

"All right, from the Sears Roebuck you get a pool and put it on the credit thing."

So I looked at a catalogue, and it said, "First time on the market—hexagonal pool—the biggest one in the country." He thought I would maybe buy a kiddy pool for teenagers? So I ordered the hugest over-ground pool known to man. It was an experimental model. Three trucks arrived at six or seven in the morning, and the men worked all day to put it up. Sal had already left for work when they came. They left about five minutes before he got home.

Our house had sliding glass doors going out to the backyard. Sal was sitting at the dinner table, eating the spaghetti when, all of a sudden, he was staring like he was seeing something from outer space. I kept busy serving the dinner, and the kids knew they shouldn't even look at anybody. It was like the man had turned to stone. It took ten minutes for him to breathe. Finally, he said, "What the hell is that?"

"They made a mistake with the order," I said, and looked him straight in the eye.

He called up Sears, but it was already done, the poles were cemented in. So he said to me, "Your pool. You take care of it." I kept it spotless, but that meant I had to learn to go with the thing and measure, mix this into that, and make sure the water was right. I had the most gorgeous purple-colored water. I'm surprised those kids didn't all die from my pool, but they had their pool, and I was happy.

But a few years later I got into this God business, and there I was in Brooklyn, trying to make normal, which meant still taking care of the pool. You had to let the water out through the outlet, and then with the filter you let new water in. So one day I was down there under the deck—the pool was about five feet deep, with decks and ladders—and as the water went rushing out, I thought, "All the water's going into my head." I felt like I was consuming water. "Now what's happening to me?"

I turned to water. I heard a voice saying, "I shall teach you, I shall take you, I shall give you water, and you shall quench the earth."

Of course the first thing I thought was, "I'll lose weight again. If I'm made of water, I don't have to eat." But it was a feeling right through the top of the head, just flowing, flowing water, never ending.

मा

That was my initiation into shakti. I didn't have a live teacher to help me, and I was scared. I didn't know what it was. For all I knew it was a brain tumor, but the flowing went right through me, and it didn't stop, ever. It started when I was fixing that pool, and it still flows through me to this day.

It is an expression of my love for my God, this shakti that flows through me and into other people. It's the same thing that you can feel in a moment of giving; it's warm and liquidy. I'll always remember being under the deck of that pool, beginning to understand, and trying to figure out how to let the water of shakti flow out for all people. In reality, it was always there within me, it just had to be felt, looked upon, touched, and heard.

That night Swami had to explain it to me. (He was talking to me now, ever since the night when he showed me the piles of ash.) He asked me what I felt when I visited hospitals and took care of the dying. I said I felt good, but sad, and I was honored that the sick, lonely, and dying trusted me enough to let me place my hands on their brows, plant a kiss on their cheeks, or just sit with them, holding hands till the end.

Swami said one simple word that got me thinking: "Why?"

I said it was because I wanted to bring a little joy to everyone. It made me happy in my heart to see the sick ones smile.

"That, my dear Jaya, is shakti. The joy you bring people and want to bring people is an actual substance that we all have dwelling within us, waiting for the holy to come activate it and tease it alive." He continued, "When shakti is awake, it melts one's resistance to love and affection. Judgment is drowned in the waters of the Mother."

"Whoa!" I said. "What are you talking about? What are the waters of the Mother? Is it like the waters that the baby floats around in before birth?"

"Yes, it's like the waters of a pregnant woman that protect her young. When you go and visit the sick, you bring them the mist of the Mother; that mist is an actual substance. It says to the one lying in the bed, 'You're a human being. You're not this disease that ravishes your body'."

"Service cannot be dry," he continued. "It must be, it has to be, soaking wet, drenched in the love of God, and you, my Ma, have the ability to bring this shakti, or soul waters, to all who cross your path. Go out and initiate them into shakti. She is the Divine One, the Mother who dwells at the base of the spine. She stays asleep there until awakened by her own self in one who cares enough to want to touch humanity, withstanding the judgment of the world."

Finally I understood. My life was coming apart at that time. Every time I seemed to get closer to my Christ, I went further from my family. I was in love with God, and the jealousy Salvatore felt went beyond even the jealousy he would have felt if I had taken a lover. After all, how could he compete with God?

"Shakti is the female power of the Goddess herself," my Swami continued. "She has to go from one vessel to another; one gives, and one receives. Shakti then rises in the one receiving, and his whole life changes. As she goes toward the different centers, or chakras, the receiver rises out of the place of indifference and enters into the world of God and the Mother. However, shakti can be dangerous without a teacher or guru. There is always a chance that one will use the serpent power, as shakti is sometimes known, for personal gain, thus limiting oneself to the feeling of power instead of bliss. Power without love is nothing. Love and power together, that's shakti."

"Swami, is it necessary to know all this?" I asked. I wanted to go on to the next subject, but Swami wouldn't let it go. He hammered the meaning of shakti into me until I fully understood. The simplest way to put it is that shakti is the movement of the Earth in the form of God the Mother. The stillness is, of course, God the Father. Shakti is the emptiness and the fullness at the same time.

CHAPTER FIFTY-TWO

Is Rudi Here?

While I was still going to Mount Manresa and seeing Swami Nityananda every night, I started going to Rudi's ashram in New York City. Rudi, or Swami Rudrananda, was an American disciple of Swami Nityananda, but of course I didn't know that at the time. I had no idea that the man in my bathroom was real. Remember, I just figured I was crazy. The first time I went to Rudi's was to take Fran there. She was into drugs at that point, and I was urging her to quit, but she had read Rudi's book *Spiritual Cannibalism* and thought Rudi could help her.

I wasn't even allowed out of Brooklyn, except to Staten Island. That was Sal's rule, which was okay with me. That's where Fran and Ritchie lived, and Sal was okay with me being around the priests. I did all my dealings in Brooklyn, especially Red Hook and Canarsie, riding around in Sal's big black Cadillac with the red interior and a sunroof that opened up electronically. We had "Sal" written in elegant script on the driver's door, and "Joyce" on the passenger door.

Manhattan was not my territory. So when Fran asked me to take her to Rudi's in Manhattan, the first thing I said was, "Don't bother me with this nonsense."

What happened next was that a nun called me and gave me this whole story about how no one would give her a ride to Harlem. With the kids in Catholic school, by this time I knew a lot of nuns. To Sal, anything Catholic was good, so I told her okay. To me, Manhattan was like another country, so I decided I'd take care of everything in New York in one day. I'd take both Fran and the nun where they wanted to go, and then they'd leave me in peace.

It was July 1973, and the temperature was over ninety degrees. The nun, you have to understand, was a cloistered nun, so she wore a habit, with the black veil. Over the habit was a white thing around her neck and shoulders that pretty soon looked purple from sweat because, as soon as we were on the road, the car's air conditioner broke.

We were the only white people driving around in the middle of Harlem on a hot summer day in that big Cadillac. Fran was talking about Rudi, Rudi, Rudi, and how he would help her. So we dropped off one nun and picked up another, who wanted a ride to Brooklyn. The new nun was sweating, we were all sweating, and I was wondering what we were gonna do with a nun while we went looking for this Rudi. We finally found the address we were looking for, and the nun asked, "Is this a religious organization?"

"I don't know," I answered, truthfully. So she decided to stay and sweat in the car.

There were twenty pairs of shoes outside the door. I caught a whiff of incense, and then this guy came out. He was wearing rosaries, I thought, because he had beads all around his neck. Now these disciples of Rudi's, they were very tuned into energy, very tuned into shakti, the same force that had been running through me so powerfully since I met the Christ. So when this guy looked at me, he felt the shakti right away, and he said, "Wow, where you been all my life?"

I said something extremely rude in Brooklynese to him, and then I asked, "Where's Rudi?"

The same look came over his face as the priests got when I asked, "Does Christ live here?" He didn't tell us anything, he just gave us the address of an antique store called Dealer's Choice. "Perhaps you'll find that information there," he said.

I'd never been in an antique store before. There were all these weird statues there. They were beautiful, and I felt this warmth come over me, really come over me a lot. I had no idea what was happening to me, but I later found out that the statues were *murtis,* statues of the Hindu gods.

The store had belonged to Rudi and his mother. Now Rudi's followers used part of it for classes. While Fran signed up for a class, I just stared at the statues. Suddenly I noticed the book *The Art of Tantra.* Now, all I knew about Hinduism I got from Donna, the yoga teacher at Jack Lalanne's. Once she had told me, "Stay away from anything about *tantra.*" She said that because, to a lot of people who don't understand the true meaning of tantra, which is the merging of man into God, the word "tantra" just means sex. So I said to the guy, Richard Smith, Rudi's chela who was running things, "Hey, you, what's this tantra?"

"It's a secret, sacred class."

"Yeah? Well, you better not touch this little girl. I know just what you people do," I said, and I stormed out of there with Fran following me.

When we were finally on the way back home, the nun started to faint, and we had to stop the car and get newspapers to fan her. None of us thought to go into a restaurant with air conditioning. Fran and I were feeling very strange. It felt a teeny, teeny drop like when I first met Christ, a very tiny drop of the same essence. And I couldn't get the statues out of my mind. As a Jew, I knew they had something to do with idolatry, like the golden calf, but still they did something to my whole being, especially the dancing man with a lot of hands and one foot up.[4] That whole night the statue just kept dancing in my head. It was like a lost world—and a world found.

I called up Richard Smith the next day and asked if I could see him. I had no intention of going to class. I just wanted to be in that store

---

4   Nataraj, the dancing Shiva.

with those statues. Fran and I started going every day to Dealer's Choice. I had never been to Manhattan without my husband, but this was something I had to do. I just had to be there every day, though I didn't know why.

Every night I was with my Swami. I'd make myself sleep maybe one hour, and then I'd get up at 4:30 every morning and begin silently cleaning the house, nothing that would make a lot of noise. Then I'd crawl back into bed just in time to wake up with Sal at six. While I made breakfast for the kids, I would start to prepare supper. The second Sal left for work and the kids were on their way to school, I shot right out of there and picked up Fran. We begged, borrowed, and stole any car we could get our hands on, because there was no way we weren't going. Her husband Richie knew what was going on, and he worked with Sal, so he would cover for us. We'd get back at one o'clock in the afternoon, just before Sal got home.

I didn't know why I was there, but more and more I felt a certain deep connection with the statues in the store. I would just sit there and watch people come in. They would sit in front of Richard, and he worked with them. They looked into each other's eyes, and they drew the shakti from him. When I tried it, I couldn't understand what was happening, because it seemed to me that Richard and the other Rudi devotees were all pulling from me instead of me pulling from them, yet these guys were supposed to be the teachers. They would say, "Pull, pull," when there was nothing to pull.

Remember, I had already met God so this power was running through me. It was more than I could handle; it was driving me crazy because I didn't know what to do with it. And here were all these people who were trying so hard just to taste a little bit of this power. I felt bad because people were starting to come in to see me instead of Rudi's teachers. Soon I saw it was going to be the same situation as at Mount Manresa, where I had gone there to learn and ended up teaching. Meanwhile, I was waiting for Rudi to show up, because he was the guru, and he would get things straightened out. Fran and I waited months for Rudi to appear, but no one ever bothered to tell us that he had been dead for over a year.

I didn't go to any classes at Dealer's Choice. I just sat there. One day I went to the bathroom, and it was filthy dirty. I had always had a thing about bathrooms, even more so since the bathroom at home had become my temple, so I began cleaning the store's bathroom, the toilet bowl especially.

I also loved to clean the statues. I'd bring my own little bottle of Pledge and make love to the statues with Pledge. One day Richard Smith turned around and saw me polishing a bench that they had in the window. The bench was perfect. It was inlaid stone, mother of pearl, and cost like $48,000. He saw me putting Pledge on it, and he screamed so loud, with such passion, that it was like the Red Sea was opening up. All of a sudden, in my hand there was a piece of inlay.

"You ruined it!"

That's when they told me I couldn't use Pledge anymore. I could only clean their toilet bowls.

CHAPTER FIFTY-THREE

Glimpses of Samadhi

Summer turned to fall, then winter. We had friends who lived in the Poconos, and we went up there for New Year's. It was Sal, the kids, and me, and Fran and her husband Richie. It was very cold.

I had just gotten my diary, and I planned to start writing in it with the new year. Although Fran and I had tried to read some books, I really knew nothing except that a very deep part of my soul was yearning for an even greater depth. So I was going to write about God and the depth of God. At that time, I had a lot of questions because Swami had begun to tell me that my guru was coming. What did that mean?

I was wondering what was to become of me. I had a little girl of six, a son, a grown daughter, and a husband. And here we were with friends. Our friend was a state trooper, and he and his wife owned a motel. It was New Year's Eve as 1973 was turning into 1974. As I watched everybody drinking, I sat in the corner, writing, writing. I wondered why I never could get intoxicated, no matter what I drank or how much I drank. When I was a teenager in Red Hook, all the old Italians would sit with me. We'd drink and drink, they'd collapse, and I would just keep going.

Everyone but me was getting drunk, but I knew that nothing in this world would ever give me the feeling that I had the first time I met the Christ. And if Christ would not come back to me, what did my life hold?

I went outside. Everybody was finally asleep, but for me sleep had stopped. The lake was freezing over, dawn was breaking, and I spotted a rowboat. I got in and went out on the lake. There was only one oar, but I just kept rowing.

Death wasn't on my mind, just life. I wanted to understand what these people felt that night. Sometimes now I could see into people's minds and know what they felt, and it scared me to see that what they felt was not ambrosia, was not the excitement they intended to feel. It was empty, it was tinny, it was a drug, it was liquor. It was forcing oneself to become happy. If the only true happiness came from seeing Christ and no one saw him, what good was life?

As I thought about all this, I kept going farther out on the lake. I have never been depressed in my life. But here I was, for the first time, feeling for the world, for the sadness of it and the loneliness of it. It was the first time I had looked at my family that way. Until Christ had come, they were my whole world, and I loved them so much. But I never looked deeply enough to see the pain in those I thought I knew.

Finally, I noticed water around my feet, and then it was rising higher. The leaky boat started to sink, down, and down, and down, and down. But I was becoming not cold, but warm. I had gone into samadhi, still not understanding what that was, and in samadhi the body is very, very cold, so cold that the icy water of the lake was warming my body. And I was slipping away.

Years later, I learned the words of the poet Ramprasad. As he was doing *puja* in the sacred Ganga, he went into the oneness of God and disappeared into the waters. In his last poem, he had written,

> *How can I slumber anymore? My slumber I have lulled asleep for evermore.*
>
> *Now I am wide awake in the sleeplessness of yoga.*

I didn't know anyone else who had ever felt as I did, but I felt the warmth of the freezing pond upon my cold body. It felt as God should feel. It felt caressing. It felt like making love. It felt like ecstasy.

Then I heard the words "Ma, Ma." Again I heard them. I saw a man with a bandanna around his head. Another Indian holy man had popped up in my life, but to me he just looked weird and wild. I was getting used to this by now, so I noticed his bandanna, and I asked him if he was the new chef. "Being that we're all crazy here, do you cook?"

"Why is it that you want to leave your body now?" he asked.

"I do not, but the warmth feels so good," I answered.

He said, "I am Shirdi Sai Baba," and he placed in my hand a little murti of Shirdi, a little brass statue. It was solid, it was real. And I began screaming, screaming at him that he didn't exist. Everybody from the motel woke up and came out, I screamed so loud. The wind came up, and the rowboat was pushed to the shore. Fran was there crying. And I was there, not feeling cold, but feeling very warm, though I was shivering. I was shivering with the excitement of what my life held. Yet my life at that very moment was in the midst of the most chaos possible.

Here was a family, a home, a husband. And here was God. There were choices to be made, and yet there was never a choice. For here was God, and the rest was just floating away. It was never really a choice, for if you put God here, what else is there? Where are your choices? You have none—no matter how fierce the world seems to you or how beautiful, no matter how it beckons you. No one—no man, no woman, no child—can give you what God can give you.

I kept that little murti. I still carry it with me everywhere, so many years later.

Shirdi Sai Baba became a frequent visitor to my bathroom temple after that day. In India he was known to both Hindus and Muslims as a holy man who often performed miracles, and he still does. In his presence I knew I wasn't crazy after all, or if I was it didn't matter. Of course I didn't know who he was, but that was nothing new. I didn't know who Swami was either, and he was with me every night. Ramana Maharshi would come to my temple sometimes, and Mary would appear in different places in my house. I would light a candle every place I saw her, including the middle of the floor, and try to remember to blow them out before Sal came home and burned himself.

CHAPTER FIFTY-FOUR

Notes from My Blue Diary

I started writing in my little blue diary on New Year's Eve and kept it up for about three months. On every page were secret mystical numbers. The secret they held was my weight, but I hid the true number in my own secret code.

Every day I did yoga and wrote down what I did. Every night Swami Nityananda came to me, and I placed a little flower before him—I drew it in the book and placed it at his feet.

What I want you to understand from the diary is that I was just like any person on a spiritual path: sometimes scared, sometimes confused, sometimes excited.

Here's my diary from January 14, 1974: "All that man must know in this life lies within himself. The search must start and end there." This is what Swami Nityananda had told me. In the very beginning, I'd say to him, "You're here to take me to my Christ. You're here for no other reason. I don't even like you." Then he'd say, "Your Christ is inside you." I'd write that in my diary, or I'd call up Fran and tell her, "Christ is inside you."

The next day, I wrote, "To know God, one must search deeply inside. To know one's guru one must wait."

Sometimes I begged him to be my guru, but on another page I wrote, "I have no guru, but all gurus have me." I wrote that in total anger, so mad at Swami, the way he seemed to be playing with me.

A few days later in January I wrote, "Jesus the Christ has become one of my dearest friends and teachers." I wrote in pencil, and on top of the page I drew a Jewish star. Sometimes it still scared me that I was Jewish and yet I loved Christ, so much so I drew a Jewish star and then I drew a cross. In code I wrote my weight that day, which was still quite a big number, but during that period of my life the weight kept me a little bit grounded, sane, in my body. On the next page, I wrote, "Spiritual life is not an easy path but it is my only way to live. I pray my children and Sal will see your light, Oh Lord, and be comforted by it. I love them all so much."

Swami once said to me, "So you think you love your husband. So you think you love your children. What is this love? MY husband, MY children, MY home. This is not love; this is possession, attachment. You don't know the meaning of love."

I, who loved my husband and children so deeply, could not understand. I stared into his eyes, this stern, hard, harsh man. In his eyes were pools and pools of love, and I knew for the first time that complete love is giving totally of yourself without ever looking to see who is taking. After the Christ, Swami was the first to show me the meaning of unconditional love.

"Do what you must," I told him. That which was precious to me seemed like so little to give up, for the truth was so much greater. I was giving up my husband who I adored, my three children, my business, my friends. I was stripped naked. I was scared and alone. I said, "Swamiji, Swamiji, what else can you take? If there is anything else, take it from me." Every day I was torn like that between my family and my God.

I remember Swami saying, "Those that you love the most—they may call you crazy for your want of God." That was already happening. Of course they thought I was crazy, and so did I. But I didn't even hesitate. "I want, I want, I want!" I, who had never wanted anything for myself, I screamed for God with great agony and great pain. You see, I had been tricked. I already had God; I was born with the awareness of God. But in leaving me, Christ had set me on the path of a seeker. I had to seek God, and I had to yearn desperately to know what most people feel on the spiritual path. How could I teach if I had not felt all this for myself?

Although I suffered as if I had a choice, in reality I had none. My only choice was that I could have gone slower. Curiosity got the best of me, so I went quite fast. Curiosity and also a vague sense of the chelas waiting for me—my students who would come when I was ready for them—hurried me on with great urgency. I had no idea where I'd end up, but I was determined to get there as quickly as I could, wherever it was, and at any cost. The only cost that mattered was my family. And so every day I would pray that they too would know God, and I would write that on a page in the journal.

On another page of the diary, I wrote, "One must conquer fear of different dimensions"—I never graduated from high school and here I was writing all this stuff—"and have faith in one's guru and God. I feel as if I am on a honeymoon with God." That was true. It was one of the most incredible times of my life.

January 23rd: "As each day passes, I go deeper and closer to you, my Lord. And fear of the unknown is gradually ceasing, as my faith in you grows stronger."

"Nityananda," I wrote, and I drew his flower.

"One believes in himself, and then one can believe in God, for God is in all human beings."

Another day: "My whole head chakra is wide open, and my heart is filled with bliss." That's how I walked around all day—in bliss, but crying, crying, crying. "The sweetness of knowing God is beyond words." I was in ecstasy all the time—ecstasy and pain, all the time, constant ecstasy and constant pain. Pain because I couldn't sit all day with God. I had cleaning, cooking, running around, taking care of children, managing what was left of my business, and keeping house. It was pain from not doing what I wanted to do.

In my diary I wrote, "I will continue to practice the spiritual exercises no matter what path I take." I had picked up that phrase, spiritual exercises, but that's not what I meant. I meant just sitting there and loving God. On another page I wrote, "Love," and then "I love God. Bless my family, please, Oh Lord, and be their father."

Every day was brand new. "What an exciting day. The work of the Lord is quite strange and beautiful. Studied with Fran. I do not know how to express my love for God, for there are no words. Went to the movie with my Sal."

Then I wrote, "When I see the light, I know." The body, as you realize when you start to leave it, is actually made of light, or the same substance as light. As you leave your body, you are that light, and your body becomes that light, and even the place where you are is light. So the whole place lights up. Every time I sat down with Swami Nityananda to learn, the whole room would light up. Everything would be just light.

I mean light in both senses of the word. It was very bright, and it was very buoyant. When you're light, you have no attachment. Attachment is what makes you heavy and dark. And so the whole house would light up. It wasn't like in the movie where God walks in a path of light. It was just that with Swami's presence the place would actually physically change. Everybody around me would see something, but not know it. They could feel something. Whenever Swami Nityananda was about to come, all of a sudden my kids would get very tired. Sometimes they'd even go to bed by themselves.

Swami Nityananda was flesh. Nityananda was the light, and he was flesh.

He began saying something to me all the time, "He is coming, he is coming." Who was coming? Christ? A guru? Or did Swami mean himself, since he always talked in the third person?

So that's what that meant: When I see the light, I know it's time to get the kids to bed.

CHAPTER FIFTY-FIVE

The Third Eye

Coming home from Rudi's one day, my third eye began to open up. There was a pulsation between my eyebrows like I had never felt before. I had never paid much attention to the third eye until then, because I actually saw Christ and Swami Nityananda and Shirdi with my physical eyes, or at least that's how it seemed to me. Now all of a sudden my third eye began to open up, and I began to suck in the universe. I was driving the car, and I began to suck in the road, right into my third eye. The car, the buildings, everything went into the third eye. Everything came into me, and I expanded while I was driving.

At the same time, my tongue began to turn up and press into the roof of my mouth, without me doing it. The next day there was a honey taste, a bitter honey, in my mouth. That was when I first tasted *amrith*, the nectar of God, which has filled my mouth and my being ever since.

In India, my Swami taught me, yogis have experiences like this in the jungles, with the opening of the third eye. Or they are initiated by their guru, and amrith begins to flow from their being. Me, it happened driving on the Belt Parkway. And I had no idea what was happening.

Another day, Fran and I were driving to Rudi's, and I began to burn. It felt like my whole body was flames. We went to Rudi's to look for the head man, Richard, because maybe he would know what to do, but he wasn't there. We drove around. All of a sudden, I spotted a new apartment building with a fountain out front. I jumped out of the car and went running right into the fountain, in the middle of New York City. White pants, nice top, soaking wet to the skin. It helped a little, but not much. I went into the water again and again and again. Finally, dripping wet, between sweat and the water, I got back in the car, and we drove to Dealer's Choice.

Richard was walking down the street. He came over to the car and I told him, "Richard, I'm burning." He explained it was *kundalini*. I knew in my heart that was absurd, "for how could the Mother rise in the Mother?" I didn't know what those words meant—I only heard them inside me. That's the kind of stuff I would hear sometimes, from this voice that I had begun to call "The Golden Man." It had been in my head since I was a kid, a kind of golden voice, which usually stayed in the background, but once in a while it would come to the front of my mind with something important to tell me.

Meanwhile, Richard was telling me that kundalini yoga is dangerous. Everybody says that, and in fact, it can be. But there was nothing dangerous left for me, and I wanted to go on.

I had physical pain too. Around the time when I first started going to Rudi's, Swami Nityananda had said to me, "This one will teach you how to take on *karma*." Karma is a substance, and so it can be transferred from one person to another. Sometimes people take on pain from those they love, and sometimes those who work with pain all day take pain into themselves and so become exhausted. Love should not hurt that way. The key is to give it all up to God. You are not big enough to hold another's pain, nor do you need to. Christ has taught us that. But, in my eagerness to help, to touch, to share, it took a long time for me to learn this fully.

मा

A few days before, when I had the experience of sucking everything into my third eye, I was sucking in nectar, but I was also sucking in the garbage that went with the beauty. I saw no difference. And now, something in me told me that I was burning up somebody else's karma.

I just began sucking in again, sucking everything into me, until a sick feeling came over me. I heard the golden voice again, the Golden Man, saying, "Why are you holding on to their impurities?" I didn't know who he was talking about. He said, "Why are they staying in you?" I looked at my body, and it was transparent.

I saw the arteries, I saw the heart, I saw the lungs, I saw every part of my being. And then I saw the blackness of Hell, all inside of me, a blackness coming from all that I had just taken in. At the same time, right above my head was the purest white light man could ever see. I began to suck in the light, and the black in me turned to white. Then I began to breathe out. As easy as that, the heat left. The karma that I had taken in was totally gone. No big deal. My body became normal again.

मा

After my third eye opened up, I had no way of closing it. So Fran and I would be driving along the streets of New York with hundreds and hundreds of people passing by, and I would look around and say, "He's not gonna live for two more days. That one has cancer. That one's gonna be raped." I would take on all this stuff; I was like the garbage pail for all of New York City. I would see sick people on the street, anywhere, and just take it all into me. Sometimes it made me sick, and sometimes, even worse, it took the form of fat or, even more terrible, pimples—the ultimate sacrifice! Finally, I learned to close it off, to shut down my third eye a little bit, because I couldn't control the whole world, because certain things must be acted out.

CHAPTER FIFTY-SIX

Faith

After the amrith began to flow, I ate very little for about six months. Even cheesecake was nothing compared to the nectar of God. The weight just came off. No matter that I was in a state of God-intoxication, when I looked in the mirror every once in a while, I liked what I saw.

One night, Swami Nityananda told me to go downstairs to the kitchen. He said that I was taking on karma and that I had to eat a huge amount of cheesecake. The working of karma is the most interesting thing you could ever learn about, and he was just starting to teach me. He had told me stories of holy people in India who take on karma in all sorts of odd ways. I still didn't understand it completely. I had this great new figure, so I hesitated. He said to me, "You will not gain weight."

I didn't believe him. "Once I start, I'm like an alcoholic. I will never stop."

Swami said, "We are here in the Western world, and I cannot tell you to do the things a sadhu in India would do. So I'm telling you to do the simplest of things. How dare you defy me?"

I wasn't defying him; I just didn't trust him. But it didn't take much to persuade me to have cheesecake, so I went downstairs, sat down with two containers of milk and a whole cheesecake and ate. And I ate and I ate and I ate, having no faith that I would not gain weight.

When I went back upstairs, he said, "Go down again and have chocolate pudding."

By now I was getting a little nauseous, so I asked, "Could I have some Alka-Seltzer, too, while you're giving me orders?"

He said, "Yes."

I had no Alka-Seltzer in the kitchen. I had Brioschi, pretty much the same thing, but I had to check if that was okay. I went running back up to ask him.

"Yes," he answered and laughed, which is something he very, very rarely did, unless he was with babies or children. He said, "Your faith is not there, is it?"

I said, "No, but I'm still doing as you say."

"And yet you came up again to ask me if you could have the Brioschi instead of the Alka-Seltzer." It was true. I would not have touched the Brioschi if he had not said I could have it. He said, "If your faith is not there, tomorrow you will gain nine pounds."

How do you force yourself to have faith? The next day I got on my scale and I had gained almost nine pounds. I was infuriated. That night I went into the bathroom screaming at him.

He just said, "You gained because you had no faith."

I was disgusted because I had just gotten this great new figure. Then he said, "Go downstairs and finish the eggplant parmesan." I went down and got out the eggplant. There were whole trays of it. I ate like I never ate before, with such abandon. Whatever happened, it was up to him now. I ate more and more. He kept sending me up and down, up and down the stairs, and I realized that I never got full. I wasn't hungry. I was enjoying the food immensely, but I wasn't getting full. There was a lightness. I looked down at my body, and I saw atoms, I saw cells. I kept eating and eating until there was nothing left in the house to eat.

When I ran to my scale the next morning, I had lost nine pounds, even though I had never eaten that much before. That was one of the greatest lessons I've ever learned. By that time, it was not so much that I didn't believe in him, but I didn't believe in myself. Yet even without faith, I still did what he said.

Of course, I prayed for a year to have that same thing happen to me for the rest of my life, so I could eat whatever I wanted, but it never happened again.

CHAPTER FIFTY-SEVEN

"Ram" on Every Page

Franny and I knew we had to study. Study what, we never knew, but we would sit together in her house or around my kitchen table. I wrote in my diary, "Today I have learned the lesson of silence—to know God one must be quiet and still. To do God's work, one must listen to the sounds of silence. Studied with Fran. Let my children, dear God, know you. And thank you for your guidance and for your teaching."

Then I wrote, "Even happiness should be quiet." I was freaked because by then I had gotten into a very silent space with Swami Nityananda.

My first yoga teacher, Donna from Jack Lalanne's, would still come to my house and give a class in the mornings. One day we had about fifteen or twenty people in my basement when, all of a sudden, I just had to get out of the house. I left a bunch of strangers in my house, not knowing what time my husband would come home, or my kids, or anything. We just took off, Fran and I, and went to my sister's house. Shirley had an apartment near Flatbush Avenue, and she had given me a key if I ever wanted to go there during the day while she was working.

We sat there, and the whole room became light—very, very light and bright. And we both heard the same thing; we heard God, God without form, talking to us. Two separate people, me not knowing who I was, Fran not knowing who she was, heard the same words, in a loud booming voice like in the movie *The Ten Commandments*. (It had to be dramatic for me to be in spiritual life.)

When I heard this voice, I said, "This is the end." I looked at Fran, and she was ashen, as white as a ghost.

"Did you hear it?" she asked.

"Did I hear WHAT?"

"Joyce, did you hear it?"

"I'll tell you what I heard and you tell me what you heard," I said. "I'll write it down." We didn't trust each other, that's how scared we were.

We both wrote and then exchanged papers. They both said the same thing: "You must know God. You must become God. You are God." This was too much. We held on to each other. She was clinging to me, and I was squashing her, and we didn't know where to go or what to do with ourselves. We called up Richard, one of the teachers at Rudi's, we were so scared. "Listen to us—God talked to us!"

At first he said, "Oh, come on."

"You've got to believe us," I told him.

We had called him right away. From being on the phone with us, he felt the light all around him. It was an amazing experience for him. Finally he said, "Okay, you made the contact with God together. It's out of my hands."

Then I had to go home and cook the lasagna.

मा

One night, as I became very light, my oldest daughter invited some friends over. Instead of going into the temple of my bathroom, I gave a yoga class for her friends. But Swami was there in the house, and I was feeling him as if I were sitting cross-legged in my temple. Right there in the midst of my daughter's Catholic friends, I cried out, "Know me, Oh Lord!" I didn't mean Swami Nityananda, and it wasn't even Christ I was calling. It was something beyond. This is the moment when I realized that I was really in search of the formless God; it was the Father I had to find. Christ was my beloved, but now I wanted beyond Christ. I had to have what he had.

Here's my diary again, for February 2nd. "Each night I can't wait to sit in meditation and feel the love of God spread through me." I was scared, yet I couldn't wait for the children to go to bed.

"Take me higher, my Lord, so I may dwell closer in your arms."

"I have never begged for anything in my life, but I beg to see the face of God, or the face of Creation. With all my heart, I beg you, Lord." Now I had to know.

This was the turning point—February 2nd, 1974. I wrote, "Deep morning meditation." I had started taking from the nights and bringing it into the day. That was my ruination. By this time, I never slept. Before, I used to be in the bathtub all night, come out of the bathroom early in the morning, and try to be a wife and mother. So I never sat during the day because I couldn't. There would have been no way to keep everything going. When I started meditating in the daytime, it was all over. All I did now was cook breakfast, send the kids off to school, and start sitting again. It had become everything. Soon I would be sitting twenty hours a day.

Still there was more to be learned, even as the fear kept growing. The mere thought of having to sit for so many hours with Swami petrified me. The sweat would pour down my face. I wanted only the Christ, yet forgot so many times his words spoken so clearly, when he said that there are many paths to the sacred heart. I would sit in the bathtub cross-legged for hours, and then there would be no breath. Then I would hear, "Breathe in!" But now there was no "in" to breathe, and no "out." That's when I would panic.

I later learned that in deep meditation, the breath gets very slight, and in samadhi there is no breath. But I had been married since I was fifteen, rarely went to school, and who knew from samadhi? Yet even in my terror I realized that the softness I felt running through me was something I had never felt before, nor had most people.

What happens is that in certain states, the throat closes, and you don't know how to open it, so you can start to choke. So there I was sitting in the bathtub, doing a breathing exercise that Swami taught me, one more powerful than the breath from Jack Lalanne's that got me into this mess in the first place. "Breathe in," said Swami. What's in, what's out? Total, total fear. After fear came hysteria, then came a huge bump on the head because I was trying to get out of the bathtub. After that, Swami taught me how to start the process of living again, by breathing *out*. If you try to breathe in once the throat starts to close, you choke and panic. But if you breathe out, the body takes over and breathes in again for you.

The body has to be trained to hold the power and love of God. Night after night Swami trained me like that, and night after night he pounded the scriptures into my head. Night after night I complained, because I never liked school and how was I supposed to remember all this? We were halfway through the *Bhagavad Gita* when I made a deal with him. I learned how to absorb the scriptures into myself without forcing wisdom through my mindless mind.

He also taught me to use my hands. There were all these *mudras* I had to learn, and I couldn't get them straight. Mudras are gestures of the hands and body that a teacher can use to help people, usually without their knowing anything has happened. Swami was trying to teach me all the things that a spiritual teacher should know, but I couldn't get it. Swami would call me "stupid" and "idiot." I would take notes, then try to use them to do my mudras, but I'd still get them wrong. Then he would slap my hands, so I'd slap him back.

This was all going on in front of Salvatore. I'd sit down with my family and pretend to watch TV, meanwhile trying to practice my hand movements. Sometimes I would get mixed up and do mudras to help the people on TV—like to help the *Star Trek* crew defeat the aliens—and I would wonder why it wasn't working. Swami would come out of the bathroom and sit in front of the TV with us. Of course, only I could see him.

My husband of twenty years who loved me so much sat with me night after night while I carried on with invisible men. What could he have thought except that I was crazy?

But I wasn't crazy, and I would even work at times with people in mental hospitals, just like I had worked with the leukemia children, so I knew the difference. I began to realize I could help them because in reality many mental problems are spiritual problems caused by the splitting of kundalini, when the spiritual power doesn't rise straight up the spine.

When you have so much to give, there has to be somebody to take it. If no one is there to take, or if you haven't learned to give, it kind of backs up inside of you, becomes stagnant, makes you tight. The river of God had flowed through me ever since I had seen the Christ, but if there was no one on Earth to receive it, then I would just give everything back to God. I would be lost in the flow between God and me, and in that state I would be partly lost to the world. But if I could help a person in need, then that force of God could flow right through me into the world, and I could live somewhat normally.

And yet, I was losing control of my own life. That's why Fran stayed close to me so much. She started to spend nights at my house and became like a second mother to my kids. I was drifting away, and she could feel it. We'd be driving on the Belt Parkway, and I would be going into God. She'd say to me, "Joyce, don't leave me."

I'd say to her, "I'm right here. I'm in the same car with you. Where could I go?"

She'd say, "You're going someplace where I can't follow you." She could feel what was happening.

Meanwhile, I kept writing in my diary, but after a while, by the beginning of March, I would just write "*Ram*" on every page—the name of God.

Photos 1971-2010

p. 334 Inscription on the Back of Ma's Painting of Christ:
Dec 19, 1991. The Christ came first in my life, Swami came next then THE BABA, this picture was painted exactly as I saw and knew my beloved Christ then and now. He always has a special place in my heart.

p. 335 Ma's Painting of Christ, 1991.

p. 336 (Top Left) With Fran, 1990s. (Top Right) Off her diet! Colorado Retreat, c. 1976. (Bottom Left) At Mount Manresa, 1994. (Bottom Right) Swami Nityananda of Ganeshpuri.

p. 337 (Top Left) With Hilda Charlton, New York, c. 1974. (Top Right) Neem Karoli Baba. (Bottom) In the Puja Room, Brooklyn, 1974.

p. 338 Ma's First Vision of Krishna, Brooklyn, 1974.

p. 339 (Top Left) Teaching in Tompkins Square Park, NY, c. 1975. (Top Right) With Michelle Jaya Gange, River House, 1993. (Bottom) With Billy.

p. 340 (Top) With Sadhu God, Los Angeles. (Bottom Left) With Paul Monette, Los Angeles, 1992. (Bottom Right) With Mr. Tillman, West Palm Beach County Home.

p. 341 (Top) With Tommy, West Palm Beach County Home. (Bottom Left) With Haagen Das, Los Angeles. (Bottom Right) West Palm Beach County Home.

p. 342 (Top Left) With Kim Bergalis, 1991. (Top Right) With Craig and Everal, 1990s. (Bottom) Ping Pong at Kashi, 1976.

p. 343 (Top) With Rabbi Zalman Schachter-Shalomi and Eve Ilsen at Kashi. (Bottom Left) Ma Doing Rounds at West Palm Beach County Home. (Bottom Right); Showing Cardinal Joseph Bernadin Pictures of People with AIDS, 1993.

p. 344 Ma at the NAMES Project AIDS Memorial Quilt Display, Washington DC, 1996.

p. 345   (Top Left) With Randy at the AIDS Quilt Display in West Palm Beach. (Top Right) At the NAMES Project AIDS Memorial Quilt Display, Washington DC, 1996; (Bottom) With Deena, Connors Nursery, West Palm Beach, 1993.

p. 346   (Top) Ma with Mel and Shirley, 1990's. (Bottom) Showing Pope John Paul II Pictures of People with AIDS, Vatican City, 1993.

p. 347   (Top) With the Dalai Lama, Miami, 2000. (Bottom) The Parliament of the World's Religions, Chicago, 1993. From left to right, Ma Jaya, Bibiji Inderjit Kaur, Swami Satchidananda, Dr. Balwant Singh Hansra, Yogi Bhajan, Dr. Irfan Ahmad Khan.

Dec 19, 1991

The Christ came first in my life, swami came next then The BABA,

This picture was painted exactly as I saw and knew my beloved Christ then and now. He always has a special place in my heart.

† † †

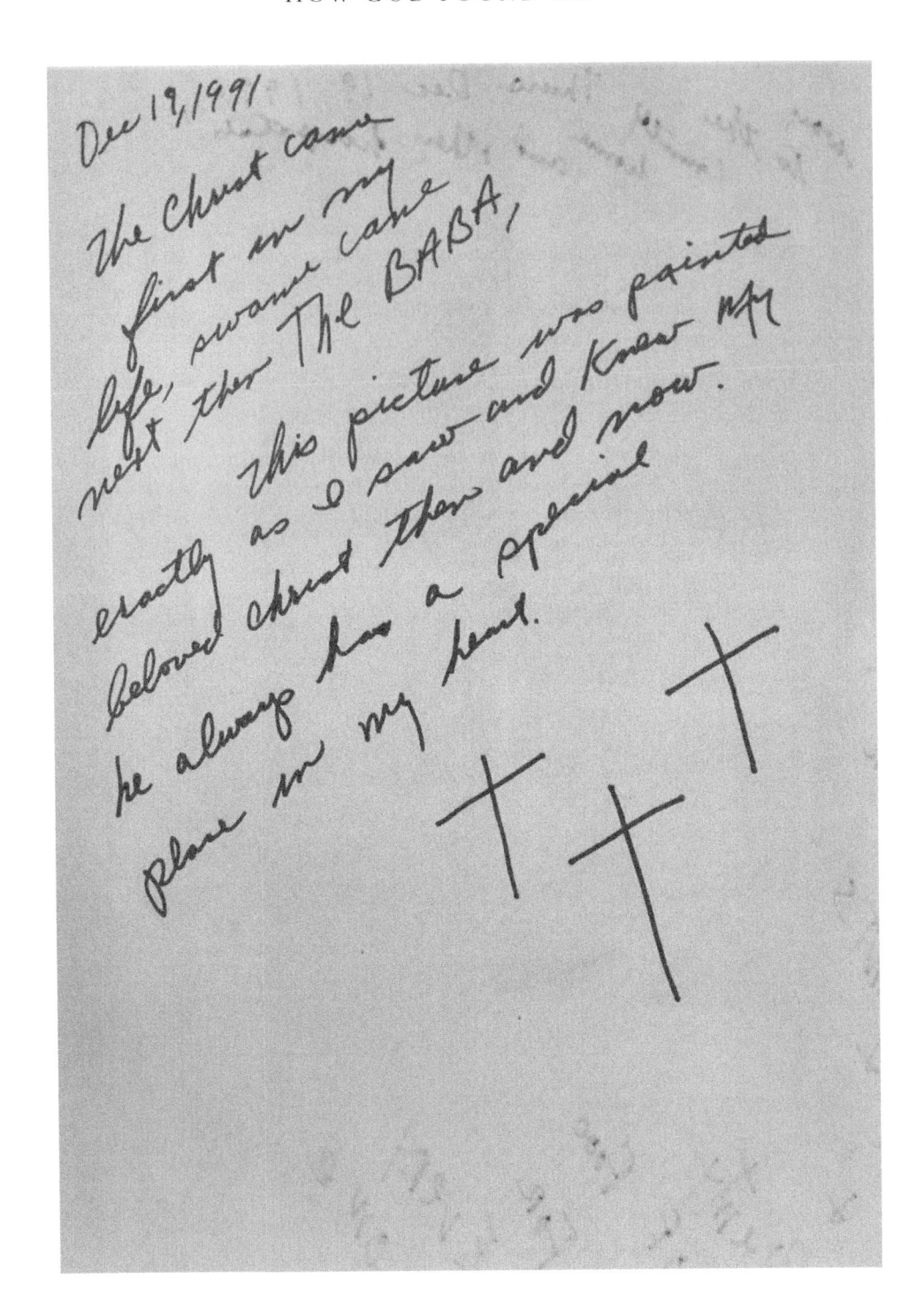

MA JAYA SATI BHAGAVATI

HOW GOD FOUND ME

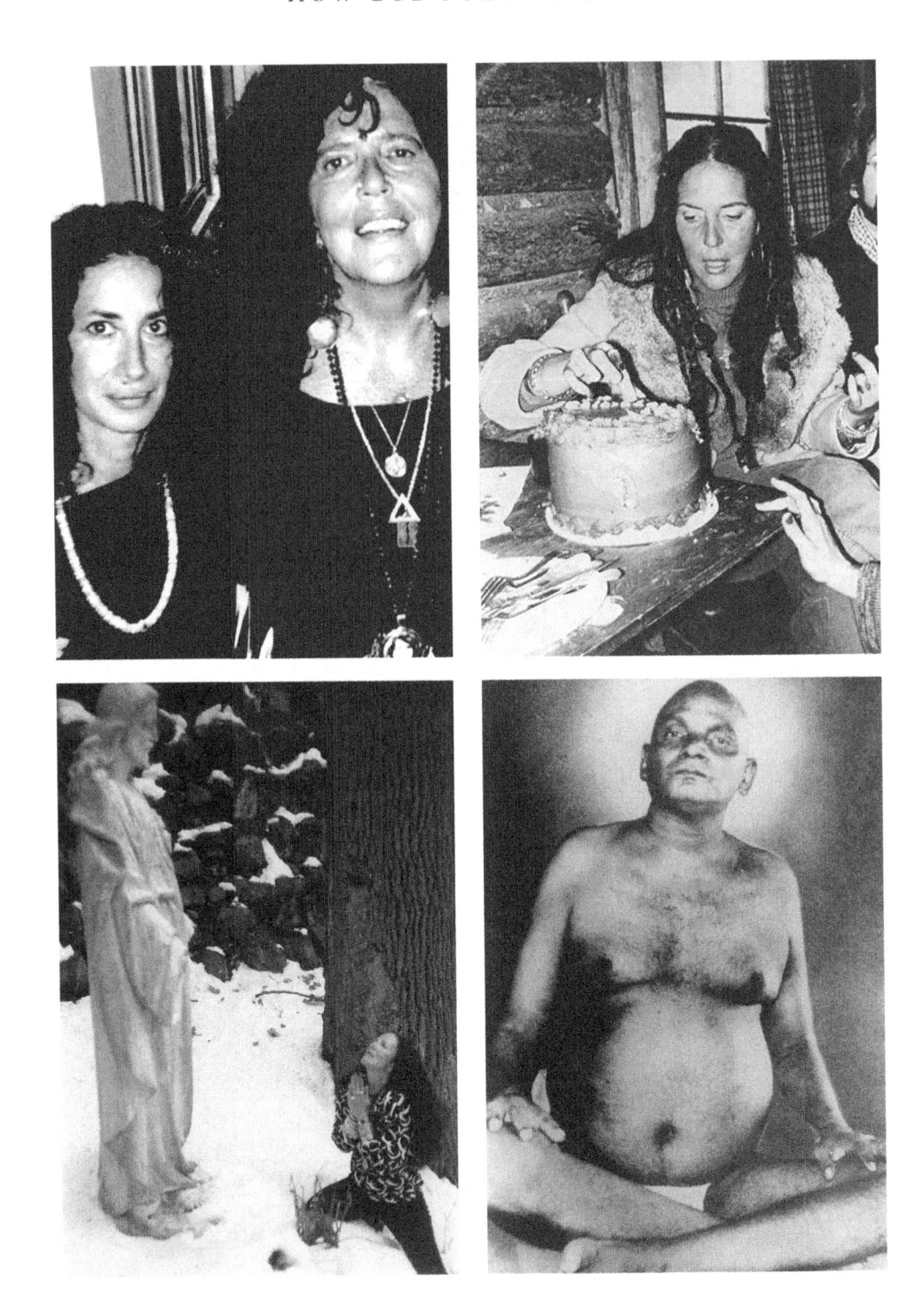

MA JAYA SATI BHAGAVATI

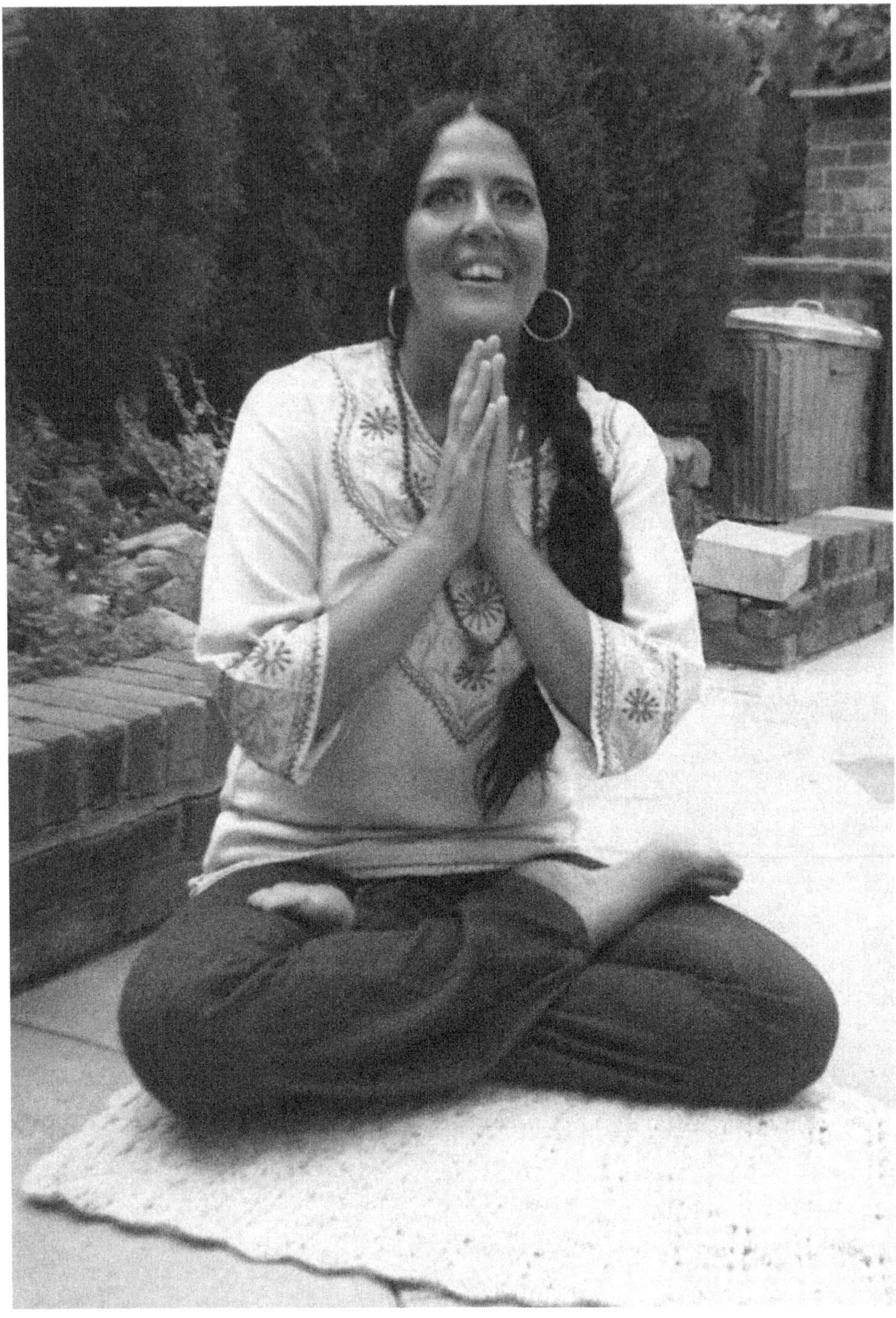

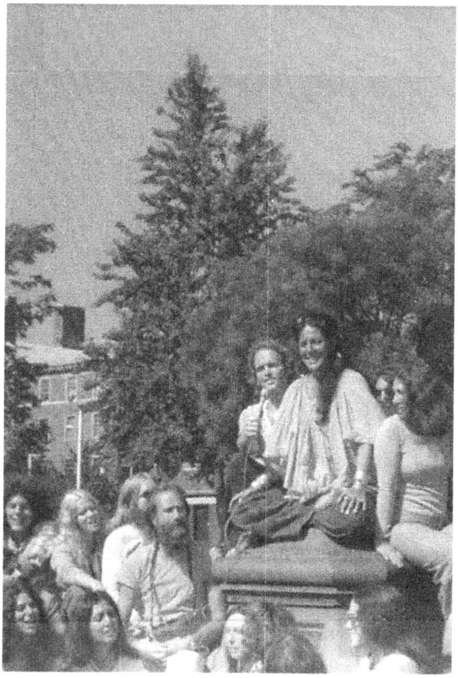

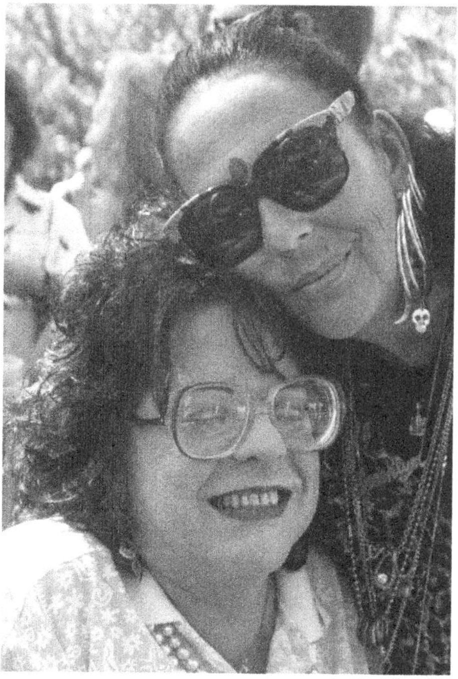

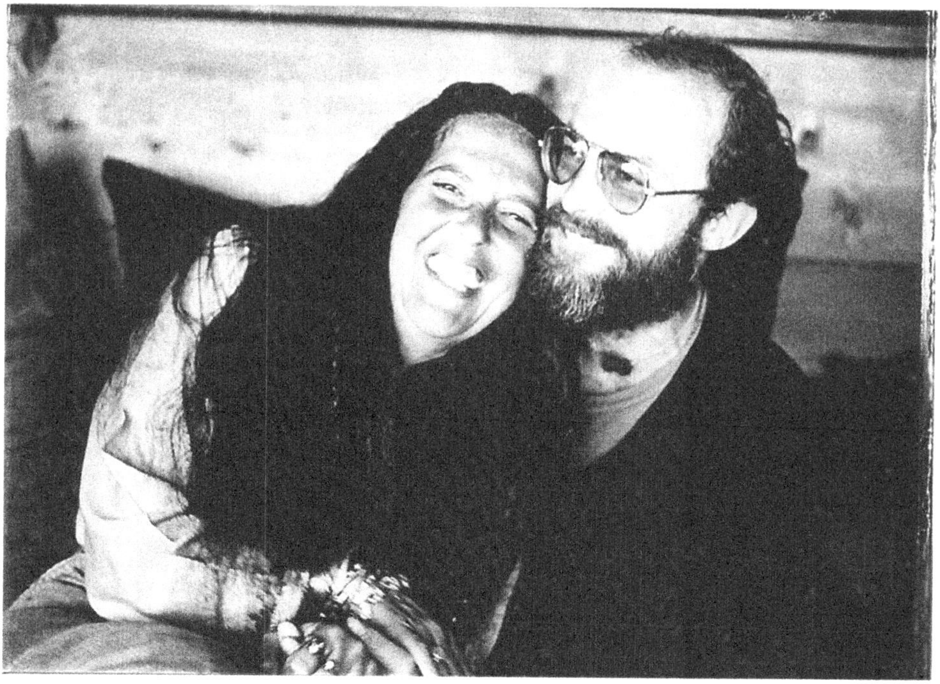

HOW GOD FOUND ME

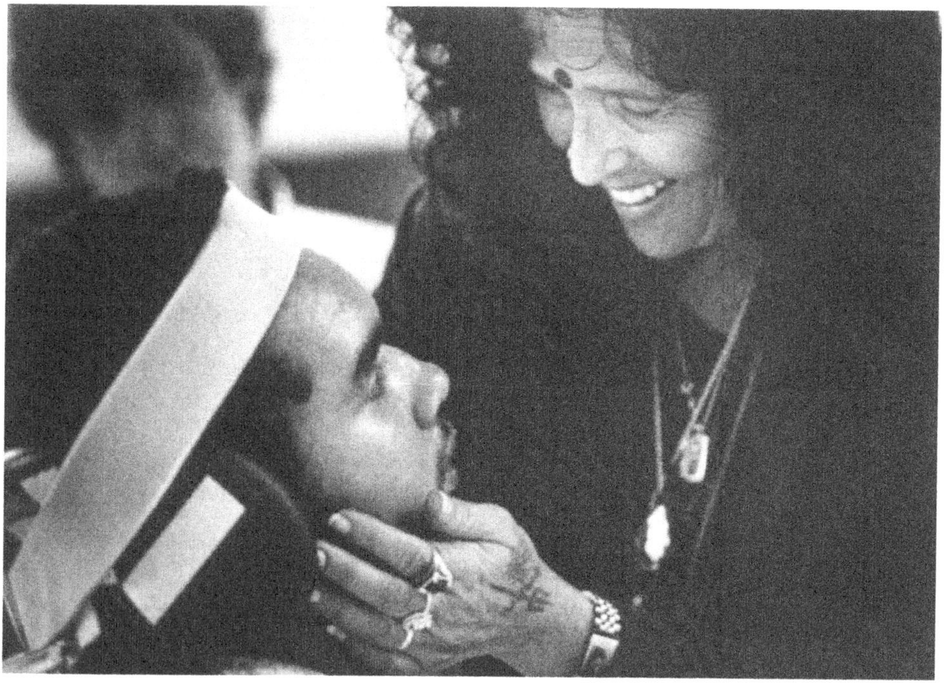

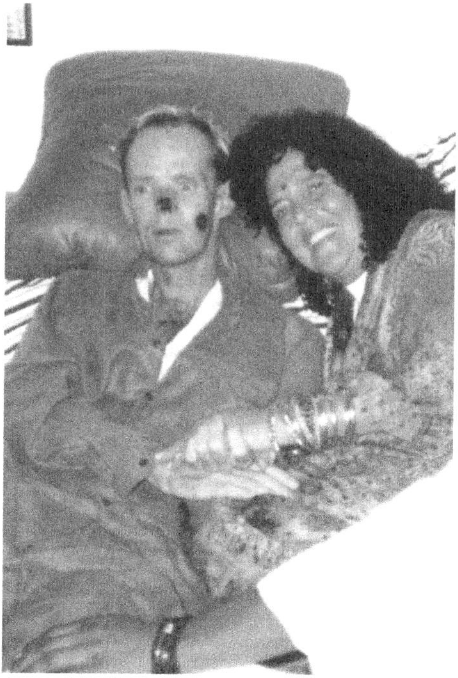

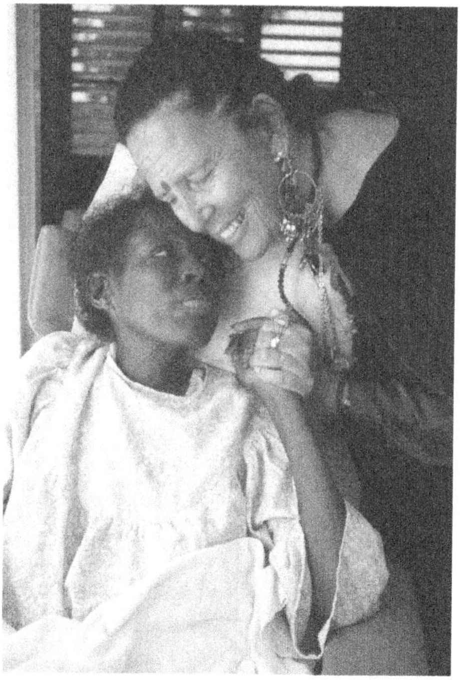

HOW GOD FOUND ME

MA JAYA SATI BHAGAVATI

HOW GOD FOUND ME

MA JAYA SATI BHAGAVATI

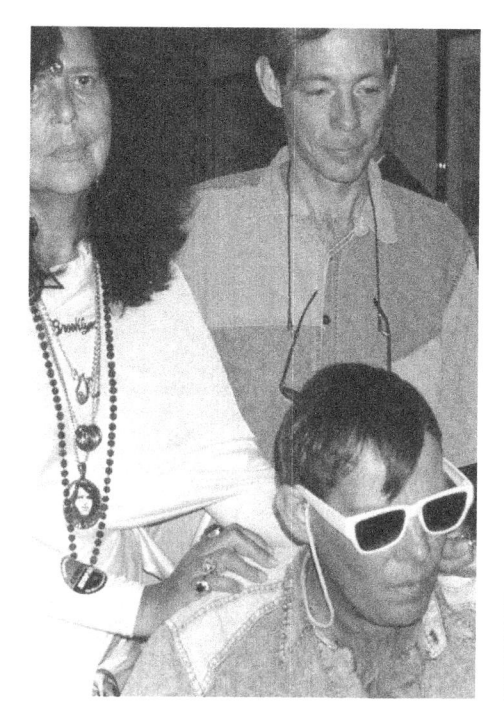

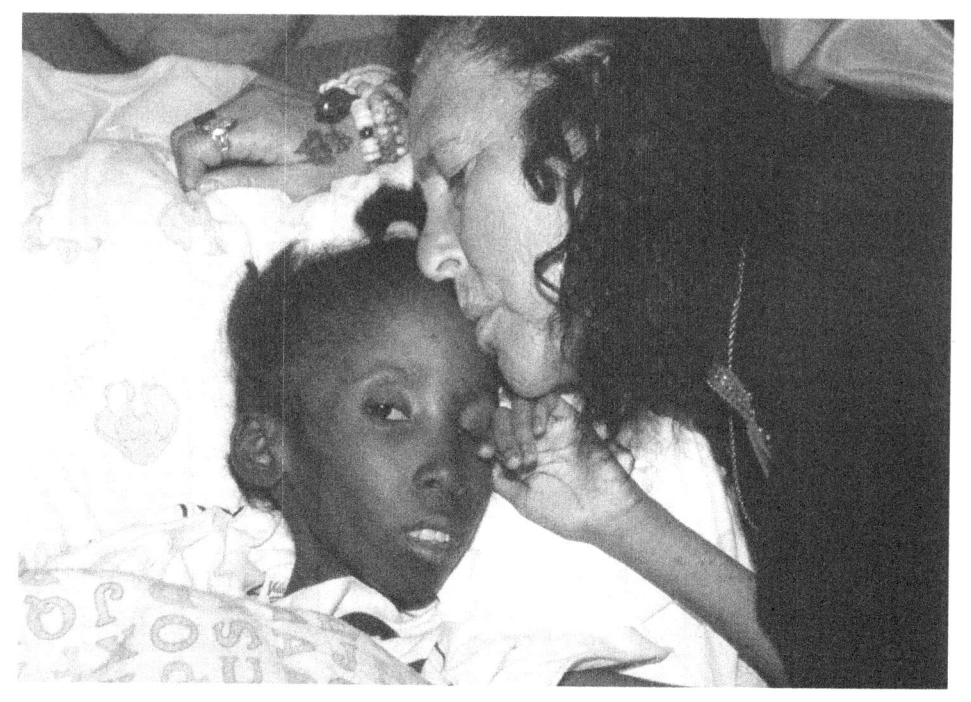

HOW GOD FOUND ME

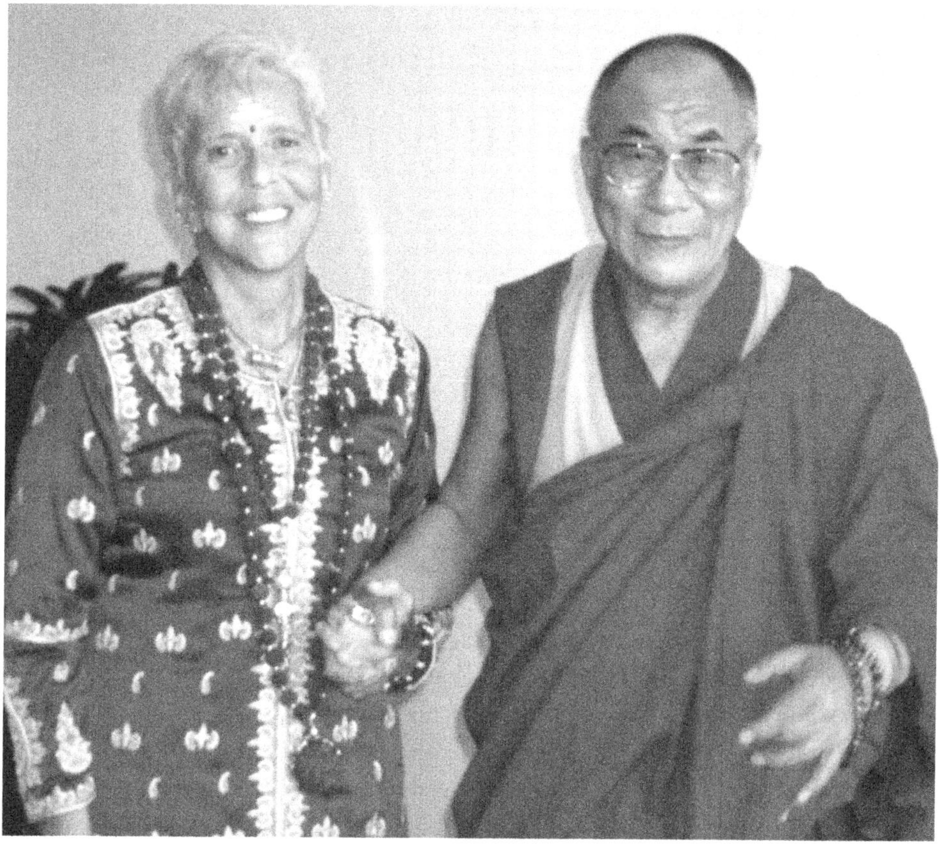

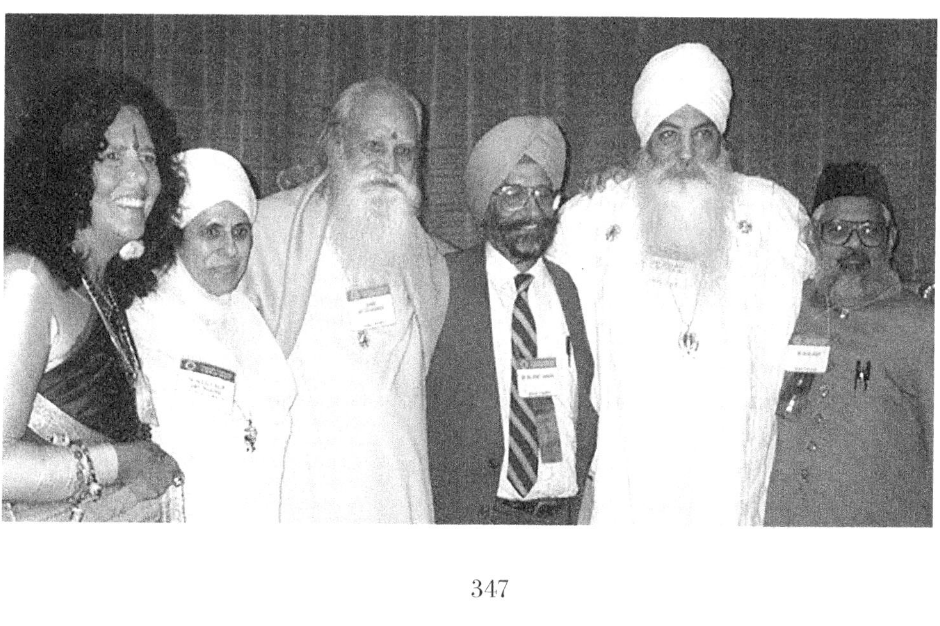

CHAPTER FIFTY-EIGHT

Swami's Birthday

Swami Nityananda had been with me almost a year, and I was still spending every night with him. So why hadn't there been a birthday party for him? Birthdays were very big in my family, and he was certainly part of the family.

I asked him about it all the time. He'd answer, "This one was never born, and will never die." That was all very nice, but I just had to have a birthday party for him. So finally, he said, "You find out my birthday."

The very next day, Fran went to Weiser's, which was a huge spiritual bookstore in Greenwich Village. She had been spending a lot of time there. She would look up stuff in the spiritual books to try to figure out what I was saying, because I would repeat what Swami told me, not knowing myself what I was talking about.

She called me up hysterical, hardly able to speak. "Joyce, there's a poster, with Swami Nityananda's name on it. The man really exists!" She read me the poster. It said, "Swami Muktananda coming to America, disciple of Swami Nityananda." And there was a phone number.

I said, "Of course he exists." But really, I had just gotten used to the idea that I was crazy, so it was a shock to hear that somebody else in this world knew his name.

So we called up the number, left a message, and a woman named Susan Weissmann called me right back. I said, very innocently, "I have this man in my bathroom, and I really would like to know his birthday. His name is Nityananda."

She said, "Excuse me?"

I said, "His name is Swami Nityananda, and I would like to know his birthday."

She answered, "He was never born and he will never die."

"You just don't know the answer," I said, "I'm gonna have to force him to tell me himself. If you find out his birthday, call me back." I hung up, real Brooklyn.

She called me back. "There was no birthday. They found him under a tree."

"My God, the weirdest places! I found him on a toilet bowl!"

Infuriated, I went upstairs and told him, "Look, I'm driving everybody crazy, so just tell me one thing: what is your birthday?"

Finally he told me: March 19th.

I kept questioning him, and that's how I found out this story:

Many years ago in India, an old lady found a baby under a tree, but the baby wouldn't come out of samadhi. He wasn't breathing, and he was just slipping away. The old lady was crying because he was such a beautiful baby. Just then a holy man passed by, and he told her, "Kill a crow and feed him the meat, for it is the lowest meat one can eat, and it will bring him out of samadhi."

But the old lady had been trained from earliest childhood never to kill, not even a crow. She didn't know what to do, so she just stood there paralyzed. Meanwhile, the baby was slipping away. So the holy man picked up a stone and killed the crow. The baby was given the meat to suck on, the grossness of it brought him into his body, and he lived. The old lady and her husband took care of him and brought him up.

You see, sometimes all a holy person needs to do is be in a human body for a few minutes to bring a blessing. But these two people grabbed hold, and by their love and desire for God they held this God-man firmly to the Earth, where he stayed for many years, blessing the Earth every moment.

I never told too many people this, but after I heard that story I spent two weeks trying to find a crow. I was having trouble with life on Earth myself, and I figured if it worked once it will work twice. I went into every kind of butcher, and every kind of health food store, but I couldn't find a crow. I was even ready to strangle a pigeon—I'm no *Brahmin*.

मा

I make light of it now, but I was desperate for a way to stay down in my body and live a normal life in spite of what was happening to me. Even going to Rudi's every day wasn't helping me much. I didn't have any place to go for help.

I could have just stayed in my bathroom until I didn't come out anymore. By now, Sal was getting desperate. I had lost track of time, so I can't tell you exactly when this happened, but he put me into a mental hospital. I looked around at all the women locked up with me. One of them peed on the floor right in front of me, and the aide hit her. I couldn't tell "crazy" from "not crazy," but I knew from pain, I knew that some mental illness comes when kundalini rises wrong, and I knew how to help. So that's what I did, I began working with some of these women, and when the observation period was over, they just sent me home.

Even so, Sal was very frightened. He would catch me not breathing sometimes, and one of his friends told him I could get brain damage like that, so he went and got these oxygen tanks on wheels and had them all around the house. It didn't matter. Sometimes I'd just go into ecstasy and fall. In those days, it didn't take much to send me into ecstasy. It could be the way the moon shone on the snow, or a moment of looking at a star.

Finally Sal hit on a new way to get his wife back. He decided we should move to Florida. Sell the house, sell the business, go! This is something you just don't do when you're part of a big Italian family, but Sal was very frightened.

He didn't know what to do, whom to turn to. But, what you must understand is that everything Sal did, he did for love. Sal was a wonderful, wonderful husband for almost twenty years. But now he had his wife's lover to fight. This is an Italian man, a Sicilian. If his wife had gone to another man, he'd know exactly what to do, but how do you fight God? Taking me away to Florida was his last big hope. So we made plans that Sal and Richie would go into business together in Florida.

My sister stayed home with the kids, and we went to Florida. It was just Sal and me, Fran and Richie, on our way to Florida to look around and get established. I saw my first palm tree at the airport, and immediately I wanted to get away from everybody spiritual. I didn't need the people at Rudi's; all I needed was my Christ. As soon as I realized Christ could live in Florida too, I wanted to stay there. I had a sick feeling and almost threw up. It was a feeling like "Run, run, Joyce, run!" I just knew I should stay in Florida—just God, my family, and me. Who needed all the rest of it? I told Sal, "We're gonna buy a house."

On the way from the Fort Lauderdale airport I saw a house for sale and made Sal stop the car. I went right in and said to the man, "How much do you want down?" We didn't have a penny. Then I told him, "Let's trade. You take the house in Brooklyn!"

Sal said, "You don't buy a house like this!"

I turned around, looked at Fran, looked at Richie, and said, "Well, THEY DO! They're not going home!"

Sal said, "What are you talking about?"

"Richie and Fran will stay here and get a house! They'll get a house for us and a house for them."

This was news to Richie, but we all decided they'd stay an extra week to find a condo, and then Sal and I would buy one next door as soon as we sold the house in Brooklyn.

On March 19th, Swami's birthday, we were still in Florida. It was the day we were supposed to fly back to New York. I had asked Swami, "How do you celebrate your birthday?" He told me, in fact he described, how in India they would have a *bandhara*, a big feast for everyone in the neighborhood, and all the sadhus would come and be fed. We needed plates made out of leaves, we needed all kinds of food, and especially mangoes because that was Swami's favorite fruit. But by then it was time to go to the airport. Fran and I spotted a fruit store, and we made Sal stop the car. We persuaded the guy in the store to sell us some banana leaves. Meanwhile Sal and Richie were outside saying we would miss the plane, so we shoved everything in a bag and got in the car.

Then we sat ourselves down in a corner of the Fort Lauderdale airport, on the floor, with canned mango juice and whatever fruit we had found. We had made ourselves little platters from the banana leaves, the way Swami said they do it in India.

Salvatore found us. "What are you doing on the floor? Get up!"

You have to picture it: there was this man, very tall, very good looking, extremely conservative, always perfectly dressed, and then there's his wife, a wild woman with long black hair, sitting on the floor and eating off leaves.

Eventually, we got on the airplane.

CHAPTER FIFTY-NINE

Hilda Charlton

The very day we got back from Florida, Susan from Muktananda's ashram called to say, "There's a woman coming tonight who will talk about her experiences with Swami Nityananda in India."

I went into absolute ecstasy. I had only just begun to believe he really existed even though he had been on my toilet bowl for a year, but to find somebody that had actually sat at this man's feet was just too much.

But I had to answer, "I can't go, I'm not allowed out at night." I never went any place at night without my husband, and I could only imagine the scene if I said to Sal, "You wanna go hear a woman talk about the man in your bathroom?" So I said to Susan, "Would you please do me a favor and tape it."

"I'll send a tape tonight."

Now the other important thing was that I asked Susan the woman's name, and she told me, "Hilda Charlton." Swami Nityananda had been saying to me, "Hilda, Hilda, Hilda," and I didn't know why. When he first started to talk to me, he would say, "Jaya, Jaya, Jaya," trying to make that be my name. Jaya sounded to me like coffee, which I never drank. I just like a good cup of tea. He kept bothering me with this, but better he should call me something besides "child," which was annoying, so I took the name Joya because it sounded like halvah, a kind of candy, and I figured I'd rather sound like halvah than coffee. Then he still kept saying Jaya, and I kept saying Joya, and I won. I'd been Joya for a while when he started saying, "Hilda, Hilda, Hilda."

I said, "No way, you're not naming me Hilda." But he had me worried.

When Susan Weissmann said the woman who was going to speak was named Hilda Charlton, I was in ecstasy because it was clear that the name wasn't meant for me.

Susan had promised to send the tape, and some people showed up at my door late that night, dressed in Indian clothes, with the saris and the dots on the forehead and the whole bit. No way could I let Sal see this! I thanked them fast and got them out of there.

I immediately played the tape of Hilda's talk. She told how a yogi had come to her in a vision when she was a young woman in Oakland, California. After that there were times when she would be in the middle of the street and feel herself disappearing into what she called "The Absolute." Later she went to India with a dance troupe. She met many holy people, and when she finally found Swami Nityananda she stayed with him at his ashram in Ganeshpuri. Only after she had been in India for years did she see a picture of Swami as a young man and recognize him as the man who had come to her in the vision!

Can you realize what this tape meant to me? What happened to Hilda seemed so close to what had happened to me: the vision, the search, finding a picture, the ecstasy running out of control. And there was no doubt that the man she had sat in front of in India was the man in my bathroom. She described how he rarely spoke, how he would walk out at three or four in the morning to bathe in three hot pools he had there, and how the ground would shake when he walked. Hilda would hide under a tree, waiting just to catch a glimpse of him.

She told how Swami would allow people to come see him for hours. He had a big chair where he loved to sit cross-legged, as heavy as he was. From sitting cross-legged, being human, and taking on the pains of the world, there was always something wrong with his knees. Hilda told how, when he got up at the end of the day, he would cry in agony, cry out in pain.

She thought he should have seen a doctor, or he should have had a massage, but most of his disciples didn't understand that. He was healing people all day and taking on their pain, so how could his pain be real? When you're a guru, you take the vow of never *ever* using your powers for yourself. That's why the holy need someone to take care of them, while they take care of the world. Hilda somehow understood this, even when she was new to his ashram.

On the tape, Hilda spoke very beautifully. She sounded young and very English. I had to talk to her right away, even though by then it was late at night. I learned later that Hilda never took calls after a certain time, but she answered the phone when I called. I was so scared to be talking to her.

My very first words to Hilda were, "How do you speak to a saint on the phone?"

"Oh, darling, I'm not a saint."

Oh, my God, my heart was beating!

She said, "You must be Joya." That name, which was still new to me. "Can you come to see me?"

I later learned that this surprised those who knew her, because she didn't usually see people just like that. I went early the next morning. I took Desiree and Denise and her friend, telling them, "This day will change all of our lives forever," and we went. It was the end of March 1974, and it was snowing.

We were ushered into an apartment on the Upper West Side of Manhattan. Hilda's assistants took the kids to another room and put me by myself in a blue room, which is where Hilda used to see people. They gave me a little beach chair to sit on. I was so nervous, the sweat was pouring down, and my false eyelashes were coming off. I tried to press them back on, and I was shaking. I was trying to sit cross-legged, but the chair was too small. I had one foot up, one foot down. I was so scared, listening for footsteps, and I just wanted to look nice.

I had pictured a young, very tall, very refined Englishwoman. When Hilda finally came in, I was in awe and disappointed at the same time because she didn't look like what I had imagined a holy woman to be. She didn't fit my molds, but then I don't fit anybody's molds, either. It didn't matter, because this was the teacher that I was looking for to tell me that I wasn't crazy. I needed desperately to find a teacher, and it had to be a woman because of Sal.

"Please tell me about Swami Nityananda. He's in my bathroom."

"Darling, get him out of your bathroom immediately!" She meant that I should put him some place nicer, of course, not realizing that my bathroom was my temple, the purest and holiest room in my house.

"I can't. I have a husband and three children."

"Get rid of them immediately and get him out of your bathroom."

It was insane, but this was my first conversation with Hilda. She didn't seem to think I was crazy, so maybe I wasn't. I made an appointment to come back the next day.

That afternoon, Fran got back from Florida. She was all excited, saying, "We got it! We got it, we bought the condo in Plantation!"

"What are you talking about? You bought a plantation?"

"The condo in Florida. Plantation, Florida. We got it!"

I didn't know what she was talking about. So much had happened in a few days that I had forgotten the whole thing about moving to Florida. "Come on," I said, "we're going to see Hilda."

"Who's Hilda? What are you talking about?"

I said, "We can't move to Florida now. I found a woman teacher!" I grabbed Fran, Denise, and Desiree, we got in the Cadillac, and we went.

At Hilda's apartment, right away I was put in the blue room alone again to wait for her. She came in, with a student named Howard. She touched my forehead and sent me shooting up into samadhi, for what seemed like it was the first time.

As soon as she touched me, I knew I had found my Ma. She would be my spiritual mother. Me, who had lost my real mother at thirteen—finally I was where I had to be. Later I would realize that I had been in a state of samadhi the whole time, I just didn't know it. But when Hilda touched me, I could go deeper into it, and for the first time I could feel where I really was, because now I had someone to take care of me. She made it safe for me to go where I was supposed to go.

She touched my head, and I went into samadhi. In this state, the body goes stiff and the breath stops while the soul returns home. This had been happening to me for months; that's what I meant when I said I would fall in ecstasy and appear to be dead. The difference was that now I could go into that state and know and remember it, not just be it.

The highest samadhi is no samadhi, beyond samadhi, where you just live in the constant flow of God, living a life that might even look quite ordinary, but you are immersed every single second in bliss. Even in the midst of pain there is bliss. Really there's no such thing as samadhi; samadhi is just a word, as Swami taught me. In those days, if I tried to describe samadhi, words would stop, and I would become it.

That day in Hilda's apartment, I went into this state. Coming down out of it, I had such a feeling of happiness. Hilda was there, and I had found my Ma. But as I began again to hear the sounds of the world,

I heard the words "Ma, Ma, Ma, Ma," not in my head, but in a new voice. It was Hilda who was calling me Ma, with tears in her eyes. In that moment, I knew I hadn't found my Ma, she had found hers. I was so hurt and so resigned, both in that one split second, realizing that there was no way that I would ever have a Ma, because the mother I had been looking for was myself. It hit me so hard, having an older woman like Hilda calling me Ma.

All that time I had been without a guru, I was cocky, saying proudly, "I have no guru," but eventually I knew I had to have one. I had wanted it to be Hilda, but it wasn't.

I found myself putting my hand upon her head, and this wonderful woman looked up and said to me, "Ma, help me teach the jewels of my life." She meant all her students. She had a lot of people looking to her. She had helped many people, especially kids she would take off the streets of New York.

So I promised to help her. But as I made that promise, I began to feel fear again. Just a few days ago, I had been running away from spiritual life to the freedom of Florida.

CHAPTER SIXTY

God Intoxication

Hilda would come into that blue room every day in a different sari and tell me stories of Swami Nityananda, Sathya Sai Baba, and other holy men she had been with in India. If it weren't for Hilda, I would have died. She taught me that I wasn't crazy, she protected me, and she tried to get me to stay down—to have the control to stay away from God so I could teach and be in the world.

I used to sit on Hilda's couch in bliss from the amrith that filled my mouth. I stopped eating. For a period of about six months after the amrith started, I didn't eat at all, and I didn't sleep either. I was in a very peculiar state then, crazed for God. With Hilda, I didn't have to mask my love for God. I was finally free. She would sit me on her couch, and I would go into samadhi. People would pass before me and touch my feet. Normally I would have thought that this was weird and pagan, but in that state I didn't care—just let me sit here in peace.

In India I might have been called a *mast*, which is a person who is God-intoxicated, so in love with God that they no longer function in the world. There are many such people in India. Meher Baba used to take care of them. He would bathe them and make them eat a little.

But I still had to keep it together at home. That wasn't easy to do. In my God-intoxication, I would fall, sprawling out in the ecstasy of God. I knocked out some of my teeth that way. One time, a tooth went through my lip, and I still went to Hilda's. She sent me home, and the next thing I knew I was on my way to see a dental surgeon I'd never met before. Both Fran and Sal had to go with me because I won't go near a dentist unless I have to, and sometimes even then.

I fear nothing in all the universe, except for one thing: the dentist.

Sal and Franny waited for me outside. They gave me sodium pentothal. Soon I was on the ceiling, staring down at myself in the dentist chair. Okay, this was nice; I thought I looked pretty sitting down there. But then the nurse fainted, the doctor started to cry, and they pronounced me dead! There was no heartbeat, no pulsebeat, because I had gone into samadhi. There was nothing holy about it. I was just escaping the dentist, because in certain states I can't feel a thing. People tell me they're scared of God, but God is easy compared to a dentist.

They called my poor husband in, and the dentist said, "Your wife is dead."

From a tooth pulled! I'm on the ceiling watching this, and I'm going, "Fucko, I'm not dead!" I mean, how dare he?

Sal started banging on my chest so unbelievably hard that he almost broke the breastbone. He was screaming at me, "You can't die on me, you bitch!" He refused to believe that I was dead.

Now, I'm still very comfortable on the ceiling, but I'm thinking I better get back in my body. But not with Sal pounding on my chest like that, no way! And I started to scream at him, "You fuck, stop banging on my chest!" And sure enough, straight from the dead, there I was, screaming "Fuck!" His love had brought me back.

That was the first time a doctor ever pronounced me dead, but it wasn't the last time. Here was a woman with no breath and no pulse, so what else could a doctor think? It bothered them a lot when I spoke to them while I was in this state.

CHAPTER SIXTY-ONE

Billy

Soon after I started going to Hilda's, she introduced me to all her students, and that was how I met Billy. Hilda first introduced him to me as "the don from England."

In Brooklyn "don" was sometimes the word we used for a big-shot pimp. Was I ever impressed with Hilda! She could take a don and change him into a spiritual seeker!

But he didn't sound like a don. "Glad to make your acquaintance," he said.

"Is this guy kidding?" I asked Hilda.

"No, darling, he is English."

"I gather you're from Brooklyn," he said.

"How can you tell that?" I wondered if he was psychic or something.

He looked to see if I was kidding. He saw before him a two-hundred pound woman in a green leotard and tight pants. By then I had lost fifty pounds. Thinking I looked great, I walked around in this kind of clothes. I wore a scarf wrapped around my head to hold back my long hair, which fell loose and wild down my back. Later, Billy told me that he was so impressed with my accent and my looks that he could hardly speak.

"You'd better get yourself another coat," I told him, eyeing his old, beat-up, thrift-store-looking coat, which I learned later he prized. "A don don't usually dress like that."

"Do you know a lot of dons, Joya?"

"Yeah, I know a few. I helped them mend their ways, though you look pretty mended."

"I guess," he answered, looking more confused than ever.

For a long time I thought Billy was a pimp, instead of a big shot at Oxford University. Then one day I called him a pimp instead of a don.

"Excuse me, Ma?"

"Pimp," I said, "is another word for 'don'."

"Indeed, I am not a pimp, nor was I ever one."

"Listen, Billy Boy, don't get all riled up, as long as you've changed your ways."

He broke up laughing. Hilda came running in. "Children, darlings, what is it? Don't yell at the Divine Mother, Billy." That broke us both up.

"I knew it all the time," I lied, "I was just kidding you."

"Oh, Ma," he said, "I've never loved this way before. Never change."

Over the years his dignity rubbed off on me, and my Brooklyn on him. We made a good pair, Billy and me.

मा

"Billy, what do you want for your birthday?" It was 1991, and I knew this would be my last May with Billy, the first man to call himself my chela. We had been through so much together, including the discovery of his leukemia several years before. Now finally the leukemia was claiming his body.

"Ma, promise to grant me the boon of being with you on Thursday."

What a strange thing to ask of me. Billy had been with me every single day of my life, but not on Thursdays. Thursday was the day I went on rounds, and Billy was much too sick to come with me. "Why would you want to come with me when you're so sick yourself?" I asked.

"Ma, the world is letting your people with AIDS die unnoticed. They're not able to keep their dignity. I have an acceptable disease; people have the time for someone with cancer."

"Okay, Billy Boy, Thursday it is."

Thursday came. It was a clear, hot Florida day. Before Billy even got in the van, he had tears in his eyes.

"Billy, if this is the way we are starting off, what will the afternoon bring?"

"Ma, this is like traveling with Annapurna." In India, Annapurna is the goddess of abundance, always overflowing, always feeding everyone.

I looked in the van, seeing it for the first time through someone else's eyes. In every available space there was food: bananas, grapes, oranges, grapefruit, cheese, crackers, and pretzels. The biggest treat was the cookies that my kids on the ashram bake. There were a few special meals in the van, too. One was for Sonny, a man without legs who'd been in the County Home for twenty-eight years and who sells Avon products in the lobby, always with a smile. There were cigarettes for the AIDS patients in the Haney Wing. There were books for Helen, who spends her life in a wheelchair reading about the romances she will never have.

"Billy," I said, ashamed of my blurring eyes, "hop in. It is going to be a hard day." After making our rounds in West Palm, we would stop at the home of Kim Bergalis, a very brave young girl who was dying of AIDS.

I was the first person Kim had told that she had HIV/AIDS. She had heard about me through one of my chelas who worked in the health department, and he had told her about my work. When doctors warned her that she might be infected with the virus, she wrote to me as she waited for the test results.

"Ma," she wrote, "I'm not writing to ask for any miracles. I'm writing because I'm very scared about all this and confused.... It's all in the hands of God now.... I haven't given up hope yet that the tests will be negative, but I'm beginning to get a frightened feeling inside. I just want the ability to cope with whatever God decides is best for me. I like to think that I'm a strong person and I'll be able to handle it, but I don't know. I also want to best prepare myself for when the time comes. I want to be truly ready and not afraid of entering another world.... Ma, maybe if you could pray for spiritual strength and guidance for me, or ask God to help me organize my thoughts and feelings and not feel so alone."

She wrote eight pages while she waited. When her test results came in, she finished her letter: "Ma, I just found out a few minutes ago that I do have AIDS. I'm so scared. I have to tell my parents and sisters now. I just want to close my eyes and open them and see that this is all a mistake—a horrible nightmare. I want to leave this hospital. I want to just run and go back to being a little girl again.... I'm so scared, Ma.... Please pray for me."

Kim received a lot of publicity later when it came out that she had been infected by her dentist. Some of the AIDS activists, including people I loved, didn't believe her. They were trying hard to remove the public's fears that it was easy to catch AIDS, and Kim's case got very political. I didn't care about the politics, I just cared about Kim.

I never ask anyone how they got the disease. I only know I have to hold them in my arms. I need to take their aloneness, their pain at rejection, their grief over losing so many friends. These beautiful people have names, faces, feelings, lovers, wives, husbands, children. Every one is an individual and unique in every way.

Billy met Kim that night on the way back from West Palm, and they kept in touch. Kim came to Kashi sometimes to sit by the Ganga. But by the time we held Kim's memorial service, Billy, too, was dead.

मा

When Billy was in the hospital, he said, "Ma, take me home to Kashi to die." Now he lay on the bed in the guest room, an oxygen tube in his nose, saline solution in his veins, and blood seeping from the incision in his chest where doctors had installed a port. I yelled at him like a spoiled child, "Billy, Billy!"

He opened his eyes and gave me a look as if to say, "Hey, lady, you taught me how to die. Now let me get on with it."

I knew the student was well rehearsed; only the teacher wasn't ready. All Billy's years passed before my eyes—a strange occurrence, for I was not the one dying. "And yet," I thought, as I gently pressed the blood-soaked towel against his incision, "I am dying."

In those early days, when I became so close to God that the Earth seemed strange, I used to say to my chelas, "You teach me to live, and I will teach you to die." One of the people I trusted the most in those days was Billy. He had traveled around India as a spiritual seeker, but when I met him he was a don at Oxford University, and he was always bothering me to write down my teachings. I didn't always listen, since I made it a practice to speak in the moment. I never taught from a piece of paper, so why would I write a book?

Billy had helped me live in the world, but I was not ready to let him go into death. My tears salted his body. I caressed his hand, the same hand that had led me through life. Now I would take him through the stages of death. He opened his eyes, returning from his place of peace. He gave me a piercing look and spoke: "Ma." Death's preparations made his other words faint, yet I caught them in my heart. "Write, Ma, write."

"I will, my son," I said, almost faint from anguish. "I will write and write until there is no more ink in my heart, simply because you asked me to."

My chelas began to gather outside. They came into Billy's room, one at a time, to bid their *gurubai* farewell. Others in the next room were singing now, "Vishwanatha Gange," a hymn to the god Vishwanath, who whispers the name of God in the pilgrim's ear, the pilgrim who has come to Kashi to die.

I never felt more like a lost child. Billy had been my lifeline to the world as I had been his to God. I am strong and I know death well, yet no mother wants her child to go before her. And all my chelas are my children.

"Write, Ma," he said with his last breath. "Let the River flow through you."

मा

Now, a year after Billy died, I write here in my temple, the candle flames swaying to the gentle breeze from the open door, and I think of all the children who are alone in the darkest part of their lives. I am writing, my Billy, to light one candle in the heart space—where the flesh can't decay and AIDS can't reach or death destroy—the heart of hearts, the place that the holy call the soul. My words will echo after death separates our flesh and life bids us farewell. I will leave my words on the papers of time simply because my chela asked me to.

I cross my legs, sitting in the sacred lotus position. I am alone as I walk through the cremation ground of the goddess Kali. As the dark is alone with its night, so I am alone with my Billy.

CHAPTER SIXTY-TWO

Let Them Touch Your Feet

The warm Florida wind was blowing my hair around my face. It was the last night of Durga Puja, the ten days of the Mother, a Hindu celebration honoring the many aspects of the goddess. The dhuni, the eternal fire of God, was burning brightly. The *pujaris* were tending the flames. Next to me was John, Billy's brother from Scotland. Now, on this sacred night, dressed in the bright red sari of Durga, I was to perform my first ceremony without Billy—his memorial service.

In a basket to my right were little jars filled with the ashes of our dead scholar. My God, would he have loved this drama! I was going to give them out to all his gurubai before I sat down by the dhuni, where the fire would lick my bleeding heart dry of its wounds. The conches were sounding, incense was burning, chelas were chanting, candles lit the sky around our pond—and Billy was gone.

या

My thoughts traveled back to India in 1977, to Haridwar, a city on the banks of the Ganga. Billy and I had gotten ahead of my other chelas. We were walking along the river's edge on a paved stretch of road. The river was raging forward; I was in bliss. We passed a group of beggars clustered together. They were very shabby looking, and their hands and feet were covered with dirty bandages and rags. I gravitated to them. In my cotton sari, worn tied behind my neck sadhu-style, with my wild hair and my tattoos, I was a sight to be seen walking with this sedate Englishman.

My Billy said, "Not too close; they are lepers." I hadn't seen lepers in Haridwar. I had seen them in Rishikesh and Kashi. Yet here they were, with bent heads hidden behind the rags with which they covered their bodies.

"Don't be afraid," I said, "I am Ma."

One small person—it was hard to tell if it was a male or a female—looked up and repeated, "Ma." In his eyes was agony and yet a certain amount of peace. I had the deepest desire to touch this person's feet. I began to bend down in the ancient custom of humility and respect, thinking he would run away, yet knowing I must try. The others stepped back, but he held his ground.

"Babaji," I said in greeting, "Namaste."

"Mataji, namaste."

When my hand reached down, there were no feet to touch. Leprosy had taken them, and he had perfected the art of walking on his heels.

"Dear God," I thought, "what courage."

He stepped back and threw himself on the ground, clutching my ankles.

"Mataji, Kali!" He called out the name of one of the most loved and feared goddesses in all of India.

This was all new to me—no one ever touched my feet—and in my shyness, I pulled back. The tears began to fall from his eyes. Billy, though appalled by his guru's behavior, whispered in my ear, "Let him touch your feet, Ma. Let us all touch the flesh of the guru and be released from the pain of the world."

I put my right foot forward. This man with leprosy kissed it gently while clutching my other foot. Just then, five men, dressed in Indian whites, came toward us shouting, "*Jao, jao*! Get out! Go!"

"Leave them!" I screamed, my heart breaking. "Leave them alone or help them."

The lepers started to run. Billy held me back from running after them. "Let them go, Ma. Let them go."

The one who touched my feet turned and, with lips that were half-eaten away by this devastating disease, smiled at me. My eyes blurred with tears. I was a stranger in a strange land—a strange land, yet so much more of a home to me than my own flesh is to my soul.

"You did it, Ma. You gave someone the blessing of the guru's feet."

"No, Billy, I received the greater blessing."

An official-looking man came over to us. "Mother, disinfect your feet well. The leper has touched you."

"I don't know how to wash my heart, nor do I want to, for that is where he truly touched me," I replied.

My Billy, being the coward he always professed himself to be, said, "Thank you, Sir, she will." We walked back the opposite way with the Ganga rushing by us.

"Billy, I know how to wash our hearts."

The Ganga runs swift and cold at Haridwar. An iron railing protects people on the banks, and yet pilgrims seek the river's blessing here, too. Together, we climbed over the rail and held on tight to the bars, letting the raging Ganga tear at our bodies and soothe our souls.

"Gange, Gange, Ki Jai! Victory to the River! Victory to the Mother," we cried out like children.

"Billy, hold on or She will get you."

He was laughing and crying at the same time. "Get me, Mother," he cried out. "Get me, Ma."

I got you, my Billy. Not only your ash, which I wear around my neck, but I have your spirit in my heart. Gange, Gange, Ki Jai!

CHAPTER SIXTY-THREE

The Stigmata

Sal had given up on Florida, but he still thought it might help me if we moved out of the house where I had seen Christ. We had plans to go look at a house in Staten Island. That morning, I looked down at my hands as I was scrubbing my refrigerator, my fancy copper refrigerator that showed every fingerprint, a record of all the people who opened it every day. And now I saw blood.

It was Good Friday, 1974, more than a year since the night Christ had first appeared to me and told me, "Teach all ways." So much had happened, but my love for Christ had only grown deeper.

There was more and more blood on my hands, and I couldn't hide it from myself. I called up my lifeline, Hilda, and said, "Something's happened, and I need to get out of this fast!"

She said, "Darling, it's only a vision. It's something you're bringing on psychically because you love him so much."

I didn't know what to do. Finally Hilda said, "Call Denise." My daughter was seventeen by then, very straight, very sensible. On this day, it was her turn to take care of the upstairs, while I cleaned the downstairs.

I tried to be calm, but maybe my voice cracked a little bit. I didn't say anything about blood. I just said, "Hey, Hilda's on the phone, would you talk to her?" We had to leave in an hour to go look at the house.

I was very afraid, and I was in ecstasy, all at the same time. When Denise first came down, I kept my hands closed, but then I showed her. When you sweat, you can watch the droplets come out on your skin. That's what this was like. It was as if the blood was sweat, seeping out of my palms. I said, "We gotta do something fast." I thought maybe I should go to the emergency room and get some stitches.

Denise said, "All right, let's calm down." She had me rinse my hands in cold water. Then we tried ice, but the blood kept building up, building up. There was no cut and no pain, but blood just seeped through the skin.

Meanwhile Hilda was telling Denise it was just something I was bringing on psychically. That's when I heard Denise say to her, "Okay, then, you get over here and wipe up the psychic blood."

That was all Hilda needed to hear. "Denise, take her to the mountain right away, take her to Mount Manresa."

"How can I take her anywhere? My father is taking us to Staten Island to get a house."

I don't remember everything that happened that day, but my daughter saw it all. This is not a story I often tell but Denise helped me with this part of it.

Sal was outside waxing his car. We had to get ready to go. The blood would come and go, sometimes one hand, sometimes both. Denise and I decided that we were just not going to pay attention to it, we were not going to discuss it, and we didn't care that it was Good Friday. Many strange things had been happening. Although I tried my best to act normal, I knew this blood came from loving Christ so passionately, something I would never deny.

Sal's parents came over to have a cup of coffee and talk about the house in Staten Island. I was wearing a scarf wrapped around my head to hold my hair back. All of a sudden Denise ran upstairs, and then she called me to come up. I didn't know what was going on until I got up there and looked in the mirror. All over my forehead were droplets of blood coming out on the skin.

At the beginning, it was more pinkish than blood red, but the longer the day went on the redder it got; it was somehow as if it was building up. I felt that I had no control anymore and asked, "Why does he want me? I am who I am." I didn't ask for any of this, but it was happening to me. I was feeling ecstasy and great fear at the same time.

We knew we had to keep it from Sal. He would have insisted that I go to a hospital. We decided we had to continue our day as if nothing was strange. The bleeding wasn't a constant thing, so I re-wrapped the scarf around my head so it would cover my forehead, pirate-style, and we all got in the car.

The sky turned black. Between the sky and the blood, it was terrifying. Sal turned to me and asked, "Joycey, you okay?" I said I was, but I couldn't even look at him. I loved him so much, but by this time I felt I had to lie to him whenever God was involved, and that was really because I didn't want to hurt him.

We stopped at a fast-food hamburger place called Roll-N-Roaster, where we used to love to eat. It was Friday, so we just ordered cheese fries. I was okay, I was with my family, the blood was hidden, and I could just sit there with them. Until all of a sudden Denise said, "Let's go to the bathroom, Ma."

Sal said, "Seventeen years old, you can't go to the bathroom yet? That's three times you called your mother to the bathroom today."

"It's the womanly thing to do, Pop!"

The bathroom wasn't even inside. You had to get a key and go outside to a little two-by-four space. We went in, and I asked, "What's the matter?"

She said, "Well, why don't you just take a look down?" Sure enough, there was blood on my feet now, too. Then my head and my hands started bleeding more heavily again. Denise stayed with me, she brought me ice, she did everything there was to do, but of course we had no control.

We couldn't stay in that bathroom. We had to go see that house, we had to make normal for Sal, so we cleaned up the blood as best we could, took all the napkins from the table, and got back in the car. At that point there was a lot of blood. It really scared me. There was still no cut anywhere, and no pain, just blood oozing through the skin, and I felt tingly all over.

In the car, Denise kept stuffing my hands with tissues. We didn't know what to do with them once they were full of blood, so we littered on the Belt Parkway. We were terrified that Sal would notice, so out the car window they went.

With Sal, everything was kosher if it was about Christ or Catholic, so I said, "On the way to Staten Island, can you just drop me off for a second so I can see Father Atherton at Mount Manresa?" I had my hands in my pockets and my pockets were getting soaked.

As I was going in, one of the statues started to talk to me—not my statue down in the grotto, but one to the left that stood all by itself. I didn't want to talk to a statue just then. I was kind of insulted because I wanted to talk to the man himself. The statue said to me, "It is not necessary for any being upon this earth to feel the pain of Christ or my Father." But I forgot that part until later.

I went on, and showed the old priest what was happening. By that time, I was bleeding from the side as well. The priest rushed me into his rooms. I tried to make light of the whole thing, saying, "You've been trying to get me in your room for a year now, huh?" When you're scared, you'll say dumb things out of nerves.

That's when he told me that I must hide what was happening to me. He said that thousands would try to come to see me and they'd make a freak out of me. He said that not all of those who would come would truly come for God. And then he frightened me even more by getting down on his knees in front of me.

I wanted to stay there at Mount Manresa and let the priests take care of me, but Sal was waiting in the car, so I had to go. We picked up Fran and Richie. Fran saw the blood too, and helped keep it from Sal. The blood was really getting hard to hide, and the sky was filling with black clouds. Sal felt something. He kept asking me if I was okay, and I kept saying yes. There was no pain, just a feeling of fullness and lightness. It was ecstasy, and I wanted it to stop.

I prayed to Christ to stop the blood. Actually, I said, "If you don't stop this, Jesus Christ, I'll never teach again." And the blood stopped. I thought I had some powers, until I looked at my watch and saw that it was three o'clock. According to tradition, that's the time the crucifixion ended.

Later, my daughter asked me, "Are you still my mother? Or are you a saint? Some kind of Jewish saint?"

"I ain't no damned saint. This is just a freak accident."

My daughter told the priest at school, and he sent her to a psychologist. I didn't tell many people what had happened. I wasn't looking to be a saint, a teacher, a holy person, and least of all a freak.

CHAPTER SIXTY-FOUR

Kali

I kept what happened that Good Friday hidden from Sal because the man had had enough. How could I show him that I had had enough, too—of the hospitals and doctors he would drag me to, the oxygen tanks he ordered, the arguments we had? He was trying every way he knew to fix me, like maybe there would be a cure for loving God. So I kept it hidden. And then the old priest warned me not to tell anyone about it or I would be made a freak in a circus show. So when it was over, we went home, and I cooked dinner and made normal as best I could.

On Easter Sunday, we always had a big, big dinner. I would be cooking for days. But the bleeding began again on Easter morning and, again, I tried to hide it. I wore my laundry gloves, and I wrapped a turban around my head while I cooked and got ready. Everybody but Shirley went off to Mass that morning, so she was there and saw the whole thing. But what could we do? We had a house full of guests coming, there was food to be served, and I had to get through the day like I did on Good Friday. As the blood kept flowing, I was on the phone with Hilda off and on all that Easter day. She would tell me, "It's nothing, dear. It happens all the time."

Billy was at Hilda's, and she had told him to listen on the extension phone. He heard what happened when Sal's mother Anna first saw me. Suddenly the old lady started screaming, "It's the Little Flower! The Judatz has turned into Saint Theresa!" She fainted away right there in the foyer.

And then Sal was yelling, "Mama, get up for Christ's sake. Are you crazy?"

Then everybody was screaming, and the dogs were barking, and I tried to act like nothing was happening, because that's what Hilda kept telling me to do. I already had my rubber gloves on, so I went and sorted the laundry until they calmed down.

When I spoke to Hilda she said, "Well, what are you waiting for, darling. You've got a family to feed. Go serve the spare ribs." And she hung up.

Later, in her practical way, Hilda said, "Let's draw all the blood up to the top of the head." She had a bunch of people at her house, so she had them pray for seventeen hours to stop the bleeding, starting that morning when I first called her and continuing into that night. She kept trying to calm me down by saying everything was normal, but of course she knew it wasn't.

This whole time, I was totally fascinated. Maybe I would have liked it better if it wasn't me this was happening to, but still I was fascinated. The guests came, the guests ate, and they went home. Throughout the day, I played the part of wife and mother as well as I could. Meanwhile, Hilda was telling me not to worry, she was sure that the blood would stop at midnight.

Finally, I was all alone in the basement, where Sal had made a meditation room for me after the thing with the bathroom became too much for my family. I stayed down there to be on the phone with Hilda. It was just me and my telephone.

Just as Hilda had said, the blood stopped at midnight, but that wasn't the end. At midnight sharp, a parade began. First the prophets came, all of them—Isaiah, Abraham, everybody came one by one. Then the gods and the goddesses of every religion known to man came, passed before me in my basement, each one more beautiful than the last.

Hilda was still on the phone with me. I described to her what I was seeing, what each one looked like. She repeated what I said into a tape recorder and told me who each one was. I would say, "He's all in white ash, he's wearing a tiger skin and carrying this pointy thing."

First she would repeat all that for the tape, and then she would say, "Oh, my dear, that's Shiva."

All of a sudden, the blackest of black appeared before me, this black blob dripping goo, and it was coming toward me. I panicked. Even though I was already in samadhi, I still panicked. It felt like, "Now I did it, I went too far, get me out of here." A black blob was coming toward me, and there was my precious Hilda on the line, what seemed like 50,000 miles away from me. I was screaming, and she was telling the tape recorder what was going on, and meanwhile the blob was coming closer. She finished speaking into the tape recorder, and said, "Oh, it must be Kali, darling."

"Just get her away from me!" Any image of the goddess Kali looks like a movie star compared to this thing that was coming at me, with fangs.

Hilda said, "No, no, darling, don't be afraid." All alone in a dark basement and don't be afraid! With this being, this ugly mass coming close. I didn't remember how to run; my legs were locked stiff with samadhi. Don't forget, I was in God already.

Meanwhile, at Hilda's they were having pizza, and I bet popcorn, while they prayed and taped everything. I could have been dying on the other end of that phone, or been getting initiated into all kinds of stuff, and Hilda couldn't answer me right away because she had to repeat for the tape what I had just said.

Here's how it went: I screamed, "Kali, coming toward me, it's Kali, she's dripping with blackness and blood and skulls."

"She's dripping with blackness and blood and skulls," Hilda repeated.

"What should I do, what should I do?" I pleaded, about to be swallowed up, while she was talking for the tape. But then, just in the nick of time, she said, "Tell her to open herself."

"Forget it, oil will come out."

See, no matter what anybody said, I was sure this was not God, this could not be God, and so it was my way out. My excuse. We all look for an excuse to get away from God, and this black blob coming toward me was my excuse.

Hilda said, "Tell her to unzip herself."

I thought, "What the fuck does that mean?" She didn't exactly have a zipper. I would have said or done anything at that moment, gotten on my hands and knees and barked, if it would have made her go away. "Please, Mother, show yourself to me," I asked the black blob. I didn't know what she was.

Hilda was still saying, "Tell her to unzip herself."

So to get rid of her, I said, "Please, Mother, unzip yourself."

And she did. She opened herself up, and a light came forth. I have never seen anything as beautiful in all the three worlds as the light that came from her. I have never seen beauty shine from a woman like that, except from the Virgin. That was the first time since seeing the Christ that I really saw, being a woman myself, what love is, what a goddess would do to herself for her children.

I saw the Golden Kali as well as the terrifying Black Mother, and they were the same. She's beautifully ugly from the karma of the world. She becomes black and horrible, her tongue protruding and her fangs coming out, so that her children can be pure. Because the lighter you get, the darker she gets. That's her beauty, her love, and her enjoyment at serving her children, taking their karma into herself.

I realized then, perhaps for the first time, what it was to be the Mother. I said, "May I serve you?"

That was it. She zipped up and said, "Yes, my daughter."

Hilda said, "Let her enter you, darling."

"What are you, nuts?" I still hesitated. And then before me came all of humanity, one by one. Not the saints and the phony holies, but humanity—the sinners, the whores, the damned. They all kept passing by me, begging me to take away the burden they didn't need. Each one had an incredible burden of karma that was carried lifetime after lifetime.

Kali said, "Take me into you."

I did, and she has been with me ever since.

CHAPTER SIXTY-FIVE

Cremation Grounds

"Touch my hand, Jaya," Swami said quietly. I gladly touched his huge hand.

"Look down at the hand," he ordered. I looked. It was covered with maggots and pus. "Hold your hand pressed to my own, tightly." Only my love and trust for my teacher allowed me to do such a thing. "Don't flinch," he said. "Ugliness is in the mind and not of the soul. The flesh of someone filled with sickness can still touch the heart space. You must love everyone as the Mother."

I bowed to my teacher and thought, "Where will I use this knowledge?"

That happened in 1974, when I was a newcomer on the path of this life. Who would have thought I would one day be telling this story to my chelas in the face of such a devastating disease as AIDS?

Meanwhile, most of the time at Hilda's, I wasn't teaching with words, but sitting in my own silence and letting people take what they could from me in that silence. Everybody was perfect to me, as long as I could sip the nectar of God.

One day Swami said to me, "Jaya, look at your children. Point out to them their imperfection."

I fought his instructions as long as I could, but one day Hilda brought me a young man. She told me that he had been in trance for three days and hadn't eaten anything. Hilda said he was in samadhi. That was okay with me because, really, I thought everybody was in samadhi anyway. We could just sit there in God together.

But there was Swami, yelling at me, telling me I must look deeper into this boy. I didn't want to, but I looked at the boy and I saw that he had just had bacon and eggs and waffles. He had stopped for breakfast on the way. Three helpings of bacon! I came down heavy on him. He jumped up and ran away, and I never saw him again.

He was just the first one. I came down heavy on a second one, and a third one, and a fourth one. Soon I had become the garbage pail for all New York City again, but now I was taking imperfections just as Kali, the dark goddess, had shown me. People seemed to understand this kind of teaching better than silence. Even though it was harsh, it turns out it was easier to take harshness than the simplicity of love. But to me, I felt as if I had put on a heavy, heavy mask.

When Kali first came to me, I was reassured by the beauty of her golden form, but as I began to teach, I longed for her darkness. With the blessing of Mother Kali, I learned to take pain into my eyes. As this happens, the man or woman looking into my eyes feels a buoyancy; the spirit rises. As he gets lighter, giving up what he fears the most, my face gets darker, until he closes his eyes.

It has taken me years to refine the process of consuming the suffering of another person without looking too weird, and without hurting myself. It is an honor that I both cherish and love. Usually, though, I allow Kali to appear only to those people who are deeply seeking God. I have never forced my beliefs on anyone simply because I believe in goodness and kindness in any form. Therefore I believe in everyone, and every religion or spiritual path is good enough for me if it teaches kindness. I place my heart on humanity's doorstep and cry out into the night: "Do not judge what you can't understand. I am here for you."

मा

Now, so many years later, I was making my rounds of hospitals and hospices in West Palm Beach. Tommy was waiting for me at the entrance to Health House, a residence for people with AIDS. He was wearing high-heeled white leather boots, just to show off for me. We admired them together, but when I took him in my arms, I could feel his fear. We both knew he didn't have very long to live. I followed him into his room, and we sat on the bed. He asked, "Can I look into your eyes?"

I was taken aback. When I go on my rounds, I am there only as one who serves and holds, kisses, and hugs. The spiritual part only comes out on request. In fact, no matter where I am, I never ask others to believe as I do.

Yet here was Tommy, who I had seen only a few times, asking me to use the power of Kali to take his fear and his pain. He was making ready to die and asking me to help. I understood that he was looking for Kali, whether he knew her name or not—the black goddess of nighttime fears; she who stalks the cremation grounds on life's shores; she whose darkness is darker than any evil, any pain, any negativity; she whose darkness can absorb pain to reveal the purity of the soul.

"Come here, closer. Look deeply," I said. He began to get lighter and lighter as darkness and pain left him.

"Ma," he said, laughing, "you are as black as night."

"No one has ever laughed before. They're usually too scared."

"Oh, Ma, it's only you playing goddess. I feel great. Now, show me what it feels like to die." I called on Yama, the god of death, who used my eyes to show Tommy the floating sensation of going into the light.

Tommy was crying now. As I held him, I wondered if we had gone too far.

"No," he said, "I'm crying from joy."

Sitting on his bed, I thought, "The young are dying. I am teaching the young to die. A generation lost to death, while so many are unaware."

मा

I feel now as if I spend many days in the cremation grounds, or sitting near the burning ghats of India. Those who come to me and offer their ego, or their small self, expose themselves to the Black Mother and to all she is capable of doing for them. I take inside myself, as Ma, simply as Ma, all the pain I can, or am allowed to take—including pain due to karmic reasons. And I hold them, I touch them, I caress them. I say to them, "Strip yourself, strip yourself of all that you do not need to go on. I love you as you are."

Is it me they come to see, or do they come to see themselves? I am available to those who seek God. Any god, it does not matter; many faces, it does not matter; many forms, it does not matter; God as form or formless, it does not matter. I am available to those who seek themselves, and this is the blessing of Mother Kali.

CHAPTER SIXTY-SIX

Hanuman and Christ

Hanuman was the last of the gods to come to me that Easter night, after Kali. In the great epic *The Ramayana*, Hanuman is an incarnation of Shiva, who came to Earth in the form of a monkey to teach us humility, and so Hanuman is the god of service. Of course I hadn't read *The Ramayana* at the time, but here was a monkey in my basement, and I felt in him the exact same essence as that of Christ. How could I explain that to my priests at Mount Manresa? I didn't know, nor did I care.

In a Tibetan store I found a tiny brass murti of Hanuman, one of the little statues of the gods that you find all over India, and I began to carry it in my hand everywhere I went. One summer day, sitting on the hill at Mount Manresa, holding this little Hanuman in my hand, I forgot all caution and common sense and began to teach the Jesuits about the monkey. I had been with them for more than a year. At first they had listened to me simply because they saw in my eyes that I had touched Christ, touched his flesh, his body. But during that year, I had learned about many spiritual paths—Hinduism, Tibetan Buddhism, the Native American traditions. I had seen the gods parade before me in my basement, and Hilda had shown me that I wasn't crazy after all.

I had shared with the priests some of what I had learned, but not all of it. I mainly spoke to them about yoga, which was still a big part of my life. I had also repeated to them things my Swami was teaching me, plus what I was absorbing from all the scriptures. What was inside me was waking up.

On July 30, 1974, I was sitting on the Jesuits' hill, and Swami Nityananda told me, "Do it now. Show them your true beliefs."

I began by telling them that I had in my hand a statue. I didn't use the word murti then. I said, "I have here a statue that is the same as Christ to me," and I told them there was no difference between the essence of Christ and the essence of Hanuman the monkey.

Just as I said that, at that moment, I had such a strong feeling of Christ. I had been searching, searching for him everywhere for a year and a half. There were times I could feel him so close, but he never came like he had before. Now finally, I was doing what he had told me to do: teach all ways. At first I had thought he meant "teach always," all the time, which I do anyway; in reality he had meant teach all the ways to God. Now, for the first time, I was talking about all the paths to God that I could, and I didn't care for the opinion of man. That's what he meant when he said, "You must teach all ways, and I will return to you when you become who you are." It wasn't like at the beginning, the four visits when he appeared to me so real and so sudden, when I was so afraid, and it was all so new. I still missed his form, but feeling his essence like that was an exquisite reunion in itself. It felt like coming home.

Some of the priests didn't like me saying that a monkey was the same as Christ, but only a few judged me for it. They all knew in the depths of their hearts that I had really seen Christ. So what if I was crazy, too? Their God was big, and their love was big—big enough that they didn't have to slam the door on forms of God that were different from their own. It's only the people who make their God small who fear other religions.

CHAPTER SIXTY-SEVEN

Neem Karoli Baba

I was watching the dancing shadows on my bedroom wall. Slowly and quietly I got out of bed. I was anxious to blow out the candle I always lit after Sal fell asleep and which I extinguished before he woke up.

"God," I thought, "it's going to be a hot one today." It was the first day of August, and in Brooklyn that meant hot. I threw on an old housedress that Sal thought was quite sexy—it was cut low in the front—and I went downstairs to make myself a cup of Lipton tea and maybe have a diet bran muffin, which I was sure had a hundred thousand calories. Anyway, I was starting my diet again the next day. Today I had planned a big steak barbecue for Sal and the kids when he got off from work.

Also that day, I had an appointment with a lady from the neighborhood who wanted help with her boredom and depression. I was to meet her that afternoon in my backyard. Though I had promised to show her how to meditate, in my heart I didn't know if I should. She might end up like me, with strange goings-on in her bathroom. I had been teaching since March. Words just came through me like a fountain that wouldn't stop. They flowed and sounded alien, yet quite beautiful, bringing many of Hilda's students to tears.

Every day I wondered if Swami Nityananda was my guru, even though he always said he wasn't.

"A guru is everything, Joya," Hilda would tell me.

"What the hell is a guru?" I was asking again, as the morning light peeked in the window that faced the yard.

Sal came down the stairs. I had made him pancakes and bacon. I joined him for the pancakes, but left the bacon off my plate. I had given up meat. He would always say, "Come on, eat with me." I loved my husband and wouldn't think of refusing him my company at breakfast, especially if it was pancakes.

"You spent the night in the bathroom again, didn't you?"

"No," I answered, "I was back in bed at 4:30."

My heart broke for this man who was losing me to Christ, after wanting me to be a Catholic for all those years we had been married. I had kept my Judaism intact, only now I was in love with the Christ of my heart, the Christ who had visited me four times. My whole life had become a waiting game: waiting for the Christ, waiting for a guru, waiting for Sal and the kids to understand my search. Waiting, yet Swami often said, "Be in the moment, Jaya." Well, I sure was in the moment now—the pancakes were delicious.

"Babe," he said, "I am losing you, and I don't want to. I will do everything I can to hold onto you, even if it hurts you."

"Just let me love God in my own way," I answered, choking on my words, the pain of want gripping both of us. To lighten the moment, I promised him the best cookout he'd ever tasted. He kissed me passionately and held me tight, as if he was going off to war. "Sal," I said, "I'll see you in a few hours."

"Okay, Babe," he said, grabbing his keys and work gloves. "Kiss the kids for me."

"Goodbye, my love," I whispered to the closing front door.

मा

I didn't know this day would mark the end of my life as I knew it. August 1, 1974: the day I was to meet my guru for the first time in this life.

"What is going on?" I asked into my cup of tea, which had grown cold. Why is it that every time I say goodbye to my husband I feel like I'm losing him more and more? Yet my love had not grown less, only more.

I began to gather the ingredients that I would need to make my sauce. I put on the tape machine. Dinah Washington was singing, "What a Difference a Day Makes."

"Yeah," I thought, "what a difference every moment makes." I got the sauce started on a medium flame. While it was simmering, I ran up the few stairs to my bathroom temple. There, as I knew he would be, was my teacher and friend, Swami Nityananda.

"Why does this day feel different?" I asked the great Swami, sounding to my own ears like the youngest grandchild that asks the Four Questions at the beginning of Passover.

"You will see," he said in his loving and stern voice. He closed his eyes as if to say, "Go on with your business and leave me to my own."

As I began cooking again, I thought about Hilda's words, "The guru is everything. The guru is everything."

After everyone had left, I proceeded to clean the huge house. If Christ came back, I didn't want him to think I was a slob, did I? Fran came over and helped me, as she had been doing because I was becoming less able to manage ordinary life. Sometimes I felt unconnected to the earth, or ungrounded, and she understood that better than anyone except Hilda.

When everything was finished, we put on our bathing suits and headed for the backyard and the pool. We climbed the steep aluminum steps that led to the narrow deck. As I sat down, I felt a strange warmth come over me. Somehow I knew it wasn't from the hot sun beating down on us.

"Fran," I said, "I forgot to take out the steaks."

Sal was expected at three, and as soon as all the kids came home we would start the big brick barbecue in the corner of the yard and begin to cook the steaks. I had sold a huge load of Anne Klein seconds and made a few extra bucks, so I had ordered about a dozen huge T-bones. If Salvatore knew how much they'd cost, he would have had a fit.

Fran said, "I'll get the steaks and we'll defrost them in the sun."

I closed my eyes for a moment, listening to Dinah Washington on the tape player, still feeling strange. As Fran brought out the steaks, I shouted to her to let the dogs loose. I was so out of it at that moment that I forgot about the steaks. The two huge Italian bulldogs had been a present from me to myself. I loved them fiercely. They were yelping and playing when someone called out to me. It was Sylvia, who I had agreed to meet with. Fran held the dogs while Sylvia climbed up the steep steps.

"I need your help desperately," she said as she took the lounge chair across from me. She was known on the whole street as a complainer. I began to say something when that same warmth that had spread over me earlier now became like hot liquid, weird but somehow pleasant. Sylvia lifted her hand to her face in horror and screamed, "You have no teeth!"

"What are you fucking talking about?" I shouted.

"You're a fat old man," she screamed, slipping down the steps and landing on the concrete. She hit the ground running. In all the excitement, the dogs went a little crazy. Giavana, the female, grabbed some steaks in her huge jaws; her brother followed her. By the time Fran got to them, my little angel pups had devoured twelve expensive T-bone steaks. At least they didn't eat Sylvia. Fran was hysterical, knowing how much they'd cost and how much I'd wanted to make the afternoon special for Sal and the kids.

I tried to tell her that something was happening to me. I felt like I was about to give birth, only without all the pain. She just yelled, "I'm going to get some more steaks." She left me up there on the deck of the pool. I never felt so crazy in all my life. She didn't even wonder why Sylvia had run away like that.

All of a sudden, there was an old fat man without teeth sitting in the chair that Sylvia had recently occupied. I was speechless, never mind scared out of my wits. "You got no teeth!" I screamed at him.

He smiled, and I saw he had three teeth. He kept smiling as if to prove to me that he did indeed have teeth.

"Who the fuck are you?" I asked. "There is no more room in my bathroom!"

It was about 110 degrees in the sun, and this toothless old man was wearing a heavy blanket, yet he was as cool as could be. The blanket was itchy-looking, and that bothered me no end. I looked into his black eyes. I heard him talk, as if from a long way off, even though he was right opposite me.

"I am your guru."

"My what?"

He said it again, "Your guru."

I began to laugh and cry at the same moment. I couldn't explain what I felt, even to myself. I hated him and loved him. I was angry at him. Yet I knew that if he left I would die. In the next moment, I wanted him out of there. But I had never felt anything like this before. This man was cool as ice in his blanket, and I was drenched in sweat and shaking all over. He was beautiful, he was ugly; he was everything, he was nothing. I felt as if a web had been spun from my last life to this life, from my heart to his heart. He was an old man, but he had stolen my heart, perhaps a thousand years ago, and had never given it back. And I hated him. My first feeling was pure hatred. Why did I hate him? Because I loved him. I loved him to the very depths of my soul.

I also knew that the Italian was about to come home. But I couldn't move as I watched the old man gracefully go down the steep deck stairs and into my house. He opened the sliding glass doors, turned, and smiled his toothless smile. I was staring at him, the sun blinding me. I thought, "This is all a dream." But Sylvia had seen him too. I followed him with my eyes. In the place where he'd been standing a moment before, was now a young man of about thirty-three, looking at me, and I knew in that instant, even as he changed back to the one who called himself my guru, that I would follow him anywhere. No matter the pain or joy, I would devote my life to this old man in the itchy blanket.

He had come for me at last, and I knew him, and he knew me. I also knew he would never leave me again, and the love I felt for him was the same love I felt for my Christ. I knew his love for Christ was the same as my own. Now I had someone to share my love with, and I understood how my Christ was keeping his promise. I knew it in every cell of my being as I climbed down the steps and followed my Baba.

CHAPTER SIXTY-EIGHT

Save the Last Dance for Me

I was walking toward the sliding glass doors when Fran returned with the steaks. "Where are the beasts?" she asked. I realized she meant my Italian bulls. I looked all around the yard for them. I couldn't see them anywhere. All the while my heart was whispering, "Go in and see the man you've been waiting for all your life."

When I went inside I heard the dogs barking playfully. I lost my breath for a moment; I thought the dogs had eaten the old man, as if a spirit could be eaten. When I found them, they were playing with the old man, yelping like little puppies instead of fierce watchdogs.

I heard Fran come in. "Did you find them, Joyce?" I was curious to see if she could see the old man. "Why the hell are those dogs jumping in the air like lunatics?" She just stared, looking at the dogs. I knew then that she couldn't see the old man but that the dogs could.

All of a sudden she looked at me and said, "Are you okay, Ma?" She never used this name for me, nor would she ever call me "Joya," the name used by Hilda and her students. I looked at Fran, and she smiled at me. Once again I was Joyce. "Hey," she said, "you'd better get started on this cookout." She grabbed the big dogs, who began crying like babies as they were dragged outside.

I went into Denise's room and picked up a small blanket she was crocheting for her sister. I placed it in front of the fireplace in our basement rec room. We had decorated it in what we thought of as Spanish style. There was a fake fireplace, red velvet wallpaper, with two huge battle axes crossed on the wall, and a six-foot knight in armor standing in the corner. You could see down into the basement as soon as you came through the front door. The old man appeared, as I knew he would, and sat cross-legged on the blanket, hiding it with his own big form. He paid no attention to the knight.

It was as if I had been struck by lightning. As he was wrapping his blanket around his shoulders, he looked at me and said, "What is your life?"

I looked right into his eyes and answered in one word, loud and clear: "Ruined."

From being with my Hilda I somehow knew to bow. I did so and left him alone in the basement. As I was about to walk up the stairs, I heard him say, "Jaya Ma, Jaya Ma, take care of the family as best you can. Try to be as normal as possible. Your children are young. One day you will be forced to leave them for a little while. They do not understand your quest for God."

I turned and said, "Guru, how can they understand, if I still don't?"

He smiled a sad smile and said these words with tears running down his face: "My Ma, they didn't understand the Christ, they didn't understand the Baba, now they will not understand you. Yet you are the Mother, and you will go past their nonunderstanding."

"Guru," I said (I still did not know how to address him), "is this for real, or am I crazy? It feels as if I'm losing my husband, I'm losing my children, I'm losing my mind."

"Have you ever been happier than at this moment?"

I looked at this old toothless man in my basement wrapped up in a heavy blanket. He was only spirit, yet I could see his flesh clearly. "No, never for one second." I was never happier. "But is it real?" I asked.

You know what he had the nerve to say to me? "Ma, it is not real."

I really went crazy then. "What did you say?" I screamed at my newly discovered guru. I didn't know where to turn. "Not real! Then what *is* real?"

"When you can share this with others, then you will know," he said calmly.

"Share what?" I asked, confused.

"Just this," he said. "Only in the sharing is it real. I am the sharing. Share me."

I bowed once again and took my leave. Fran was outside in the hot sun giving the dogs a lecture on manners. In the kitchen, I grabbed the big salad bowl I'd taken out and began to make my famous salad. As I was tearing the lettuce leaves, dipping them into a mixture of oil and bread crumbs, Fran came in and said, "I don't know what's going on here, but I beg you, don't leave me behind."

"Fran, will you share me with others?"

"Share what?" she asked.

"Everything. It is all in the sharing."

"Joyce, where did you get those words from?"

"From my guru. He's downstairs in the basement in front of the fireplace."

Fran didn't blink an eye and said, "I will share you with the world only if I can always be with you and if I never have to call you Joya, because it's not your name."

"What is my name?" I asked, as I began to shred the water mozzarella for my salad.

She grabbed her keys off the counter. "Why, 'Ma,' of course."

She was on her way to pick up the two little ones from school. I ran to the top of the stairs. When she got to the foyer, she looked down the steps leading to the basement and pranamed, putting two hands together and bowing her head.

"Who are you bowing to?"

"To your guru, of course."

"Can you see him?"

"No, not really, but you can, and that's good enough for me."

I hung over the banister and said, "Old man, I don't know if I have the same faith as Fran, but if you make trouble I want you out of here."

The words didn't sound convincing at all, even to me. I heard the old one just chuckle and say in a singsong voice, "Ma, Ma, Ma." My heart stopped. It was the voice I had heard all my life. I ran back to the kitchen and the comfort of food. I thought if I ate something it would take that sound away, the sound of "Ma, Ma." I grabbed a huge box of Oreos and began eating. The words got louder, the voice ringing through the whole house. I began to sway with the sound of it. I looked down and saw I had eaten the whole box.

"Well," I said, as loud as I could, "you're really getting out of here. The Christ at least helped me to lose weight. I wouldn't even think of eating in his presence. With you I don't even know I'm eating."

"Feed everyone," said the voice of the guru coming from the basement into my heart.

"Okay, okay, I'm trying," I yelled back.

"Trying what, Babe?" I jumped out of my skin. It was Salvatore. I hadn't heard him come in.

"I'm trying to make the best cookout you ever had." I had boiled the corn on the cob earlier. Now I was going to wrap the ears in tinfoil with lots of butter and pieces of bacon around them. Then I was going to put them on the barbecue and toast them nice, melting the butter. Suddenly I thought, "I didn't even light the barbecue." I hurried to the backyard. To my surprise I found about two dozen teenagers and a few younger kids out there. The big brick barbecue was going something fierce. How long had I been inside?

"Take out the chopped meat," I screamed through the kitchen window. "We gotta have more to serve these kids. Twelve steaks aren't enough."

Just then Denise came home. She came right out to the back yard. Ignoring her brother, sister, father, Fran, and the crowd, she marched right over to me. I thought, "What now?"

"Mama," she whispered in my ear, "who the hell is in the basement, and why, for God's sake, can't Papa see him? Or better yet, why can I see him if Papa can't?"

"Oh, Denisey," I said, "I'm not crazy after all. I love you."

Salvatore was smiling as he came out with the corn. I ran to him. Someone had turned on the stereo, which piped music outside. Our song was playing, "More" from the movie *Mondo Cane*. He put down the pot, and we began to dance in the backyard in front of all the kids. Yet I kept thinking of another song I loved, "Save the Last Dance for Me." Was this to be the last dance with my husband, now that I was dancing to a different tune and with God, that tune simply being the singsong way the guru said "Ma, Ma"?

CHAPTER SIXTY-NINE

Baba's Blanket

The music kept blasting, the kids kept eating, and I kept thinking of the old man. My saving grace was that Denisey saw him too, so either we were both crazy or there really was a toothless old man in my basement.

Johnny Boy, a neighbor's kid, came over and put his thin arms around me. He was about thirteen and real cute. "Aunt Joyce," he said, "are you okay?"

"Yeah, baby, I sure am."

"Well, you look kinda strange."

I did feel pretty strange at that moment. I loved being with the kids and the family, but I couldn't wait to get downstairs to see what having a guru meant, what it was that I had been asking for these many months.

I felt my heart swell up and said silently, "Dear God, don't take my kids away from me. I'm all they've got."

I heard in my head, "They're *all* your children, the young and the old."

Johnny went back to helping me clean up the yard with the other kids. Night had fallen, warm and pleasant. It was about nine.

Fran came out of the house and said there was a phone call for me about the business. I immediately knew that it was Hilda. That was her code, a business call, and I would always take it downstairs out of earshot of the family. I ran in. In the basement, as I expected, was my guru. Fran was right behind me, and I asked her, "Don't you see anything?"

"No," she answered softly, "but my heart has been beating fast ever since this morning, and I feel peculiar, as if my heart is about to burst."

I walked over to the old man who was simply smiling and saying "Ma, Ma" over and over. Fran was having a hard time with Hilda. I heard her tell her, "She'll call you right back." They were not exactly real fond of each other.

"What a mess," I thought. "My life has gotten more and more complicated since the Christ. And his instructions were for me to be simple." Well, this here guru he sent didn't look too simple to me. In fact, right in front of me he kept turning into this very young and handsome person with long hair and a kingly bearing. In the very core of my being, I was sure I knew him.

"What do you want me to tell my teacher?" I asked, meaning Hilda. I knelt by his blanket. "Strange," I thought, "he smells almost like a little baby fresh from the bath. My God do I love this man like I've never loved before. How can this be?" I had such a strong desire to lay my head on his lap and let his blanket cover me and the world.

I wanted to touch his feet in the worst way. Instead I pranamed. He called my name as I was about to stand up and go to the phone. "Ma," he said, "always do what your heart tells you to do."

I didn't want him to read my heart or mind. I simply answered, "My guru, what is it that you want from me, and what do you want me to call you?"

"From you, my Ma, I have everything. You may call me whatever is in your heart."

A strange word came to me in that very second of time and space. The word was "Laxman." It seemed to be his name. I thought, "This guy is a Jewish guru!" Of course I didn't know it then, but that really was one of my Baba's many names, especially when he was young. He began to laugh before I could put words to my thoughts.

"I am everything," he said, "as you are everything. It is all in the sharing." I got up, walked over to a silent Fran and took the phone out of her hands.

Before I could say a word, Hilda began, "Darling, what is going on there at your house? My whole body is trembling."

"Hilda," I said, "my guru is here, but I want him out of the house. He reads my mind and knows what I'm going to say before I do." I said this all in one breath.

Hilda didn't even skip a beat. "How nice," she said. "Darling, who is he?"

I yelled to him. He was sitting only about ten feet away. "Who are you?" I asked.

"Your guru."

"No," I said, "what is your name, my guru?"

"My name is sometimes Neem Karoli Baba."

Now I thought, "Maybe he's Italian." I repeated what he said.

I could hear Hilda gasp on the phone. "Darling," she said, "what is he wearing?"

"An itchy blanket," I answered.

"What else, darling?"

"Hilda," I said, "how the hell should I know?"

"Well, give him my love, darling, and I will see you tomorrow after Salvatore goes to work."

I said goodnight to her. The kids were coming into the house with wet clothes from the pool. I ran up the stairs screaming at them, telling them that I was going to murder them if they ruined my floors. After having snacks outside under the Brooklyn sky, most of the kids went home. The rest dug in and fell asleep in the basement. I thought, "At least my guru isn't alone." I kissed the kids goodnight.

Denise came over to me as I was about to go into my bathroom temple. "Well, Mama, what are we going to do with you now?"

"I don't know, Denisey, I don't know."

I sat in front of my Swami and said, "So this is what it is to have a guru."

He looked at me and said, "This is just the beginning, Jaya Ma, just the beginning." I began to weep. I wept until there were no more tears to be shed. I was weeping from fear, from bliss, but mostly I was weeping because I knew in my heart of hearts that my Christ had returned and I would never be without him again so long as I lived, in this life or any other. I was weeping because my guru was downstairs protecting my sleeping children, and because my teacher, the swami, was in front of me. I was weeping for all the pain and the joy that would come to me in the form of a teaching I was yet to have and to give.

मा

Those days—from late 1972 to the summer of 1974—had been the hardest, the saddest, the most wonderful days of my life. Somewhere I didn't believe any of it—not the Christ, not the Swami, not the Guru, and not the Virgin Mother, who was now with me always, ever since her son had left me. And somewhere I was afraid and excited that it was all too true. In my mind's eye, I kept catching glimpses of things that I seemed to remember from long, long ago.

My tortured, wonderful youth had begun to make a whole lot of sense. Back in those days I'd loved to be in the company of the holy, and I thought that everyone had holiness in them. I loved God, my Mac, with all my heart. Then my Christ stole my soul and my life. No one, though, could come near the way I felt about the toothless old man in my basement.

To say that I was confused is putting it mildly. To say I was lonely in the company of the great ones is to speak truth. My flesh separated me from them, and that caused me unhappiness. Yet, I never thought of dying, of ending my life. I loved breathing too much, and I loved the joy I could bring to others. It was as if I knew, in an ancient place deep in the roots of my heart, that there would always be a way to go into a timeless place where I could just *be*.

At times, I miss those simple, complicated days of newness and adventure. Even the pain and suffering, which I surely went through, was a deep awakening.

CHAPTER SEVENTY

Guru Is Everything

Although my tears were falling like waterfalls, I never once took my eyes off my Swami. It was later that night, as he sat there as usual on his throne—my toilet seat with the top down—on one of my prettiest towels, one I'd bought especially for him at John's Bargain Store. He was staring at me, and all of a sudden I knew I didn't want anything to change.

I still felt safe in my life of selling "hot" goods, taking care of my own kids, and feeding the other kids in the neighborhood. I loved the way the kids called me Ma or Aunt Joyce. It seemed I had a million names and perhaps a million faces. I had Hilda and Mount Manresa, where I went to find my beautiful Christ. I had my Jesuits and my nuns. In other words, I had my life. Now I had what I'd been searching forever for, or maybe it was just in this life. "My guru." I said the words over and over, "My guru."

"Swami, what is a guru? Is it someone who will take all that I love away from me? Will he take you from me? Swami, talk to me!" But I never gave him a chance to answer; I just kept asking him questions about my worst fears and my deepest desires. "Swami, will the guru take my children from me, and Salvatore? Swami, who will feed the kids? And what about Hilda? If I have a guru, who is Hilda to me? Who are you? Swami, tell me please." By then I was sobbing into a thick towel. I was afraid the kids or Sal would hear me.

"Ma, Ma," my Swami answered, "sit in the silence of your own tears and hear these words. Some you will understand, and some will have no mental meaning for you. Now listen closely and say no more."

I nodded my head, telling him with my eyes that I wouldn't interrupt. He began, "In the days of Radha and Krishna…"

"Who the hell are they?" I asked.

"This one shall not speak another word if you interrupt again." But his eyes were laughing. Here is what he told me:

> After Radha and Krishna had made love, she lay in her beloved's arms and wished for the moment never to end. When she opened her eyes, she saw that she was alone. "Where is he?" she cried into the morning light. "Where has he gone? Why," she pleaded to the mist coming over the Yamuna River, "why has my beloved gone?"
>
> Her pain almost made her faint, but she heard someone coming toward her. Thinking it was her Krishna, she jumped up, unashamed of her nakedness. Instead it was a young cowherd girl, a *gopi*, who was also weeping.
>
> "What is it you weep for?" asked Radha.
>
> "I weep for the sight of my master Govinda."
>
> Radha felt ashamed, for in her passion she wanted more than simply the sight of her Govinda, who was her own Krishna. How greedy I am, she thought. She quickly dressed in her sari and held her arms out for the young one. The little gopi felt Radha's passion for Krishna and felt safe and loved.
>
> Radha began to understand now more than ever before— My wanting him will lead others to feel his love. I will show my devotion at any cost, and others will follow my lead. From that day on Radha always remembered her longing and gave freely of her love. You see, *it is all in the sharing.*

My Swami stopped talking and asked, "Do you understand, little Mother?"

His eyes were so tender. Looking into them, I asked, "Did Radha lose everything?"

"Yes, she lost her family and her friends."

"Swami, will I lose everything?"

He answered in one simple word: "Yes."

I began to cry again. "Will I lose you, my teacher?"

Again, "Yes."

"And my life?"

"Yes."

"I will lose it all?"

Again, "Yes."

I nodded with the understanding I had always sought. After being a good wife and mother for almost twenty years, I would lose it all for a guru, a God, and humanity.

"Nay," said my Swami reading my mind, "you will not play the martyr. You will lose everything because you will be unable to live here without getting hurt badly, both physically and spiritually, and without you hurting those you love."

"What is a guru?"

"Everything and nothing," he answered. "It is he you live for. It is he that you would die for. It is he that you acknowledge as goodness, and it is he that will show you how to consume evil. It is he that has given you the boon of using your eyes to take pain, heartache, and even karma from those who will come and sit in front of you. It is he that will take that same pain from you. He is the heart that beats inside of you and the soul that occupies the flesh. He is the silence your soul longs for. He is you. You will go on in life always in the heat of your passion for your guru and your God. Others will see it in you and ask to sit at your feet. And the time will come when you, too, will be called guru and your name will come to mean Mother. You will be the Mother to all who are willing to give up attachment to the world."

I looked at my Swami and said, "If this comes to pass, then I will become the Mother to all, not just the holy. I will call to me those I knew in my youth, those under the Boardwalk that the world was afraid of, those who could teach the world the wisdom of the streets. I will be Mother to all, or no Mother at all."

My Swami was still. The sound of my breathing was the only sound in that small temple. When he spoke again, there was a different tone in his voice. He was the most tender I had ever heard him. "Jaya," he said, "you have just spoken like the Ma you are at the feet of your guru."

I had been sitting for hours in a bathtub filled with water, wearing my flannel nightgown. This is as crazy as one could get, I thought.

Once again my Swami spoke. "No, it is not. It can get crazier than this."

I jumped out of the tub, which had turned ice cold. Soaking wet, I ran downstairs. And there he was, my guru. The children, unaware of his presence, were sleeping in a horseshoe around him. He was saying "Ma, Ma" over and over.

I watched it all, dripping, from the top of the steps. "Dear God, protect me from myself and my own attachments. I need to be clear in my life." I felt a presence, turned, and there in all his splendor was my Jesus, my Christ. "Am I who I am?" I asked, with as many tears falling as the water dripping from my nightgown. He had said he wouldn't return until I'd become who I was.

The Christ looked at me and said, "You're getting there."

I had to laugh, and when I did, the Christ smiled at me and disappeared into my beating heart, a place he has never left.

As I climbed the wet stairs, thinking that I'd better change, I stopped for a moment and said out loud, "My God, even the Christ has a sense of humor." He had said I was getting there, but disappeared before I could ask, "Getting where?"

I walked up the stairs and into the bathroom to get my robe. It was almost morning, and I needed to get into bed and lie next to my husband for a few minutes. I looked at my Swami and said, "I don't know if I can do this thing. I need to think about it. I don't want to hurt anyone."

"What a night," I thought as I lay in bed. I heard words coming through the floors from the basement.

"What a life, my Ma, what a life."

The night passed as if the whole house was embraced in a mist, a mist that warmed me and frightened me at the same time. I lay next to my husband and watched his breath go in and out. "I'm going to lose you, Salvatore," I thought, as I stroked his dark hair. "You're never going to understand my love for God or guru. How can I expect you to understand my love if I can't figure it out for myself? All I know is to serve and feed everyone."

My mind raced back over the years to Chicky's words to me: "Love costs less than hate," and a short time later, "and you get a lot more for your money, too, with love."

I began to wonder, "Are there many gurus in someone's life?" Chicky had taught me so much, and Tirza, in her own way, had taught me lessons I'd never forget. And Mama—didn't I learn all about courage and perseverance from her? Yes, that's it, I decided, one guru isn't the answer. The old man in my basement had to go and go fast if I was to save my life and my marriage.

I cuddled up closer to Sal's muscular back. Feeling safe and comfortable, I drifted into sleep. There in my dreams was everyone who had ever taught me life's lessons—so many drifted by me. I tried to catch hold of the moment. I was twirling and turning, glancing all around. I awoke with a start. Looking at the clock I saw to my astonishment that no time had passed at all. Taking in a few deep breaths, I gave up the thought of sleep. It was almost time to start the day anyway.

"Where are you going?" Sal asked, as I was getting out of bed.

"I'm going to start the batter for the pancakes."

He grabbed my arm, none too lightly, and said, "Stay with me, Babe. Don't leave."

"I need to make the kids' lunches and start the sauce."

"Babe, I don't want to lose you. Do you hear me? I'm not gonna let you go to God or man. I'll fight. Do you understand?"

"I understand. Now it's your turn to understand. I love God." I began to cry. "I love God. Sal, please believe me. You've been the only man for me since we were just kids, but I need to be with God in a different way, not the way of man and woman. I need to serve, I need to nourish, I need to give. Will you let me?" I asked with hope in my voice and heart. "Will you let me?" I asked again. This time I found myself begging, a thing I thought I'd never do: "Will you let me?"

He didn't answer. We were both crying now. I went into his arms and just held on for my life. He whispered to me with his face buried in my hair, "I thought we could grow old together, Babe."

My heart was breaking as I asked a question that would change our lives forever. "Will you share me, Sal?"

"I can't," he answered. "I can't."

I slipped out of his arms, grabbed my old terry robe, and walked down the stairs, sobbing. I went straight down into the basement. The kids were still sleeping. The old man was just sitting there on the floor, looking at me as if he knew I would be coming down the stairs. "One guru, one guru only," he said. "One mother can give birth, one guru can give life and teach of death. Many teachers, one guru."

I turned and ran back up the stairs. "I want it all! I want it all!" Dawn came. Children woke up. Dogs woke up and realized they were dogs and barked at the dawn. I fed them all. There was a stillness in the house, a haze. We all felt it and kept silent. With Sal at work and the kids off to school, I quickly dressed in a cotton housedress and let my long black hair hang wild. In the empty house there was the presence of something profound. "Is this the holiness I want? But what's to happen to me?" Then I thought, "Will there be enough of me to go around?"

I looked toward the old man. He smiled his toothless smile and said, "Feed everyone, Ma. Everyone needs the Mother."

Before Baba came to me, I used to ask Swami all the time, "Are you my guru?" From being around Rudi's, I knew that word, but never the depth of it. And he would say, "No. Your guru is to come." That's when I wrote in my diary "No man is my guru." I was so angry. I wanted desperately to have a teacher, to have a guru.

CHAPTER SEVENTY-ONE

Ram Dass

The doorbell rang. It was Hilda's students, the ones I'd been teaching when Fran and I would sneak into Manhattan. Billy came over to me and pranamed. "How are you, Ma?"

"There," I thought, "he called me Ma again." It was a name I was getting used to hearing out loud even though I had already heard it all my life.

Billy, who had traveled all over India looking for God, said, "Ma, we heard that Baba was with you."

Himalaya walked over, the mop already in her hand. She was one of Hilda's students who would come over to help me clean the house. (Many years later she would be the first woman to whom I would give the title of "Swami.") "Is it true, Ma," asked this attractive blond woman in her twenties, "is Ram Dass's guru here?"

"Who the fuck is Ram Dass?" I asked, getting annoyed that everyone knew my business.

Just then my friend Joan walked in. "Joyce. Joyce. I heard through the grapevine that Ram Dass is coming. Can I stay?" She shoved a purple book at me.

"What the hell is this?" I asked.

"It's Ram Dass's book, *Be Here Now*." I recognized one of the books Fran had found at Weiser's bookstore, but we hadn't paid very much attention to it. Now Joan was all excited about its author.

It was all too much for me. When I saw Fran come through the door, I asked her to man the phones and the door. I went down to the basement and sat down to the left of the old man, who was sitting on his special blanket near the fireplace. He began to talk to me, but all I remember him saying was, "My son is coming." I tried to listen, yet something beyond myself was calling. I went to that place of timelessness and felt only bliss.

Someone was calling to me. "Joya, Joya, darling." The scent of rosewater reached inside my consciousness. I opened my eyes and, to my surprise, there in front of me was my beloved Hilda and an old bald man. On closer look I saw he was actually a younger man, about forty, with a gray bushy beard and no hair. And what pain!

I said aloud, "Who the fuck is he?"

"Joya, darling, this is Ram Dass."

Embarrassed to be caught unaware in samadhi, I answered, "I don't care who he is." I pointed to Baba. "Does that dirty old man belong to him?" This happened the day after Baba had come to me, and I still wasn't too happy about it.

I was pissed off and wanted to be left alone. Then Baba began talking. I looked to see if anyone else could hear him. Billy had come in and was sitting near me. He whispered, "Joan fainted when she saw Ram Dass going down the stairs." That was it. I turned to the startled Ram Dass.

"Get this old man out of here—and yourself as well!"

Hilda was just humming to herself and looking at me with great love and pride.

"I am going nuts," I thought, "really nuts."

"Tell him what I am saying," said the toothless one. I turned my head and looked straight into his eyes. God, did I love him. He turned into someone so familiar, yet strange and haunting, young and powerful. I began to speak as he whispered into my very being.

Here, in Ram Dass' own words, is what happened next:

> I looked over and I didn't see anything on the blanket. So I said, "Well, I don't know whether that's my Guru or not." At which point she, Joya, went into another state of consciousness and Maharaj-ji started to speak through her. And he proceeded to discuss with me a number of things that he and I had talked about in India before he'd left his body—things about the temple and the temple trust and various sorts of little incidental things about the life in India at the temple that we would relate to each other, none of which I would talk about in the West—and there would be no reason for this woman to know any of that stuff.
>
> And after about ten or fifteen minutes there was no doubt in my mind that Maharaj-ji's consciousness was in this space with me. My consciousness kept being pulled by this woman…the quality of this woman, the quality of Maharaj-ji. The most critical quality of both of them was the degree of their purity, for I had never met beings this pure.[5]

That first day I was just letting my Baba speak through me. I had gone into the same state I used to be in when I would teach at Hilda's. Who cared what I said, as long as I could sit there in bliss? Now I looked at this bearded man and began to wonder what the hell I was talking about. I looked toward my Billy. He nodded and there were tears in his eyes. Ram Dass had tears in his eyes, too.

---

5   Ram Dass often told this story in his lectures. This quote is from a talk in Gainesville, Florida, in October of 1975, recorded on a tape he shared with his own students.

Only Hilda was calm and unemotional. "There, darling," she said to Ram Dass. "Isn't she wonderful?"

"Hilda, can he get this old man out of here?"

"Of course not, darling. Can Billy tell you what to do? After all, you are Billy's guru, you know."

"I am *what?*" I asked.

"Yes, darling, you certainly are."

Billy was all smiles. Ram Dass was sighing. I was fuming. Billy was always asking me who he was to me. I immediately thought of the old holy man in my bathroom who always said, "Who am I?" I looked straight into my Billy's eyes and told him, "Ramana Maharshi is your guru." He looked deeply hurt, yet I knew he loved this man. I threw in Baba's words: "You can have only one guru and many teachers."

"Wow!" I thought, "That was close." I was not about to admit to being anyone's guru!

The bearded one, Ram Dass, tried to touch my feet. I almost kicked him. Billy had already tried that. Before he left, Ram Dass bowed to the blanket in front of the fireplace. I saw the look on the old man's face. There were tears in his eyes. He loved this man Ram Dass, whoever he was.

"Well, I'll get the dirt from fainting Joan," I thought. She seemed to know him well.

Now Baba was swaying back and forth again saying, "Ma, Ma, Ma."

"Did you hear that?" asked Billy to Ram Dass. Ram Dass paid no attention to Billy.

"Shit," I thought, "this guy is a little afraid of Billy's light. They should live together." What was I thinking? The last thing in the world I wanted was to organize people's lives.

Baba was talking to me again. "Why not?" he asked simply, "Doesn't it feel good to take someone's pain?" The old man had read my mind again and, yes, it did feel good to take someone's pain, real good. But again I thought, "Will there be enough of me to go around?"

I looked toward the old man. He smiled his toothless smile and said, "Feed everyone, Ma. Everyone needs the Mother."

CHAPTER SEVENTY-TWO

Learning to Teach

Before Baba came, I had gone through a period when I didn't eat or sleep; I just lived on amrith. Now I needed to get more control of my life, and be more grounded. My whole struggle in those days was not to find bliss, but to get far enough away from bliss so that I could live, teach, and take care of my family.

India is full of people in bliss, but if I just sat, lost in the bliss of God, who would understand? Why did I bother to take a human body if I didn't intend to live a fully human life? So Baba said I had to start eating again to get a little more connected to the Earth. In fact, Baba had the nerve to say he'd like me to be a little more chunky! That really made me mad, but the more I thought about Chunkys, the more sense it made. I must be the only person in history to come out of a state of God-intoxication and break a six-month fast with Chunkys.

या

When Swami first came to me, I said, "Show me the universe." I tried it on Baba soon after he came to me. We were in the basement in my new puja room. Swami Nityananda stayed upstairs in my bathroom.

"Let me take you from star to star," Baba said. I closed my eyes. It was so cold. When I opened my eyes again, there I was, flying with my Baba. It was kind of like the Superman movie, where he takes Lois Lane flying, only this was really happening to me, and it was ecstasy. After it was over, he said to me, "Child, don't ever want this again."

"Why, Baba?"

"There is so much more than this. There's man into God."

I understood what he meant. Beyond all the glory, the visions, and the spiritual experiences, beyond all the ecstasies, there is nothing more profound than the merge of a human being and God.

"How can I serve you?" I asked him again. "What can I do for you, how can I serve you?"

"You must take the hard ones," he said, "those that are filled with the want of God, that no one in the world would touch except you and me." He said, "You will love them. They will hurt you. Your heart will burn and your heart will bleed, but you will love them. You will love them from the morning to the night, and from the night to the morning. Your whole life will revolve around every single one of them. They will come one by one and touch your feet, as you touch their hearts."

"And how shall I teach them?" I asked him that a thousand times.

"Any way you wish, for what is expressed will come to pass, if they listen, and hear." He asked me, "Do you want this responsibility?"

"No," I said, "But I will accept it, because I do not know what else to do with my life. But," I said, "I must know who is calling me. Let me feel what they feel, let me see what they see, and let me know what they know."

"Are you sure?"

"Pain or sorrow means nothing to me. I must feel it."

Still he looked at me kind of strange, and he said, "It does not work like that. You can just give a blessing when you hear them calling. You needn't know who called."

At this time I didn't have my own chelas, except that I knew that Billy and a few others I had met at Hilda's were truly mine. Hilda had asked me to help her teach her kids so that's what I was doing. But I knew deeply that others would come. I said, "No, I must know who calls."

"Are you sure?" he asked again.

"I am positive."

With tears on his face, he actually begged me not to ask this. "Don't ask for that, for not even your heart is so big that it will not rip at each name calling you around this very small world of ours."

But I insisted. How could I teach if I did not go through everything?

मा

When Baba was first teaching me how to teach, he would dance in front of me in his little *langoti*, this big fat man, and tell me dirty jokes. I would laugh and answer him back, and he would say, "Ma, you're gonna end up in a loony bin, you can't do that." I had to learn how to keep my face like stone. We would do it for hours each day, training me not to laugh or not to acknowledge the deities as they came.

Mother Kali would come before me, the same way as she came before Ramakrishna. *The Gospel of Sri Ramakrishna* describes how he would be talking with his chelas and the Mother would come to him. His body would go stiff, right in the middle of a sentence, and he would be lost in bliss. But unfortunately we're not in Calcutta, where these things are understood. Sometimes, even to this day, I may get kind of a blank look on my face; that's what's going on, I'm listening to my Baba.

मा

Baba also asked me to take two vows as a teacher. I thought they were kind of strange at the time, but I understand them now. The first was: "Never use one person for another unless both go toward

God." The second vow was: "Never use the power of suggestion." When I lead people into meditation and they are wide open, it would be easy to tell them what to feel. They might feel so deeply that they become attached to me, the teacher, instead of going more deeply into the truth of their own being. Or, it would be quite easy through the power of suggestion to make people think they are feeling something, perhaps a visit from the psychic world.

Meanwhile, I was spending every day with my beloved Hilda, who loved the psychic world so profoundly. Hilda had students who could see with their third eyes a little bit, but not fully. They would be telling Hilda, "Oh, Baba's over there, he's blessing us," but meanwhile he was on the other side of the room, dancing a jig and giving everybody the finger.

This was not new for Baba; he always acted like that. When Western disciples first went to him in India, whatever he would say to them, the translator would say, "Oh, Baba blesses you." Finally, one young man learned enough Hindi to find out what Baba was really saying and, boy, did he get a shock! (Baba often called people "sister fuckers.") With a guru though, it doesn't really matter what words he says. The translator had it right; it was all a blessing.

My Baba was well known throughout India, but by many different names and in many different stories. As a young sadhu, he was called Laxman, and then as he traveled all over India he had other names. He would pop up here and there, touching people profoundly and then disappearing. One name was Neem Karoli Baba, named for a place where he once showed a little bit of who he was. The story is that the porters threw him off a train because he had no ticket, so he just went and sat down under a Neem tree. The train wouldn't start, no matter what they tried.

Finally, someone figured it out and invited him back on the train, and then off they went. Sometimes he was called Maharaj-ji, "great king," or simply Baba, which just means "father." Only near the end of his life did he settle for part of the time in temples or ashrams, at Kainchi, Allahabad, and Brindavan, and that's when the first Western disciples came to him. Ram Dass was the first to write about him and bring his story to the West.

Baba left his body in September, 1973. Almost a year later, he moved into my house, and he never left.

CHAPTER SEVENTY-THREE

Steam Rollin' Mama

I still had very little control, so at times I would just go into the stiffness of samadhi. But this was Brooklyn, not Calcutta, and one time I was picked up off the street by the police, and I woke up in the morgue with a tag on my toe. That's when Ram Dass went out and got me one of those medical alert bracelets, only mine was gold and had "Yogic Trance: Do Not Bury" printed on it.

Sometimes I couldn't see. My third eye was wide open. I could see God, but I couldn't see the world. I couldn't live like that. There were Sal, the kids, and the house, all falling into chaos. My children were young, and they still needed their mother. It was very sad, in a way. I loved God passionately, I only wanted to be married to God, and I had to fight God all the time just so I could be with my family. It was very hard, on me and on them. I desperately needed something to bring me into my body so I could live a normal life.

Hilda came one day and offered me a way out. When she was in India, she had bought a topaz ring, earrings, and brooch. The brooch was very special to her. Even when she had no money, she wouldn't sell it. Now she wanted to give it to me. She had the brooch made into a pendant and hung it on a heavy gold chain. She said, "When I touch your stone, it will bring you down quite fast into your body." She had a necklace made for her, too, from one of the smaller stones in the set, and she put hers on.

I was about to put on the chain with the topaz, when my Baba told me "no." He had been training me to live in the world, and if I had listened to him I would have gradually learned how to fit comfortably into my own flesh. Swami Nityananda appeared, too, and said, "Do not put that chain on your neck."

For the first and only time, I went against them. This was my beloved Hilda, who had been my lifeline for so long, offering me a present. She promised me that if I put on the stone, I would be able to know God and function in the world, too. That was what I wanted so desperately.

I put the necklace on, and Hilda touched the topaz. My body burned like a thousand razor blades were going through it, because her touch on the topaz made me come back into my body too quickly. I felt the way an ice cube must feel when it is dropped in boiling water. But the world became clear, reality became illusion once again, and I could live more easily in the world. Putting on the stone was the first time I ever went against the gods, and the very last time. With the gods screaming in my ears, I did not listen. And it was the beginning of a horrendous journey.

Hilda got an eight-by-ten photograph made. It showed us together, and in it I have the stone around my neck. When she couldn't touch the stone itself, she would hold the photo and rub the stone in the picture, just rub it continuously. And I, feeling the stone, would have some ground. The real power of the stone just came from the love and trust I had for Hilda, love that had helped keep me down for months already. But now, with the stone, something changed.

There was something else in the stone besides love; there was power, there was jealousy, there was the fear of losing me. I was too young in God then, too much in love, and I went for it. The psychic world can invade reality, and soon I was becoming a slave to it. I began to depend on Hilda to bring me down with the stone, even though it was agony.

By now I was teaching with Hilda sitting on one side of me, Ram Dass on the other, and more and more people were coming. At first I had been Hilda's big secret. Everyone that came was brought to me by Hilda. Now Ram Dass began to bring people, too, mostly those who had been with Baba in India. "Maharaj-ji's animals," Hilda would call them, because they were usually wilder than her kids, and also smellier. They were all hippies in those days, walking around New York City like sadhus, dressed in grubby blankets. They were all what we in Brooklyn would call "skeevy." At one point I got so tired of hippies that I told all the women they should wear polyester slacks and nice little sweater sets. They pretended they hadn't heard me, but still they did start to clean up their acts.

Now there was always a tension between Hilda and Ram Dass. At times, Hilda would shock my system with her overwhelming love. She had such incredible beauty when in the realm of love that a light would shine from her being, and that's why she sometimes used the name Lazuma, Goddess of Light. Hilda was connected to astral beings called the Masters of the Great White Lodge, although Billy could never accept that part of her teaching. He used to upset Hilda when he called them "a bunch of spooks."

The psychic world was becoming more and more important to Hilda and some of her students. It got so they were always looking for astral beings, trying so hard to see the other worlds. Hilda had little pillows on the floor around her apartment for all the "invisibles" to sit on, and she'd demolish any yogi who made the mistake of stepping on one.

By the end of 1975, we had thirteen little ashrams all over Queens, houses where everybody chipped in and paid the rent. Nothing was ever public in those days. You only got in if Hilda or Ram Dass said you could come to see Ma.

The biggest class was on Friday mornings in a borrowed yoga studio on the West side. Hilda would sit next to me rubbing the stone in the picture, and any time I went too far into God, she would say, "Draw, kids," meaning everybody had to breathe in and pull the shakti from me before the pull of God took me too far away. Meanwhile, Ram Dass sat on the other side, never speaking, but also helping me stay down. I had found that he and, in fact, all who had been with Baba in India, made me feel very comfortable because they held his essence.

Except for Friday, we had no regular place, and the classes kept growing. I began having secret early morning classes, and then secret secret early early classes, plus once a week I taught yoga in the backyard at my house in Brooklyn.

I was teaching pretty steadily, never missing a class. Hilda was my guardian angel, but when Baba came, and then Ram Dass and others who had been with Baba in India, it was the beginning of a change between Hilda and me. Nothing ever changed how I loved her, but I was starting to go beyond her. Now Ram Dass, too, began to take care of me and teach me how to live in this world. The tension between Hilda and Ram Dass was growing, and Hilda was going more into the dryness of the psychic realms.

Finally, that winter, in a Friday class, I decided to make my stand. I said, "It is far better to feel what you don't see than to see what you don't feel."

The psychic realms are real, very beautiful, and so seductive that seekers have wasted whole lifetimes exploring them and never knowing God. The merge into God comes with the rising and falling of kundalini, up and down from the base of the spine to the top of the head and beyond, vertically. The psychic world, if you get caught in it, takes you horizontally, takes you nowhere. God, samadhi, the merge with the Formless, comes as a feeling, which I could never describe without going into it and becoming unable to speak. I just used to say that going into God was like sitting in a freezing cold bathtub and turning on the hot water.

Now here was a large roomful of people, and many of them had given up homes and businesses and moved to New York looking for God. How could I offer them a lesser teaching? I wanted to give them straight God. I walked in that Friday morning singing, "I'm a steamrollin' mama," and then I told them, "I'm like a steamroller for God. I'll roll over anyone who doesn't want God. I'll roll over Hilda, I'll roll over Ram Dass, I'll even roll over Joya if they don't want God."

By the time spring came, I would know how true that was.

CHAPTER SEVENTY-FOUR

Freedom

All this time, I was teaching Ram Dass, spending time with him in between classes, and also on my day off, Monday. I would take him to my sister's apartment and lead him into meditation. Just as he entered the highest of the high, I would jump up, and say, "I want ice cream! Take me to Carvel." He would shake, or he would get angry, but I was trying to teach him how to go up into God and bring that essence back down to Earth. Besides, I really did want ice cream.

I would teach him with a lot of the essence of Kali, always chipping away at the ego. I did that with all my chelas, but I gave Ram Dass more than the others because he could take it. In his purity and his want of God, he could keep consuming whatever the Black Mother had to give. The beauty of Ram Dass was that he could absorb very fast. Even if I showed him something very painful about himself, still he would be right there, ready for more. That gave me a kind of freedom and a comfort in being with him.

The same way Hilda let me be free to go into God while I was with her, Ram Dass gave me the freedom to teach as I wanted. Before most of the others understood, he knew what you have to do when your ego begins to die: consume it, stay open, and keep going. Any spiritual path at some point demands the death of the ego, because the ego is the small self that keeps you from God. It has to die, but it fights very hard to live. That's why the scriptures of India are so full of battles and demons. Sometimes they symbolize cutting off worldly attachments, and sometimes they show the agony of the dying ego.

Hilda was the first to give me the freedom of the heavens, and now Ram Dass was starting to give me the freedom of the Earth. I told him, "I'll teach you to die, and you teach me to live." He needed me to kill his ego so he could go more fully into God. I needed him to teach me how to live in the world. He could do that because he carried the essence of his Baba so fully. It was an exquisite dance that we carried on.

I was still tied to Hilda with the stone, and now Ram Dass began to tell me that I could learn to live without it. He said he would help me, just through love.

One day I was with Ram Dass and a few other people. We drove out to Manhattan Beach and sat on the rocks. It was beautiful there by the ocean, but I was barely in my body enough to enjoy it. Hilda wasn't there, and I usually counted on her to bring me down with the stone. Suddenly, Ram Dass asked if I would kiss his cheek. Sure, why not?

Then he kissed my cheek and gently said, "Come down. Feel the sand and see this ocean." I came into my body and felt the Earth fully for the first time in two and a half years. And I just cried and cried. He brought me down with that gentle kiss. I'll be forever grateful, because that was the beginning of getting more grounded. After that I trusted Ram Dass more and more.

Still, it seemed like everybody wanted to control me—especially Sal, Hilda, and Ram Dass. They all loved me, and they all wanted to take care of me, but everything just got too crazy until I needed to get free of everyone. So I took Fran, my two daughters, and Shirley, and off we went to Florida. I hardly knew my own name just then, but I had to go.

I really didn't know what would happen without the stone. Hilda had told me that I would burn up from the power of the shakti running through me unless I could share it by teaching. Besides that, there is a limit of about three days that a person can stay in samadhi and still get back into the body. So she had me very scared—not scared of dying but scared of not being able to take care of all who would come. I really didn't know what would become of me, but I had to find out.

That first night in Fort Lauderdale, I left the stone in the hotel room and went out on the beach alone. I stayed there all night, in samadhi, and in the morning I was able to bring myself back into my body. So I was free, truly free for the first time since I was a kid, alone at dawn on the big empty beach.

The only power that a holy person ever really responds to is the power of love, and Hilda surely loved me. But she was also intrigued by the power in the stone. It took me a while to realize it, but the stone had worked by mutual consent. I had agreed to be bound to it, and so I was.

I called Hilda, and I told her, "We're free now, we're equals, now we can dance." But all the strain of the past few months was very hard for both of us, because in the beginning we just used to laugh and laugh and play together in the psychic realms.

As soon as I got back to New York, I began to make plans to go to Florida again, only this time I would take everybody with me who wanted to go. On the first trip, I had discovered Sanibel Island and its miles of beach with nobody on it. We went in March, about seventy-five of my chelas and me. The day we left for Sanibel, I saw Hilda for the last time.

CHAPTER SEVENTY-FIVE

Montauk to Miami

By the time we got back from Sanibel, rumors about me and Ram Dass were going around. It was all getting to be too much. Most of all I just wanted to be free, so I sent back some gifts he had given me. We began that spring to go our separate ways.

For several weeks we held the big Friday class at Mount Manresa, where the Jesuits loaned us a meeting room. But that couldn't last. Mount Manresa had been a second home to me, but where was home now? Not with Sal, not with Hilda, not with Ram Dass, and at last not with the Jesuits.

When I was a child, the beach was my home. I turned there now, and my chelas followed, first to Jones Beach and then to Montauk at the end of Long Island. Every Friday morning we drove three hours to Montauk, a caravan of yogis in twenty cars, often staying late at night around a campfire before driving back to the city, or sometimes cramming into a motel for the night and gathering on the beach at dawn.

As spring turned to summer, we rented a house across the street from the beach and made plans to hold retreats there. I figured twenty people at a time would come out from the city for a week for an intense teaching, straight God, no foolishness.

I left my home in Brooklyn and moved to Montauk—the hardest thing I have ever done. Christ himself, then Swami, and then Baba had told me that I would lose my family. I had fought them all for as long as I could, forgetting the second thing they had told me: that I would get them all back. For now, my battle to hold my family together was ending. The steamroller had rolled over all of us, and there was nothing left but God.

People would be coming, but how would I teach? I walked on the beach in Montauk with Billy. In front of us was a big piece of driftwood which was bleached right down to the bone, pure white. If it stayed another ten years out in the sun, it would be pure ash. It was bare and, in its bareness, it was the most exquisite thing I had ever seen.

Baba said to me, "Ma, that is the first teaching of the Skull: bareness, the very bareness of life. If you have no attachment, then you can have everything because truly you want nothing. The real essence of God is the complete and total emptiness of the void. The Skull speaks from a place where there are no words, sees where one cannot see, and therefore sees all." He told me this was a Tibetan teaching on detachment and the void.

We planned to start the retreats on the Fourth of July weekend, 1976. Meanwhile Sal came out from Brooklyn to talk to me and try to get me to come back home. Everything changed for me that weekend. Out of love for my family, I'm skipping over a lot that happened, but I knew it was time to go.

Florida had become my refuge, the place to go when everything in New York became too much.

One of my chelas had an International van that he let me borrow. He had bragged to me that it had two gas tanks and that, furthermore, you could start the engine with the hidden gas key. That was good because, as we were arguing, Sal had grabbed the other keys. When I left Sal's motel for the last time, I didn't turn back toward the Montauk house, I turned toward Florida. I made it as far as the Belt Parkway. Right in front of me in the traffic, a little bright red car stopped short. It said "newly married" all over it, and there were two shiny new bikes in a rack on the back. I couldn't hit them with my big van and ruin their honeymoon, so I swerved, ran off the road, and crashed into something. By the time the ambulance got there, I had gone into samadhi, same as I did at the dentist that time. The paramedics thought I was dead because I had no pulse. On the way to the hospital, I started talking to them, freaked them out something awful. At the hospital, it turned out all I had was a concussion and a lot of bruises. So they let me go home, except that I didn't have a home.

Some of the yogis picked me up from the hospital and took me back to one of the houses in Queens. But Florida still called me, and I couldn't predict what Sal might do if I stayed around. Somebody had a credit card, and they got me a plane ticket to Miami. I wouldn't let anyone come with me. "Take this credit card," they said, "and as soon as you get there, go get a Hertz Rent-a-Car." I got on the plane with my face all bruised up from the accident. I looked so bad the ticket guy offered me a wheelchair.

All this, from Sal arriving in Montauk to me landing in Miami, had taken less than forty-eight hours, the Fourth of July weekend. Meanwhile there were twenty people at the house thinking they were on a spiritual retreat.

Of course nobody knew it at the time, but according to a history of the AIDS plague this may have been when the AIDS virus came into the United States, when so many people were in New York from all over the world for the bicentennial celebrations.

I had gone into God again on the plane, so when we landed I hardly knew where I was. All I could remember was "Hertz Rent-a-Car." But I couldn't get a car because the credit card wasn't in my name. Now I had no car, no money, no place to go. I had a concussion, there wasn't a spot on my face that wasn't black and blue, and I kept losing control and going in and out of samadhi. An older man working at the Hertz counter finally said, "You're badly hurt. I'm a married man. I'll call up my wife and you come home with me."

Truly people have been good to me my whole life, but I never saw someone take care of a stranger like that. I could have been anybody.

The man called his wife, who got on the phone. She said, "I have children of my own. Come home with him. You can trust him; ask anyone how long he's worked for Hertz."

But I couldn't put them in jeopardy like that, because where was Sal? I was imagining him arriving on the next plane, although in reality he'd had enough sense to go back home to Brooklyn. Finally the Hertz man called the airport hotel and set it all up for me, even arranging to have me seen by a doctor at the hotel. He called a cab and paid for it. By then I couldn't talk, I was so overwhelmed by the generosity of a stranger, but I never found out this good man's name.

The next day I called for Billy to come down to Florida, and then a few of the others. We looked at the map. How far could we get from Brooklyn? We drove straight to Key West. But nothing there was good enough for Billy, who preferred to keep driving in the hundred-degree heat, so we turned back north, looking and looking for a place to go.

Finally, after days of driving around Florida, going from motel to motel, we stopped in a place called Vero Beach. Billy, the scholar, said he thought maybe Vero was a Spanish word for "truth," because it sounded like the Latin word *veritas*. I liked that, "Truth Beach," so we stayed there and rented a house right by the beach.

Soon we had a dozen people living in the Vero Beach house, and every week a group would come down from New York for a week and then go back. Then I started flying up to New York on the weekends to teach up there. By now Sal had calmed down so I was able to see my kids.

Every day I would take a long walk with several of my chelas and teach on the beach. Sometimes we'd get as far as a very exclusive community called John's Island, and we'd jump in their pool. Nobody was around, it was August after all, and we weren't bothering anyone. Another time I saw the cops harassing one of my black chelas who was just sitting on the beach like anybody else. I went running over screaming that she was the princess of Ethiopia or some such nonsense, and they left us alone after that. Even so, this was an exclusive beachfront neighborhood, and we didn't quite fit in.

I thought maybe we should have a big dinner party for the neighbors so they could know we were okay. We did, and everybody was on their best behavior except me. There was this young man from the neighborhood who came, and over dinner I just asked him straight out, "Are you a homosexual?" I didn't care if he was or not, but he seemed to be in pain, and I felt he could get past it if he acknowledged what was bothering him. Things kind of went downhill after that. In fact, Billy took to calling that dinner "disaster night."

The real disaster was later that night, when the mayor and the police chief came knocking on the door. They counted thirty people sleeping on the floor. "Just house guests," I said, "they're all leaving in the morning." They were very polite, but of course they knew I was lying. So we were evicted, and the landlady gave us an excellent reference to get rid of us. Soon we found our new home: two houses and a pond on seven acres in Sebastian, the next town up the road. To me, straight out of Brooklyn, everything looked like the wild frontier, so we started calling it "The Ranch." That was October, 1976.

CHAPTER SEVENTY-SIX

Tell Them How I Died

When I received an invitation to speak at the 1993 Parliament of the World's Religions in Chicago, I was asked to submit a description of my work. Well, exactly how would I describe my work?

I was thinking about this in Connor's Nursery, sitting with other volunteers on the blue couch with the yellow flowers. Connor's was a place in West Palm Beach that took in abused children and babies with AIDS. I would go there every week after the County Home.

Some of the babies were sleeping and tucked into their cribs. Little Nisha had just turned nine months. Joey was crawling around the floor. William, our oldest little boy, had been playing with a caregiver's lipstick and had fallen asleep on the couch. With the lipstick smeared all over his face, he looked like a little old lady who had had too much to drink. He was three and proud of the feeding tube that came out of his little belly. If he liked you enough, he'd let you put his food in the tube.

"Ma, I don't feel well," my little Deena said to me as she tried to put her thin arms around my neck. It wouldn't be long before death claimed her for his own. Deena's life hadn't been a pretty story. After being raped at seven by her babysitter's boyfriend, she became HIV-positive and developed AIDS. I had known Deena since she came to Connor's Nursery about six months before. Two weeks ago, she had told me that she wanted to die. Now I held her close to my breast and laughed as she asked for barbecued chicken.

"I thought you wanted to die," I said.

She laughed. "Yeah, but first I want barbecued chicken." Fran said she'd go out and get some for her. While Deena waited, she looked into my eyes and asked, "Is it okay if I don't eat it and only smell it?"

"Of course."

She continued, "If I smell the chicken now, then I will still be able to smell it when I die." Then, with a startling intensity, she whispered in my ear, "I think I'm dying." Nine years of age and already through with life.

I kissed her forehead and went into the glass-enclosed office. There my dear friend Jean was conducting the business of putting the right medicines out for the children. She treats these suffering children as she would treat any child, sick or not. They all love her; her gruff voice fools no one. I grabbed her hands and pulled her off the chair. "Get over here, and let's have a hug."

For a moment she forgot her toughness and let her heart show. "There are two dying, Ma, and one very sick."

"I know," I said, as I whispered into her hair that I loved her.

"Okay, enough bull. Let's get to work."

She picked up a very sick little boy who was so ill I didn't recognize him at first. It was little Brad, who couldn't walk on his feet because he had muscular dystrophy as well as AIDS.

"Here, Ma, give him ice and Gatorade every half hour."

For a moment, all was silent except for the sound of the dying children's labored breathing. My mind traveled back to the burning ghats in India, where bodies burn all day and night. Children and holy men are not burned but placed gently in the sacred Ganga. There is no place holier than Kashi on the banks of the Ganga. Now, as I sat in Connor's Nursery, the silence was comforting. To no god in particular I said, "I have found a place as holy as my precious Kashi, a place where children are loved and cared for as they wait for the river to claim them."

Jean came in. "Girls, there is a new baby coming in." Everyone was excited—and then sad. How many more, dear God, how many more?

या

With the Parliament's gathering of religious leaders approaching, I couldn't help thinking about all the church and temple doors that are closed to my people with AIDS just when they need the openness of religion the most.

I had gone to see the Pope in Rome six months earlier. I brought my pictures of everybody I knew who had died of AIDS. There were a lot of pictures by now—I had been keeping these little photo books for months. So many were dying, and I feared I might forget even one name. If the Pope could see what I had seen, he would embrace my people—how could he not? I wanted him to put his arms around just one person with AIDS, in public, and let the world see that his compassion had no limits. The world would follow his example, I thought, and with that one gesture he could put an end to the stigma of AIDS and the prejudice that was literally killing people all over the world.

I had an appointment for a private audience at the Vatican, but suddenly there was a schedule change, and the audience was canceled. We stayed on in Rome hoping for another chance, and a few days later I ended up in the controlled chaos of a general audience, where the Pope would walk through a huge crowd giving blessings. Of course everybody wanted to stand right along the path where he would walk, but I didn't grow up in Brooklyn for nothing. I pushed right to the front; it didn't matter who I stepped on—nuns, priests, whoever, I didn't care. People were holding up crucifixes and rosaries for the Pope to touch and bless, and I held up one of my picture books, right in his face. He touched my forehead, and I guess my pictures all got a blessing. But I don't think he really saw, and nothing changed.

या

Sitting with Deena at Connor's, I knew that some of the babies would be dead and most would be very ill by the time I spoke at the Parliament. I thought of Timmy, who had just recently died at Connor's, and of all the little dead babies being placed gently in the Ganga in India after their bodies had been rubbed with sweet-smelling jasmine and sandalwood oils. After Timmy died, I found myself gently rubbing his little neck, so tiny and thin. His face looked as if it was carved out of the best black marble. He looked like a little African prince asleep on his bed, waiting for the morning sun to come and waken him to the new day. I just kept massaging his little body, so new to death that my Timmy still felt alive, but already the funeral home van was there to take him away.

A big group of us carried Timmy outside—me and my chelas and all the caregivers from Connor's. The man in charge opened the door and pulled out the gurney. "Ma, I can't do this," said the sobbing Elaine, Timmy's caregiver, and handed me his body. I held the little boy and then placed him on the soft blue blanket on the gurney. I wrapped the top of the blanket around his little head, making sure he looked cozy and comfortable, and I kissed him. Was I acting crazy? I didn't care. I kissed Timmy one more time, and the man smiled at me. He tied the straps, slid the gurney into the van, and said goodbye. We all stood there as if we were turned into stone. The van drove off. I waved and saw the others waving, too.

"Goodbye, my darling," I said out loud into the cool late afternoon breeze. I went to the weeping Elaine and assured her that they would take good care of our baby. She told me that the last funeral people who came to take away a baby refused to touch him when they heard he had AIDS. They wanted to put the little boy on the floor of the van.

I gasped in shock, then wondered why I would be shocked. AIDS is a disease that has such a stigma on it. I found myself in a place of rage and didn't know how to get out of it. The worst part was that I wasn't sure I wanted to stop my rage. Too many religious leaders refuse to give comfort to my people, many of whom are the street people of this world. Where was the compassion of my Christ, who had told me to teach All Ways, for All Ways were his? How would I address the Parliament?

Waking me up from my memories, Deena said in her high-pitched voice, "Ma, you'll be able to do it. Just take us all with you. And Ma, tell them about me and how I died."

CHAPTER SEVENTY-SEVEN

The Parliament of the World's Religions

Arriving in Chicago, we entered the hotel lobby and were surrounded by people of all religions and cultures of the world. The Palmer House would be my home, and the home of hundreds of spiritual leaders, for the next ten days. At first it was like a huge playground. I put my hands together and pranamed to everyone I saw. To my happy surprise they all answered in their own way, some bowing, some smiling, and others pranaming right back. For the first time since my visions of the Christ and my guru, I did not feel strange and out of place in this gathering. I was just another woman in a sari with a dot on my forehead.

The next evening for the opening ceremony, I sat in the ballroom thinking of everyone I had lost; they were all sitting there with me. Local and Parliament dignitaries spoke eloquently, welcoming us. Many of the world's problems were mentioned, but not AIDS.

"Okay," I said to myself, "take it easy, girl. This is just the first night."

The next morning, I looked out my hotel window and addressed the rising sun. "Please let this be a day of understanding. Let us all rise in unity in the love of one God."

Now it was my turn to be on the stage in front of thousands of people. I was scheduled to read two poems, one about my river, the Ganga, and one called "On the Wings of a Butterfly," about my dying children. The presenters would each be given seven minutes, and no more.

"Ma, I am here," said my little dead Deena. I greeted the audience and began to speak. I didn't stop and, to the credit of the Parliament people and the lady who had selected me to speak, I was allowed to continue. After a little while, I read my poetry. There was a silence when I finished. I thought, "I blew it." Then, just as I was about to give up and retreat gracefully, I heard applause. I put on my glasses and saw tears on many of the leaders' faces. I felt humbled by my own words; I knew I had gotten something across. Then I heard the sound of my Lord Christ's voice: "Not enough. It is not enough. These are only tears of the moment. There must be tears in all moments."

या

The most important function I would be attending at the Parliament would be the three-day assembly of more than two hundred religious leaders, where global problems would be aired and discussed. Finally, here would be my chance to speak about AIDS. I would bring them all—the children, the gays, the forgotten—to the feet of the spiritual leaders and beg the leaders to acknowledge them. I would also have a chance to meet His Holiness, the Dalai Lama. If I could get him to address AIDS and all its problems, the world just might listen.

"What's next?" I asked God as I prayed the night before the assembly of spiritual leaders was to begin.

"From your heart—speak from your heart." This was the Christ of my early spiritual journey. This was not the voice of fire and brimstone. This was the gentle Jesus lying in his mother's arms after the crucifixion. My children, my men, and my women are being crucified now, only, unlike the Virgin Mother, many of their mothers refuse to hold them while they are dying.

Those of us chosen to be in the assembly were seated seven to a table with a Parliament person running the show. I was happy to share a table with Brother Wayne Teasdale, a Catholic who followed the path similar to that of a Hindu *sannyasin*. Across the room I spotted my new friend Yogi Bhajan, also known as the Siri Singh

Sahib, leader of the Sikh Dharma for North America. I had met him a few days before. He was at the Parliament, in spite of a double bypass heart operation and the advice of his doctors, to share his vision of world peace.

"Will all the Catholics please stand," asked the president of the Parliament.

I, who had walked into the Parliament with the Christ in my heart and whispering in my head, stood up. Yashoda whispered in a high screech, "Sit down, Ma." She pulled on my sari. This was the beginning of the sari almost falling off.

"Who here are Hindus?" said the president.

I, of course, stood again. I love Hanuman, and I follow the Hindu path of unity. By now I had caught the eye of the other spiritual leaders. I just smiled, holding tight to my sari, grateful that we had used huge diaper pins to hold everything in place.

"Who here is of the Jewish faith?"

Why, of course I was Jewish. By this time, Yashoda had given up. I stood up for all the religions as the Parliament president called them out. I wasn't trying to be funny. I love all ways and all ways are the Christ, and I had to honor the God inside of myself. Anyway, my people with AIDS are of all different faiths and religions.

श्या

The last day of the assembly dawned wet and foggy. It was cold, and I felt the wind beating against my hotel window was trying to tell me to be true to myself and my people. After all, wasn't this the same town that had hosted the Parliament a hundred years before when Swami Vivekananda spoke of world peace and understanding? Yogi Bhajan and Brother Wayne didn't want to wait another hundred years for world peace, and neither did I. Letting the sound of the wind enter my heart, I walked to the Assembly feeling like a warrior of God.

In the assembly room, cards were displayed on the walls, summarizing the subjects we had talked about during the past three days. I watched as His Holiness the Dalai Lama entered, and I pranamed to this great man. He pranamed back. When I had been introduced to His Holiness the previous day, I had shown him my photo albums of the dead, the same ones I had carried to Rome. He looked at each photo, taking his time to ask about each one. "Please, Your Holiness, do something," I begged without shame. He touched my face with a caress I can still feel to this day and said, "Yes."

Now I scanned the lists on the walls looking for the words "AIDS" and "HIV." I was open and vulnerable; little six-year-old Jack had just died at Connor's that morning so my heart hurt deep inside. Nowhere did I see those words, and I was furious, to say the least.

We sat down, and continued to discuss a document called "A Global Ethic," which was supposed to be signed by all the spiritual leaders. A lot of the leaders wanted one thing or another changed. Would we ever reach agreement? I was okay with it as long as the phrase "for all people in spite of their sexual orientation" was added to it. A microphone was going around. Brother Wayne and I both raised our hands—Wayne to speak about his mission of nonviolence and me about my vision of open hearts toward AIDS and, of course, a cure.

"Wayne, if you get the mic, give it to me, and I'll give it to you if I get it."

"Okay," he said, his orange robes as wrinkled as my sari.

After a while, and still no microphone, I just stood on the chair. Shodie, still doing her thing with my sari, could not stop me from waving my hand like a wild woman.

Yogi Bhajan got the mic and said in his powerful voice, "Sign it already. We will figure it all out later. Just let us all sign it now. Let us forget our differences. We are all here under our God. Sign the damned thing!"

Harvard Professor Diana Eck, to whom I had given the spiritual name "Ganga Ma" the night before, said, "Why don't we just call it, *'Toward* a Global Ethic'?" It was the right thing to say, and it calmed everyone, that is, everyone but me with my dead weighing like a heavy stone in my heart. All of a sudden I got the mic!

"Your Holiness," I said, turning toward the Dalai Lama, "I am Ma and I have no shame crying in front of you. On the way here I received a message that a little boy of six had just died. I am now begging the spiritual leaders of the world…."

The gavel went down, stunning me.

"With all due respect, Madam," said the president, "you are out of order."

"Sir," I said with tears falling down my face, tears I had not shed so freely since the plague started, tears that have stayed in my heart causing a huge river of grief to well inside of me. "Sir," I said, refusing to give up the mic. I looked at the Dalai Lama, who was urging me with his hands, eyes, and heart to go on.

"Sir, I am not out of order. I am about AIDS. I am about the thousands of women, men, and children dying alone in every city, in every country around the world. I have no shame or embarrassment about getting down on my knees and revealing to you my broken heart. Please listen, you who lead. Please tell those who follow you, tell them about AIDS."

I was too choked up to continue, but I couldn't let go of the mic. It was my weapon of nonviolence. Finally, Wayne took it out of my hands. You could hear a pin drop and then the applause. But I wondered, where were these clapping leaders when I was told that I was out of order? Why hadn't they said something then? "Shame on all of you," I said into the loud applause.

या

That night, in front of thousands of people in Grant Park, His Holiness spoke eloquently and, perhaps for the first time, mentioned AIDS. I pranamed and bowed my head. I knew that one great spiritual leader had heard me. Even though his own people were being slaughtered in Tibet, he had the patience and holiness to hear about my people's suffering.

The next day it took me three hours to say goodbye to everyone and leave the hotel and the Parliament. The Parliament was wonderful, but it was not enough because the pain of the world goes on.

"Did I blow it, Deena?"

"You did good, Ma," I could hear my Deena telling me. "Don't stop."

Please listen, everyone who has a heart. Keep the unity going. Keep the love going. Keep your God alive. Keep his word strong.

I will never forget my little Deena, Shiva Baba, Mr. Tillman, Mr. Daniels, Haagen Das, Randy, and the hundreds of others who have died in my arms. And when forever is finished, I shall never forget all the heroes who fought this plague so gallantly, carrying the mightiest weapon of them all: love.

CHAPTER SEVENTY-EIGHT

My Sacred Kashi

When I went to India in 1977, I kissed the ground right in the airport. Mother India! The place where I had lived with my Baba in the flesh last life, or so many lifetimes ago, the place where my river flows through the sacred city of Kashi. When I returned to Florida, I named our home "Kashi."

I was young, still in my thirties, and so were most of my chelas. There were only about twenty people living at Kashi in Florida at first. Others would come and go from their houses in New York, California, and Colorado. Every few months I would travel and teach, and of course the teaching grew and grew until more than a hundred people were living at Kashi. Then there were children so we started a school. We bought more land, and we began to build our temples. As soon as the Hanuman Temple was built, I asked my chelas to hold *arati* every morning, a ceremony of sharing the light in honor of gods and gurus. And they began to take turns in the temple singing "Shri Ram Jai Ram, Jai Jai Ram" around the clock.

People have asked me, "Why Florida? Why not California?" Sometimes I reply that we needed to consume the bigotry. Sebastian was still a small town then, and in those early days we got at least one visit from the Ku Klux Klan, or maybe they were just Klan wannabes who liked to burn things on our front lawn. The word got around town that we worshipped a monkey because we had a temple to Hanuman, and who knows what else people thought we were up to. It would take years for people in the community to get used to us, but eventually they did.

Besides, I liked the heat of Florida. In India, the snows of the Himalayas symbolically represent a place to stay in the solitude of one's own being. That's for the monks, the holy men, the renunciates. But warmth is for chela and warmth is for teaching, so Florida was perfect. I found that the heat helped me stay away from the stiffness of samadhi, so it allowed me to teach.

By this time, in the late seventies, if I had wanted to say, "Bless you, my child," to everyone who came along, I could have had thousands and thousands of chelas. All I had to do was be nice. But I'm not nice, thank God, and I never will be, because truth is not nice, truth is reality, and truth can be very harsh. I want desperately for you to know God, to know the bliss of God, and so I go right to the core.

I used to say, "If you sit before me and pretend to want God, I will pretend not to know you are pretending." But I always knew who really wanted God with every part of their being. I watched as people came begging for God, I watched as some of them went away again, and I watched as some of them turned with great anger and tried to hurt me as they left. With the power of Kali, I had begun to strip them naked; I had begun to kill their pettiness, their greed, their attachments, their small egos. They came, they fell in love with God, and they said, "Kill my ego, Mother, for it is God I want." But once you say those words, once you really mean it for even a split second, Kali gets right to work.

Is the desire for God strong enough to carry you through the Black Mother's cremation grounds, at any cost? For some of my chelas the answer has been no, and they have run, sometimes screaming, "cult," and sometimes declaring, "I will destroy you." The great love that a chela has for a guru can flip over and become great anger. It's the same thing you see sometimes in a bad divorce, but multiply that by a million, because we're talking here about the love affair between mankind and God.

"Touch me, God, but not too hard." Who hasn't said that at one time or another? I said it myself in those beginning days when I still tried to keep my family together, when I still held tight to who I used to be. It's not easy, this death of the ego. Physical death is nothing compared to the pain of ego death.

So, yes, I have been attacked many times over the years. Things have been said and written about me. Did it hurt? Of course, but the best advice I ever heard was given to me in India by Siddhi Ma, the very beautiful woman who was closest to my Baba. She told me, "Walk on like an elephant, and let the little dogs bark at your heels. But always walk forward." She was right, and I have always walked forward. If I had my whole life to live over, I would do everything the same, with no regrets.

In the early days, I used to beg my Baba, "Don't make me be a guru." I was very shy. I couldn't bear the thought that people would want to bow to me, or touch my feet like they do in India. To me, Baba was the guru, and that was all I could imagine. With Billy, Fran, and a few others, no matter how I denied it, their hearts told them the truth, and little by little I had to acknowledge them as chelas. I kept confusing the others for as long as I could get away with it, repeating lines like, "A woman can't be a guru." (That's true, but it's also true that a *man* can't be a guru, because a guru is way beyond that kind of duality. The soul, in its perfection, has no gender.)

Meanwhile, my greatest joy was to touch my Baba's feet, although I wouldn't let anyone come near mine. One day I went to touch his feet, and he pulled them away from me. I was devastated. How could he do such a thing to me? But I saw what I was doing to my chelas, and little by little I began to let them honor me as a guru is honored in India.

What is a guru? This is a word not well understood here in the West. It is a word that is even feared. That's why, the day my Baba first came to me, I felt it all—great love and great fear—at the same time. The love won my heart right away, but sometimes it takes a little longer.

I have been talking and writing about the guru and what it means to have a guru for what seems like forever. Here is what I wrote, back in 1978:

> The guru is in your heart. He dwells there, waiting and watching. He sits there and wonders when you will come home. You are completeness, and he sits there waiting for you to know this. You are love and he sits there waiting for you to acknowledge this.
>
> The guru lies in the depth of your being. You are the answer to your own question.
>
> The earth is like a puzzle. God puts a man or a woman upon it with many roads, with many paths, and man walks up and down a thousand times a thousand roads, creating illusion for himself. But God waits, for there is no time in God.
>
> A thousand times a thousand lifetimes pass, and man still stumbles because he is afraid, afraid to merge into the ultimate Godhead.
>
> A thousand times a thousand. How many lifetimes do you need to know who you are? How many pains do you need? How much heartache and separation do you need until you find out who you are? How many agonies must you feel until you realize you are loved by God and God alone? That you have no friends except for God. How much teaching do you have to absorb until you realize there is no place in this world except at the guru's feet?

Of course when I said "guru" in those days, I was writing about my Baba, as I was still not ready to accept the name of guru for myself.

And who am I now? Guru to many, teacher to many more, and Mother to all.

To all I say the same thing: God is inside of you, God is your true self, and guru brings you to that true self. Surrender to the guru? Yes, by all means—surrender to that true self.

मा

It took a few more years for my chelas to understand what it really is to live on an ashram. When they were ready, I renamed our "Ranch." It became Neem Karoli Baba Kashi Ashram, or just Kashi Ashram. I began calling it just "my sacred Kashi," because that's what it became to me. When AIDS came along, we began to put the ashes of the dead in our pond, sometimes with two or three memorial services in a single week. That's when it truly became the Ganga, with Kashi on her shores.

Our first temple turned out looking exactly like a phone booth, but as time went on we built and built until now the pond is surrounded by shrines dedicated to many of the world's religions. My Baba has his own temple and so does my Swami Nityananda. A white marble Christ stands in his own grove of bamboo, an exact copy of the one I found in the grotto at Mount Manresa so many years ago.

We never had much money in the early days at Kashi, and we never had enough space. Some people were always sleeping on the floor, and there was always somebody standing in line for the bathroom. They all had to share the refrigerator and try to work together and not kill each other. Plus, of course, I demanded celibacy, vegetarianism, kindness, truth, meditation, health, hard work, cleanliness, and service. And in the middle of it all there was their Ma, sometimes swinging Kali's sword, sometimes just loving them, always stirring the pot. Whenever they looked like they might just get it all organized, we would jump in our cars and drive across the state to Sanibel, stay on the beach all night and greet the dawn together.

I had been given a choice by my Baba, to teach the scriptures or to live them. I chose to live them, and to teach them through living, which in those days meant through our life at Kashi.

"Kashi is not for the weak," I would often say, because to really live on an ashram, you have to get past your small self every single day in every single moment. In every moment there is the choice to live in the awareness of God or to pay heed to the small ego.

It wasn't easy, and yet it was magnificent. I used to say, "I only teach the teachers," and when it came time to go out into the streets and serve, and especially when AIDS came along, my chelas were ready.

We had been at Kashi for a few years when AIDS first came into our lives. I had no idea what it was, or what it would become.

मा

"I don't know what I have," a young man said. "My body is turning red, and the skin's falling off." By the time I met him in California, he had been to many doctors, but nobody knew what was wrong. The redness was crawling up his body month after month. He told me, "I know when this redness reaches my heart I'm going to die."

He died before he could be diagnosed with Kaposi's sarcoma, the "AIDS cancer," but now I believe that's what it was. As he was dying, his wife was by his bedside, and I stayed on the phone with her. My chelas listened as I guided him into death. This would be the first of many, many calls like that.

Then in 1983 another young man came from San Francisco to visit one of my chelas. While he was here, he became sicker and sicker, but I still hadn't met him. One day, I was outside working with a group of abused children, and someone brought him over to me. He was so sick, I said, "Get him to the emergency room, and I will be there as soon as I have somebody to watch these children." I would regret those words.

या

We got to the hospital, and I asked, "Where is Morgan?" They said he was in the emergency room. An hour passed, two hours, three hours. I had just met him, but still I was frantic to find him.

Finally we were told, "There's nobody by that name here." As soon as they figured out he had AIDS, they had transferred him to Shands Hospital in Gainesville. They wouldn't tell anyone where he was, and I only found this out later. From there, the state of Florida chartered a private jet, which at that time cost something like $14,000 dollars, and shipped him back to San Francisco, all alone. There was such fear, such ignorance, and they didn't want anyone with AIDS in Florida.

Soon everybody was talking about AIDS. Somehow Morgan's story became public—I think San Francisco filed suit against Florida—and then the word started going around that Kashi had brought AIDS to Florida.

One day we were told that if we let a child with AIDS attend our ashram school we could lose everything. This was no idle threat. We had been hearing all the time about the prejudice faced by people who were HIV positive or had AIDS, which also seemed to build on top of the ancient prejudice against gays and lesbians. Things got so bad that a family in another part of Florida got burned out of their home after the courts ruled their HIV-positive son could go to public school. As a private school, we could do what we wanted, but not without risk. I called everyone together and said, "There is no in-between path here. You're either with me with in this or you're against me, but we're taking this child in our school, and we could lose our ashram." I asked them, "If you're with me, stand up." Every person who lived here, they all stood up.

That's how it began—so many stories, so many memorials, so many ashes in our sacred Ganga pond. Too many, too young, and too close to our hearts.

I began to speak more and more about service, which is, in fact, the fastest way to know God. We opened up our doors wider and wider, until all kinds of people were coming and we were truly honoring Baba's instructions to "Feed Everyone."

People came from many religions and from no religion. Nobody had to convert to anything and nobody had to accept me as their guru. Nobody even had to believe in God. They just had to practice kindness. I had always said the teaching was "interfaith" and definitely not a religion. Then I realized that the word "interfaith" didn't include everybody as long as gays and lesbians faced so much prejudice in churches and temples. That's when I began to say that Kashi offered "a vacation from hate," and we threw the doors open even wider.

CHAPTER SEVENTY-NINE

Home

The Boardwalk was lit up. People were walking, talking, and just hanging out in spite of the time. It was about two in the morning. The night air was cool and refreshing. The ocean called out to me as it did when I was a child. I had spent the day teaching in New York, and now I was home on the Boardwalk with a few of my chelas to show them my youth. One thing my Baba asked of me many years ago was to share my life with my chelas, and I had begun to tell them about Big Henry, Chicky, Chews, Hudson, Tirza, and Joe Joe.

We went down the stairs to look for my home under the boards, and I started to weep in the deepest reaches of my soul. Most of the space had been packed with sand so the homeless couldn't live there anymore. The sounds on the Boardwalk reaching down to the beach did nothing to ease the pain in my heart. This had been my home for most of my early childhood, and now it was nothing but broken bottles and dirty sand. How could I explain the beauty of a cold night under the stars with the fires going in the wire garbage cans and the scent of roasting old potatoes filling the senses? The breeze whispered to me that the ghosts of my friends were still there. The mist from the ocean felt like it was weeping with me.

"My home," I said, "my true home, the only home that I knew." I snuck a look at my sister as she wiped a tear from her eye. She was remembering, too, only her memories were not like mine. She hadn't known the sea or the beach, nor did she have my people. She had just worked and taken care of us all in any way she could.

We climbed back up the stairs to walk the boards for a while. We stopped in front of one of those stands where you swing a big hammer and try to ring the bell. I had put my tears away for now, and some of my yogis wanted to give it a try. I turned to the guy running the stand. "Did you ever know Tirza the Wine Bath Girl?" I asked him.

"Why do you want to know?" He sounded very suspicious.

"She was my babysitter," I said simply.

He looked hard at me, clearly not believing me. I was ready to walk away. "Joyce?" he said. "Joyce, is that you?"

"Yes, and who the hell are *you*?"

"Of course I know Tirza. I'm her son!"

He was shy, but I hugged him tight anyway, and we talked about Tirza for a few minutes. He said she was still alive and well, but she had retired to Florida. There wasn't much more to say, so we walked on.

"Ma," I heard one of my chelas say, "there really *was* a Tirza! I thought you were making it all up."

My heart broke for the second time that night. What else did he think I was making up? Was my story too much to be believed? It would be years after that before I could fully share the stories of my crazy wonderful youth, or the story of how God found me, and I never thought I could put it all into a book. In truth, I could write a whole chapter about every single day of my life, but I wondered, who would listen?

And yet, once I began to teach full time, it wasn't just my story anymore—it became also the story of all the people whose lives have touched mine.

We write it together, every day.

AFTERWORD

And Then What Happened?

Ma ends the personal part of this story with the move to Florida. Besides her work during the height of the AIDS epidemic, what else happened after 1976?

First, she added to her family, with a grandson whom she adopted at birth in 1978. In 1980, she married Tae Kwon Do Master Soo Se Cho, an 8th degree black belt from Korea. Together they quickly adopted four more children, and together the family went through the heartbreak of having to give up one of those children who, after seven years, was taken back by her biological parents. This happened in the context of the "cult" fears of the 1980s. As a charismatic teacher of Eastern spirituality, and as a woman, Ma was an easy target. She was also a mother, and she felt the loss of a child as deeply as any mother.

Around 1980, an interracial family with three children moved from New York to be with Ma. On the first day of public school, the youngest came home and asked his mother about one of the names he had been called. Within days, Kashi Ashram opened its own school. At first there were few books and no classrooms, but it had a name: The River School. Several ashram residents had teaching credentials or miscellaneous advanced degrees, and Billy, the Oxford Don, taught Latin.

The school remained unusual in several ways, especially as Ma led the community to deeper involvement in service. Her grandson, Tony Cho, remembers those days:

> By the time I was in high school, the school had grown to have a lot more students besides the ones that lived at the

ashram. Ma began teaching these other kids about service along with the ashram kids, just by letting them share in what she was doing. Some of my friends in high school, I know it changed their lives. It was powerful to be with Ma and watch how she'd gracefully be with people who were on their deathbed or in their last days. There was a realness that Ma brought to everyone. At the same time she brought a sense of humor to the situation, which cut through a lot of the heaviness and pain. Sometimes she was able to show us death as a joyful experience, but without airbrushing the pain.

We also had the River House, which had space for eight people who were dying, usually from AIDS, and ashram people staffed that around the clock, sleeping on the couch in case someone needed help in the night. Sometimes us kids would go with Ma from school straight to the River House and the bedside of someone who died right in front of us, with maybe one of us holding their hand. Then back to class, normal day. Ma wanted us to see death as a part of life and not be afraid.

In the early 1980s, Ma began painting. Although at first she insisted that she couldn't even draw a stick figure, the paintings arose from her own meditations. "I wait for the mother to come into me. She guides my brush, and I find that I make her exact image in that moment on the canvas," she wrote. Although she was at first reluctant to show her work, within a few years she was invited to exhibit in galleries in the US and Europe, with the proceeds often going to AIDS charities.

Spiritual life with Ma could be physically strenuous. For several years the ashram had horses, and every day Ma would lead a group of about a dozen riders out before dawn, never mind the weather. Later came rollerblade hockey—Ma captained her own team— and step aerobics, followed by weight training and Zumba. Almost everyone studied Tae Kwon Do, and many including Ma earned their black belts. In between all this, Ma taught yoga, but it was not until about 2000 that she developed Kali Natha Yoga in a systematic way, working from ancient roots to integrate breath, sound, and meditation as well as asanas. She said, "Everything is sacred in Kali Natha Yoga. You are building a temple in your body to hold the essence of God and Goddess."

Ma was always interested in providing homes for vulnerable people. The destructive hurricanes of 2004 made it clear that there was very little affordable housing for low-income seniors in the area, and Ma inspired the development of a forty-one bed facility on land adjoining the ashram. Little by little, through the simple practices of openness and service, most of the neighbors had stopped worrying about cults.

All this time, the ashram has kept taking care of the poor—some locally, and some in Africa and India. These projects still follow Ma's example of making personal connections with people in need. As she often said, "There are no throwaway people."

Ma had several health challenges over the years. At the start of 2012 she was diagnosed with terminal pancreatic cancer. Tony Cho tells us about that time:

> In those last months as Ma withdrew, my wife Sharada and I came up from Miami every single week to be with her in a very intimate setting which I hadn't had with her in a long, long time. We were living her whole teaching again about death and dying, and how when it comes to the end, and you're going through that with someone, it gets really real really fast.
>
> Those last three months of her life were some of the most powerful times I ever spent with Ma. Everything was just in the flow. We knew it was for a limited time and it was

precious. Being around death makes you realize how temporary this physical body is, and makes you realize how important the moment is. So many people live in fear, but if you can have a respect and a reverence for death and embrace it, then you don't live in fear and your life is a lot more fulfilled. Ma had always taught that, and here we were living it with her.

For the last few days, people were coming from all over just to see her, even though she was rarely awake. On the last day everyone knew it was coming to an end and they came one by one to touch her feet. Then around 10:30 that night my aunt Denise gathered me and Sharada and the rest of Ma's family and told us we should come back in to her bedroom. We surrounded Ma. Her breaths were coming further and further apart. Her eyes were closed, my brother Soo Se and I were holding her hands. Finally Soo Se said in a strong voice, "Mommy, it's OK, you can let go." She took her last breath and there was this amazing spirit energy. I felt it like a cool breeze, but Sharada remembers it like pressure and a bubble breaking, time slowing way down, as Ma's spirit was leaving her body. And just then, the rain, a huge storm broke over us, the heavens opening up and cleansing the world. Soo Se yelled "Jai Ma!" and then we all did, and that was the moment of her passing, joyous and almost happy, and it was very much how Ma taught us to celebrate death.

Tony continues:

I didn't know if the Kashi community would survive without Ma, but it has grown. There's a retreat center, and a yoga school focused on Kali Natha Yoga, and a permaculture project that my brother created. Ma's paintings hang on every wall, her teachings are becoming available as books and videos, and the temples still hold their essence.

Ma often said that she and Kashi were one. She wrote:

> This Kashi has stolen my heart and buried it under its sacred soil. I shall never find my heart again, simply because I do not care to look for it. I am content to leave my heart where it is, and you who come are blessed again and again.

Acknowledgements

There are many people to thank for their love, support, and encouragement to write these stories of my life.

To my Billy, Dr. Thomas Byrom, who encouraged me to write. I miss you, my Billy.

To those who have dedicated their lives serving others; you have my deep gratitude as you serve humanity with your hearts.

To everyone at Kashi Publishing and to all those who have encouraged and advised me in the making of this memoir; thank you for your dedication in sharing the written words of your guru.

To the heroes of the AIDS community and all who serve them, I am with you always.

There are not enough words to express my love and dedication to my Kashi Ashram, which holds me and keeps me safe in her holy womb.

Thank you my students and chelas, you are my heart and every breath I breathe. I love you; this book is for you.

Suggested Reading

Buck, William. An English retelling of *The Ramayana*. University of California Press, 2012.

Byrom, Thomas. *The Heart of Awareness: A Translation of the Ashtavakra Gita*. Shambala, 2001.

Harding, Elizabeth. *Kali: the Black Goddess of Dakshineswar*. Nicholas-Hayes, Inc.,1993.

Monette, Paul. *Borrowed Time: An AIDs Memoir*. Harcourt, 1988.

Mukerjee, Dada. *By His Grace, A Devotee's Story*. Love Serve Remember Foundation, 2014.

Ram Dass. *Miracle of Love; Stories About Neem Karoli Baba*. Love Serve Remember Foundation, 2014.

Sen, Ramprasad. *Grace and Mercy in Her Wild Hair: Selected Poems to the Mother Goddess*. (Seely and Nathan, Translators), Hohm Press, 1999.

Swami Muktananda. *Bhagwan Nityananda of Ganeshpuri*. Syda Yoga Foundation, 1996.

Glossary

Adonai
Part of the traditional first line of many Jewish blessings, *"baruch atah Adonai Eloheinu, melech ha'olam,"* which may be translated as "Blessed are you, lord our God, king of the universe."

Amrith
The nectar of immortality, the delicious ambrosia of the gods, which in holy people may drip down on the tongue from the roof of the mouth.

Annapurna
The goddess of food and great abundance.

Ashram
A religious community, home to a guru and the guru's chelas.

Avadhut
A mystic or saint who is beyond ego-consciousness, duality and common worldly concerns and acts without consideration for standard social etiquette.

Baba, Babaji
Terms of respect for an Indian man, similar to "father." In this book, Baba specifically refers to Ma's guru, Neem Karoli Baba.

Bandhara
A public feast, often given to celebrate a special occasion.

Bhagavad Gita
Part of the epic *Mahabarata*, the *Bhagavad Gita* contains the instructions given by the god Krishna to the warrior Arjuna about how to behave on the battlefield of life. It is among the most important sacred texts to Hindus.

Bhagawan
Absolute truth. When used as part of a person's title, it is equivalent to "Lord."

Bentsch licht
To recite benedictions over lit candles on the Sabbath and holidays.

Brahmin
A member of the highest caste in India, the priestly and scholarly class.

Chela
Spiritual student, disciple of a guru. The connection between guru and chela is more profound than the student-teacher relationship as understood in the West. It is a deep connection of the heart and soul, and extends beyond this life.

Chidakash
The heart space over the head, a teaching of compassionate detachment and awareness, which Ma learned from Swami Bhagawan Nityananda.

Darshan
"To have the darshan of a saint" means to catch a glimpse of a holy being and thus to be blessed. The word can refer to any gathering with a guru, which may include instruction, meditation, or worship.

Daven
To pray, in the Jewish tradition.

Dhuni
The sacred fire of Shiva that reminds us that God's light is constantly burning in our hearts. The dhuni is also understood as a purifying fire.

Ego
The small self. Identification with the ego keeps us separate from God, the universal self.

Ganesh, Ganesha
The elephant-headed god, the remover of all obstacles, who is called upon at the beginning of all pujas.

Ganga, Ganges, Gange
The most sacred river for Hindus in India. The holy city of Kashi is on her shores.

Ghats
Areas on the banks of the Ganga. On a few ghats, the dead are cremated and their ashes are placed in the waters. It is believed that Kali dwells in the cremation grounds, and Shiva in the form of Vishwanatha imparts the mantra of illumination to the dying.

Gopi
A young woman who herds cows in India. In a well-known story, the gopis are the lovers of Lord Krishna, representing humanity loving God, and God embracing all.

Govinda
A name of Lord Krishna, in a youthful aspect.

Goy, Goyim, Goyisha
Non-Jewish.

Guru
An enlightened being who serves as a spiritual teacher and guide, offering the chela the most profound and enduring connection of heart and soul.

Gurubai
Spiritual brothers and sisters. Those who have the same guru are gurubai.

Hanuman
The Hindu god of service; an incarnation of Lord Shiva who came to earth in the form of a monkey to teach humility. (See also: *Ramayana*)

Hilda Charlton
(1906-1988) An American disciple of Swami Bhagawan Nityananda, Sathya Sai Baba, and others; she taught in New York City for many years.

Kali
The Hindu goddess Kali, though terrifying in appearance, assists those on the spiritual path by consuming their impurities and bad karma.

Karma
The law of cause and effect; the results of the action of the laws of karma.

Kashi
The Indian holy city on the banks of the Ganga. It is considered auspicious to die at Kashi, releasing the soul from bondage. (Kashi's modern names are Banares or Varanasi.)

Krishna
A very beautiful blue-skinned Hindu god, most often portrayed with a flute.

Kundalini
The power of God that rises within us.

Langoti
A simple garment worn by Indian men on the lower part of the torso.

Laxman
When Ma's guru, Neem Karoli Baba, was a young man, he was known as Laxman. Laxman is a hero of the Indian scripture *The Ramayana*, and is closely linked to Hanuman.

Ma, Mataji
Mother, used as a term of respect for women in India.

Maharaj-ji
"Great king," a name sometimes used for Neem Karoli Baba.

Mast
One who is "intoxicated with God," a mast may appear to be mad or out of touch with ordinary reality. This state is best understood in terms of spiritual experience.

Meher Baba
(1894-1969) An Indian holy man who established centers in India, Australia, and the United States.

Mezuzah
A representation of a sacred Jewish scroll, which may be attached to the doorpost of a house or worn on a chain around the neck.

Mudra
Special gestures known to yogis, which may be used in worship, healing, and prayer.

Murti
An image of the deity, usually a statue, that is inbued with the essence of what it represents.

Neem Karoli Baba
(d. 1973) Ma's guru and one of the great spiritual masters of our time. He is believed by some to be an incarnation of Shiva.

Om
A mystical sound, known as "the sound of the universe," Om (or AUM) is part of many prayers and invocations in Hinduism and other Eastern religions.

Namaste
An Indian greeting, sometimes translated as "The God in me greets the God in you," or "My soul greets your soul."

Payot
Long ringlets of hair worn in front of the ears by Orthodox, Yemenite, and Hasidic Jewish men.

Pranam
An Indian gesture of worship or respect, with the palms pressed together.

Pranayama
Yogic breathing exercises that bring one to the awareness of the breath and help one attain a higher state of consciousness.

Puja
Worship, or moving prayer, often with candles, incense, bells, and the like. The word may also refer to a personal shrine or altar.

Pujari
A person who performs the rituals at a puja, or who takes care of a shrine.

Radha, Radhe
The primary gopi, devotee, and consort of Lord Krishna, she represents all who are in love with God.

Ram
A name of the formless God, which is repeated in many mantras. A "Ram shawl" is covered with names of God.

Ramana Maharshi
(1879-1950) One of the most revered spiritual teachers of modern India, he is remembered especially for teaching the great mantra, "Who am I?" which helps us realize our true identity as eternal, pure consciousness.

Ramayana
One of the best-loved epic scriptures of India, which tells the story of how Sita is captured by a demon and later rescued by Hanuman and others.

Ramprasad Sen
(c. 1718-1775) A Bengali poet, a great devotee of Mother Kali.

Rudi, Swami Rudrananda
(1928-1973) A Brooklyn-born devotee of Swami Bhagawan Nityananda. He taught in and around New York.

Sadhu
A wandering ascetic who travels through India with no fixed home and very few possessions.

Samadhi
A state of profound union with God. In some stages of samadhi, awareness of the material world is lost in bliss. The body may become stiff, without a detectable heartbeat or pulse.

Sannyasin
A Hindu renunciate who has been initiated into a lineage and given the title "Swami."

Sathya Sai Baba
(1926-2011) A modern spiritual master in India, with a large following world-wide.

Shabbos
The Jewish Sabbath, which begins at sundown on Friday and ends at sundown on Saturday.

Shakti
The female energy of the universe, which is love and power combined.

Shanda
Shame or impropriety.

Shiksa
A non-Jewish female.

Shirdi Sai Baba
(d.1918) An Indian holy man who taught by simple parables, and lived in harmony with all religions. It is said that his presence conveyed a direct experience of the divine.

Shiva
One of the three chief Hindu gods, he who destroys and rebuilds. His incarnations are believed to include Hanuman and Neem Karoli Baba.

Shtick
A special bit of acting, a routine.

Sit Shivah
In Judaism, to participate in a vigil for the dead.

Stigmata
Appearance of bodily wounds corresponding to the crucifixion wounds of Jesus Christ

Swami Bhagawan Nityananda
(1897-1961) An Indian holy man, believed by many to have been a perfect master from birth. After traveling widely in India, he established an ashram at Ganeshpuri.

Tantra
Hindu or Buddhist philosophy and spiritual practice with the goal of merging with the divine.

Torah
First five books of the Hebrew scriptures.

Yahrzeit
A memorial candle, which is lit during a period of mourning for the dead and also on the anniversary of a death.

Yama
The Hindu god of death.

Photo Credits

p. vii   Ram Giri.

p. 188   (Top) Shirley Green. (Bottom Left) Shirley Green. (Bottom Right) Anna Green.

p. 189   (Top) Melvin Green. (Bottom) Shirley Green.

p. 190   Shirley Green.

p. 191   (All) Shirley Green.

p. 192   (Top) Shirley Green. (Bottom) AP Photo/Jack Kanthal.

p. 193   (Top Left) Shirley Green. (Top Right) Murray Korman, Used by Permission. (Bottom) Shirley Green.

p. 194   (All) Shirley Green.

p. 195   Shirley Green.

p. 196   (Bottom) Shirley Green.

p. 197   (Top Left, Top Right, Bottom Left) Shirley Green. (Bottom Right) Lincoln High School Photo.

p. 198   (All) Shirley Green.

p. 336   (Top Left) Durga. (Top Right) Photographer Unknown. (Bottom Left) Yashoda. (Bottom Right) Photographer Unknown.

p. 337   (Top Left) Photographer Unknown. (Top Right) Ram Giri. (Bottom) Shirley Green.

p. 338   Shirley Green.

p. 339   (Top Left) Photographer Unknown. (Top Right) Durga. (Bottom) Photographer Unknown.

p. 340   (All) Durga.

p. 341   (All) Durga.

p. 342   (Top Left) Durga. (Top Right) Durga. (Bottom) Photographer Unknown.

p. 343   (All) Durga.

p. 344   Kailash Shankara.

p. 345   (All) Durga.

p. 346   (Top) Durga. (Bottom) Vatican Photographer.

p. 347   (All) Yashoda.

Made in the USA
Monee, IL
28 February 2020